LEXICOGRAPHICA Series Maior

LEXICOGRAPHICA

Series Maior

Supplementary Volumes to the International Annual for Lexicography
Suppléments à la Revue Internationale de Lexicographie
Supplementbände zum Internationalen Jahrbuch für Lexikographie

Edited by
Sture Allén, Pierre Corbin, Reinhard R. K. Hartmann,
Franz Josef Hausmann, Ulrich Heid, Oskar Reichmann,
Ladislav Zgusta

95

Published in cooperation with the Dictionary Society of North America
(DSNA) and the European Association for Lexicography (EURALEX)

The Perfect Learners' Dictionary (?)

Edited by
Thomas Herbst and Kerstin Popp

Max Niemeyer Verlag
Tübingen 1999

Die Deutsche Bibliothek – CIP-Einheitsaufnahme

[Lexicographica / Series maior]
Lexicographica : supplementary volumes to the International annual for lexicography / publ. in cooperation with the Dictionary Society of North America (DSNA) and the European Association for Lexicography (EURALEX). Series maior. – Tübingen : Niemeyer.
Früher Schriftenreihe
Reihe Series maior zu: Lexicographica

95. The perfect learners' dictionary (?). – 1999

The perfect learners' dictionary (?) / ed. by Thomas Herbst and Kerstin Popp. – Tübingen : Niemeyer, 1999
(Lexicographica : Series maior ; 95)

ISBN 3-484-30995-4 ISSN 0175-9264

Gedruckt auf alterungsbeständigem Papier.
Druck: Weihert-Druck GmbH, Darmstadt
Einband: Nädele Verlags- und Industriebuchbinderei, Nehren

Contents

The Perfect Learners' Dictionary (?)

Since this volume is not a piece of crime fiction but a collection of academic articles, it is no violation of the principles of the text form to indicate the ending right at the beginning. *The Perfect Learners' Dictionary (?)* is, of course, as much a reality as is the ideal native speaker. At least, at the symposium entitled *The Perfect Learners' Dictionary (?)*, which was held at the University of Erlangen-Nürnberg in April 1997, it soon became apparent that the participants were generally agreed that there was not much point in taking the title question too seriously, despite the ambiguity of the phrase, since neither are there perfect learners nor could one really imagine perfect dictionaries.

Nevertheless, it is remarkable that at the end of the twentieth century it does not seem totally unjustified to ask a question of that kind and to perhaps even use the word *perfect* in a lexicographical context at all – at least in a sense similar to that given in OALD5 under 4: 'excellent; very good', particularly perhaps in the case of English. The reason for talking about perfect learners' dictionaries – and, in fact, the reason for considering it worthwhile organizing a conference discussing this question – is the dramatic development of English learner lexicography in the last two or three decades of this century. The fact that four major EFL dictionaries were published in the same year, 1995, speaks for itself. Even if up to a point it may be a coincidence that the fifth edition of the *Oxford Advanced Learner's Dictionary* (OALD5), the third edition of the *Longman Dictionary of Contemporary English* (LDOCE3), the second edition of the *Cobuild English Dictionary* (COBUILD2) and the *Cambridge International Dictionary of English* (CIDE)[1] appeared more or less simultaneously, it certainly shows that the EFL dictionary market is (or at least was) considered by the publishing firms to be an extremely important and potentially expanding one. What is even more important from the users' or, from a world-wide EFL, point of view is that with now four major learners' dictionaries of roughly the same size aiming at very much the same target group it becomes more important to compare and review these products.

The assessment of dictionaries, however, is a very difficult and tricky task. Not surprisingly, dictionary reviewers and metalexicographers are often criticized, mainly for two reasons: Firstly, of course, it is much easier to review a dictionary than to write one, especially if the review concentrates on one aspect of a dictionary the reviewer happens to be particularly keen on while neglecting the whole. This kind of criticism, mostly raised by dictionary makers, is of course often more than justified and there is very little metalexicographers can do about that (if they actually lack the experience of genuine lexicographical work), apart from pointing out that the weaknesses they identify indeed do exist and that discussing them may indeed result in improvements in further editions. The second major problem any dictionary review is faced with is that of how to assess the

---

1 Since these dictionaries will be referred to in all articles in this volume, their references are only given at the end of this introduction.

quality of a work of several thousand pages with 50,000 or more entries. As far as general features such as layout or grammatical coding system are concerned, this is relatively easy, but judging the quality of the definitions or the usefulness of the examples is a much more complex task. There is a rather widely used impressionistic method – browsing through the dictionary and noting down a few awkward definitions, badly chosen examples etc.,[2] which makes the review appear thorough and critical. In extreme cases of this reviewing practice, a very convincing body of such negative quotations from a dictionary is followed by a very positive conclusion about the character of the work as such. In any case, this approach makes it difficult for the reader to judge whether the examples quoted happen to belong to the details that unavoidably go wrong in any enterprise of such proportions or whether they are typical of the overall quality of the work reviewed.

The basic idea of the symposium *The Perfect Learners' Dictionary (?)* was to attempt to overcome such weaknesses of dictionary reviewing practice by bringing together experts working in different fields of lexicography, metalexicography and linguistics. Thus it was possible to devote one or even several papers to very specific features of the new generation of English learners' dictionaries. This again meant not only that key aspects of these dictionaries could be discussed in great detail, but also that in many papers a quantitative approach could be pursued and that the assessment of the feature in question and the comparison of the four dictionaries could be based on relatively large and thus also relatively representative samples of text, overcoming a purely impressionistic approach. Although, unfortunately, it was of course not possible to invite all scholars who would have had a valuable contribution to make, we were happy that all linguists approached accepted the invitation to come to Erlangen and that we were thus able to have papers by renowned experts from various European countries on different aspects of these dictionaries. In particular, the organizers of the conference are grateful that each of the four dictionaries which formed the main subject of the conference was represented by their editors or by senior members of the respective lexicographical teams. Guided by the insight that the brackets round the question mark in the title would have to be dropped anyway, the purpose of the conference was not one of a comparison resulting in any kind of ranking, but one of a thorough investigation of different policies and the way they were realized in the four dictionaries with the aim of discussing their merits or faults within the framework of the particular dictionary and in the light of the ongoing metalexicographical discussion.

From an outside observer's point of view, it is not only the differences between the four English learners' dictionaries published in 1995 that are of great interest, but also what they have in common. There can be no doubt that they all represent a very high standard of lexicographical achievement. Furthermore, they can indeed be seen as members of a particular generation of dictionaries, which might be called the post-Hornby pre-CD-ROM generation, referring to the beginnings of EFL lexicography and possible future

---

2 Cf. Jehle, Günther (1990): Das englische und französische Lernerwörterbuch in der Rezension. Theorie und Praxis der Wörterbuchkritik. — Tübingen: Niemeyer (Lexikographica Series Maior 30).

developments (both of which also received considerable attention during the conference). What makes the 1995 EFL dictionaries perhaps more homogeneous as a generation than, say, the 1987 LDOCE2, COBUILD1 and the 1989 OALD4 seen together, is that they are all, in varying degrees, based on similar policy decisions in a number of important issues:

The first and certainly most important aspect in this context is that they are all based on corpora. Admittedly, the extent to which corpus evidence (in the form of quoted or modified examples, frequency indicators, highlighted collocations, phrases and gramma-tical patterns) is actually incorporated in the dictionary varies. Nevertheless, the fact that extensive corpus research forms the basis of all four dictionaries is most remarkable – not only with respect to earlier English learners' dictionaries but also in comparison with such dictionaries for languages other than English.

While the most important impetus for using large-scale corpus analysis in EFL lexicography came from the first edition of COBUILD (1987), it is probably fair to say that it was the publication of LDOCE1 in 1978 that instigated competition with respect to user-friendliness. Again, it is interesting to see that many issues, some of which even formed the subject of passionate debate following the publication of LDOCE1, LDOCE2 and COBUILD1, seem settled and certain lexicographical principles seem to be fairly established, at least as far as English lexicography is concerned. This concerns relatively trivial as well as central points. For instance, amongst the four dictionaries discussed here, there is not a single one that would not spell out the headword of an entry in the example sentences (and use an abbreviation or a tilde instead), which increases the readibility of the examples considerably. Similarly, none of the four dictionaries uses non-mnemotechnical or non-transparent coding systems for the indication of information on verb valency. As far as the crucial question of providing semantically accurate but simple and thus comprehensible definitions is concerned, the approach of making (modified) use of a limited defining vocabulary seems to have become generally accepted.

Nevertheless, important differences between the four representatives of this generation of English learners' dictionaries remain (as continuations of the lines of tradition in which they have to be seen) or have emerged through different policies or different implementations of similar policies. It is the aim of the present volume to highlight the central features of these dictionaries. While the majority of the papers is thus concerned with a detailed analysis of particular issues (such as syntactic information, examples, structure, vocabulary selection, sociolinguistic aspects etc.), others consider this new generation of English learners' dictionaries along the lexicographical dimensions of time (looking at the origins of learners' dictionaries and possible future developments), system (analysing the relationship between more specialised EFL dictionaries and general learners' dictionaries) and region (comparing EFL dictionaries on the basis of the experience with similar dictionaries for other languages).

The editors would like to express their gratitude to all participants for taking part in the symposium, hoping that they enjoyed their visit to Erlangen both academically and personally as much as we did. We would also like to thank the Deutsche Forschungsgemeinschaft and the Dr.-Alfred-Vinzl-Stiftung for their support, without which this symposium could not have been carried out, as well as the Rektor of the Friedrich-

Alexander-Universität, Prof. Dr. G. Jasper, and our Erlangen colleagues especially Prof. Dr. F. J. Hausmann, David Heath, Rosemary Zahn, Dr. D. Barnickel and Dr. M. Klotz for their support in the process of organizing the conference and preparing this volume. Finally, we would like to thank Frau Disch and our student helpers Tanja Becker, Hedwig Erhard, Katrin Götz, Nina Heidemann, Yücel Özyürek, Christina Sanchez, Birgit Steinbügl, Renate Wech, Sibylle Welz and Karola Wenninger.

Thomas Herbst Kerstin Popp

The 1995 English learners' dictionaries — bibliographical references

Cambridge International Dictionary of Englisch (1995): Paul Procter (ed.). — Cambridge: CUP. [CIDE]

Collins COBUILD English Dictionary (^{2}1995): John Sinclair (ed.). — London: HarperCollins. [COBUILD2]

Longman Dictionary of Contemporary English (^{3}1995): Della Summers (ed.). — Harlow: Longman. [LDOCE3]

Oxford Advanced Learner's Dictionary (^{5}1995): Jonathan Crowther (ed.). — Oxford: OUP. [OALD5]

I. The new generation of English learners' dictionaries: historical background – assessment of specific features – the perspective of the user

Anthony P. Cowie

Learners' dictionaries in a historical and a theoretical perspective

1 Introduction

The monolingual learners' dictionary, which the present volume celebrates, analyses and forecasts the future of, came into existence over sixty years ago, in the mid-1930s. By the early 1940s it had taken on characteristics recognizable in varying degrees in all the advanced-level dictionaries of the 1990s.

The circumstances in which learners' dictionaries first appeared were exceptionally favourable, since not only were their editors - the founding fathers of EFL lexicography - teaching in the Far East when their dictionaries were compiled, but all were contributors to, and beneficiaries of, innovative and fruitful programmes of lexical research. Of these, none had a deeper or more widespread effect on the early history of the monolingual learners' dictionary than the so-called 'vocabulary control' movement of the 1920s and 1930s. In fact it would be no exaggeration to say that vocabulary limitation gave birth to the learners' dictionary - and that its parental influence endures to this day. Harold Palmer, the acknowledged leader of the movement, but with no awareness at the outset that its most remarkable and enduring achievements would be lexicographical, produced in 1938 a pioneering encoding dictionary - *A Grammar of English Words* - to which his own structured word-lists had paved the way. Michael West, also a major contributor to the movement, drew from research into vocabulary limitation the simplified defining vocabulary of the very first EFL dictionary - the *New Method English Dictionary* of 1935. That was an initiative whose repercussions we are still witnessing. A. S. Hornby, who played a leading part in a scheme of phraseological research which ran parallel to collaborative work on word-lists, was the originator of the 1000-word-list which provided much of the macrostructure of *A Grammar of English Words*. In return, the Palmer dictionary, with its verb-pattern scheme, its labelling - for the first time in any dictionary - of the countable-uncountable distinction, and its original approach to indicating variation in examples, left its mark on Hornby's *Idiomatic and Syntactic English Dictionary* (later to be the *Advanced Learner's Dictionary*) and helped to shape its strongly 'productive' character.

In this brief historical and critical survey, I shall begin by referring to Harold Palmer's crucial role, describing the particular character which research took on under his leadership, and tracing the gradual emergence of learners' dictionaries from his highly structured word-lists. Of Palmer's various contributions to dictionary design I shall focus on his notion of the 'skeleton' example as one which endures and deserves to be more widely understood. I shall then turn to Michael West and to his notion - not, as it happened, shared by Palmer and Hornby - that a limited vocabulary should be used for purposes of definition in a learners' dictionary. Finally, I shall consider the development, within the wider movement, of phraseological research, and how its findings were channelled into learner lexicography. Here A. S. Hornby's role was central, and here too there are clearly links with the present concerns of EFL lexicographers.

2 Harold Palmer and the Vocabulary Control Movement

Harold E. Palmer was from 1923 to 1936 director of the Tokyo Institute for Research in English Teaching (or IRET), and it was largely through his leadership and intellectual authority that IRET became during those years a research centre of world-wide reputation and influence. Palmer's interest, since the beginning of the century, in vocabulary control was motivated by the desire to ease the learning burden of the foreign learner by presenting only (or at least initially) those words which could be shown to carry the main weight of everyday communication. This interest was closely linked to the preparation of simplified reading texts. Pedagogically, the aim was that those texts would be prepared within the radius of a given limited vocabulary (3000 words, in the case of IRET's *First Interim Report on Vocabulary Selection* of 1930). They would then serve, in the classroom, to consolidate that vocabulary through motivation and repeated exposure. The *validity* of the word-list could later be tested by the simplification of other unabridged texts, since words which never or seldom occurred in those texts would have a poor claim to be retained, while words which occurred frequently but were not already present in the list might be thought of as good candidates for inclusion.

Until his *Essay in Lexicology* of 1934, which included a number of specimen entries for a possible 'learner's dictionary' – none was in fact 'in contemplation or preparation' at the time – Palmer gave no sign that vocabulary control could lead to and indeed inspire dictionary designs for the foreign learner (1934b: 1). However, those samples, and the specimens which Palmer provided in a deeply perceptive paper of 1936, were remarkably similar to entries in learners' dictionaries, as we shall see in a moment.

With hindsight, it is not hard to see why the word-lists produced in the early 1930s by Palmer and his immediate colleagues, and later by Palmer, West and Lawrence Faucett in collaboration, should evolve into macro- and microstructure dictionary designs appropriate for foreign learners. We need to bear in mind that Palmer's word-lists were shaped by an almost obsessive preoccupation with the definition of lexical units. When in 1927 he was first asked by IRET to compile a controlled vocabulary (for middle-grade Japanese schools) he saw his task initially as one of category definition. (The titles of two papers of 1929, 'What shall we call a word?' and 'What is an idiom?', reflect his dominant concerns.) He was also aware that a word-list was a more complex affair than an alphabetical inventory of spelling-forms, based on frequency of occurrence, such as the American exponents of quantitative word-counts, led by Edward Thorndike, had been promoting since the early 1920s. (It will be clear incidentally that at that early stage - all of seventy years ago - Palmer was addressing problems that have resurfaced in the wake of the computer revolution). Acting on theoretical assumptions that were diametrically opposed to those of their American colleagues, Palmer, West and later Hornby succeeded in producing, from 1930 onwards, what were in fact a number of structured lexicons. Their word-lists, that is to say, were alphabetical arrangements of 'word-families' (to use Palmer's term), each entry being headed by a simple word, or root, and consisting of a cluster of inflectionally and/or derivationally related forms and common compounds. Structured lexicons reached their most sophisticated level with the addition of phonetic transcriptions and word-sense divisions (as in Palmer and Hornby's *Thousand-Word English* of 1937) and above all of plentiful examples and collocations (as in the *General Service List* of 1936, where incidentally the collocations and idioms were provided by Hornby). Some idea can be gained of the levels of complexity reached, and of the potential relevance to learners, from the two extracts at (1)(a) and (1)(b):

(1)(a) **HARD** [hɑ:d], *adj.*
(I. = not soft)
(2. = intense, as in *hard work, hard fight*)
hard [hɑ:d], *adv.* (as in *work, fight hard*)
hardness ['hɑ:dnis], *n.*
(Palmer and Hornby 1937).

(b)	**HARD**	
	hard, adj.	(1) (*hard to the touch*)
		A hard bed
		Hard ground
		(2) (*resulting from much force, requiring much effort*)
		A hard blow
		Hard work
		Hard to understand
		(3) (*not gentle, severe*)
		A hard heart, nature
		Be hard on a person
		Hard words
		Have a hard life
		Hard winter
	hard, adv.	(1) (*not soft.*)
	harden, v.	Freeze hard
	hardness, n.	Boil an egg hard.
	hard-working, adj.	(2) (*vigorously, strenuously*)
		Try hard
		Work hard
		(Faucett, Palmer, Thorndike and West 1936).

(c) **HARD**
I. hard [hɑ:d], harder ['hɑ:də], hardest ['hɑ:dist], *adj.*
1. = firm to the touch. *Contrasted with* SOFT
Stone is very hard.
The ground was very hard.
A hard sort of wood.
The bed seems very hard.
2. = vigorous
a hard blow.
3. = laborious, difficult
hard work.
a hard question.
This hill is hard to climb.
He leads a hard life.
¶**be hard on sy.**
¶ **be hard up** (for sg.)
Comp. hard-hearted ['hɑ:d'hɑ:tid], *part. adj.*
Comp. hard-working ['hɑ:d'wəkin], *adj.*
Δ **harden** ['hɑ:dn], *v.*
Δ **hardness** ['hɑdnis], *n. Uncount.*
II. hard [hɑ:d], *adv.* = strenuously, painfully, with difficulty.
He worked very hard.
They tried hard to succeed.
It is raining hard.
(Palmer 1938).

Extract (1)(b), by comparison with (1)(a), shows an extended range of meanings, but more interestingly, an attempt to give the zero-derivative ***hard***, adv., a prominence not granted to ***harden***, ***hardness*** or ***hard-working***, first by the absence of indentation and second by the specification of meanings of its own: ('*not soft*'), ('*vigorously*', '*strenuously*'). Palmer, as can be seen from extract (1)(c), builds on this ordering of priorities in *A Grammar of English Words*, first by making ***hard** adv.* a numbered sub-entry, but second by pushing ***harden*** and ***hardness*** back (since they are derivatives of the adjective, not of the adverb).

By the time the *General Service List* was compiled, Palmer was aware that he had the essential framework of a dictionary, but one quite different in form and purpose from the *Concise Oxford* or an American collegiate dictionary. He was not even then (the date was early 1936) fully aware that this dictionary would have a strongly productive character, yet most of the elements for encoding were already in place. Though none of the published word-lists contained syntactic information, research into verb-patterns and the so-called 'anomalous finites' (modal and primary verbs) had proceeded in parallel with work on vocabulary control, and major reports had already appeared (Palmer 1934a, 1935a). Second, extreme vocabulary limitation gave special prominence to structural words, the essential building blocks of sentence construction. Third, the Palmer-Hornby approach to lexical analysis had, as we have just seen, bequeathed an entry structure in which derivatives were clustered around their roots, with potential benefits for encoding. Fourth, and this is a point I wish to develop at greater length, Palmer had given careful thought to the role of examples as models for sentence-building. His recommended models, as incorporated in *A Grammar of English Words*, and - with Hornby's modifications - in the *Advanced Learner's Dictionary*, became standard patterns, and need to be included in any critical discussion of examples in learners' dictionaries.

3 Palmer, Hornby and dictionary examples

Palmer became convinced of the importance of illustrative examples in vocabulary lists while serving as a member of the Carnegie Committee, whose *Interim Report on Vocabulary Selection*, published in 1936, incorporated the *General Service List* in its first version. He was of course aware that examples would help to show what words (in their various senses) meant. However, of even greater value, in his view, were illustrative sentences designed to show the lexico-grammatical patterns by which items in their particular senses were realized. In the 1936 paper on vocabulary lay-out to which I referred earlier, he illustrated the point with reference to adjectival *used to*:

(2) to be used to something or somebody
to get used to something or somebody
to be used to doing something
to get used to doing something (Palmer 1936b).

Now, of course, these are not examples at all, if by examples we mean instances of *performance*, grammatically complete or incomplete, real or simulated. They are simplifications and abstractions - what I have elsewhere called 'minimal lexicalized patterns' (Cowie 1995, 1996) - and their value has long been recognized in French and Italian monolingual lexicography. Palmer referred to them as 'skeleton-type examples' and he and Hornby were responsible for introducing them into the monolingual learners' dictionary. Especially worth noting is that the type allows for internal variation, and also for degrees of abstraction. Consider the skeleton at (3), which is a conflation of the first two examples at (2), and in which the square brackets indicate alternatives while 'something' and 'somebody' (unlike *this* and *that*) represent nominal sub-categories:

(3) to be [get] used to something [somebody, this, that, etc.] (Palmer 1936).

Palmer, of course, also allowed in his overall scheme for sentence examples that showed no abstraction or alternation at all - what he appropriately called the 'sentence-sample type'. He did not, it is true, point out at that stage what the particular advantages of the skeleton-type were - that they, unlike sentence-samples, could clearly indicate which elements in a sentence or phrase were fixed, which optional and which substitutable, and in so doing help to prevent unacceptable flexibility or undue rigidity in production. The skeleton-type, incidentally, has descendants in the boldface pattern frames of OALD4 and 5, the 'generalized example sentences' of COBUILD1 and 2 and the 'pattern illustrations' of LDOCE3 (Herbst 1996). Interestingly, Palmer did recognize that the example-type chosen for illustrative purposes in a given dictionary would depend on the preferences of its users, and specifically whether they liked information to be set out fully and in detail, or in a concise, organized form.[1] In practice, this would often mean providing a *variety* of example types, as Hornby was to demonstrate in the *Idiomatic and Syntactic English Dictionary* of 1942. As I have shown in a recent analysis of a run of 506 entries and sub-entries in ISED, Hornby provided, out of a total of 258 examples, 129 phrase and clause examples that were simplified in a more or less standardized way (Cowie 1995). The clauses typically consisted of a transitive verb in the infinitive form, and a noun with little or no modification functioning as direct object. They were also ideally suited to encoding, as they constituted core collocations which could be inflected for tense and number and syntactically manipulated. Compare Hornby's skeleton examples to the left at (4) with the possible expansions to the right:

(4)	to man a ship	(⇒ The ship has been fully manned)
	to manage a horse	(⇒ I found the horse difficult to manage)
	to master the English Language	(⇒ She had not completely mastered the English Language) (Hornby et al. 1942).

In that same run of entries, though, there was an almost equal number (115) of sentence examples which, because of their grammatical completeness, came closer to simulating actual speech or writing, and could be used to convey cultural or encyclopaedic information (Cowie 1995: 286). Notice at (5), for example:

(5) Can you manage another slice of cake?
I don't like his manners at all.
Winds from the sea are generally moist. (Hornby et al. 1942)

[1] "A lay-out must be in conformity with the requirements of the learner for whose benefit it has been composed" (Palmer 1936b: 6).

4 Michael West and the 'minimum adequate definition vocabulary'

In the years immediately prior to the Carnegie Conference, Michael West had been engaged in compiling a learners' dictionary that would appear in 1935 as *The New Method English Dictionary* (NMED). As an entirely original feature, West's dictionary contained definitions based on a 'minimum adequate definition vocabulary' and, in the same year as the dictionary itself, West published *Definition vocabulary*, an account of how the defining vocabulary had been systematically chosen, checked and revised. The research necessitated compiling a preliminary version of the dictionary, in which a defining vocabulary of 1799 words - eventually to be reduced to 1490 - was used to define 23,898 vocabulary items (West 1935: 34-41).

In *Definition vocabulary*, West pinpointed and attempted to solve a number of the problems that were later (in the 1970s and 1980s) to face lexicographers wishing to devise limited defining vocabularies for advanced learners' dictionaries. The discussion is in fact remarkable for the range of theoretical issues he raises. West identified several of the characteristic weaknesses of definitions in the mother-tongue dictionary - the fondness for defining the known (say, *pencil*) in terms of the unknown ('instrument'? 'tapering'?), and the tendency to resort to 'scatter-gun' techniques, whereby 'one fires off a number of near or approximate synonyms in the hope that one or other will hit the mark and be understood', as in: 'sinuate = tortuous, wavy, winding' (1935: 8).

West also faced up to the problems of dictionary *size* presented by a limited defining vocabulary. He realized that in defining within a small wordstock, especially for foreign users, we are often forced to expand the definitions and possibly provide more examples. He saw, too, that at times we may be forced to use double definitions (as in the definition of *gherkin*, in which first *pickles* has to be defined, and then - as part of the definition of *pickles* - *vinegar*). Such requirements will tend to increase the length of the dictionary to an unacceptable extent. Of course, double definitions can be avoided, as Palmer was aware, by treating any defining word from outside the limited vocabulary as a cross-reference to its own place in the dictionary. This device was later to be a standard feature of LDOCE1 (1978).

One class of items that cannot with confidence be removed from the list of dictionary headwords is the defining vocabulary itself, since the compiler cannot be sure that these are already known by dictionary users. It was partly with this in mind that Gabriele Stein later put forward the idea of a 'bridging' bilingual dictionary designed to teach the definition vocabulary used in the appropriate advanced monolingual dictionary (Stein 1990).

As for the criteria used to limit the defining vocabulary, one question of crucial importance is the extent to which one can assume some degree of inference on the part of the user. West includes the commonest prefixes and suffixes (e.g. *dis-*, *in-*, *-able*, *-en*) in the defining vocabulary, and in the definitions he allows these to be attached to various words - provided their meanings are regular. So the deverbal suffix *-able* can be added to *drink, eat, read*, etc., on the assumption that the user will infer the meanings of *drinkable*, *eatable* and *readable* (cf. West 1935: 16). In this way great economies can be made. All the same,

West, like Palmer and Hornby in their work on *Thousand-Word English*, was aware of the danger of introducing into definitions derivatives or compounds whose meanings were not straightforwardly relatable to those of their elements (cf. Stein 1979, Cowie 1990).

As I have already shown, West's systematic approach to testing and refining the limited defining vocabulary of the *New Method English Dictionary* involved taking a word-list and then attempting to write a preliminary version of the dictionary within it, in the process modifying the vocabulary first selected. This was in fact a word-list already used by West for producing simplified readers. While it is not necessary to describe here the various processes through which the vocabulary was passed before it became suitable for use in NMED, one final theoretical point needs to be made. While drafting definitions, West realized that to provide a satisfactory definition in a large number of cases it was necessary to 'force in' 61 additional words. These are included, specially marked, in the list of words that constituted the defining vocabulary. Interestingly, several of these items, including *behaviour, belief, engine, insect, instrument, metal, noun, quality, relation, science, skill, solid, surface, vegetable*, are superordinate terms of some generality thought essential for defining many specific objects, substances, animals and plants.

5 Phraseology: the Palmer-Hornby legacy

The decision to set up a programme of research into phraseology at IRET was made in 1927, at the same time as the decision to compile a limited word-list, and was prompted by Harold Palmer's incisive observation "that it is not so much the *words* of English nor the *grammar* of English that make English difficult, but that that vague and undefined obstacle to progress in the learning of English consists for the most part in the existence of so many odd comings-together-of-words" (Palmer 1933: 13). The resulting project, the first, and - for English - the only, large-scale analysis of phraseology to be undertaken with the needs of the foreign learner in mind, was directed by Palmer but later greatly extended by A. S. Hornby. Its detailed findings were published in 1933 as the *Second Interim Report on English Collocations*. The *Interim Report* was a major landmark. Not only did it provide a detailed and meticulous classification of word-combinations in English; but it also revealed the prevalence of ready-made sequences in everyday speech and writing, and helped pave the way for the strong upsurge of interest in phraseology in the 1980s and 1990s.

5.1 The analytical approach

The descriptive approach adopted by Palmer had a number of salient characteristics, not all of which have survived into later frameworks. An undoubted and enduring strength, though, is that having put to one side 'sentence-like' combinations such as sayings, catch-phrases and familiar quotations, Palmer embarked on a rigorous classification of the much larger group of 'word-like' units.[2] These could be broken down initially into verb-collocations, noun-collocations, adjective-collocations, adverb-collocations and preposition-collocations, but much finer sub-categories were eventually recognized within those broader divisions, as for instance the adverb-collocation 'PREP x a *or* an x NOUN' (no. 35113), with examples that included:

(6) After a fashion
At a blow
At a disadvantage
At a distance
At an end
(Palmer 1933).

5.2 Limitations of the approach

The Palmer-Hornby approach had certain limitations. Few phraseologists would now apply the term 'collocation', as they did, to the whole range of word-combinations which they recognized - or even to the very large sub-class of 'word-like' combinations treated in the *Interim Report*. Most would now limit the term collocation to word-like combinations ('nominations') which are not idioms (that is, not more or less invariable and opaque) but which lie in the 'fuzzy' region between idioms and free word-combinations. Since neither Palmer nor Hornby recognized a scale of idiomaticity cutting across the grammatical classes of their scheme they - naturally enough - provided no procedures for distinguishing between the more and the less idiomatic.

The most obvious consequence of failing to recognize this descriptive dimension is that, in *A Grammar of English Words* and the earliest editions of ALD, as in the *Report* itself, idioms are not always given the special prominence that their status calls for. In the list at (6), the phrase *after a fashion* is both invariable and unmotivated, and thus an idiom, while *at a disadvantage* - quite apart from having a complementary term in *at an advantage* - can be internally modified, as in *at a serious disadvantage* and *at something of a disadvantage*, and is thus a collocation.

Of course, some features of the analytical approach adopted by Palmer and Hornby have had a lasting effect on the treatment of phraseology in learners' dictionaries. One interesting mark of their influence is that long before corpus-based studies revealed that short, stylistically colourless idioms (*in a sense, in a word, on the whole*) occurred much more frequently than culturally marked expressions (such as *buy a pig in a poke* or *put something on the back burner*), Palmer and Hornby were giving much greater prominence to the former both in the *Interim Report* and in their early dictionaries.

---

[2] Palmer provided a sub-classification of sentence-like units ('propositions'), in 1942, some years after retiring from his post as head of IRET.

Another enduring aspect of the Palmer-Hornby legacy is the emphasis now laid in several British phraseological dictionaries on the syntactic categorization of idioms and collocations. We also owe to the *Interim Report* the greater depth of analysis that is now common. Once the practice had been established, in the *Report*, of classifying multi-word units according to form and function, the natural next step was to provide a more detailed description, particularly by indicating transformational possibilities and restrictions. We find this finer specification in both volumes of the *Oxford Dictionary of Current Idiomatic English* (1975/1983) and in the *Longman Dictionary of English Idioms* (1979).

6 Conclusion

With the notable exception of Michael West's *New Method Dictionary*, the learners' dictionaries of the 1930s and 1940s are especially noteworthy as aids to encoding. Even Hornby's pioneering bilingual learners' dictionary of 1940 - *A Beginner's English-Japanese Dictionary* - was designed not to teach an intermediate vocabulary to middle-school Japanese learners but to familiarize them with verb-patterns and basic grammatical terms. It partly met the requirements of a 'bridge' dictionary recently set out by Stein (1990).

Hornby's *Idiomatic and Syntactic English Dictionary* of 1942 aimed to teach a general vocabulary, literary and spoken, up to university entrance level, but its title, its elaborate grammatical introduction, and the text itself suggested encoding priorities. It was only with the second (1963) and third (1974) editions, and the introduction, in LDOCE1 (1978), of a defining vocabulary based on West's innovative scheme, that something like the present balance between help for the writer and support for the reader was achieved.

Bibliography

A Beginners' English-Japanese Dictionary (1940): Albert S. Hornby, Rinchirou Ishikawa (eds.). — Tokyo: Kaitakusha.

A Grammar of English Words (1938): Harold E. Palmer (ed.). — London: Longmans, Green.

Collins COBUILD English Dictionary (First edition) ([1]1987): John McH. Sinclair et al. (eds.). — London and Glasgow: Collins.

Idiomatic and Syntactic English Dictionary (Photographically reprinted and published as A Learner's Dictionary of Current English by OUP, 1948; subsequently, in 1952, retitled The Advanced Learner's Dictionary of Current English) (1942): Albert S. Hornby, Edward V. Gatenby, Harold Wakefield (eds.). — Tokyo: Kaitakusha.

Longman Dictionary of Comtemporary English ([1]1978): Paul Procter (ed.). — Harlow: Longman.

Longman Dictionary of English Idioms (1979): Thomas H. Long, Della Summers (eds.). — Harlow: Longman.

Oxford Advanced Learner's Dictionary of Current English ([3]1974): Albert S. Hornby, Anthony P. Cowie, Jack Windsor Lewis (eds.). — London: OUP.

Oxford Advanced Learner's Dictionary of Current English ([4]1989): Anthony P. Cowie (ed.). — Oxford: OUP.
Oxford Dictionary of Current Idiomatic English ([1]1975): Anthony P. Cowie, Ronald Mackin (eds.) (Volume 1). — London: OUP
Oxford Dictionary of Current Idiomatic English (1983): Anthony P. Cowie, Ronald Mackin, Isabel R. McCaig (eds.) (Volume 2). — Oxford: OUP.
The Advanced Learner's Dictionary of Current English ([2]1963): Albert S. Hornby, Edward V. Gatenby, Harold Wakefield (eds.). — London: OUP.
The Concise Oxford Dictionary of Current English ([3]1934): Henry W. Fowler, H.G. Le Mesurier (eds.):— Oxford: Clarendon Press.
The New Method English Dictionary (1935): Michael P. West, James G. Endicott (eds.). — London: Longmans, Green.

Cowie, Anthony P. (1990): "Language as words: lexicography". — In: N. E. Collinge (ed.): An Encyclopaedia of Language (London: Routledge) 671-700.
— (1994): "Phraseology". — In: R. E. Asher (ed.): The Encyclopedia of Language and Linguistics, Volume 6 (Oxford, New York: Pergamon) 3168-3171.
— (1995): "The learner's dictionary in a changing cultural perspective". — In: B.B. Kachru, H. Kahane (eds.): Cultures, Ideologies and the Dictionary (Tübingen: Niemeyer) (=Lexicographica, Series Maior 64) 283-295.
— (1996): "The 'dizionario scolastico': a learner's dictionary for native speakers". — In: International Journal of Lexicography 9/2, 118-131.
Faucett, Lawrence, Harold E. Palmer, Edward L. Thorndike, Michael P. West (1936): Interim Report on Vocabulary Selection for the Teaching of English as a Foreign Language. — London: P. S. King & Son.
Herbst, Thomas (1996): "On the way to the perfect learners' dictionary: a first comparison of OALD5, LDOCE3, COBUILD2 and CIDE". — In: International Journal of Lexicography 9/4, 321-357.
Palmer, Harold E. (1930): First Interim Report on Vocabulary Selection. — Tokyo: Kaitakusha.
— (1929a) "What shall we call a 'word'?". —In: IRET Bulletin 54, 1-2.
— (1929b): "Editorial: what is an idiom?". — In: IRET Bulletin 56, 1-2.
— (1933): Second Interim Report on English Collocations. — Tokyo: Kaitakusha.
— (1934a): Specimens of English Construction Patterns (Based on the general synoptic chart showing the syntax of the English sentence). — Tokyo: IRET.
— (1934b): An Essay in Lexicology in the Form of Specimen Entries in Some Possible New-Type Dictionary. — Tokyo: Kaitakusha.
— (1935a): The Theory of the 24 Anomalous Finites. — Tokyo: IRET.
— (1935b): "When is an adjective not an adjective?". — In: IRET Bulletin 114, 1-10.
— (1936a): "The history and present state of the movement towards vocabulary control". — In: IRET Bulletin 120, 14-17 and 121, 19-23.
— (1936b): "The art of vocabulary lay-out". — In: IRET Bulletin 121, 1-8 and 14-19.
Palmer, Harold E., Albert S. Hornby (1937): Thousand-Word English. — London: George Harrap.
Stein, Gabriele (1979): "The best of British and American lexicography". — In: Dictionaries 1, 1-23.
— (1990): "From the bilingual to the monolingual dictionary". — In: T. Magay, J. Zigány (eds.): BudaLEX '88 Proceedings (Budapest: Akadémiai Kiadó) (=Papers for the EURALEX Third International Congress) 401-407.
West, Michael P. (1935): Definition Vocabulary (=Bulletin no. 4 of the Department of Educational Research). — Toronto: University of Toronto.

Flor Aarts

Syntactic information in OALD5, LDOCE3, COBUILD2 and CIDE

1 Introduction

"Dictionaries", said Dr. Johnson, "are like watches. The worst is better than none, and the best cannot be expected to go quite true". In the history of English lexicography a lot has happened since Johnson's famous pronouncement. The dictionaries we have now are infinitely superior to those of the 18th century. This is true of their coverage, their definitions and their use of corpus-based real-language examples. But the perfect dictionary does not yet exist.

The same is true of learners' dictionaries. Since the publication of the first edition of Hornby's *Oxford Advanced Learner's Dictionary* (OALD) in 1948, a lot of progress has been made, not only in coverage but also in the way meanings are defined and exemplified. And, of course, we now have four major learners' dictionaries instead of one. The OALD is already in its fifth edition, the *Longman Dictionary of Contemporary English* (LDOCE) is in its third, the *Collins Cobuild English Dictionary* (COBUILD) in its second and there is, of course, a newcomer on the market: the *Cambridge International Dictionary of English* (CIDE).

The question mark in the title of this conference ('*The Perfect Learners' Dictionary?*') would seem to suggest that the organizers agree with Dr. Johnson and assume that perfect learners' dictionaries exist only in ideal worlds. Indeed, none of the four dictionaries uses slogans claiming to be perfect, although all of them make us offers that we cannot refuse. COBUILD2 "helps learners with real English", CIDE "gives today's users of English unrivalled access to the English they need", LDOCE3 offers "a complete guide to written and spoken English" and OALD5 claims to be "the dictionary that really teaches English". Whatever the value of these claims may be, there is no doubt that all four dictionaries have achieved exceptionally high lexicographical standards. Perfection, unfortunately, is not yet for sale.

Perhaps we had better ask what a *good*, rather than a *perfect*, learners' dictionary is and in terms of what criteria we should evaluate it. Randolph Quirk, in the preface to LDOCE3 (p. ix), mentions coverage and definition as two core features. David Crystal, in *The Cambridge Encyclopedia of Language* (1987: 111), lists no less than twenty questions that we should ask when buying a dictionary. They concern coverage and definition, but also usage and information about word class, inflectional endings and "other relevant features of grammar".

In this paper I shall focus on the information that OALD5, LDOCE3, COBUILD2 and CIDE provide on what Crystal calls "other relevant features of grammar". More particularly, I want to concentrate on the syntax of verbs as well as on the way in which syntactic information is presented.

As has often been pointed out, learners' dictionaries should serve a dual purpose. They should enable students to decode what they do not understand and, at the same time, serve as instruments that enable them to produce their own texts. In other words, learners' dictionaries should serve the needs of both readers and writers. They can only fulfil this second role if they contain adequate syntactic information.

A.S. Hornby was the first lexicographer to come up with the idea that the syntactic properties of verbs could be represented by means of codes. He first set out this idea in detail in *Guide to Patterns and Usage in English*, published in 1954. In the preface to the second edition of his *Guide* (1975) Hornby writes: "A knowledge of how to put words together in the right order is as important as a knowledge of their meanings. The most important patterns are those of the verbs. Unless the learner becomes familiar with these he will be unable to use his vocabulary". Hornby's *Guide* contains 25 verb patterns, which consist of the symbol VP, followed by a number and a capital letter. Thus VP2A stands for an intransitive verb. Hornby's idea was brilliant, but the format of his codes was useless. Students, as we all know, do not bother to read prefaces to dictionaries, let alone explanations of what complicated verb codes stand for (cf. Béjoint: 1981). As a result, Hornby's codes were inaccessible to students, except to those who were prepared to learn them by heart.

Lexicographers began to realize that it was necessary to do something about the codes if they were to have any use at all. In 1987 and 1989, respectively, LDOCE and OALD published new editions with completely revised and considerably improved verb code systems. COBUILD's first edition (1987) also contained codes that could be regarded as a step forward.

Two years ago things changed again. The year 1995 may be regarded as a high point in the history of English learners' dictionaries. Not only did it see the publication of yet another edition of OALD, LDOCE and COBUILD, it was also the year of the appearance of a competitor, the new *Cambridge* dictionary. This provides us with an ideal opportunity for comparison (cf. Boogaards: 1996 and Herbst: 1996).

In what follows we will first look at the way in which the four dictionaries organize verb entries (Section 2). The entry for the verb *believe* will serve as an example.

Section 3 looks at the symbols that the four dictionaries employ in their verb codes. In section 3.1 we will examine the symbols that are used for the verb in the earlier editions (Table 1) as well as in the 1995 editions (Table 2). Section 3.2 compares the symbols used for elements that come after the symbol for the verb (Table 3).

Section 4 shows how these dictionaries encode syntactic information on major verb patterns. For OALD, LDOCE and COBUILD a comparison will be made with the earlier editions.

Section 5 contains a summary.

2 The organization of verb entries

In all four dictionaries verb entries provide information on pronunciation, word class and (where relevant) on spelling, usage and register. In addition, a verb entry contains definitions, examples and codes, which account for the semantics and the syntax of the verb in question.

The way in which verb entries are structured is just as important to students as the information they contain. When we compare the entries for the verb *believe*, we can see how practice varies.

2.1 OALD5

believe /bɪ'li:v/ *v* (not in the continuous tenses) **1(a)** to feel sure of the truth of sth: [Vn] *She believed everything he told her.* ○ *I refuse to believe it.* ○ *I'll believe it/that when I see it* (ie I will not believe it until I have solid evidence). ○ *I'm told he's been in prison, and I can well believe it* (ie it does not surprise me). ○ *Don't believe what you read in the papers.* **(b)** to accept the statement of sb as true: [Vn] *I don't know which of them to believe.* **2** to think; to suppose: [V.*that*] *People used to believe (that) the world was flat.* ○ *It was widely believed that he had betrayed his country.* ○ *I believe I should congratulate you on becoming a father.* ○ *It happened on 22 February, a Monday I believe.* ○ *The police believed him to be guilty.* ○ *I genuinely believe it to have been a mistake.* ○ *'Is he coming?' 'I believe so/not.'* [also V.*wh*]. **3** to have a religious faith: [V] *He thinks that everyone who believes will go to heaven.* PHR V **be'lieve in sb/sth** to feel sure of the existence of sb/sth: *I believe in God.* ○ *Do you believe in ghosts?* **be'lieve in sth/sb; be'lieve in doing sth** to trust sth/sb; to feel sure of the value or truth of sth: *She has doubts about him, but I believe in him implicitly.* ○ *Do you believe in nuclear disarmament?* ○ *He believes in getting plenty of exercise.* **'believe sth of sb** to accept that sb is capable of a particular action, etc: *If I hadn't seen him doing it I would never have believed it of him.* IDM **believe it or 'not** it may sound surprising but it is true: *Believe it or not, we were left waiting in the rain for two hours.* **be-lieve (you) 'me** I can tell you confidently: *Believe you me, this administration won't meddle with the tax system.* **don't you be'lieve it!** it is not true; it will not happen: *'He's only 34.' 'Don't you believe it — he's at least 40.'* **give sb to believe/understand** ⇨ GIVE[1]. **make believe (that...)** to pretend: *The boys liked to make believe (that) they were astronauts.* See also MAKE-BELIEVE. **not believe one's 'ears/'eyes** to be unable to believe that what one hears or sees is real because one is so suprised: *I stared at her, scarcely able to believe my ears.* **seeing is be'liev-ing** (*saying*) one needs to see sth before one can believe that it really exists or happens. **would you be'lieve (it)?** (expressing great surprise or shock) although it is hard to believe: *Today, would you believe, she came to work in an evening dress!*

▶ **believable** *adj* that can be believed: *an entirely believable explanation/scenario* ○ *a play with believ-able characters.* Compare UNBELIEVABLE.

believer *n* a person who believes, esp sb with religious faith: *a message to all true believers of Islam.* Compare UNBELIEVER. IDM **be a (great/firm) be-liever in sth** to feel sure that sth is important or valuable: *I'm a great believer in (taking) regular physical exercise.*

The OALD5 entry for *believe* tells us that it is not possible to use this verb in the continuous forms. There are four sections: the first is concerned with the various meanings, the second treats the phrasal verb *believe in* and the third deals with idioms. Derivatives are listed at the end of the entry. The structure of the entry is clearly indicated by means of black boxes with capital letters, marking those sections that deal with phrasal verbs and idioms.

Meanings are separated by numbers, or, if closely related, by letters. The arrangement is according to frequency. Each meaning is defined. Definitions are in telegram style and they are written within a 3,500-word vocabulary (printed in Appendix 10). Each definition is followed by one or more examples, based on the British National Corpus.

The syntactic codes are given in square brackets and precede the examples. OALD5 claims that "when an example follows another one illustrating the same pattern or patterns, the code is not repeated" (Study page, B 8). Note that the example under 1 (b) has been given the wrong code and that the last four examples under 2 should have been given their own codes instead of the code [V.*that*]. Moreover, at the end of 2 we find a code, viz [V.wh], without an example.

Phrasal verbs do not have codes. If a phrasal verb is transitive, the position of the direct object is said to follow from its position in the entry. Thus the object comes last in *look after sb/sth*, but immediately follows the verb in *call sth off*. Unfortunately this does not tell the reader that the object can also follow the phrasal verb, as in *call off a deal*, provided the object is not pronominal. The reader is probably supposed to infer this from the examples.

2.2 LDOCE3

S1 W1 **be·lieve** /bɪ̈ˈliːv/ *v* [not in progressive]
1 ▶ BE SURE STH IS TRUE ◀ [T] to be sure that something is true or that someone is telling the truth: *You shouldn't believe everything you read.* | **believe (that)** *I can hardly believe he's only 25!* | **believe sb** *I don't believe her – it can't be true.* | **believe sth of sb** *Stealing? I would never have believed it of him!* | **not believe a word of it** *spoken* (=not believe something at all)
2 can't/don't believe *spoken* used to say that you are very surprised or shocked by something: *It's still raining – I don't believe it!* | *I can't believe he's expecting us to work on Sunday as well!* | *My mum couldn't believe it when I dyed my hair green.*
3 believe it or not *spoken* used when you are going to say something that is true but surprising: *Well, believe it or not, they've given me a loan.*
4 would you believe it! *spoken* used when you are surprised or angry about something: *And then he just walked out. Would you believe it!*
5 believe (you) me *spoken* used to emphasize that something is definitely true: *There'll be trouble when they find out about this, believe you me!*
6 you'd better believe it! *spoken* used to emphasize that something is true
7 don't you believe it! *spoken* used to emphasize that something is definitely not true
8 can't believe your eyes/ears *spoken* to be very surprised by something you see or hear: *I could hardly believe my eyes when he took a gun out of his pocket.*
9 if you believe that, you'll believe anything *spoken* used to say that something is definitely not true, and that anyone who believes it must be stupid
10 ▶ HAVE AN OPINION ◀ [T] to think that something is true, although you are not completely sure: **believe (that)** *I believe you two have met already.* | **believe so/not** (=think that something is true or not) *"Have they arrived yet?" "Yes, I believe so."* | **believe sb to be sth** *The jury believed Beyers to be innocent.* | **be widely believed** (=a lot of people believe this) *They are widely believed to be planning a takeover bid.* | **have reason to believe (that)** (=have information that makes you believe something) *We have reason to believe that she knew the victim quite well.*
11 seeing is believing *usually spoken* used to say that you will only believe that something happens or exists when you actually see it
12 ▶ RELIGION ◀ [I] to have a strong religious faith: *She says that those who believe will go to heaven.* —see also **make believe** (MAKE[1] (19))
believe in *phr v* [T] **1** to be sure that someone exists: *Do you believe in God?* | *It's amazing how many people believe in ghosts.* **2** to support or approve of something because you think it is good or right: *I don't believe in all these silly diets* | **believe in doing sth** *They believe in letting children make their own mistakes.* **3** [T **believe in sb**] to be confident that someone can be trusted: *The people want a President they can believe in.* | *You've got to believe in yourself, or you'll never succeed.*

The entry for *believe* in LDOCE3 shows that this verb is among the 1,000 most frequently used words in spoken as well as in written English. The entry also tells the reader that this verb does not occur in the progressive form.

Three major senses of *believe* are distinguished. This is done by means of a new and very useful feature, viz so-called 'signposts', that is, short phrases and words in capital letters that serve as a visual index. Meanings are given in order of frequency and they are numbered. All meanings begin on new lines (at least in longer entries). Phrases and idiomatic expressions do not appear at the end of the entry, but are listed together with the sense of the headword to which they belong. Idioms are treated as separate meanings and they are also numbered separately. The phrasal verb *believe in* is given at the end of the entry.

In LDOCE3 meanings are usually defined in telegram style by means of a 2,000-word defining vocabulary (printed at the end of the dictionary). Definitions are illustrated by examples based on the Longman Corpus Network.

Syntactic codes are given within square brackets and precede the definitions of the major senses. The coding system in LDOCE3 has been considerably simplified in comparison with the 1987 edition. For the verb *believe* we find, in fact, only two codes: [T] for the first two senses and [I] for the sense 'have a strong religious faith'. This means that a number of syntactic patterns in which *believe* can appear (for example, those in which it can be followed by a finite or non-finite clause) have not been given special codes. These patterns are illustrated by collocations in dark type (for example, **believe (that)**).

In LDOCE3 idioms do not have codes, but phrasal verbs do. A phrasal verb is any type of multi-word verb. If a phrasal verb has an object that can occupy two positions, this is indicated by a double arrow (*hand sth ↔ out*).

2.3 COBUILD2

believe /bɪliːv/ **believes, believing, believed** ◆◆◆◆◆

1 If you **believe** that something is true, you think that it is true; a formal use. You can say **'I believe'** to indicate that you are not completely sure that what you are saying is accurate or to make a statement sound more factual and less emotional. *Experts believe that the coming drought will be extensive... I believe you have something of mine... The main problem, I believe, lies elsewhere... We believe them to be hidden here in this apartment... 'You've never heard of him?'—'I don't believe so.'*
VERB =think V that V n to-inf V so/not Also V n adj

2 If you **believe** someone or if you **believe** what they say or write, you accept that they are telling the truth. *He did not sound as if he believed her... Never believe anything a married man says about his wife... Don't believe what you read in the papers.*
VERB ≠disbelieve V n

3 If you **believe** in fairies, ghosts, or miracles, you are sure that they exist or happen. If you **believe** in a god, you are sure of the existence of that god. *I don't believe in ghosts... Do you believe in magic?*
VERB V in n Also V

4 If you **believe in** a way of life or an idea, you are in favour of it because you think it is good or right. *He believed in marital fidelity. ...decent candidates who believed in democracy.*
VERB V in n

5 If you **believe in** someone or what they are doing, you have confidence in them and think that they will be successful. *If you believe in yourself you can succeed.*
VERB V in n

6 **Believe** is used in expressions such as **I can't believe how** or **it's hard to believe that** in order to express surprise, for example because something bad has happened or something very difficult has been achieved. *It was awful. We couldn't believe what they were doing but we never thought it would make a difference... Many officers I spoke to found it hard to believe what was happening around them... I was a physical and emotional wreck – I still can't believe how I ever got any work done.*
VB: with brd-neg PRAGMATICS V wh Also V that

7 If you say that you cannot **believe your eyes** or cannot **believe your ears**, you are emphasizing that you are very surprised about something you have seen or heard. *I could not believe my eyes. She was far more beautiful than I had imagined.*
PHRASES V inflects, with brd-neg PRAGMATICS

8 You can use **believe it or not** to emphasize that what you have just said is surprising. *That's normal, believe it or not.*
PHR with cl PRAGMATICS

9 If you say **would you believe it**, you are emphasizing your surprise about something. *And would you believe it, he's younger than me!*
PHR with cl PRAGMATICS

10 You can use **believe you me** to emphasize that what you are saying is true. *It's absolutely amazing, believe you me.*
PHR with cl PRAGMATICS

In this dictionary the frequency of the verb *believe* is indicated by means of five black diamonds in the margin. This means that this verb belongs to the 700 most frequently used words in the language. COBUILD2 does not mention any restriction on the use of *believe* in the progressive form.

The entry for *believe* is divided into ten sub-entries, all of which are numbered. In COBUILD2 numbers are always printed at the beginning of the left-hand margin. The order is determined by frequency. *Believe* has two main senses, which, interestingly, are listed in a different order from those in OALD5 and LDOCE3: the 'believe = think' meaning precedes the 'accept the truth of' meaning. The intransitive ('religious') use of *believe* (as in: *I do not believe*) is not listed. The phrasal verb *believe in* is dealt with in sub-entries 3-5, idiomatic expressions in 6-10.

An important feature of this dictionary is that it usually defines meanings in full sentences containing the word or expression to be defined and showing how it is commonly used. For example: *If you say* Would you believe it, *you are emphasizing your surprise about something*. The importance of defining meanings by means of full sentences is that verb entries provide two types of information in COBUILD2: the codes tell us how a verb subcategorizes and the definitions specify its selectional restrictions. Most of the words in COBUILD2's defining vocabulary are among the 2,500 most frequent words in English. Definitions are followed by examples, the majority of which are taken from *The Bank of English*, a corpus of 200 million words.

Grammatical, semantic and pragmatic information in COBUILD2 is printed in the so-called 'Extra Column'. This is a useful feature of this dictionary because it means that the text of an entry contains only definitions and examples without being interrupted by codes. COBUILD2 claims that "in the case of verbs, we give examples for all the main grammatical structures in which they are used. The examples are given in the same order as the patterns shown in the Extra Column" (p. xxii). As we can see, this claim does not hold for the entry for *believe*. For example, for sense 1 we find 5 examples and 4 codes. However, the third example does not have a code and the fourth code does not correspond to an example. Of the examples for sense 2 the third should have been given its own code (Vwh) and under 3 the code 'Also V' should have been exemplified. COBUILD2 is the only dictionary that has no examples of passive *believe*-sentences.

Phrasal verbs are coded in COBUILD2. Transitive phrasal verbs are given two codes to show the position of the direct object. For example, *pick up*, in its transitive sense, has the codes 'VnP' and 'VPn (not pron)'.

•

2.4 CIDE

be·lieve *(obj)* /bɪ'liːv/ *v* to think that something is true, correct or real • *Strangely, no one believed us when we told them we'd been visited by a creature from Mars.* [T] • *He believes* **that** *all children are born with equal intelligence.* [+ *that* clause] • *She's arriving tomorrow, I believe.* [+ clause] • *"Is she coming alone?" "We believe* **not/so** (= We think she is not/is)." [+ *not/so*] • *You wouldn't believe* **who** *Ed's going to marry.* [+ *wh-* word] • *I believe her* **to** *be the finest violinist in the world.* [T + obj + *to* infinitive] • *The robbers are believed* **to** *have escaped via Heathrow Airport.* [T + obj + *to* infinitive] • *All the crew are missing, believed dead.* [T + obj + adj] • To believe **in** something is to be certain that it exists: *Do you believe in reincarnation?* [I always + prep] • To believe **in** someone/something is to have confidence in that person or thing: *I believe in the fundamental goodness of human nature.* [I always + prep] • *So he told you she was just a friend, did he? I don't* **believe a word** (= any) *of it!* • *He's upstairs doing his homework,* **believe it or not/would you believe it?** (= it is true, although it seems unlikely). • *She* **could hardly/couldn't believe** *her* **eyes/ears** *when she saw/heard* (= was so surprised that she thought she imagined) *what happened on the bus.* • *I* **couldn't believe my luck** (= was very surprised and very pleased) *when I heard that I'd inherited my uncle's fortune.* • To **make believe** something is to pretend it: *Let's make believe we are pirates and search for treasures.* See also MAKE-BELIEVE. • If you say you **will believe** something **when** you **see it** you mean it seems so unlikely that you will not think it is true until you see proof of it: I'll believe someone on a motorcycle can jump over seventeen cars when I see it. • *"When my love swears that she is made of truth,/ I do believe her, though I know she lies"* (William Shakespeare, Sonnett 138) • *"Believe it or not"* (title of a newspaper column by R.L.Ripley, 1893-1949)

be·liev·a·ble /bɪ'liː·və·bl̩/ *adj* • *I didn't enjoy the film because I didn't think the characters were believable* (= like real life).

be·liev·er /£bɪ'liː·vəʳ, $·vɚ/ *n* [C] • A believer is a person who has a religious belief or who has confidence in the good of something: *She's became a believer after she survived a terrible accident.* ○ *Harvey's a* **(great)** *believer* **in** *health food.* ○ *I'm a* **(great)** *believer* **in** *allowing people to make their own mistakes.* • *"Then I saw her face, now I'm a believer"* (song written by Neil Diamond and sung by The Monkees, 1967)

The Cambridge dictionary does not tell the reader that *believe* is a frequent verb in English nor does it say that *believe* cannot occur in the progressive. The entry first defines and exemplifies this verb and then goes on to deal with the phrasal verb *believe in*. Idioms and derived words are treated at the end of the entry.

The entry for *believe* differs in several respects from those in OALD5, LDOCE3 and COBUILD2. First, we notice that no distinction is made between the two senses of *believe*, viz *believe* = 'think' and *believe* as antonym of *disbelieve*. This is strange, since each sense has its own, characteristic, syntactic patterns. Secondly, CIDE does not use numbers, but large dots, to separate meanings, definitions and examples. This means that the text in this entry runs on and that the reader's only guide to what he is looking for is what is printed in bold face. In entries with more senses, however, CIDE has so-called 'guide words', which are reminiscent of the 'signposts' in LDOCE3. A third difference is that codes appear in two different positions.

Definitions are in the traditional, brief style and written within a controlled defining vocabulary of less than 2,000 words (printed at the end of the dictionary). Occasionally CIDE defines meanings by means of full sentences in a style we associate with COBUILD2 (see, for example, s.v. *mean*). Meanings are usually listed in order of frequency. Definitions are followed by examples from the *International Cambridge Language Survey* of 100 million words (which includes a learner corpus).

Codes are given before the definition of a word, if the word always appears in the same syntactic pattern. If this is not the case, the codes appear after the examples. The coding in this entry is very systematic: there are no examples without codes nor codes without examples. Some of the codes are wrong, however. Thus, the phrasal verb *believe in* is given the code [I always + prep] and the passive sentence *The robbers are believed to have escaped via Heathrow Airport* is coded [T + obj + *to* infinitive], which is the code for its active counterpart.

Note that the headword is immediately followed by the symbol *(obj)*. In CIDE this means that *believe* is used both transitively and intransitively. When used in this way, the symbol *obj* refers to a verbal subclass, viz 'transitive'. However, when used in the codes, it has a different meaning, for example in [T + obj + *to* infinitive], where it refers to a sentence constituent. This is confusing.

In CIDE phrasal verbs are coded, but idioms are not. Information about the place of the direct object of transitive phrasal verbs is provided before the definition of the headword, by printing the headword twice (as in cross out *obj*, cross *obj* out) and by a code, *v adv* [M], where [M] denotes that the adverb is movable.

The information in the four entries for *believe* and the way in which this information is presented can be summarized as follows:

1. Information about frequency of headword	in LDOCE3 and COBUILD2
2. Information about use of progressive form	in OALD5 and LDOCE3
3. Use of numbers	in OALD5, LDOCE3 and COBUILD2
4. Numbers on new lines	in LDOCE3 (longer entries) and COBUILD2
5. Meanings in order of frequency	in all four dictionaries
6. Use of 'signposts'/'guide words'	in LDOCE3 and CIDE
7. Definitions in full sentences	in COBUILD2
8. Defining vocabulary	in all four dictionaries

9. Use of codes	in all four dictionaries
10. Place of codes	OALD5: before examples LDOCE3: before definitions COBUILD2: in 'Extra Column' CIDE: before definitions or after examples
11. Idioms	at end of entry: OALD5, LDOCE3 and CIDE in text of entry: LDOCE3
12. Phrasal verbs	before idioms: OALD5, COBUILD2 and CIDE at end of entry: LDOCE3

In order to be maximally accessible to readers, a verb entry should meet the following requirements:

1. all senses should be numbered;
2. each sense should start on a new line;
3. if the headword has several senses, 'signposts' or 'guide words' should be used;
4. definitions should always be followed by one or more examples;
5. codes and examples should be systematically paired, that is, a code should always be accompanied by one or more examples and an example should always have a code;
6. it should be quite clear which code(s) go(es) with which example(s);
7. sections dealing with verbal idioms and phrasal verbs should be clearly marked.

3 The symbols used in the verb codes

3.1 The symbols for the verb

Table 1: Symbols for the verb (1987-1989 editions)

	OALD4 (1989)	LDOCE2 (1987)	COBUILD1 (1987)
Intransitive verb	I	I	V
Linking verb	L	L	V
Monotransitive verb	T	T	V
Ditransitive verb	D	T	V
Complex transitive verb	C	T	V
Ergative verb	-	-	V-ERG
Reciprocal verb	-	-	RECIP

As Table 1 shows, COBUILD1 had only three symbols to indicate verbal subclasses: V, V-ERG and RECIP. V was used for intransitive verbs and linking verbs, as well as for the three classes of transitive verbs. V-ERG was the symbol for ergative verbs (like *open*) and RECIP denoted reciprocal verbs (like *meet*). The meaning of these symbols was explained in boxes. LDOCE2 used three symbols and OALD4 as many as five.

Table 2: Symbols for the verb (1995 editions)

	OALD5	LDOCE3	COBUILD2	CIDE
Intransitive verb	V	I	V	I
Linking verb	V	linking Verb	V-LINK	L
Monotransitive verb	V	T	V	T
Ditransitive verb	V	T	V	T
Complex transitive verb	V	T	V	T
Ergative verb	-	-	V-ERG	-
Ergative link verb	-	-	V-LINK-ERG	-
Ergative reciprocal verb	-	-	V-RECIP-ERG	-
Reciprocal verb	-	-	V-RECIP	-

A comparison with Table 2 shows the changes that have been introduced. COBUILD2 now uses V-LINK for copular verbs and V-RECIP for reciprocal verbs. It employs two new symbols, V-LINK-ERG and V-RECIP-ERG, for ergative link verbs (eg. *keep*) and ergative reciprocal verbs (eg. *alternate*), respectively. This means that COBUILD2 now has six symbols for the verb. Although these symbols are explained in the grammar section of the dictionary, students will probably find them difficult to interpret.

LDOCE3 still has three verb symbols and so has CIDE. OALD5, however, has reduced the number of symbols from five to one. If a verb is intransitive, the code is simply V. In all other cases V is followed by additional symbols to indicate particular syntactic patterns.

In my view, OALD5 now has the simplest system. As I have pointed out elsewhere (Aarts, 1991: 572), there is no need to use symbols such as I, L, T, D and C. Many students do not understand what these symbols mean nor do they bother to look up what they stand for. If a student does not know how a particular verb is used, there are, in fact, only two questions that he should find an answer to in his dictionary, viz 1. can this verb be used on its own? and 2. if not, by how many elements and by what type of elements must it be followed? If the verb can be used on its own, it is intransitive and the code is simply V. If the verb requires complementation, V is followed by additional symbols which automatically assign a category value to V.

3.2 The symbols used after the verb symbol

Table 3: Symbols used after the verb symbol (1995 editions)

	OALD5	LDOCE3	COBUILD2	CIDE
adj	+	+	+	+
adv	+	+	+	+
adv [M]	-	-	-	+
-ed	-	-	+	-
inf	-	-	+	-
inf (no to)	+	-	-	-
infinitive without to	-	-	-	+
-ing/ing	+	-	+	-
n	+	-	+	+
obj	-	-	-	+
P/p	+	-	+	-
pr(ep)	+	+	+	+
that	+	-	+	-
that clause	-	-	-	+
to inf(initive)	+	-	+	+
v-ed	-	-	-	+
v-ing	-	-	-	+
wh	+	-	+	-
whether/if	-	-	+	-
wh-word	-	-	-	+
	10	3	12	12

Table 3 shows how many symbols the four dictionaries employ in their verb codes (apart from the symbol for the verb).

There is hardly any difference between OALD5, COBUILD2 and CIDE, with 10, 12 and 12 symbols, respectively. They thus differ strikingly from LDOCE3, which, in comparison with the 1987 edition, has reduced the number of symbols from 13 to 3: *adj*, *adv* and *prep*. This has important consequences, which will be discussed in section 4.

Note that, with the exception of the symbol *obj* (in CIDE), all symbols denote grammatical categories, rather than grammatical functions: they refer to word classes, verb forms or clause types.

4 The major verb codes

In this section we will examine the major verb codes employed by the four dictionaries. Following the classification in Quirk et al. (1985: § 16.20 ff.), we will distinguish five categories of verbs: copular, intransitive, monotransitive, ditransitive and complex transitive. Each category is represented by one or more verbs in Tables 4-7. Examples will be given of codes for 22 major verb patterns (for a very detailed survey of simple and complex verb patterns in English, see Sinclair: 1996). For OALD, LDOCE and COBUILD we will also list the codes that are to be found in the preceding editions.

Table 4: The major verb codes in OALD (1989 & 1995)

	OALD4	OALD5
Copular		
1. become angry/president	La; Ln	V -adj; V -n
Intransitive		
2. faint	I	V
Monotransitive		
3. admire sb/sth	Tn	Vn
4. believe (that...)	Tf	V.*that*
5. doubt (whether sth is true)	Tf	V.*wh*
6. wonder (what to do)	Tw	V.*wh*
7. refuse (to leave)	Tt	V.*to* inf
8. enjoy (singing)	Tg	V.*ing*
9. want (sb to do sth)	Tnt	V. n *to* inf
10. hate (sb doing sth)	Tsg	V. n *ing*
Ditransitive		
11. send (sb sth)	Dn.n	Vnn
12. teach (sth to sb)	Dn.pr	Vnpr
13. promise (sb that...)	Dn.f	Vn. *that*
14. ask (sb whether...)	Dn.w	Vn.*wh*
15. show (sb how to...)	Dn.w	Vn.*wh*
16. advise (sb to do sth)	Dn.t	Vn.*to* inf
Complex transitive		
17. drive (sb mad)	Cn.a	Vn-adj
18. elect (sb chairman)	Cn.n	Vn-n
19. know (sb to be a liar)	Cn.t	V. n *to* inf
20. make (sb do sth)	Cn.i	Vn. inf (no *to*)

21. set (sb thinking)	Cn.g	Vn. *ing*
22. get (sth repaired)	-	-

The 1995 edition has a completely revised and considerably simplified coding system, for which Keith Brown is responsible.

There are at least two important differences with the 1989 edition. First, there is only one symbol for the verb (viz V), instead of five. Secondly, a number of opaque symbols, such as f (for finite clause), w (for *wh* -clause), t (for *to-* infinitive), g (for *-ing* clause), sg (for constructions like *We dread Mary /Mary's taking over)* and i (for infinitive without *to*) have been changed as follows:

f > that	g > *ing*
w > wh	sg > *n ing*
t > *to* inf	i > inf (no *to*)

As in the 1989 edition, OALD5 employs category symbols only (such as n, adj and pr), rather than symbols denoting sentence functions. In all, OALD5 has 19 different verb codes for the major syntactic patterns. There is no code for example 22.

A new feature is the use of two typographical devices (a dot and a dash) to distinguish codes that would otherwise have been identical. Compare, for example, code 16 (Vn.*to* inf) with codes 9 and 19 (V. n *to* inf). In 9 and 19 the place of the dot, immediately after V, shows that the n is not the object of the V, but the subject of the following infinitive. The same applies to codes 10 and 21. OALD5 also distinguishes between Vnn (code 11) and Vn-n (code 18) and between Vn (code 3) and V-n (code1). These devices are supposed to illustrate underlying syntactic differences. In my view, they make the codes too difficult to interpret.

Note that no distinction is made between finite and non-finite *wh* -clauses, as appears from codes 5 and 6 and codes 14 and 15.

Table 5: The major verb codes in LDOCE (1987 & 1995)

	LDOCE2	LDOCE3
Copular		
1. become angry/president	L, L	linking verb
Intransitive		
2. faint	I	I
Monotransitive		
3. admire sb/sth	T	T (not in progr.)
4. believe (that)	T+ (that)	T
5. doubt (whether sth is true)	T+ if/whether	T (not in progr.)
6. wonder (what to do)	T+ wh-	I; T

7. refuse (to leave)	T+ to-v	I
8. enjoy (singing)	T+ v-ing	T
9. want (sb to do sth)	T+ obj + to-v	T
10. hate (sb doing sth)	T+ obj + v-ing	T (not in progr.)
Ditransitive		
11. send (sb sth)	T+ obj (i)+ obj (d)	T
12. teach (sth to sb)	T (to)	T
13. promise (sb that...)	T+ obj + (that)	T
14. ask (sb whether...)	T+ obj + wh-	T
15. show (sb how to...)	T+ obj + wh-	T
16. advise (sb to do sth)	T+ obj + to-v	T
Complex transitive		
17. drive (sb mad)	T+ obj + adj	T
18. elect (sb chairman)	T+ obj + n	T
19. know (sb to be a liar)	-	T(not in progr.)
20. make (sb do sth)	T+ obj + ~~to~~-v	T
21. set (sb thinking)	T+ obj + v-ing	-
22. get (sth repaired)	-	-

In LDOCE3 the symbols I and T for the verb have been retained. The symbol L has been replaced by 'linking verb'. In other words, the reader is still told that, for example, *become* is a linking verb, that *faint* is intransitive and *admire* transitive. However, complementation patterns are no longer specified in terms of codes (as in the 1987 edition), but illustrated by means of collocations. The only codes that bear some resemblance to those in the earlier edition are [T always + adv/prep], for example for the verb *put*, and [I always + adv/prep], for example for the verb *sit*. Symbols for verb forms and clause types (*inf, -ing* and *-ed*) have also disappeared. So has the function label *obj*. Note also that pattern 7 has the wrong code (viz I instead of T) and that there are no codes for patterns 21 and 22.

What this comes down to is that the new code system describes most verbs only in terms of their membership of the classes 'linking verb', 'intransitive verb' and 'transitive verb', but not in terms of their subcategorisation features. This means that LDOCE3 leaves it to the reader to infer from the examples and the collocations that *become*, as a linking verb, can be followed by both nominal and adjectival complements, that *believe* can have clausal as well as non-clausal complementation and that *enjoy* can be followed by a non-finite *-ing* clause. It also means that monotransitive verbs (like *admire* and *believe*), ditransitive verbs (like *send* and *promise*) and complex transitive verbs (like *drive* and *elect*), all have the same code [T], in spite of the fact that they have widely different complementation patterns.

There is no doubt that the new code system in LDOCE3 has been greatly simplified. We are not told why this has been done and one wonders whether this simplification has not been too radical. The editors probably believe that phrases and collocations can do the same job as codes. This is a question which deserves further research.

Table 6: The major verb codes in COBUILD (1987 &1995)

	COBUILD1	COBUILD2
Copular		
1. become angry/president	V + C	V adj; V n
Intransitive		
2. faint	V	V
Monotransitive		
3. admire sb/sth	V + O	V n
4. believe (that)	V + REPORT-CL	V that
5. doubt (whether sth is true)	V + REPORT-CL	V whether/if
6. wonder (what to do)	V + REPORT-CL	V wh
7. refuse (to leave)	V + *to*-INF	V to-inf
8. enjoy (singing)	V + -ING	V n/ing
9. want (sb to do sth)	V + O + *to*-INF	V n to-inf
10. hate (sb doing sth)	-	V n-ing
Ditransitive		
11. send (sb sth)	V + O + O	V n n
12. teach (sth to sb)	V + O + A *(to)*	V n *to* n
13. promise (sb that...)	V + O + REPORT-CL	V n that
14. ask (sb whether...)	V + O + REPORT-CL	V n wh
15. show (sb how to...)	V + O + REPORT-CL	V n wh
16. advise (sb to do sth)	V + O + *to*-INF	V n to-inf
Complex transitive		
17. drive (sb mad)	V + O + C (ADJ)	V n adj
18. elect (sb chairman)	V + O + C (NG)	V n n
19. know (sb to be a liar)	-	V n to-inf
20. make (sb do sth)	V + O + INF	V n inf
21. set (sb thinking)	V + O + -ING	V n -ing
22. get (sth repaired)	V + O + PAST PART	V n -ed

Apart from V-ERG and RECIP, the verb codes in the first edition of COBUILD employed only one symbol for the verb, viz V, irrespective of whether the verb was copular, intransitive or transitive. In the 1995 edition V has been retained, but copular verbs are now labelled V-LINK. Also new are the codes V-RECIP, V-LINK-ERG and V-RECIP-ERG (see Table 2 above).

The new verb codes have been improved on a number of points. The most important change concerns the function labels C (for Complement), O (for Object) and A (for Adjunct), all of which have gone. Complementation patterns are now described in terms of category labels, such as *adj, n, adv, prep* and *pron*, so that, for example, the code for the ditransitive verb *send* has changed from V + O + O into Vnn. We also notice that the label REPORT-CL has been dropped. Codes for verbs that can be followed by clauses now contain the symbols 'that', 'whether' or 'wh'. The label PAST PART has been replaced by '-ed'.

For the major syntactic patterns COBUILD2 now has 18 verb codes. The COBUILD2 system is virtually identical to that in OALD5.

Table 7: The major verb codes in CIDE (1995)

	CIDE
Copular	
1. become angry/president	L
Intransitive	
2. faint	I
Monotransitive	
3. admire sb/sth	T
4. believe (that)	+ *that* clause
5. doubt (whether sth is true)	+ *wh*-word
6. wonder (what to do)	+ *wh*-word
7. refuse (to leave)	+ to infinitive
8. enjoy (singing)	+ v-ing
9. want (sb to do sth)	T + obj + *to* inf
10. hate (sb doing sth)	+ obj + v-ing
Ditransitive	
11. send (sb sth)	+ two objects
12. teach (sth to sb)	T
13. promise (sb that...)	+ obj + *(that)* cl
14. ask (sb whether...)	T + obj + *wh* -word
15. show (sb how to...)	-
16. advise (sb to do sth)	T + obj + *to* inf
Complex transitive	
17. drive (sb mad)	T + obj + adj
18. elect (sb chairman)	T + obj + n
19. know (sb to be a liar)	T + obj + *to* be n/adj
20. make (sb do sth)	+ obj + infinitive without to

21. set (sb thinking)	+ obj + v-ing
22. get (sth repaired)	+ obj + v-ed

When we examine the verb codes in the Cambridge dictionary, we must conclude that it has missed an opportunity to profit from the shortcomings in the earlier editions of its competitors. The consequence of this is that the objections that could be raised to the earlier codes in OALD4, LDOCE2 and COBUILD1 still apply to the code system in CIDE. These objections can be summarized as follows:

1. CIDE uses the function label *obj*, which is not transparent (and which the other dictionaries have dropped).
2. In the case of transitive verbs the headword is immediately followed by the symbol *obj*, no matter whether the verb in question is monotransitive, ditransitive or complex transitive. This use of the symbol *obj* does not supply any information that is not also supplied by the symbol T or by the codes that accompany the examples.
3. In some codes the symbol *obj* refers to a constituent that does not function as the direct object of the preceding verb, but rather as the subject of the following non-finite clause (see, for example, codes 9, 10 and 19). This is confusing.
4. Apart from the function label *obj*, CIDE also uses category symbols, such as *n* and *adj*. This means that many codes contain both function and category labels (see, for example, codes 17 and 18).
5. Like LDOCE3, CIDE has separate symbols for linking verbs (L), intransitive verbs (I) and transitive verbs (T), instead of simply using V.
6. In codes 5, 6 and 14 the use of the code *wh*-word is confusing. The verbs in question are followed by *wh*-clauses, rather than *wh*-words.

A comparison of the verb codes in Tables 4-6 shows that OALD5, LDOCE3 and COBUILD2 have completely revised their verb code systems. In the 1995 editions OALD5 and COBUILD2 have virtually the same codes. The only difference is that OALD5 uses two typographical devices (a dot and a dash) to keep certain syntactic constructions apart and that it lacks a code for pattern 22.

5 Summary

This paper deals with what OALD5, LDOCE3, COBUILD2 and CIDE have to say on syntax, more particularly on the syntax of verbs. Section 2 takes the entry for the verb *believe* to show how verb entries are organized. Syntactic information on verbs is mainly supplied in the form of codes. The symbols used in these codes are examined in section 3. Section 4 shows what codes the four dictionaries use for 22 major syntactic verb patterns in English.

More than ten years ago Lemmens and Wekker (1986: 14 and 99ff.) suggested six minimal conditions for a coding system in pedagogical dictionaries (cf. Sinclair 1987, for some critical remarks). Lemmens and Wekker also gave suggestions for the format of verb codes (*op. cit.*, §4.1). Since then further proposals have been made to improve verb codes (Aarts 1991).

In Tables 4, 5 and 6 we can see what changes the verb code systems in OALD5, LDOCE3 and COBUILD2 have undergone since the previous editions. LDOCE3 has done away with most of the codes in the 1987 edition in an attempt to simplify things. In LDOCE3 syntactic information is now mainly supplied implicitly by means of phrases and collocations. The verb codes in OALD5 and COBUILD2 are now not only virtually identical, but also very similar to those proposed in Aarts (1991).
In my opinion, verb codes, if they are to be accessible to students, should meet the following conditions (Aarts, *op.cit.*: 577):

1. the number of codes and the number of symbols should be kept to a minimum;
2. symbols should be transparent;
3. there should only be one symbol for the verb: V;
4. codes should contain category symbols only, not symbols denoting sentence functions;
5. codes should represent surface syntactic structures; underlying differences between structures can be ignored.

The verb codes in OALD5 and COBUILD2 meet these conditions. Both dictionaries use category symbols rather than function labels. Their codes are transparent, require no further explanation and are accessible even to students with little knowledge of English syntax.

Bibliography

Aarts, Flor (1991): "Lexicography and syntax: the state of the art in learner's dictionaries of English". — In: J. E. Alatis (ed.): Georgetown Round Table on Languages and Linguistics 1991 (Washington, D.C.: Georgetown University Press) (=Linguistics and language pedagogy: The state of the art) 567-582.
Béjoint, Henri (1981): "The foreign student's use of monolingual English dictionaries: A study of language needs and reference skills". — In: Applied Linguistics 2/3, 207-222.
Bogaards, Paul (1996): "Dictionaries for Learners of English". — In: International Journal of Lexicography 9/4, 227-320.
Crystal, David (1987): The Cambridge Encyclopedia of Language. — Cambridge: CUP.
Herbst, Thomas (1996): "On the way to the perfect learners' dictionary: a first comparison of OALD5, LDOCE3, COBUILD2 and CIDE". — In: International Journal of Lexicography 9/4, 321-357.
Hornby, Albert S. (^{2}1975): Guide to Patterns and Usage in English. — London: OUP.
Lemmens, Marcel, Herman Wekker (1986): Grammar in English Learners' Dictionaries. — Tübingen: Niemeyer (=Lexicographica, Series Maior 16).

Quirk, Randolph, Sidney Greenbaum, Geoffrey Leech, Jan Svartvik (1985): A Comprehensive Grammar of the English Language. — London, New York: Longman.

Sinclair, John (1987): "Grammar in the Dictionary". — In: J. Sinclair (ed.): Looking Up. An Account of the COBUILD Project in Lexical Computing (London, Glasgow: Collins ELT) 104 - 115.

— (ed.) (1996): Grammar Patterns, 1: Verbs. — London: HarperCollins.

Michael Klotz

Word complementation in English learners' dictionaries – a quantitative study of CIDE, COBUILD2, LDOCE3 and OALD5

Grammatical information and more specifically complementation information has always been a central concern in learners' dictionaries ever since the concept of verb patterns was developed in the late 30s and early 40s in Palmer's *Grammar of English Words* and Hornby's *Idiomatic and Syntactic English Dictionary*. Correspondingly, this topic has been widely discussed by a large number of authors.[1] However, while most studies discuss the advantages and disadvantages of different encoding strategies, relatively few of them include statistical information, which would inform the reader how well these strategies are put into practice across a larger number of entries. This, however, as Jehle (1990) emphasises in his doctoral dissertation on lexicographic reviews, is an important part of dictionary assessment. Amongst the few studies that include statistical information are those by Herbst (1984 and 1984a), who compared the third edition of the *Oxford Advanced Learner's Dictionary* (OALD3) and the first edition of the *Longman Dictionary of Contemporary English* (LDOCE1) with respect to verb and adjective complementation. At the time he concluded that LDOCE1 was slightly more comprehensive than OALD3 and that in general the information given on adjective complementation was not satisfactory. For example, Herbst found that the dictionaries covered only about 20 per cent of infinitival and clausal patterns for adjectives.

The following study will provide some statistical information on the coverage of the complementation of verbs, adjectives and nouns in the 1995 editions of the *Cambridge International Dictionary of English* (CIDE), the *Collins COBUILD English Dictionary* (COBUILD2), LDOCE3 and the OALD5. The study is based on a sample of 50 verbs, 50 adjectives and 51 nouns taken from various letters of the alphabet. All of these 151 words can also be found in the English valency dictionary, which is currently being prepared at the Universities of Erlangen, Augsburg and Reading.[2] Since this dictionary aims at accounting for the valency of English verbs, adjectives and nouns as comprehensively as

---

1 See for example articles by Cowie (1987), Heath (1982, 1985), Herbst (1984, 1984a, 1989) and Sinclair (1987). With Lemmens/Wekker (1986) and McCorduck (1993) there are even two monographs which are exclusively dedicated to the topic of grammar in dictionaries. With regards to the latest editions of the four large English learners' dictionaries, the treatment of syntactic information is discussed by Aarts (elsewhere in this volume) and also by Bogaards (1996) and Herbst (1996) in their general reviews of the four dictionaries.

2 An account of this project can be found in Herbst/Klotz (1998) and Klotz (1997). For a discussion of the relationship between a theoretical approach and a practical lexicographical approach to valency, providing the background for the English valency dictionary, see Herbst (this volume).

possible, the patterns listed in this dictionary will serve as a basis for the current study; all in all the English valency dictionary lists 1260 patterns for the 151 words in question:

Sample Size:	
50 verbs	552 patterns
50 adjectives	298 patterns
51 nouns	410 patterns
151 words	1260 patterns

These numbers beg the question of what counts as a pattern. In this respect the current study tries to be as explicit as possible. In particular, different formal types of complementation following a preposition are counted as different patterns. For example, *account for N, account for V-ing, account for N V-ing* and *account for wh-CL,* as illustrated below, count as four different patterns:

(1)	*Members of the armed forces should be called to account for the actions and for the casualties sustained in the conflict in Slovenia.*	+ for N
(2)	*It is the third time she has been unable to account for having a fortune in her hands.*	+ for V-ing
(3)	*Perhaps tougher sentencing policies of the courts account for more people being sent to prison for longer terms.*	+ for N V-ing
(4)	*Perhaps this accounts for why we have so many more men than women in prison.*	+ for wh-CL

Furthermore, all combinations of complements are also considered as separate patterns. This seems justified in that the listing of patterns with single complements in an entry does not necessarily mean that the complements can be combined into more complex patterns. Vice versa, the complements given in a complex pattern cannot always occur individually on their own. Thus *lecture to N on N* is counted separately from *lecture to N* and *lecture on N*:

(5)	*... lectures to first year students ...*	+ to N
(6)	*... lectures on subjects such as porcelain, dance and local history ...*	+ on N
(7)	*... her lectures to her servants on the need to be clean and orderly ...*	+ to N + on N

A basic methodological problem for counting patterns is posed by the fact that one pattern can occur several times in one entry for different senses of the lemma. For example, all four dictionaries distinguish two senses of the adjective *parallel*: firstly, the literal mathematical sense as illustrated in (8) and (9) and secondly a figurative sense as in (10) and (11). Both meanings allow complementation by a *with-* or *to*-phrase as illustrated below:

literal

(8)	*To reach the town centre continue ahead along a descending path parallel to the road.*	+ to N
(9)	*All sections are easily accessible from the A567 which runs almost parallel with the canal.*	+ with N

figurative

(10)	*Ryans' results are roughly parallel to Barnes' findings.*	+ to N
(11)	*I suppose that the rise of the model went parallel with the rise of the modern fashion designer.*	+ with N

COBUILD2 lists both patterns twice - for the literal and figurative meaning respectively. The other three dictionaries, however, only include these patterns with the literal, but not with the figurative meaning. Obviously, in this specific case the syntactic information given by COBUILD2 is more comprehensive than the information given in the other dictionaries.

Ideally, a statistical study of complementation patterns should take this into account. What should be counted is not the number of patterns given for any one lexeme, but rather the number of patterns given for a specific sense of the lexeme.[3] In practice, however, this turns out to be quite difficult. The difficulty simply results from the well known fact that dictionaries often draw the line between different senses in different places, so that the senses established in this way cannot be compared across several dictionaries. Any attempt to count patterns per sense would force the analyst into a large number of fairly arbitrary decisions about what counts as a sense. For the purposes of the following statistics it was therefore decided to count patterns per lexeme. This means, however, that the statistics do not take into account whether a pattern is actually given for all relevant senses of a lexeme, as long as it is given for the lexeme at all.

The first statistics to be discussed is the overall coverage of patterns, as it is shown in chart 1.

---

[3] Cruse (1986: 77) calls this notion of "the union of a lexical form with a single sense" the *lexical unit* and distinguishes it from the *lexeme*. For an application of this concept in the assessment of dictionaries see Bogaards (1996: esp. 278) and Popp (this volume).

Chart 1: Overall Coverage of Patterns

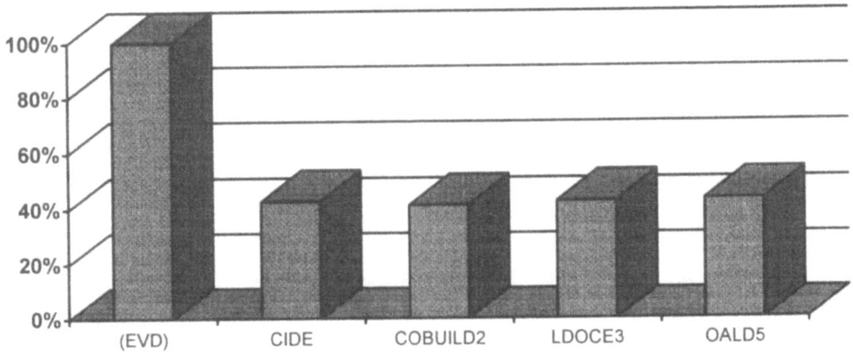

All four dictionaries show remarkable similarity in this respect, covering about 40% of the patterns listed in the English valency dictionary. Although this figure may appear to be rather low at first sight, it has to be put into the right perspective. Even though word complementation is a central concern in English learners' dictionaries, it is certainly not the only or even the single most important one. The most basic purpose of a learners' dictionary is obviously to provide information on meaning and there is also a wealth of other information on pronunciation, spelling, collocations, style, etc. Since the learners' dictionary has to serve such a variety of purposes, it cannot reasonably be expected to show the same coverage as a specialised dictionary like the English valency dictionary in that dictionary's special field. Furthermore, it can even be argued that a complete account of all possible patterns wouldn't necessarily be desirable in a general learners' dictionary. Any attempt at completeness would certainly increase the length of the entries considerably, and that in turn would make it more difficult for the users to find the information they are looking for.

In connection with these considerations it is interesting to see to what extent there is agreement among all four dictionaries about which patterns should be included. A high degree of agreement would arguably indicate that the dictionaries indeed include all the more important patterns and leave out the less important ones. Vice versa, a low degree of agreement would indicate that the line between more and less important patterns is difficult to draw and that it is therefore likely that none of the four dictionaries lists all the important patterns. The second chart throws some light on this question by showing which percentage of patterns found in the English valency dictionary are listed in how many of the four learners' dictionaries:

Chart 2: How many pattens are contained in how many dictionaries?

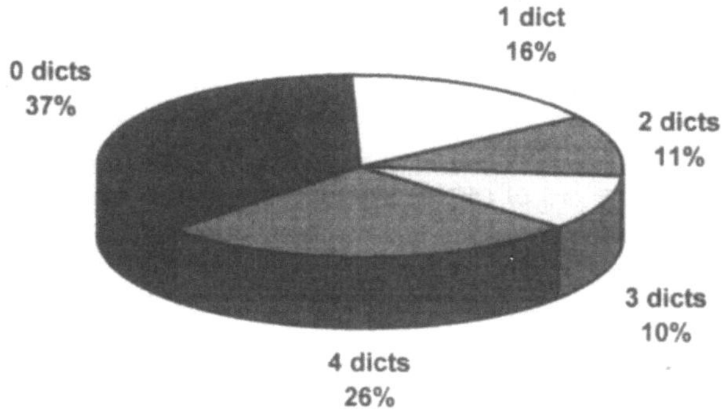

About 26% of all patterns can be found in all four learners' dictionaries. About 10% are found in three out of four dictionaries, another 11% in two and about 16% in only one dictionary. Finally, approximately 37% of all patterns which are given in the English valency dictionary are not listed in any of the four learners' dictionaries at all. Assuming that these latter patterns have not been included, because they are of a less important nature, there are still about 37% of patterns which were deemed important enough to be included in at least one of the dictionaries, but which are at the same time missing in other dictionaries. From this, it can be concluded that the line between more and less important patterns is indeed difficult to draw, and that it is fairly safe to assume that there are useful patterns missing in all four learners' dictionaries.

The coverage of patterns for verbs, adjectives and nouns separately is shown in chart 3:

Chart 3: Coverage of Patterns by Part of Speech

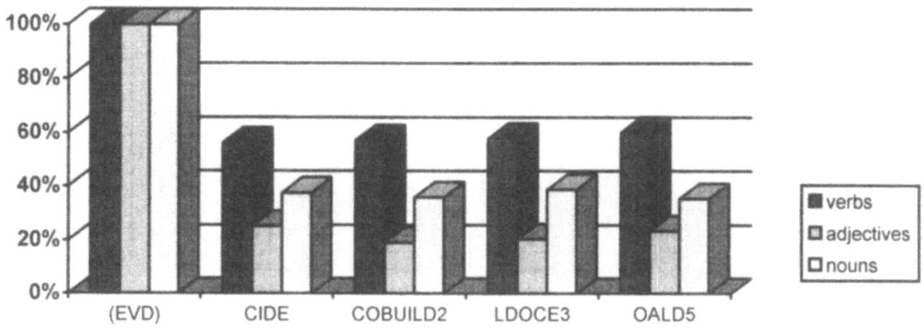

In all four dictionaries pattern coverage is distributed similarly, though not evenly across verbs, adjectives and nouns. Verbs are generally represented quite well, approaching a coverage between 56 and 60%, whereas for adjectives only 19-25% of all patterns are given. For nouns the coverage varies between 35 and 38%. The slight differences between the four dictionaries are statistically not significant, considering the size of the sample.[4] What emerges quite clearly, however, is the fact that all four dictionaries treat verb complementation much more comprehensively than adjective or noun complementation.

In order to find out which types of pattern are typically treated less comprehensively by the dictionaries, all patterns are subdivided into the following five categories:

Pattern Type	
• nominal	+ N; + ADJ; + 0[5]
• clausal	+ *that*-CL; + *wh*-CL; + *to*-INF; + V-*ing*; etc.
• prepositional	all PPs, except for those included in "adverbial"
• adverbial	adverbs and PPs with a spatial meaning
• complex	all patterns with more than one complement following the lemma

Chart 4 shows the distribution of verb patterns across these different categories. All four dictionaries cover all patterns of the adverbial category. However, since there are only seven such cases in the sample, this is not very significant. More interesting is the difference between the nominal and clausal categories on one hand and the prepositional and complex categories on the other. Coverage of the former categories seems to be comparatively better than of the latter.

Chart 4: Coverage of Verb Patterns by Pattern Type

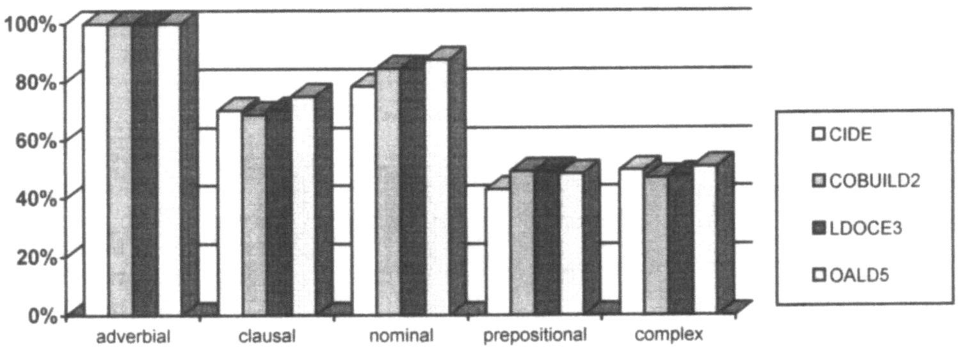

---

[4] Here and elsewhere in this study the level of statistical significance was calculated on the basis of a χ^2 test. A description of this test can be found in Woods/Fletcher/Hughes (1986: 139-151).

[5] The code + 0 signifies the monovalent construction with no complements following the lemma.

In the prepositional category, the comparatively low coverage is largely due to the fact that the dictionaries normally indicate the prepositional patterns with a noun phrase following the preposition, and often ignore participle constructions, *wh*-clauses and *wh to*-infinitives that can also follow the preposition. For example, the pattern *decide on N* as in *Have you decided on a new car?* can be found in all four dictionaries. The corresponding patterns with a participle or a *wh*-clause following the preposition as in *Have you decided on buying a new car?* and *Have you decided on whether you want to buy a new car?*, however, are not indicated in any of the four dictionaries.

The low count in the complex category can be partly justified by arguing that these complex patterns can be derived by combining patterns which are given in the entry. However, while this is certainly true for many of the missing complex patterns, it does not account for all of them. For example, neither *educate N that-CL* as in *The government tries to educate the public that the future of Europe depends on a single currency* nor *match N for N* as in *He didn't match his opponent for strength* can be derived in this way and both patterns are missing in all four dictionaries.

Chart 5: Coverage of Adjective Patterns by Pattern Type

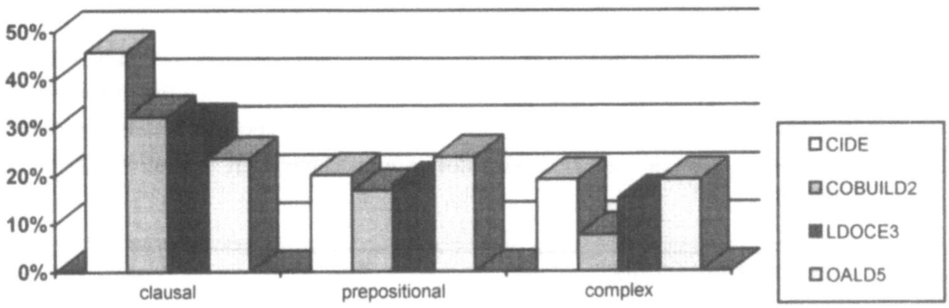

The corresponding chart 5 for the adjectives shows that the coverage of clausal complements for adjectives seems to be a strength of CIDE. 27 of the 59 clausal adjective patterns, which are contained in the sample, are also given in CIDE. The OALD5 in comparison only gives 14 of these patterns. For example, *fantastic that*-CL as in *It's fantastic that the boy is back*, *eccentric to*-INF as in *It is not wholly eccentric to wear a belt and braces* and *obvious wh*-CL as in *It was pretty obvious how they'd spent their night* are only given in CIDE.

Chart 6: Coverage of Noun Patterns by Pattern Type

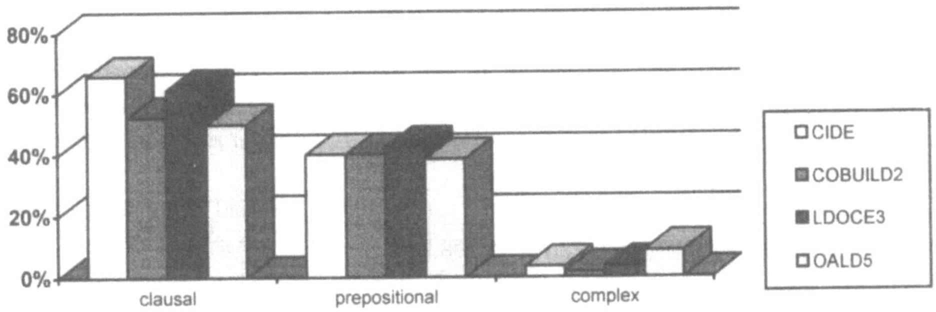

Chart 6 for noun patterns shows that the coverage of clausal complements is generally quite satisfactory, ranging between 50 and 66%. Again, the slight differences between the dictionaries is statistically not significant, if one takes the sample size into account. What can be seen quite clearly, however, is the fact that complex patterns for nouns are hardly covered at all in any of the dictionaries. As with the verbs it can be argued that many of these complex patterns can be gained by combining the underlying patterns, provided that these are given in the entry. That this is certainly not always the case is illustrated by the fact that only about 40% of the prepositional patterns for nouns are covered by the four dictionaries.

The remaining three charts will deal with the indication type, i.e. the way, in which the four dictionaries give complementation information. Three such indication types must be distinguished:

Indication Type:	
	• indication by example
	• indication by code
	• indication by code & example

Obviously, the third case is the most desirable one;[6] illustrating patterns just by examples makes it difficult for the user to find the relevant information; vice versa, indication of a pattern just by a code, albeit a transparent one, might mean asking too much of users because of the technicality of codes. This consideration has also prompted lexicographers at Longmans' - and to a lesser extent at Oxford University Press - to replace codes by what Herbst (1996: 329) has called "pattern illustrations".[7] For example, instead of giving a code

[6] The advantage of giving both codes and examples to indicate complementation information is argued quite convincingly and in greater detail by Heath (1982).

[7] This development was already foreshadowed in the *Longman Language Activator*; cf. Klotz (1994).

of the type *ask* N *to*-INF LDOCE3 now has a pattern illustration *ask sb to do sth*. For the purposes of this study, these pattern illustrations also count as codes.

The following charts show the number of patterns indicated by code, example or both for verbs, adjectives and nouns respectively.[8]

Chart 7: Coverage of Verb Patterns by Indication Type in Percent of Patterns Contained

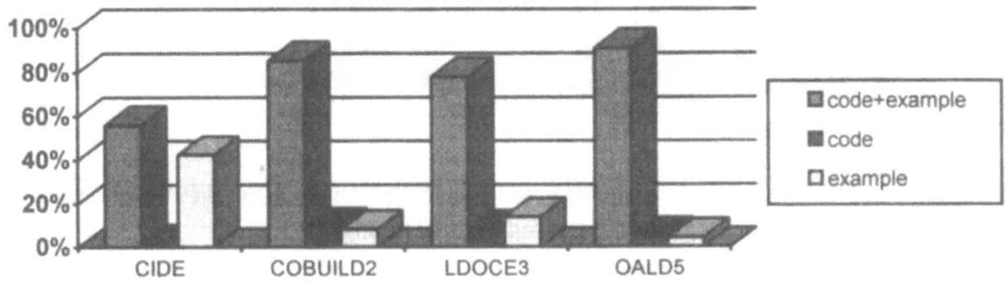

Verb patterns are indicated rather consistently by code and example in COBUILD2, LDOCE3 and OALD5. In CIDE a large number of verb patterns are just illustrated by example; this, however, is not an inconsistency, but rather a conscious policy decision: prepositional patterns in CIDE are generally indicated by having the preposition in the example in bold print.

The high degree of consistency in indicating patterns both by code and example disappears, however, as soon as we look at the adjective and noun patterns.

Chart 8: Coverage of Adjective Patterns by Indication Type in Percent of Patterns Contained

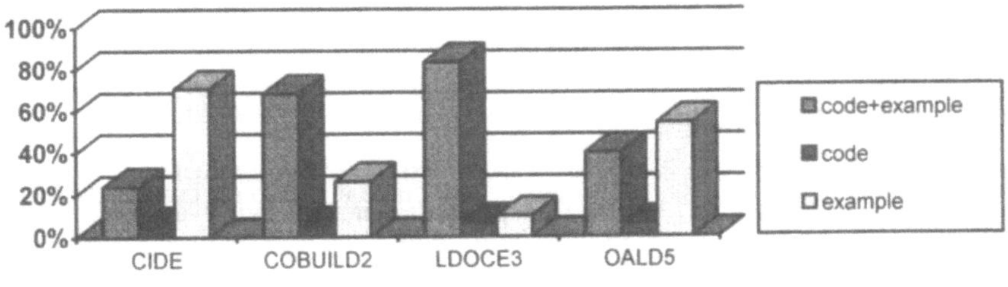

For the adjectives LDOCE3 is still quite consistent: about 84% of all adjective patterns in LDOCE3 are illustrated by code and example. COBUILD2 and especially OALD5, on the other hand, illustrate a larger number of patterns just by example.

---

8 Note that the percentages given in charts 1 and 3-6 relate to the number of patterns given in the English valency dictionary, whereas the percentages for the illustration type in charts 7-9 have to be interpreted in relation to the patterns contained in the respective dictionary.

Chart 9: Coverage of Noun Patterns by Indication Type in Percent of Patterns Contained

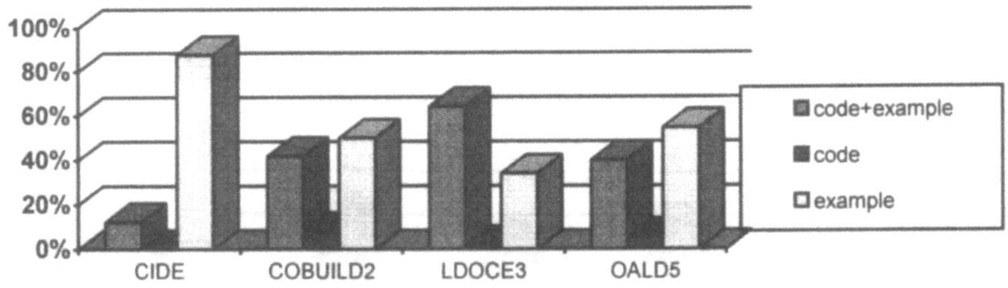

With respect to the noun patterns, finally, even LDOCE3 has given up its consistent policy and illustrates 34% of the contained patterns just by example.

Summing it all up, it seems fair to draw the following two conclusions: firstly, from a quantitative point of view, none of the four dictionaries is clearly better than the others with regards to complementation information. On the contrary, the degree of correspondence between the dictionaries is quite considerable. This also holds true if one looks at verb-, adjective- and noun patterns separately, although the statistics seem to indicate that CIDE gives slightly more information about the clausal complementation of adjectives. However, even though all four dictionaries contain roughly the same number of patterns, this does not mean that they contain the same patterns. From this we can conclude that in all four dictionaries there are patterns missing, which could profitably be included.

Secondly, the statistics show quite clearly that in all four dictionaries the treatment of adjective and noun patterns has not yet reached the same standard as the treatment of verb patterns. Although the impression prevails that considerable progress has been made in this field since the days of OALD3 and LDOCE1,[9] the coverage of adjective and noun patterns is still much less comprehensive than for verbs. Furthermore, the indication of noun and adjective patterns in terms of codes and examples is less consistent. It seems as if the insight that adjective and noun patterns should be given the same careful treatment as verb patterns is presently still not fully acknowledged.

It remains to be hoped that dictionary makers will take that into account in the next editions of their dictionaries, in order to turn good dictionaries into even better ones, which would be a further step towards the perfect dictionary.

---

9 Unfortunately, a direct comparison with Herbst's findings from 1984, which would be very instructive, is not possible, since the underlying listing of patterns used in Herbst (1984, 1984a) and in the present study are not identical.

Bibliography

Aarts, Flor (this volume): "Syntactic Information in OALD, LDOCE, COBUILD and CIDE."

Bogaards, Paul (1996): "Dictionaries for Learners of English". — In: International Journal of Lexicography 9/4, 277-320.

Cruse, D. A. (1986): Lexical Semantics. — Cambridge: CUP.

Cowie, Anthony P. (1987): "Syntax, the dictionary and the learner's communicative needs". — In: A. Cowie (ed.): The Dictionary and the Language Learner (Tübingen: Niemeyer) 183-192.

Heath, David (1982): "The treatment of grammar and syntax in monolingual English dictionaries of advanced learners". — In: Linguistik und Didaktik 13/49, 95-107.

— (1985): "Grammatische Angaben in Lernerwörterbüchern des Englischen". — In: H. Bergenholtz, J. Mugdan (eds.): Lexikographie und Grammatik (Tübingen: Niemeyer) 332-345.

Heath, David, Thomas Herbst, Ian Roe, Dieter Götz (eds.) (forthcoming): English Valency Dictionary. (working title)

Herbst, Thomas (1984): "Adjective complementation: a valency approach to making EFL dictionaries". — In: Applied Linguistics 5, 1-11.

— (1984a): "Bemerkungen zu den Patternsystemen des Advanced Learner's Dictionary und des Dictionary of Contemporary English". — In: D. Götz, T. Herbst (eds.): Theoretische und praktische Probleme der Lexikographie (München: Hueber) 139-165.

— (1989): "Grammar in Dictionaries". — In: M. L.Tickoo (ed.): Learners' Dictionaries: State of the Art (Singapore: SEAMEO Regional Language Centre) (=Anthology Series 23) 94-111.

— (1996): "On the way to the perfect learners' dictionary: a first comparison of OALD5, LDOCE3, COBUILD2 and CIDE". — In: International Journal of Lexicography 9/4, 321-357.

— (this volume): "Designing an English Valency Dictionary: combining linguistic theory and user-friendliness."

Herbst, Thomas, Michael Klotz (1998): "A valency dictionary of English — a project report". — In: A. Zettersten, V. H. Pedersen, J. E. Mogensen (eds.): Symposium on Lexicography VIII. Proceedings of the Eighth International Symposium on Lexigography May 2 - 4, 1996, at the University of Copenhagen (Tübingen: Niemeyer), 65-91.

Jehle, Günter (1990): Das englische und französische Lernerwörterbuch in der Rezension. — Tübingen: Niemeyer.

Klotz, Michael (1994): "Review: Longman Language Activator". — In: Zeitschrift für Anglistik und Amerikanistik ZAA XLII/4., 381-383.

— (1997) "Ein Valenzwörterbuch englischer Verben, Adjektive und Substantive - Vorstellung eines Projektes. – In: Zeitschrift für Angewandte Linguistik 27, 93-111.

Lemmens, Marcel, Hermann Wekker (1986): Grammar in English Learners' Dictionaries. — Tübingen: Niemeyer.

McCorduck, Edward S. (1993): Grammatical Information in ESL Dictionaries. — Tübingen: Niemeyer.

Popp, Kerstin (this volume): "Lexical units, suffixation, suffixes in OALD, LDOCE, COBUILD and CIDE".

Sinclair, John (1987): "Grammar in the dictionary". — In: J. Sinclair (ed.): Looking up (London and Glasgow: Collins COBUILD) 104-115.

Summers, Della (ed.) (1993): Longman Language Activator. — Harlow: Longman.

Woods, Anthony, Paul Fletcher, Arthur Hughes (1986): Statistics in Language Studies. — Cambridge: CUP.

Gabriele Stein

Exemplification in EFL dictionaries

Monolingual learners' dictionaries, and above all those for learners of English as a foreign language (EFL), show a number of distinctive characteristics if compared to monolingual general-purpose dictionaries: (1) a very explicit grammatical description of the headwords, (2) meaning paraphrases in what is assumed to be simple language, (3) exemplification of the headwords in phrases or sentences, (4) no etymologies. The unparalleled, world-wide demand for EFL dictionaries at the present time has led to such a relentless rivalry between the leading EFL dictionary publishers that with each new edition of their dictionary new or improved approaches to the handling of grammar, definitions and exemplification are offered. This experimenting spirit of the respective lexicographical teams is not matched by similar activities in lexicographical research. The hard-pressed dictionary compilers are thus not given the scholarly support so urgently called for to help them in their lexicographical decisions in order to improve particular aspects or areas in their dictionaries.

The present paper is meant as a contribution to such support: it will raise questions that have to be addressed when tackling the issue of illustration in monolingual EFL dictionaries. By illustration I shall be referring only to linguistic and not pictorial illustrations. The paper will attempt to develop an operational framework which encompasses the intricate relations between linguistic, lexicographical, pedagogical and corpus-data aspects. Exemplification is restricted to the main open word classes: nouns, verbs, and adjectives, and it will take into account main entries only.

Research shows a certain preoccupation with the distinction between examples and quotations. It might therefore be appropriate to specify more precisely that building block within a dictionary entry that we are going to look at. The building block under focus is a *language sample which includes the headword itself.* This differentiates it from such other blocks as the headword (spelling), its pronunciation transcription, its grammatical specification, regional, stylistic and subject labels and the meaning paraphrase itself. All these components of a dictionary entry are usually distinguished typographically.

The function to which such language samples are put decides on their form and status. Those that serve as textual or authentic evidence to document the use of a specific sense or construction by a specific writer at a specific time are commonly termed *quotations*. Those which have an exemplificatory function and for which the source has no attesting role are regarded as *examples*. Such examples - phrases or sentences - may be drawn from text corpora or be non-corpus-based. The advantages and disadvantages in the use of these two kinds of examples have repeatedly been discussed in the literature.

We might call the exemplificatory part of a dictionary entry the *demonstration part* and the one providing the spelling, pronunciation, grammar, restrictive usage labels and the meaning paraphrase the *descriptive part*. Lexicographical traditions vary from country to country and this is also reflected in the arrangement of these two components. For monolingual dictionaries published in Great Britain the usual order is descriptive part followed by demonstration part. In other countries such as France we often find the demonstration part preceding the descriptive part. In such cases there are no meaning paraphrases without exemplification. This does not necessarily hold for a formatting where the descriptive part precedes the demonstration part. All the four market-leading EFL dictionaries, OALD5, LDOCE3, COBUILD2 and CIDE, fail their users in this respect. A closer look at these dictionaries makes one wonder whether the allocation of examples is not almost as random as the inclusion of pictorial illustrations (cf. in this respect Stein 1991). The four publishing houses highlight the rich provision with example sentences and phrases as a characteristic feature of their product, but the editors do not enlighten users why so many entries have no examples at all. Is the omission a mere cost factor affecting the size of the dictionary? But even if a financial restriction was involved, how does the lexicographical team decide what to exemplify and what not?

COBUILD2, which is most explicit and detailed on the choice and function of their verbal illustrations, is the only EFL dictionary to address the non-supply of examples:

> Nearly all the words and meanings in the dictionary have at least one example. The main exceptions are concrete nouns such as **bathmat**, **seahorse**, and **trombone**, and a few other words where an example would add nothing to the information given in the definition (xxii).

The syntactic-semantic characterization remains rather general: nouns and concreteness. Since *bathmat* and *seahorse* are noun compounds, one may wonder whether there is a morphological restriction on specific word-formation structures. The third example denotes a musical instrument. COBUILD's example refers to an individual case, not the category as such. A brief check reveals that there is an example for *piano* and *violin*, there are none for all the other musical instruments. This may be justified by claiming that *piano* and *violin* are the instruments most played by amateurs. COBUILD justify their decision by arguing that an example would not add any information that goes beyond the definition itself. This may well be a sound point since the verb used with all instruments (as with all games) is *play*.

Instead of arguing here for or against a decision taken by a specific lexicographical team let us consider some nouns and test our own reaction and expectancy: would we expect example illustrations for *baby tooth*, *baccarat*, *bachelor's degree*, *bacillus*, *backbone*, *backdoor*, *backgammon*, *backhand*? One of our EFL dictionaries has no examples at all. We might agree. But why? Because we cannot envisage difficult syntactic construction patterns?

We find a similar situation with verbs and adjectives. A random test for verbs and adjectives yielded rather unexpected results. I randomly chose one of the EFL dictionaries (it happened to be LDOCE3), opened it under the letter *B* and then excerpted verbs and adjectives for which no examples had been provided. I then looked up the verbs and adjectives in the three other EFL dictionaries. Here is the list for some twenty verbs (Fig. 1):

Lexical item	LDOCE3			OALD5			COBUILD2			CIDE		
Verbs	**ex**	**s**	**phr**	**ex**	**s**	**phr**	**ex**	**s**	**phr**	**ex**	**s**	**phr**
beautify	–	–	–	–	–	–	+	+	–	+	+	–
belabour 3 'attack'	–	–	–	+	+	–	+	+	–	+	+	–
belong 3 'feel comfortable'	–	–	–	not listed			+	+	–	+	+	–
bestride *lit.*	–	–	–	not listed			+	+	–	+	+	–
betake *lit.*	–	–	–	not listed			not listed			not listed		
betoken *lit.*	–	–	–	+	–	+	+	+	–	+	+	–
bewail *lit.*	–	–	–	+	–	+	+	+	–	+	+	–
bewilder	–	–	–	+	+	–	+	+	–	+	+	–
bewitch 'get control'	–	–	–	+	+	–	+	+	–	+	+	–
bias	–	–	–	+	+	–	+	+	–	+	+	–
billet[2] (on/with)	–	–	–	+	+	–	+	+	–	not listed		
blanch 3 'make pale'	–	–	–	not listed			not listed			–	–	–
bleat 1 'make the sound'	–	–	–	–	–	–	+	+	–	+	+	–
bleed 'take blood'	–	–	–	+	+	–	not listed			not listed		
blemish[2]	–	–	–	+	+	+	+	+	–	+	+	–
blench	–	–	–	–	–	–	not listed			+	+	–
bloom[2] 'produce flowers'	–	–	–	+	+	–	+	+	–	+	+	–
blunt[2] 'make less sharp'	–	–	–	+	–	+	not listed			+	+	–
bow[4] 'bend'	–	–	–	+	+	–	+	+	–	+	+	–
braise	–	–	–	+	–	+	+	+	+	+	–	+
breastfeed	–	–	–	+	+	–	+	+	–	+	+	–
breathalyse	–	–	–	–	–	–	+	+	–	+	+	–
bulk[3]	–	–	–	+	+	–	not listed			+	+	–

Fig. 1

ex = example(s) provided
s = sentence example(s)
phr = phrase example(s)

The comparison speaks for itself: where LDOCE3 has no exemplification, COBUILD2 and CIDE in general provide sentence examples, OALD5 is not as rich as the former and tends to vary between phrase examples and sentence examples.

These observations with respect to the lexicographical practice in the four dictionaries also hold for the adjective sample (Fig. 2)

Lexical item	LDOCE3			OALD5			COBUILD2			CIDE		
Adjectives	**ex**	**s**	**phr**	**ex**	**s**	**phr**	**ex**	**s**	**phr**	**ex**	**s**	**phr**
bearish[1]	–	–	–	+	+	+	not listed			+	+	–
bed-ridden	–	–	–	–	–	–	+	+	+	+	+	–
bewigged	–	–	–	not listed			not listed			+	+	–
biblical	–	–	–	+	–	+	+	+	+	+	+	–
biddable	–	–	–	+	+	–	not listed			not listed		
bionic	–	–	–	–	–	–	+	–	+	+	+	–
bird-brained	–	–	–	+	–	+	not listed			–	–	–
bitsy	–	–	–	not listed			not listed			not listed		
blonde	–	–	–	–	–	–	+	+	–	+	–	+
bog-standard	–	–	–	not listed			+	+	–	+	+	–
bootleg	–	–	–	+	–	+	+	–	+	+	+	–
boss-eyed	–	–	–	–	–	–	not listed			–	–	–
botanical	–	–	–	–	–	–	+	+	+	+	+	–
bottom-up	–	–	–	not listed			not listed			not listed		
bourgeois 2/3	–	–	–	+	–	+	+	+	–	+	+	–
brand-new	–	–	–	+	+	–	+	+	–	+	+	–
brassy	–	–	–	–	–	–	+	+	–	+	+	–
bruised	–	–	–	not listed			+	+	–	+	+	–
bug-eyed	–	–	–	+	–	+	+	+	+	not listed		
bull-necked	–	–	–	–	–	–	not listed			not listed		
buxom	–	–	–	–	–	–	+	+	–	+	+	–

Fig. 2

ex = example(s) provided
s = sentence example(s)
phr = phrase example(s)

What emerges from these two samples is that research on illustrations in dictionaries will have to address more thoroughly the conditions which may make exemplification dispensable or indispensable. Scholarly investigations have sought to determine what is regarded as the semiotic status of examples, unfortunately overlooking a similar use of example sentences in all language teaching, and to set up a typology of examples as well as quality maxims (cf. in particular Nikula 1986, Zöfgen 1986, Hermanns 1988, Harras 1989, Martin 1989). Such conditional studies may in turn determine example typologies and provide criteria for quality assessments.

If we accept that in an EFL learners' dictionary with the entry format descriptive part (DesP) followed by demonstration part (DemP), for reasons of size and/or cost, not all the lexical items will be illustrated with examples, we will have to analyse the relation between the two components of a dictionary entry more closely. For the purposes of this paper I leave aside, as mentioned above, the third possible component, pictorial illustrations and drawings, which one might regard as recastings in a different medium of the meaning paraphrases.

What are examples supposed to contribute? Since dictionaries are compiled for users, a binary relational model would clearly be unsatisfactory (Fig. 3):

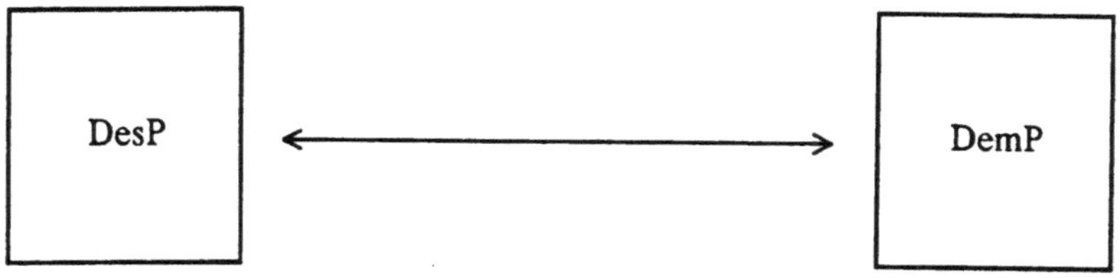

Fig. 3

The envisaged users, their assumed social and cultural background, age, world knowledge and linguistic competence, influence the overall structure of the learners' dictionary, the choice of headwords, the grammatical representations, the meaning paraphrases. A user-inclusive, triadic relational model would thus be more appropriate (Fig. 4):

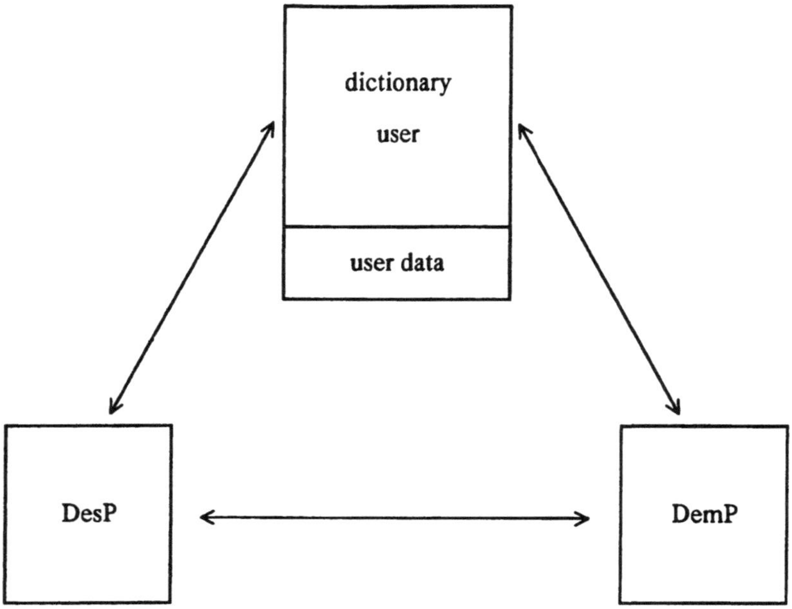

Fig. 4

Dictionaries, as other reference works, are consulted to fill a suddenly experienced gap of knowledge of some kind. The information supplied in an entry takes a form of which the compilers assume that users will understand it. We therefore have to include the lexicographical team in our model (Fig. 5):

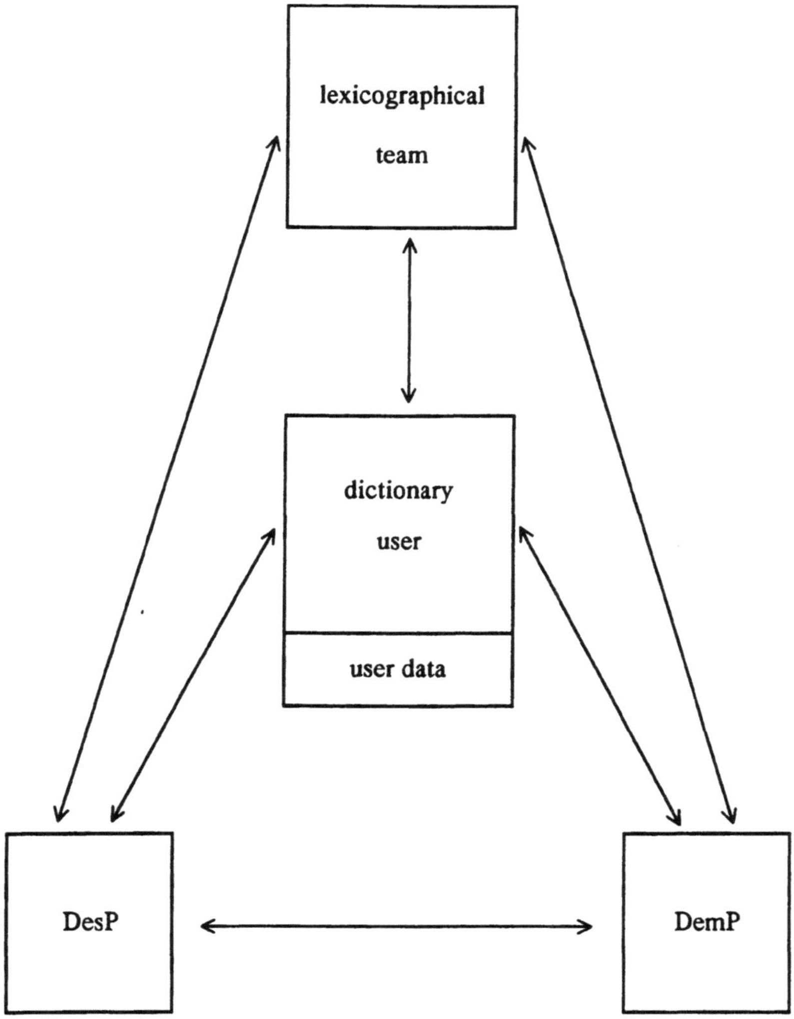

Fig. 5

For dictionaries editorial teams have to decide whether their dictionary is meant for receptive or productive use, or whether they advocate an undifferentiated use of comprehension in general. A good dictionary is usually based on an elaborate editorial policy. We therefore have to include this aspect in our model.

All the four EFL dictionary publishers now have huge computerized text corpora which the lexicographical team can consult for the selection of headwords, their senses and verbal illustrations. If incorporated into our model, we get the following structure (Fig. 6):

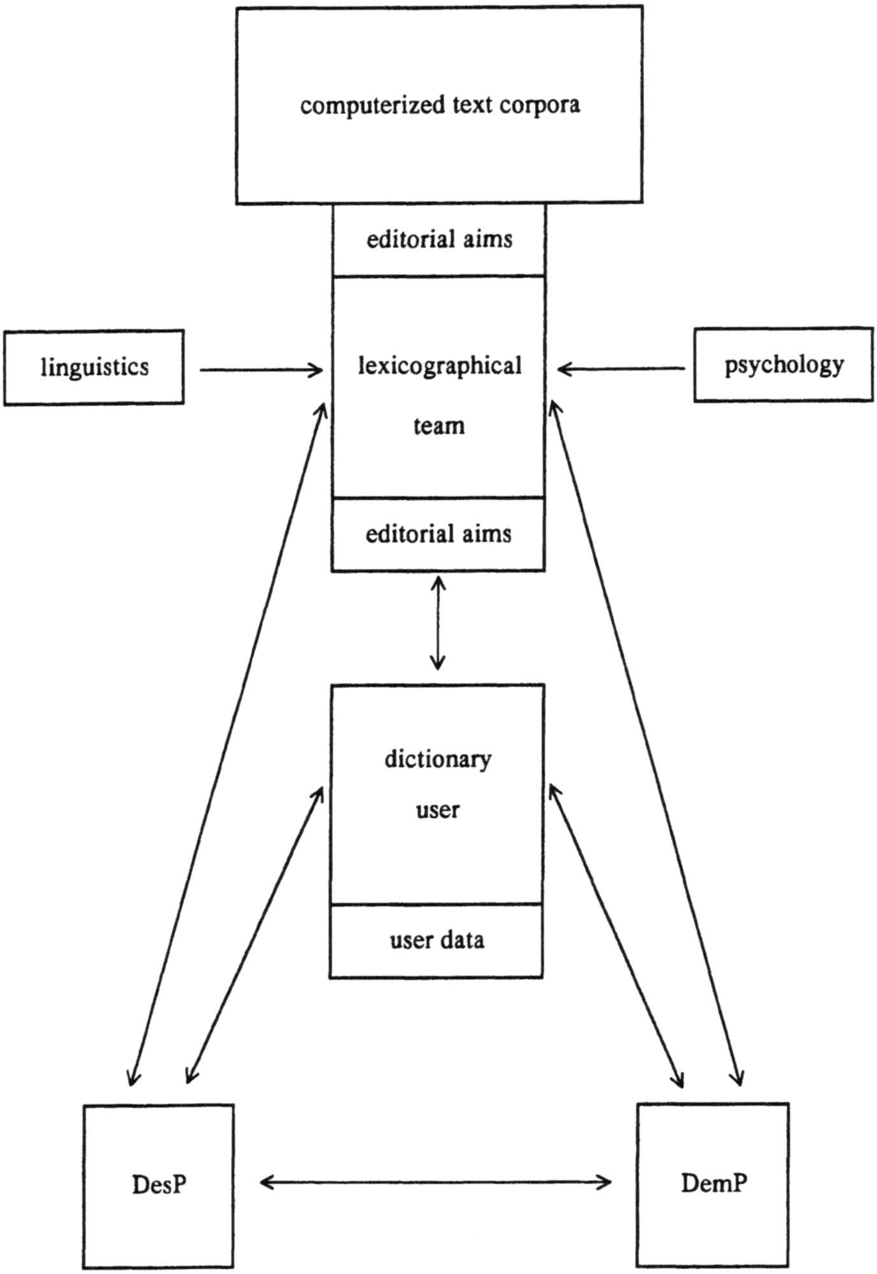

Fig. 6

I have added two further boxes to the left and right of the top box to indicate that a lexicographical team's decisions are also influenced by research findings in particular fields of science. As examples I have inserted psychology and linguistics.

Lexicographers, as human individuals, cannot escape the historical and social situation in which they find themselves. One might therefore distinguish between two layers of aims pursued by a dictionary team. At a 'deeper' level we have those aims which relate to what lexicographers might regard as their calling, as their role in a given society. Do they see themselves as objective transmitters of the culture and knowledge they are describing or as committed transformers? These 'deeper' aims are closely tied up with their personal beliefs and attitudes towards life and people and they may not always have been formulated as lexicographical policies. Yet they do not only have a bearing on the semantic paraphrases given for a particular lexical item, they also influence the choice of examples, whether taken from a computer corpus or constructed for a particular purpose. Ideologies are a well-known case. We are all aware of the endeavours to get away from social stereotypes: today's women in dictionary examples (or grammar ones) are engineers and scientists and men are cooking and changing nappies (see in this respect Gershuny 1977, Whitcut 1984, Cowie 1995). The educational policies embraced, as far as they can be inferred from dictionaries at this 'deeper' level, seem to have become rather sterile: linguistic illustrations lack edification. Where knowledge and life wisdom could be imparted as valuable experiences, precepts for adolescent learners, we are inundated by trivial examples which, in addition, are mostly cast in the unvarying form of statements. Learning through entertaining and variation seems to have been forgotten as a pursuable teaching aim. In short, the point I would like to make is that these 'deeper' aims in the compiling of a dictionary should not only be given more conscious and serious attention, they should also come more to the forefront of the lexicographical enterprise. They might then be used as criterial guidelines when lexicographers have to choose between thousands of corpus instances.

We come to the second type of aims which tends to be stated in the introductions to the dictionaries. The chief EFL dictionaries seek to expound the standard language in a social and cultural context which is generally and implicitly that of British life and institutions. Their lexicographical descriptions are meant to help learners understand and use the language correctly and appropriately. What characterizes these policy statements is their generality and vagueness which means that they are of little consequence for the actual dictionary compilation. A much sharper profile is needed. I would therefore like to take up some lexicographical issues, discuss them in the context of the relational model developed and show how they might contribute to a more consistent handling of exemplification in EFL dictionaries.

Let us begin with an example. The descriptive part of a dictionary typically takes into account eight parameters: spelling, pronunciation, grammar, currency, region, subject field, attitude and meaning, as shown in the diagram (Fig. 7):

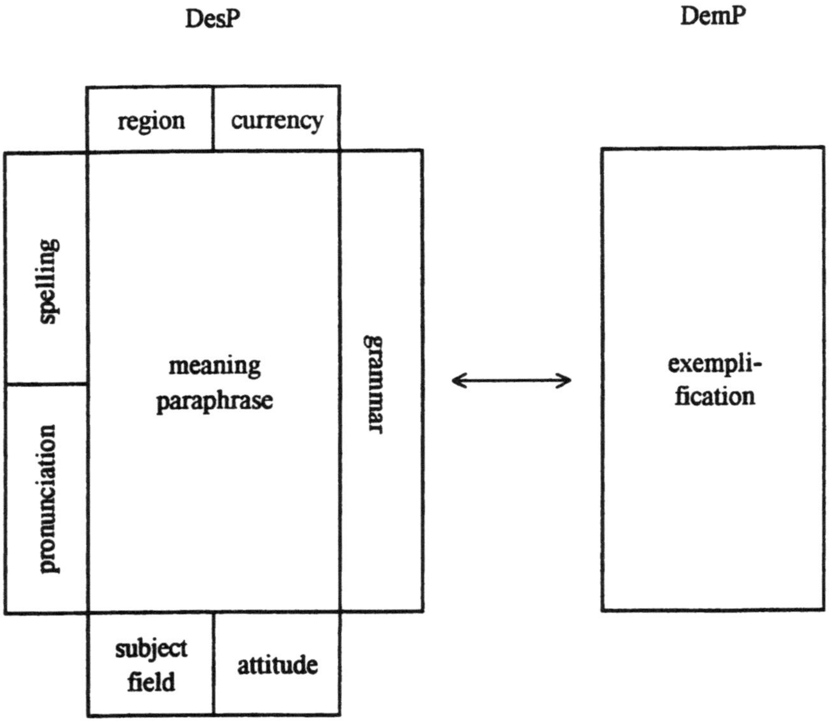

Fig. 7

In an unmarked case, a decoding situation, learners will at least call up two parameters: spelling and the meaning paraphrase. For pronunciation and grammar the intake may be less conscious. Under the noun *paramedic*, for instance, they might find the following paraphrase: "a person whose job is helping doctors, etc. with medical work" (OALD5). They understand what they read, but they cannot relate it to any job description in their experience: Is it the English correspondence for 'nurse', 'anatomist', 'homeopath' or even just a helpful bystander? When they turn to the example "*ambulancemen and other paramedics*", they will realize that they have to eliminate nurses, anatomists and homeopaths and other 'medical helpers' because paramedics are a kind of ambulancemen. A better meaning description might have made the example superfluous. Another dictionary (LDOCE3) describes a paramedic as "someone who has been trained to help people who are hurt or to do medical work, but who is not a doctor or nurse" and dispenses with the illustration. The quality of a semantic description is thus intricately linked to the need of exemplification.

When a lexical item is marked for region, currency, subject field or attitude, do we expect examples to reflect all this? In such a case, our relational model would have the structure below (Fig. 8):

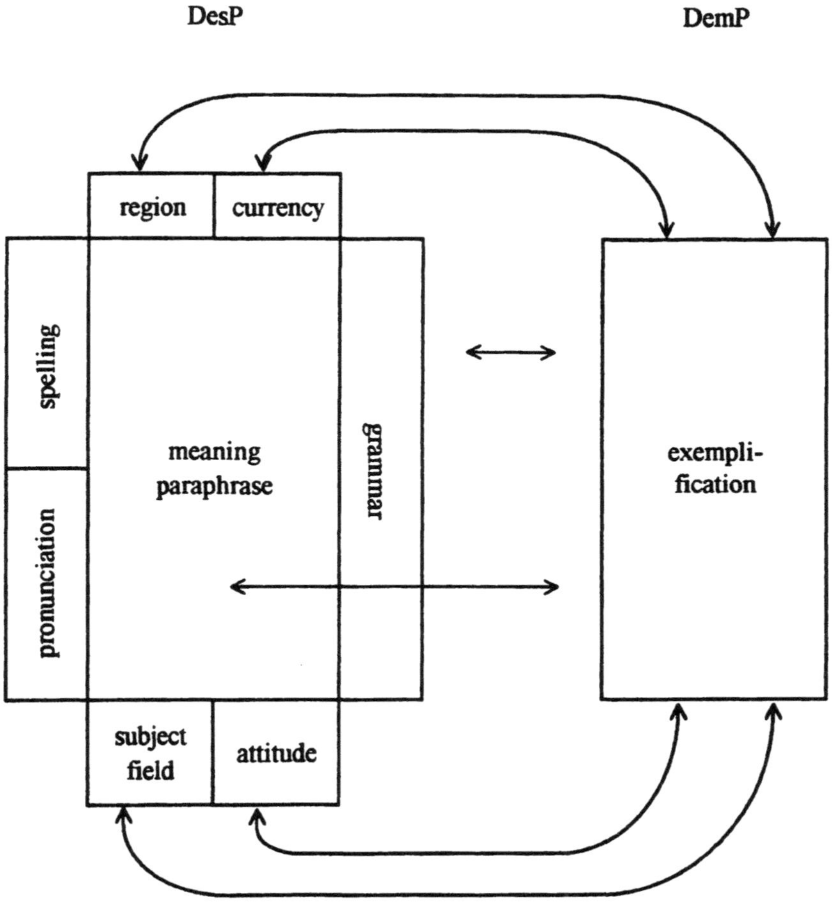

Fig. 8

Do the text-corpora held by the publishing houses supply a lexicographical team with substantial data for such an approach?

Or is there a tacit understanding that one-sentence examples, taken out of context, cannot satisfy such requirements and what lexicographers are therefore trying to do is to concentrate on the relation between meaning and grammar (Fig. 9):

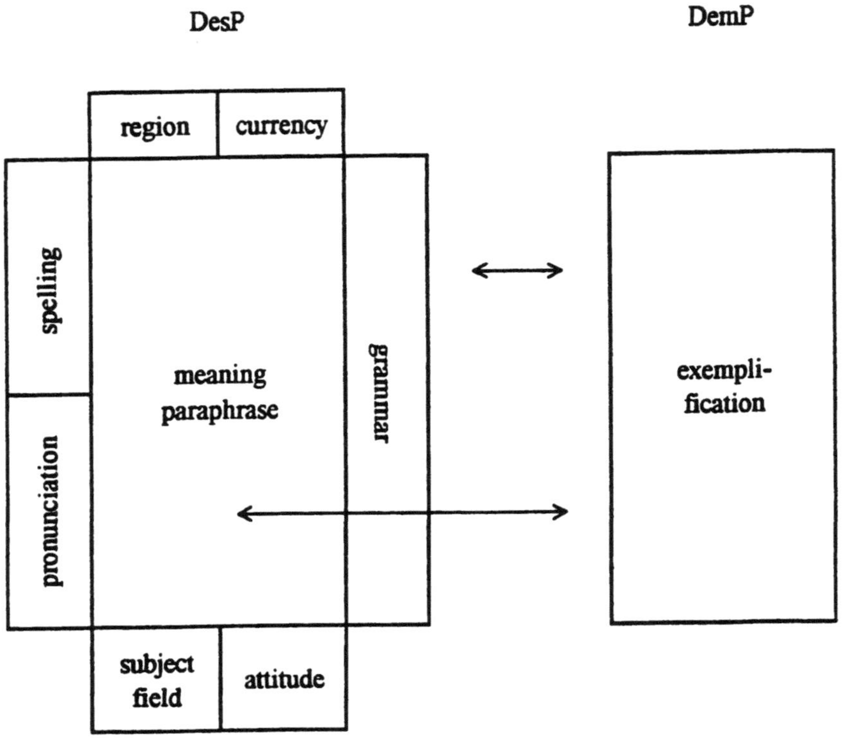

Fig. 9

If space does not allow exemplification for each word and sense, could a case be made for concentrating on the unmarked part of the vocabulary which includes the heavy-use items, those very items which are characterized by polysemy, idiomatic lexicalizations and multiple syntactic construction patterns, all calling for appropriate exemplification? This unmarked core would be the one learners are expected to use productively, the marked lexicon would be regarded as constituting the receptive vocabulary. A clearer stand taken with respect to the productive and receptive vocabulary might lead to a more effective channelling of work resources: the time gained when not illustrating the receptive lexicon might be redeployed to improve its semantic descriptions, thus justifying the editorial decision to dispense with examples.

Yet a sharper distinction between production vocabulary and reception vocabulary may not have to go that far. Less radical but still principled decisions could be taken. For instance, that items with regional and subject field markings only will not be provided with examples. Attitude and currency, because of their immediate relevance for social appropriateness in the learners' use of language would be fully covered by illustrations.

The parameters specified themselves are, as we know, not monolithic, but display a whole gamut of gradience. Take attitudinal labels. When a scale has such distinctions as *formal - neutral - informal - slang - taboo*, one might consider whether to divide it into a productive and a receptive section. Taboo words and senses are obvious candidates for restriction to the decoding lexicon.

The urgent need for a better focused editorial policy with respect to the relation between the envisaged users and the lexicographical team in our model can be shown with a striking example from the field of currency markers.

Under currency I have here subsumed such labels as *old, old-fashioned, obsolescent*, etc. In view of the constant revision of the EFL dictionaries under review we might expect that their linguistic coverage is up-to-date. Would we expect archaisms in EFL dictionaries? Would the data-banks which all the four publishers hold supply them with 'old' words in such numbers that their inclusion as headwords would be justified? It is well-known that within English lexicography the currency scale is not consistently marked. Even if a dictionary tells us, as for instance the fifth edition of OALD, that it has included 2 300 new words and meanings, we cannot easily identify them within the dictionary. There is no label 'neologism'. Archaisms, however, are clearly marked. New language use seems to make exemplification imperative so that users can see how these new words or senses are used. But would foreign learners of English speak or write in old language use? Do they need examples to document old language use?

In order to see what the lexicographical treatment of 'old words' is in the EFL dictionaries under review I again looked at a randomly chosen letter of the alphabet, excerpted a number of archaisms from one dictionary and compared the findings with the other dictionaries. Here is a list of 30 nouns from the letter *B* which LDOCE3 labels as *old-fashioned* or *old use* (Fig. 10):

A comparison of nouns marked *old-fashioned* (*of*) or *old use* (*ou*) in LDOCE3 with the markings in OALD5, COBUILD2, CIDE

Lexical item	LDOCE3			OALD5			COBUILD2			CIDE		
	l	m	ex	l	m	ex	l	m	ex	l	m	ex
balderdash *of*	+	+	–	+	+	+	+	+	+	+	+	+
bastard *of* 'parents not married'	+	+	–	+	–	+	+	+	+	+	+	+
bastardy *ou*	+	+	–	–	–	–	–	–	–	–	–	–
bathe *BrE of* 'a swim'	+	+	+	+	–	+	+	–	+	+	–	+
bather *BrE of*	+	+	–	+	–	–	+	–	+	+	–	–
bathing *BrE of*	+	+	+	+	–	+	–	–	–	+	–	–
bathing trunks *BrE of*	+	+	–	–	–	–	+	–	–	+	–	–
beast of burden *ou*	+	+	–	+	–	–	+	–	–	+	–	–
beau *of*	+	+	–	+	+	–	+	+	+	+	+	–
benefactress *of*	+	+	–	+	–	–	–	–	–	+	–	–

betrothal *ou*	+	+	–	+	+	–	+	+	–	+	+	+
bilge *of* 'nonsense'	+	+	–	+	–	+	+	–	+	+	+	+
bill of fare *of*	+	+	–	+	+	–	+	+	–	+	+	–
black Maria *BrE of*	+	+	–	–	–	–	–	–	–	+	+	–
bloomers *of* 'women's underwear'	+	+	–	+	–	+	+	–	+	+	–	–
bloomer *BrE hum, of* 'mistake'	+	+	–	+	+	+	–	–	–	+	+	+
bluestocking *BrE of*	+	+	–	+	–	–	+	–	+	+	+	–
bobby *BrE inf. of*	+	+	–	+	–	–	+	+	+	+	+	+
bodice *ou* 'corset'	+	+	–	–	–	–	–	–	–	+	–	–
boffin *BrE of*	+	+	–	+	–	–	+	–	+	+	–	+
Bolshevik *of* 'insulting term'	+	+	–	+	–	–	–	–	–	–	–	–
boob *AmE of* 'stupid person'	+	+	–	–	–	–	–	–	–	–	–	–
booby hatch *AmE of*	+	+	–	–	–	–	–	–	–	–	–	–
boor *of*	+	+	–	+	–	+	+	–	–	+	–	–
borstal *BrE of*	+	+	+	+	+	+	+	–	+	+	+	+
boudoir *ou*	+	+	–	+	+	–	+	+	+	+	–	+
bounder *BrE of*	+	+	+	–	–	–	+	+	+	+	+	+
bovver *BrE of slang*	+	+	–	–	–	–	–	–	–	+	–	–
bower *ou* 'woman's bedroom'	+	+	–	–	–	–	–	–	–	–	–	–
brethren *of* 'term of address'	+	+	–	+	–	+	+	+	+	+	+	–
brick *of* 'good person'	+	+	+	+	+	+	+	+	+	+	+	+

Fig. 10

l	=	listed in this sense in the dictionary
m	=	marked as of restricted temporal currency
ex	=	provided with an example

Fig. 11 focusses on the illustrations:

Nouns: marked archaisms

LDOCE3			OALD5			COBUILD2			CIDE		
marked lexical items	examples		marked lexical items	examples		marked lexical items	examples		marked lexical items	examples	
		%			%			%			%
30	5	16,6	8	4	50	10	8	80	15	9	60

Fig. 11

LDOCE3 provides examples in 5 cases. Of these 30 items, 22 are listed in OALD5 and 8 of them labelled. Half of them are provided with an example (4). COBUILD2 registers only 20 items, 10 of them are marked and 8 of these exemplified. CIDE lists 26 of the 30 items, marks 15 and provides examples for 9 of the 15. The rate of exemplification is higher for COBUILD2 (80 %) and CIDE (60 %).

If instead of LDOCE3 we take as our basis 30 nouns marked as *dated* or *archaic* in OALD5 and compare these with the other three learners' dictionaries, the results are as follows:

Lexical item	OALD5			LDOCE3			COBUILD2			CIDE		
	l	**m**	**ex**	**l**	**m**	**ex**	**l**	**m**	**ex**	**l**	**m**	**ex**
dairymaid *(dated)*	+	+	–	+	–	–	–	–	–	–	–	–
dalliance *(dated)*	+	+	–	+	+	–	+	+	+	+	–	+
damnation (2) (*dated* as an *interj*)	+	+	+	+	+	–	+	–	–	–	–	–
damsel *(arch)*	+	+	+ [boldface]	+	+	–	+	+	–	+	+	+
dandy^1 *(dated)*	+	+	–	+	+	–	+	–	+	+	–	+
deep^3, the 'the sea' (*dated* or *fml*)	+	+	–	+	+	–	+	–	+	+	–	–
dekko 'look' (*dated Brit sl*)	+	+	–	–	–	–	–	–	–	+	–	+
derring-do (*arch* or *joc*)	+	+	–	+	–	–	+	+	–	+	+	+
deuce^2 (*dated infml euph*)	+	+	+	+	+	+	–	–	–	+	–	+
dickens, the (*dated infml euph*)	+	+	+	+	–	+	–	–	–	+	+	+
die^3 'dice' (*dated*)	+	+	+ [boldface]	+	–	–	the idiom **'the die is cast'** is listed			+	+	+
doll^1 (2) 'attractive female' (*dated sexist sl esp US*)	+	+	+	+	–	–	–	–	–	+	–	–

dolly-bird (*dated Brit infml sexist*)	+	+	–	+	+	–	–	–	–	+	+	–
draught (2b) 'drink with some powerful property' (*esp. arch*)	+	+	+	–	–	–	+	+	+	–	–	–
drawers (*dated*)	+	+	–	+	+	–	+	+	–	+	+	–
duffer (*dated infml*)	+	+	+	+	+	–	+	+	+	+	+	+
eminence (2) 'a hill' (*dated* or *fml*)	+	+	+	+	–	–	–	–	–	–	–	–
escort[1] 'a person accompanying s.o. on a particular social occasion' (*dated* or *fml*)	+	+	–	+	–	+	+	–	+	+	–	+
faggot (3) 'a male homosexual' (*dated infml offensive*)	+	+	–	+	–	–	+	–	–	+	–	–
the fallen 'people, esp. soldiers, killed in war' (*dated* or *fml*)	+	+	–	+	–	–	+	–	+	+	+	+
fare[2] 'food' (*dated* or *fml*)	+	+	+	+	+	+ [bold-face]	+	–	+	+	+	+
fealty (*arch*)	+	+	+	+	+	–	+	–	–	–	–	–
fisticuffs (*arch* or *joc*)	+	+	+	+	+	–	+	+	–	+	+	+
flapper (*dated infml*)	+	+	–	+	–	–	–	–	–	+	+	–
flick (3a) 'a cinema film' (*dated infml*)	+	+	–	+	+	–	–	–	–	+	+	+
flicks, the (3b) 'the cinema' (*dated infml*)	+	+	+	+	+	–	–	–	–	+	+	+
foot[1] (5) 'a manner of walking' (*arch*)	+	+	+ [bold-face]	–	–	–	–	–	–	–	–	–
foundling (*dated*)	+	+	–	+	+	–	+	+	–	+	+	+
fount[1] 'source' (*arch* or *rhet*)	+	+	+	+	–	+ [bold-face]	+	–	+	+	–	+
free love (*dated*)	+	+	–	+	–	–	+	+	–	+	+	+

Fig. 12

l	=	listed in this sense in the dictionary
m	=	marked as of restricted temporal currency
ex	=	provided with an example

The figures for marked archaisms and their exemplification with OALDCE5 as our basis are:

OALD5			LDOCE3			COBUILD2			CIDE		
marked lexical items	examples		marked lexical items	examples		marked lexical items	examples		marked lexical items	examples	
		%			%			%			%
30	15	50	15	2	13,3	9	3	33,3	15	12	80

Fig. 13

If we combine the two tables of exemplified archaisms for nouns, the figures are as follows:

OALD5			LDOCE3			COBUILD2			CIDE		
marked lexical items	examples		marked lexical items	examples		marked lexical items	examples		marked lexical items	examples	
		%			%			%			%
45	7	15,5	38	19	50	19	11	57,8	30	21	70

Fig. 14

The results speak for themselves: LDOCE3 has the highest number of markings and the lowest rate of exemplification; CIDE, the newcomer in EFL dictionaries, has the highest exemplification rate.

Let us briefly look at adjectives described as *old-fashioned* or *old use*:

A comparison of adjectives marked *old-fashioned* (*of*) or *old use* (*ou*) in LDOCE3 with the markings in OALD5, COBUILD2, CIDE

Lexical item	LDOCE3			OALD5			COBUILD2			CIDE		
	l	**m**	**ex**	**l**	**m**	**ex**	**l**	**m**	**ex**	**l**	**m**	**ex**
barren *ou* (of a woman...)	+	+	–	+	+	–	+	+	+	+	–	+
beastly *of*	+	+	+	+	–	+	+	+	+	+	–	+
becoming *of*	+	+	–	+	–	+	+	+	+	+	+	+
bespoke *BrE of*	+	+	–	+	–	+	+	–	+	+	–	+
betrothed *ou*	+	+	–	+	+	+	+	+	+	(only as n)		
bothersome *of*	+	+	+	+	–	–	+	+	+	+	+	+
bucked *BrE of*	+	+	+	+	–	+	–	–	–	–	–	–

Fig. 15

l = listed in this sense in the dictionary
m = marked as of restricted temporal currency
ex = provided with an example

The rate between marked adjectives and exemplification is as follows:

Adjectives: marked archaisms

LDOCE3			OALD5			COBUILD2			CIDE		
marked lexical items	examples		marked lexical items	examples		marked lexical items	examples		marked lexical items	examples	
		%			%			%			%
7	3	42,8	2	1	50	5	5	100	2	2	100

Fig. 16

In the following table we have made OALD5 our basis of comparison:

Lexical item	OALD5			LDOCE3			COBUILD2			CIDE		
	l	**m**	**ex**	**l**	**m**	**ex**	**l**	**m**	**ex**	**l**	**m**	**ex**
damnable (*dated infml*)	+	+	+	+	+	+	+	+	+	+	+	+
dastardly (*dated*)	+	+	+	+	+	+	+	+	+	+	–	+
dicky (*dated Brit infml*)	+	+	+	+	–	+ [bold-face]	–	–	–	+	–	+
dishy (*dated infml*)	+	+	–	+	+	–	+	–	–	+	–	+
divers (*dated* or *infml*)	+	+	+	+	+	–	–	–	–	+	+	+
devine[1] (2) 'wonderful' (*dated infml*)	+	+	+	+	+	+	+	+	+	+	–	+
doughty (*arch* or *rhet*)	+	+	+	+	–	+	+	+	+	+	–	+

Fig. 17

l = listed in this sense in the dictionary
m = marked as of restricted temporal currency
ex = provided with an example

The rate between marked adjectives and exemplification is as follows:

OALD5			LDOCE3			COBUILD2			CIDE		
marked lexical items	examples		marked lexical items	examples		marked lexical items	examples		marked lexical items	examples	
		%			%			%			%
7	6	85,7	5	3	60	4	4	100	2	2	100

Fig. 18

For COBUILD2 and CIDE the illustration rate is again 100%. If we combine the two adjective samples the exemplification rate is as follows:

LDOCE3			OALD5			COBUILD2			CIDE		
marked lexical items	examples		marked lexical items	examples		marked lexical items	examples		marked lexical items	examples	
		%			%			%			%
12	6	50	9	7	77,7	9	9	100	4	4	100

Fig. 19

As with noun archaisms LDOCE3 has the highest number of markings and the lowest illustration rate; the illustration rates for COBUILD2 and CIDE are higher than that for OALD5.

Are these tendencies in the exemplification of temporally marked items confirmed for verbs? Our first sample is based on LDOCE3 and takes into account verbs listed under the letter *B*:

A comparison of verbs marked *old-fashioned* (*of*) or *old use* (*ou*) in LDOCE3 with the markings in OALD5, COBUILD2, CIDE

Lexical item	LDOCE3			OALD5			COBUILD2			CIDE		
	l	m	ex	l	m	ex	l	m	ex	l	m	ex
bandy *of* 'quarrel'	+	+	–	+	+	+	+	–	+	+	+	+
bath *BrE of* 'wash oneself ...'	+	+	–	+	–	–	+	–	+	+	–	+
bed *of* 'have sex ...'	+	+	–	+	–	+	–	–	–	+	+	+
beget *ou* 'become father ...'	+	+	–	+	+	+	+	+	+	+	+	+
behold *lit* or *ou*	+	+	–	+	+	+	+	–	+	+	+	+
belabour *ou* 'beat someone ...'	+	+	–	+	+	–	+	+	+	+	+	+
beseem *ou*	+	+	–	–	–	–	–	–	–	–	–	–
bethink os. *ou*	+	+	–	–	–	–	–	–	–	–	–	–
bide *ou* 'wait ...' *intr.*	+	+	–	+	+	–	–	–	–	–	–	–

Fig. 20

l = listed in this sense in the dictionary
m = marked as of restricted temporal currency
ex = provided with an example

The rate between marked verbs and exemplification is as follows:

Verbs: marked archaisms

LDOCE3			OALD5			COBUILD2			CIDE		
marked lexical items	examples		marked lexical items	examples		marked lexical items	examples		marked lexical items	examples	
		%			%			%			%
9	-	-	5	3	60	2	2	100	5	5	100

Fig. 21

The corresponding table with *OALD5* as our basis of comparison is:

Lexical item	OALD5			LDOCE3			COBUILD2			CIDE		
	l	**m**	**ex**	**l**	**m**	**ex**	**l**	**m**	**ex**	**l**	**m**	**ex**
carry (5) 'be pregnant' (*dated* or *fml*)	+	+	+	+	+	–	+	–	+	+	–	+
chum up (with sb) (*dated infml*)	+	+	–	+	+	+	–	–	–	+	–	+
cleave[1] (1) 'to split' (*dated* or *fml*)	+	+	+	+	–	+	+	–	+	+	+	+
cleave[1] through (2) 'to make a way through sth' (*dated* or *fml*)	+	+	+	–	–	–	–	–	–	–	–	–
cleave[2] 'to remain attached' (*arch*)	+	+	+	+	–	–	+	–	+	+	–	+
cobble[2] 'to repair shoes' (*dated*)	+	+	–	+	+	–	–	–	–	–	–	–
cuckold (*arch usu derog*)	+	+	–	+	+	–	+	–	+	+	+	+
dig[1] (2) 'to enjoy, appreciate' (*dated infml*)	+	+	+	+	+	+	+	+	+	+	+	+
do with sth (2) 'to tolerate' (*dated Brit*)	+	+	+	–	–	–	–	–	–	+	–	+

Fig. 22

l = listed in this sense in the dictionary
m = marked as of restricted temporal currency
ex = provided with an example

The rate between verb markings and exemplification is given in the following table:

OALD5			LDOCE3			COBUILD2			CIDE		
marked lexical items	examples		marked lexical items	examples		marked lexical items	examples		marked lexical items	examples	
		%			%			%			%
9	6	66,6	5	2	40	1	1	100	3	3	100

Fig. 23

If we combine the two verb tables, the figures are as follows:

LDOCE3			OALD5			COBUILD2			CIDE		
marked lexical items	examples		marked lexical items	examples		marked lexical items	examples		marked lexical items	examples	
		%			%			%			%
14	2	14,2	14	9	64,2	3	3	100	8	8	100

Fig. 24

If we combine the figures for the three word classes, the picture is as follows:

LDOCE3			OALD5			COBUILD2			CIDE		
marked lexical items	examples		marked lexical items	examples		marked lexical items	examples		marked lexical items	examples	
		%			%			%			%
71	15	21,1	61	35	57,3	31	23	74,1	42	33	78,5

Fig. 25

The overall trend in the treatment of archaisms and their exemplification according to our samples is as follows: LDOCE3 has the highest number of markings and the lowest rate of exemplification. Less than a quarter of the lexical items described as *old-fashioned* or *old use* are provided with an example. OALD5 marks fewer items than LDOCE3, but many more than COBUILD2 and CIDE. More than half of the *dated* or *archaic* words are shown in example sentences or phrases. The two EFL dictionaries which entered the competitive market after Oxford University Press and Longman had already had revisions of their respective dictionaries, COBUILD and CIDE, include fewer items with restricted temporal currency, and about three quarters of those listed are provided with an example.

One may of course wonder whether the examples provided for old language use are meant to enlighten users on the meaning or to help them use archaisms appropriately. Who would these users be?

Having looked at the marked vocabulary let us now turn to the unmarked core vocabulary. The earlier quote from COBUILD2 has revealed editorial endeavours to identify vocabulary areas where exemplification might not be necessary from a linguistic, pragmatic or cultural point of view, unless there is a specific grammatical or lexical use. Musical instruments were a case in point. Others might be:

names of games, e.g. *canasta, chess, cribbage*
names of illnesses, e.g. *appendicitis, flu, meningitis*
names of sciences, e.g. *biology, geography, philosophy*

names of animals, e.g. *puma, sheep dog, tiger*
names of flowers, e.g. *bluebell, marigold, tulip*

In the field of word-formation, the following types might have to be considered:

nouns:	noun + noun compounds on a part-whole relationship, e.g. *desktop, door knob, mountainside*
adjectives:	adjective formations in *-ed* from nouns and noun phrases expressing a HAVE relation, e.g. *barbed, bearded, striped*

A principled investigation of such semantic areas where words can stand on their own and an explicit acknowledgment of them may free lexicographers from that tedious burden to look for an example at any price and turn their full attention to where support by examples is needed.

One such area, for instance, might be collective nouns where foreign learners are often left at a loss by our four EFL dictionaries. They have learnt that nouns denoting a group of people may be used with a singular or a plural verb, according to whether unity or membership is emphasized. But they are not sure whether this rule applies in all cases. Here is a list of 10 such collective nouns and the lexicographical specification given (Fig. 26):

Collective nouns denoting a group of people

Lexical item	LDOCE3				OALD5				COBUILD2				CIDE			
sense 'group of people'	l	c	ex	hex	l	c	ex	hex	l	c	ex	hex	l	c	ex	hex
ballet	+	–	+	–	+	+	+	–	–	–	–	–	–	–	–	–
band	+	–	+	–	+	+	+	–	+	+	+	–	+	–	+	–
batch	+	–	+	–	+	–	+	–	+	–	+	–	+	–	+	–
board	+	+	+	–	+	+	+	+	+	–	+	–	+	+	+	+
body	+	–	+	–	+	+	+	+	+	–	+	–	+	–	+	–
bodyguard	+	–	–	–	+	+	+	+	+	–	+	–	+	+	+	+
bourgeoisie	+	–	–	–	+	+	+	–	+	+	+	–	+	+	+	–
(the) brass	+	–	–	–	+	+	+	+	+	–	+	–	+	+	+	+ (in para-phra-se)
bunch	+	+	+	–	+	+	+	–	+	–	+	–	+	–	+	–
bureaucracy	+	–	–	–	+	+	–	–	–	–	–	–	+	–	+	–

Fig. 26

l	=	the item is in this sense listed in the dictionary
c	=	there is a grammatical code specifying that the item in this sense can be used with a singular or plural verb or is used in the singular/plural only
ex	=	the sense is illustrated with an example
hex	=	the example is helpful, showing the use in the singular and plural, or in the plural, thus suggesting that both singular and plural are acceptable

As you can see from the column *hex* (helpful example), OALD5 and CIDE are explicit in some cases. For the rest, foreigners do not know whether the respective lexicographical teams were oblivious of the foreign learners' needs or whether the grammatical-semantic rule is not applicable. Checks with native speakers seem to suggest that the grammatical treatment of these collective nouns vacillates. In some cases, usage is restricted to a singular verb, in others a plural verb can be used. We may be witnessing a gradual linguistic change. It is here where I return to my earlier model: the linguist can provide a lexicographical team with guidelines what to look out for in their huge data-banks. Is *ballet* or *bourgeoisie*, for instance, ever used with a plural verb?

What have I tried to show in this paper? If one leaves aside those lexical items that show a complex grammatical or lexicalized behaviour, one finds that example allocation in EFL dictionaries not only varies considerably but also seems random. A framework was developed outlining the relations that may have to be taken into account when lexicographers have to decide whether or not to support a meaning paraphrase by usage examples. A number of issues were raised to urge a more consistent and principled lexicographical practice.

Bibliography

Cowie, Anthony P. (1978): "The place of illustrative material and collocations in the design of a learner's dictionary". — In: P. Strevens (ed.): In honour of A. S. Hornby (Oxford: OUP) 127-139.

— (1989): "The language of examples in English learners' dictionaries". — In G. James (ed.): Lexicographers and their works (Exeter: University of Exeter) (=Exeter Linguistic Studies 14) 55-65.

— (1995): "The learner's dictionary in a changing cultural perspective". — In: B. B. Kachru, H. Kahane (eds.): Cultures, ideologies and the dictionary (Tübingen: Niemeyer) (=Lexicographica Series Maior 64) 283-295.

Drysdale, Patrick D. (1987): "The role of examples in a learner's dictionary". — In: A. Cowie (ed.): The dictionary and the language learner (Tübingen: Niemeyer) (=Lexicographica Series Maior 17) 213-223.

Fox, Gwyneth (1988): "The case for examples". — In: J. M. Sinclair (ed.): Looking up. An account of the COBUILD project in lexical computing (London, Glasgow: Collins ELT) 137-149.

Gershuny, Henny L. (1977): "Sexism in dictionaries and texts: omissions and commissions". — In: A. P. Nilsen et al. (eds.): Sexism and language (Urbana, Ill.: NCTE) 143-159.

Harras, Gisela (1989): "Zu einer Theorie des lexikographischen Beispiels". — In: F. J. Hausmann et al. (eds.): Wörterbücher. Dictionaries. Dictionnaires, Vol. 1 (Berlin, New York: de Gruyter) 607-614.

Hartmann, Reinhard R. K. (ed.) (1984): LEXeter '83 proceedings. — Tübingen: Niemeyer (= Lexicographica Series Maior 1).

Hausmann, Franz Josef (1985): "Kollokationen im deutschen Wörterbuch. Ein Beitrag zur Theorie des lexikographischen Beispiels". — In: H. Bergenholtz, J. Mugdan (eds.): Lexikographie und Grammatik (Tübingen: Niemeyer) (=Lexicographica Series Maior 3) 118-129.

Hausmann, Franz Josef et al. (1989-1991): Wörterbücher. Dictionaries. Dictionnaires, 3 vols. — Berlin, New York: de Gruyter.

Hermanns, Fritz (1988): "Das lexikographische Beispiel. Ein Beitrag zu seiner Theorie". — In: G. Harras (ed.): Das Wörterbuch. Artikel und Verweisstrukturen. (Düsseldorf: Schwann) (Jahrbuch 1987 des Instituts für deutsche Sprache. Sprache der Gegenwart 74) 161-195.

James, Gregory (ed.) (1989): Lexicographers and their works. —Exeter: University of Exeter (=Exeter Linguistic Studies 14).

Kachru, Braj B., Henry Kahane (eds.) (1995): Cultures, ideologies, and the dictionary. Studies in honor of Ladislav Zgusta. — Tübingen: Niemeyer (=Lexicographica Series Maior 64).

Landau, Sidney I. (1989): Dictionaries. The art and craft of lexicography. — Cambridge: CUP.

Laufer, Batia (1992): "Corpus-based versus lexicographer examples in comprehension and production in new words". — In: H. Tommola et al. (eds.): Euralex '92 proceedings (Tampere: Yliopisto) (Studia translatologica A, 2) 71-76.

Martin, Robert (1989): "L'exemple lexicographique dans le dictionnaire monolingue". — In: F. J. Hausmann et al. (eds.): Wörterbücher. Dictionaries. Dictionnaire, Vol. 1. (Berlin, New York: de Gruyter) 599-607.

Minaeva, Ljudmilla (1992): "Dictionary examples: Friends or foes?". — In: H. Tommola et al. (eds.): Euralex '92 proceedings (Tampere: Yliopisto) (Studia translatologica A, 2) 77-80.

Nesi, Hilary (1996): "The role of illustrative examples in productive dictionary use". — In: Dictionaries 17, 198-206.

Nikula, Henrik (1986): "Wörterbuch und Kontext. Ein Beitrag zur Theorie des lexikographischen Beispiels". — In: W. Weiss, H. E. Wiegand, M. Reis (eds.): Textlinguistik contra Stilistik? - Wortschatz und Wörterbuch - Grammatische und pragmatische Organisation der Rede? (Tübingen: Niemeyer) (=Kontroversen, alte und neue. Akten des VII. Internationalen Germanisten-Kongresses Göttingen 1985, Vol. 3) 187-192.
Nilsen, Alleen P. et al. (eds.) (1977): Sexism and language. — Urbana, Ill.: NCTE.
Reichmann, Oskar (1988): "Zur Funktion, zu einigen Typen und zur Auswahl von Beispielbelegen im historischen Bedeutungswörterbuch". — In: K. Hyldgaard-Jensen, A. Zettersten (eds.): Symposium on lexicography III. (Tübingen: Niemeyer) (=Lexicographica Series Maior 19) 413-444.
Stein, Gabriele (1991): "Illustrations in dictionaries". — In: International Journal of Lexicography 4, 99-127.
Strevens, Peter (ed.) (1978): In honour of A. S. Hornby. — Oxford: OUP.
Wiegand, Herbert E. (1977): "Nachdenken über Wörterbücher: Aktuelle Probleme". — In: G. Drosdowski, H. Henne, H. E. Wiegand (eds.): Nachdenken über Wörterbücher (Mannheim, Wien, Zürich: Dudenverlag) 51-102.
Whitcut, Janet (1984): "Sexism in dictionaries". — In: R. R. K. Hartmann (ed.): LEXeter '83 proceedings (Tübingen: Niemeyer) (=Lexicographica Series Maior 1) 141-144.
Zgusta, Ladislav (1971): Manual of lexicography. Janua linguarum. —The Hague, Paris: Mouton (= Janua linguarum. Series Maior 39).
Zöfgen, Ekkehard (1986): "Kollokation - Kontextualisierung - (Beleg-)-Satz. Anmerkungen zur Theorie und Praxis des lexikographischen Beispiels". — In: A. Barrera-Vidal, H. Kleineidam, M. Raupach. (eds.): Französische Sprachlehre und bon usage (München: Hueber) (=Festschrift für Hans-Wilhelm Klein zum 75. Geburtstag) 219-238.

Robert F. Ilson

The treatment of meaning in learners' dictionaries – and others

1 Introduction

There are two reasons for my choice of subject. One is that at the Exeter conference in 1983 where Euralex was founded, Betty Kirkpatrick roused me from summer somnolence by insisting that learners' dictionaries should not fob off their users with second-rate explanations simply because we lexicographers think we know English better than they do. The other is my growing dismay at how little attention explanations get in most reviews of dictionaries – mine, alas, included! An outstanding exception to this comparative neglect is Sidney Landau's Review Article on The American College Dictionaries (Landau: 311-51). It is in his footsteps that I seek to walk.

So I shall examine explanations in various monolingual learners' dictionaries of English to see whether they are second-rate. Second-rate in comparison to what? In comparison to explanations in two American college dictionaries for native speakers of English (W10; RHWCD). And in comparison with explanations in several monolingual dictionaries of other languages: two French dictionaries (DFC for learners; PR for native speakers) and two German dictionaries (LGDF for learners; RSD for native speakers). I need hardly remind my international colleagues, though I fear I may have to remind some Anglophone monolingual lexicographers, that lexicography, whilst perhaps a dying profession, is an international discipline - and has been for thousands of years (see Boisson/Kirtchuk/Béjoint 1991: 261-315).

I shall investigate the dictionary entries for *lamely/lameness*, *reggae*, and *still life* (see the Appendixes to this article). A surprising selection, I agree. The last two items are by no stretch of the imagination part of the core vocabulary of English; one may indeed question their presence in learners' dictionaries at all. But there is some method in my madness. First, I want to concentrate on how dictionaries treat Meaning and Reference rather than Use. In this endeavour, items with valency problems (e.g. verbs) would be a distraction. Second, I want to minimise (but not exclude entirely) the problem of polysemy: I have too little space/time at my disposal to consider whether for item X the one sense in dictionary A, the two senses in dictionary B, and the three senses in dictionary C do or do not cover the same ground. Third, the very fact that *reggae* and *still life* are not part of the core vocabulary - and that the word *reggae* may well, like a proper name, have a similar form in many languages - favours my comparison of English with non-English dictionaries: I am assuming that *reggae* in English and French, and *still life, nature morte*, and *Stilleben* all have essentially the same meaning and reference, so that my interlinguistic comparison of them will not be misleading.

Anyway, here goes!

2 Investigation

2.1 *Lamely/lameness*

These are both derived from *lame adj*. Morphologically, they can be treated as so-called run-ons - appended after the entry for *lame adj* with no explanation of their own. And, indeed, this is exactly what is done by three of the dictionaries in my sample: the smallest (RHWDAE, for learners) and the two largest (W10 and RHWCD, for native speakers). But *lame adj* has at least two senses (in W10 and RHWCD it actually has four!): the literal 'crippled' (as in "a lame leg") and the metaphorically figurative 'ineffectual; unsatisfactory' (as in "a lame excuse"). By convention, if *lamely* and *lameness* are run on at the end of the entry for *lame*, the derivatives may be supposed to inherit all the senses of their source. Thus the following would all be acceptable:

1) He hobbled away lamely from the scene of the accident (literal)
2) He excused himself lamely (figurative)
3) the lameness of his leg (literal)
4) the lameness of his excuse (figurative).

Their acceptability is strongly implied by RHWDAE, W10, and RHWCD.

At the other extreme come COBUILD and CIDE. These two dictionaries have radically different macrostructures when it comes to main entries: COBUILD maximises polysemy (here with one entry for *lame* comprising two senses); CIDE maximises homonymy (here with two entries for *lame*, one for the literal sense, one for the figurative). But their macrostructures treat run-ons in remarkably similar ways. In COBUILD, *lameness* is run on to the literal sense of *lame* and *lamely* to the figurative sense. In CIDE, *lameness* is run on to the literal homograph of *lame* and *lamely* to the figurative homograph. So for both COBUILD and CIDE, examples 2 and 3 above are acceptable but examples 1 and 4 are not.

LDOCE takes a different line. *Lameness* is run on to *lame*[1]*adj*, which has both the literal and the figurative sense. But *lamely* has been promoted to a main entry, with its own explanation. And that explanation is of the figurative sense only. So for LDOCE, examples 2, 3, and 4 are acceptable but example 1 is not.

Finally, OALD seems to take the same line as RHWDAE, W10, and RHWCD. *Lame adj* has two senses and its run-ons *lamely* and *lameness* inherit both. So for OALD, examples 1, 2, 3, and 4 above are all acceptable. Yet at the same time OALD provides *lamely* (but not *lameness*) with an example. The example is figurative (like my example 2) rather than literal (like my example 1). OALD's combination of placement and status (both *lamely* and *lameness* as run-ons) with exemplification (of *lamely* only) conveys to its users the covert message that whereas *lameness* is equally at home literally or figuratively, *lamely* is typically figurative - but not exclusively so. So for OALD, all four of my examples are acceptable, but example 1 is marginal. Of all the dictionaries, OALD's treatment of *lamely* and *lameness* is most in accord with my own intuitions.

But what about corpus evidence? All the dictionaries claim to have used corpuses (I assume that RHWDAE's claim to have been "Created from the Random House *Living Dic-*

tionary Database^{TM} " is a reference to one such). So it is fascinating to see how different their assessments of the meaning of *lamely* and *lameness* are. That is a salutary reminder of the role of human fleshware in a world increasingly dominated by hardware and software.

And what about the so-called 'user perspective'? Merriam-Webster have made no secret of the primacy they accord to decoding over encoding. They are satisfied if any instance of *lamely* and *lameness* encountered by W10 users can be understood by reference to one or other sense of *lame adj.* Given that W10 users are typically native speakers of English, I think the Merriam-Webster line is defensible. Essentially the same line is taken by the Random House analogue of W10: RHWCD. But a treatment justifiable in a native-speaker dictionary like W10 or RHWCD is not necessarily justified in a learners' dictionary like RHWDAE. Decoding-wise, a learners' dictionary should give its users an inkling of what is more likely and what is less likely to occur. Encoding-wise, a learners' dictionary should help its users to model their own usage on the *typical* usage of native speakers. But I think it is wrong for a learners' dictionary to highlight the typical by precluding the possible. Explanations that do so are, in Betty Kirkpatrick's sense, "second-rate". Striking a balance between the typical and the possible is hard. But who ever said lexicography was easy? If RHWDAE gives too little guidance as to the typical, COBUILD, CIDE, and especially LDOCE disarm their users in the face of the possible. So, as I have said, OALD seems to be the best of the five learners' dictionaries here, informing about both the possible (covertly) and the typical (overtly) with admirable concision.

2.2 *Reggae*

The best way to understand reggae is to hear some. Bob Marley singing "No Woman No Cry" will do the trick better than any definition. Such auditory Illustration is in fact possible in multi-media computerised reference works. But not, alas, in the ten dictionaries under discussion here. These have got to use words when they talk to us.

All the dictionaries agree that reggae is a kind of music. Thereafter, however, each makes a different selection from the following types of feature: level (popular), function (dance), rhythm and structure (strong, marqué, répétitive, regular), analysis of rhythm (strong second and fourth beat, accent on offbeat, syncopated), tempo (moderate), origin (West Indies, Jamaica, Noirs jamaïquains), prototypical artist (Bob Marley), affinities (native styles, blues, calypso, rock, soul). The problem is that *reggae* seems less like a technical term (*penicillin; phoneme*) than like a proper name (*Churchill, Winston; Freud, Sigmund*). The only complete explanation of a proper name is a complete biography. Of a potentially vast number of features, lexicographers, with limited space, must select the most important and useful. For my colleague Claire Hershman, who did some work for Marley, the most important thing about reggae is its lyrics of social protest - which none of the dictionaries mentions. For me the most important thing about reggae is that I can dance to it (mentioned only by OALD). Though the English-language native-speaker dictionaries W10 and RHWCD offer more information about reggae than PR or the learners' dictionaries, neither W10 nor RHWCD says it is danceable - and neither mentions Bob Marley! NHDAE's treatment is clearly the worst, but none is clearly the best - though for a learners' dictionary I would give the palm to OALD had it mentioned Marley.

The relation of Bob Marley to reggae is interesting. Lexicographically, it is like the relation of John Wesley to Methodism (or of Jesus Christ to Christianity). An explanation of *reggae* should mention Marley, just as an explanation of *Methodism* should mention Wesley. Whether an explanation of *socialism* need mention Marx (as an explanation of *Marxism* must), or an explanation of *psychoanalysis* Freud (as an explanation of *Freudianism* must), is somewhat less clear.

Since I am (still) a working lexicographer, I feel obliged to practise what I preach. My explanation of *reggae* for a learners' dictionary would be:

> dance music that was popularised by the Jamaican singer-songwriter Bob Marley, is moderately fast and strongly syncopated, and is related to blues, calypso, and rock'n'roll

I make no apologies for using the hard word *syncopated*. It (or *syncopate*) is in all the learners' dictionaries save NHDAE and LDOCE; it is important, it is short, and it is right. To replace it with a paraphrase is almost to be second-rate.

2.3 *Still life/nature morte/Stilleben.*

The best way to understand still life is to see a still life. Since pictorial Illustration is well within the capacity of a book dictionary, one might expect the entry for *still life* to be illustrated. The American Heritage Dictionary (3rd edition, 1992) uses for this purpose a black-and-white reproduction of Paul Lacroix's "Fruit" (1868). But none of the dictionaries discussed here does this. Why not? Perhaps because the analogy between *still life* and *reggae* is misleading. A prototypical reggae number (Marley's "No Woman No Cry") is sufficiently representative of its genre to leave no doubt in the hearer's mind whether any other music he hears is reggae or not. But though there are equally prototypical still lifes (Pisarro's "Bouquet de Fleurs", 1878; Manet's "Pêches", 1880), it is less clear whether having seen these the viewer will know with certainty how far the prototype can be extended - or, as Saul Kripke might say, how rigid a designator *still life* is. Yes, we know that Baugin's "Le Dessert de Gaufrettes" (about 1630), with its flask and glass of wine and its dish of wafers, is a still life, as is Chardin's famous "La Raie" (1728), with its jugs, bottles, kitchen utensils, shellfish, and fish (including the enormous ray) - yet the picture also shows a live and very agitated cat! But what about Rembrandt's "Le Bœuf Écorché" (1655), with its huge ox-carcass hung in a butcher's and, peeping gingerly round at it to one side, the shadowy figure of a woman, like Mary at the Crucifixion? We know also that a still life is not a landscape or a portrait - they have different names, haven't they? But just why is it that when Van Gogh paints sunflowers in a vase, the product is a still life, whereas when he paints sunflowers in a field, the product is a landscape? We must confront not only the extension of the prototype, but also the boundaries between it and other prototypes.

Moreover, *still life* (like *landscape*, but probably not *portrait*) presents an inescapable problem of polysemy. The example "His wonderful still lifes attest to his mastery of still life" (compare "His wonderful portraits attest to his mastery of portraiture") shows that *still life* has at least two senses: one referring to a token, the other to the type (or genre) to which the token belongs. These senses may be related by a kind of metonymy; but their specific relation seems not to have been named either in classical rhetoric or in contemporary lexical semantics.

Reluctant as I am to deal with polysemy here, I cannot not point out that only the token, countable, sense is shown in RHWDAE, LDOCE (despite its C, U code), DFC, and LGDF; and that NHDAE's treatment is hopelessly confused (or wonderfully ingenious?), with a definition of the type (the genre) and an example of the token. RSD is marvellously clever in its use of *Darstellung* as genus of *Stilleben*: *Darstellung* covers both type and token at once; and the artful ambiguity is maintained by the absence of either article (*eine* oder *die*). RHWCD could have achieved the same effect (and not needed its strange sense 2) had its sense 1 read "representation chiefly of inanimate objects, as painting of a bowl of fruit". Unfortunately, mainstream Anglophone lexicography requires a choice of *a(n)* or *the* in definitions.

In the following discussion I shall draw promiscuously on *all* the explanations to be found in my dictionary sample, whether the information is formally addressed to the token sense or the type sense.

What is a still life? Although all my dictionaries agree that reggae is a kind of music, there is less agreement on what a still life is. It can be a painting/*tableau*, a drawing, perhaps a photograph, or (more generally) a picture/*Bild* or a representation/*Darstellung*. Dictionary evidence implies weakly that the typical still life is a painting and implies strongly that it cannot be a sculpture. Even RSD restricts *Stilleben* to *Malerei* 'painting'. That is by no means self-evident. Yet it is true that in all the discussion surrounding the exhibition by Damien Hirst of a pickled calf in a glass case, the work in question was never called a still life, however reminiscent it was of Rembrandt's "Bœuf Écorché". The safest genus-word would be *picture/Bild*. Unfortunately, there is no French equivalent: no French word that covers paintings, drawings, and photographs. *Tableau* may have a wider extension than *peinture*, but though it seems to subsume etchings it seems not to subsume drawings or photographs. This shows that the problems of formulating lexicographic explanations are not only dictionary-internal (due to differing lexicographic conventions or traditions) but dictionary-external (due to differences in the languages in which the dictionaries are written).

There is more dictionary agreement about the subject-matter of still lifes. It is objects/*Gegenstände*, inanimate objects, *objets ou êtres inanimés*, unmoving objects, objects that do not move, objects which are not living/*leblose Gegenstände*/*objets ou animaux morts*. There is also some dictionary evidence of what the typical inanimate objects are: flowers or fruit/*Früchte oder Blumen*. But for the sake of Chardin's dead ray and living cat, a hedge is desirable, such as "predominantly" (W10), "*le sujet essentiel*" (PR), "chiefly" (RHWCD), or *bes* "*besonders*" (LGDF). Two important questions remain.

One is why sunflowers in a vase can constitute a still life whereas sunflowers in a field constitute a landscape. COBUILD, CIDE, and LDOCE have independently hit on the same elegant answer: they all speak of "an *arrangement* of objects". RSD's solution is even
better: the "leblosen Gegenstände" are represented "in künstlerischer Anordnung" ('in an artistic arrangement'). Also admirable is DFC's "groupés en un ensemble artistique".

The second question is whether Rembrandt's "Bœuf Écorché" is a still life. Here we are dealing not with the *boundary* between two categories (*still life* v *landscape*) but with the *borders* of one (*still life* itself). Rembrandt's ox is an inanimate object artistically displayed. His picture of it can thus be considered a still life. But an ox is not a bowl of fruit. So Rembrandt's picture is a marginal still life, not a typical one. Just as a whale is a true but not a typical mammal, so Rembrandt's ox is a true but not a typical still life. A book on art history can say all this explicitly. A general-purpose dictionary cannot and need not. A good explanation of *still life* plus a judicious hedge ("typically", "such as", "besonders") will suffice.

Of all the explanations of *still life/nature morte/Stilleben* on offer here, none is entirely satisfactory. The reason is that the three key notions 'chiefly', 'arrangement', and 'typically' do not co-occur in any of them. But that is just as true of the native-speaker dictionaries as of the learners' dictionaries, and just as true of the French or German dictionaries as of the English-language ones. In other words, none of the dictionaries offers us something like:

1 [C]: a picture consisting chiefly of an arrangement of inanimate objects, typically flowers, fruit, bowls
2 [U]: still lifes collectively as an artistic genre

These Definitions can, of course, be supplemented with Exemplification, Illustration, and Discussion.

3 Conclusions

I began this investigation in trepidation, not knowing what I should find. I have been pleasantly surprised. With the possible exception of those in the American NHDAE, the smallest of the English-language dictionaries, the explanations in monolingual learners' dictionaries of English are not second-rate. That is, they measure up pretty well to those in native-speaker dictionaries of English and in dictionaries of French or German (whether for learners or native speakers). If that is partly because none of the dictionaries offers ideal explanations, it is also because the explanations in EFL dictionaries are not half bad. EFL dictionaries will not mislead learners with their explanations - at least no more than any other dictionaries will!

Neither the virtues nor the faults of these explanations are due primarily to corpus evidence. They are due to the sound or unsound judgement of the lexicographers who wrote them, who must evaluate distinctive features, grasp prototypes, and decide what to say and what to imply. What a shame, then, that (at least in Britain) lexicography is a dying profession! There are more and more dictionaries, fewer and fewer of us lexicographers. In the *directory Occupations* 1997 (Indy Leavesby, Ed., Thames Ditton, Surrey: Careers and Occupations Information Centre) *lexicography* is not even listed as a career option. Yet without good lexicographers there can be no good dictionaries. It is not, of course, that lexicographers know, or ever can know, all the answers. But only lexicographers can ask the right questions!

Bibliography

Der Große Duden Rechtschreibung (RSD) (1942) — Leipzig.

Dictionnaire du français contemporain illustré (DFC) (1980) — Paris: Larousse.

Langenscheidts Großwörterbuch Deutsch als Fremdsprache (LGDF) (1997): Dieter Götz, Günther Haensch, Hans Wellmann (eds.). — Berlin, München: Langenscheidt.

Le Petit Robert 1 (PR) (1989): Alain Rey (ed.). — Paris: Le Robert.

Merriam Webster's Collegiate Dictionary (W10) ([10]1993) — Springfield: Merriam-Websters.

Random House Webster's College Dictionary (RHWCD) (1991): Robert Costello (ed.). — New York: Random House.

Random House Webster's Dictionary of American English (RHWDAE) (1997): Gerald Dalgish (ed.). — New York: Random House.

The American Heritage Dictionary ([3]1992) — Boston: Houghton Mifflin.

The Newbury House Dictionary of American English (NHDAE) (1996): Philip Rideout (ed). — Boston: Heinle & Heinle.

Boisson, Claude, Pablo Kirtchuk, Henri Béjoint (1991): "Aux origines de la lexicographie. Les premiers dictionnaires monolingues et bilingues." — In: International Journal of Lexicography 4/4, 261-315.

Landau, Sidney (1994): "The American College Dictionaries." — In: International Journal of Lexicography 7/4, 311-51.

Appendix I: *lamely/lameness*

NHDAE: not entered

RHWDAE: **lame** ...–**lamely**, *adv*. **lameness**, *n*.

OALD: **lame** ... ➔**lamely, adv**: "*What's next?"she asked lamely*. –**lameness** n. [U].

COBUILD: **lame ... 1 ... lame in one leg ◆lameness**
2 ... lame excuse ◆ lamely *'lovely house,' I said lamely.*

CIDE: **lame** UNABLE TO WALK – **lameness** *n*.
lame NOT SATISFACTORY – **lamely** *adv*. *"I think I must have lost my ticket," she told the inspector lamely.*

LDOCE: **lame** ➘ *adj 1* ... **go lame**
2 ... some lame excuse ... – see also LAMELY ... – **lameness** *n* [u]
lamely *adv* if you say something lamely, you do not sound confident and other people find it difficult to believe you: *"But I still love you," he added rather lamely.*

W10: **1 lame** *adj* ... – **lamely** *adv* – **lameness** *n*

RHWCD: **lame 1** *adj*. ... – **lamely**, *adv*. – **lameness**, *n*.

Appendix II: *reggae*

NHDAE: a kind of music that began in the West Indies: *Bob Marley was one of the most famous reggae artists.*

RHWDAE: a style of Jamaican music blending blues, calypso, and rock

OALD: a type of West Indian popular music and dance with strong rhythms

COBUILD: **Reggae** is a kind of West Indian popular music with a very strong beat. *Many people will remember Bob Marley for providing them with their first taste of Reggae music.*

CIDE: a type of popular music from Jamaica with a strong second and fourth beat

LDOCE: a kind of popular music from the West Indians with a strong regular beat

W10: popular music of Jamaican origin that combines native styles with elements of rock and soul music and is performed at moderate tempos with the accent on the off beat

RHWCD: a style of Jamaican music blending blues, calypso, and rock and characterized by a strongly syncopated rhythm

DFC: not entered

PR: Musique des Noirs jamaïquains, à rhythme marqué, à structure répétitive.

LGDF: not entered

RSD: not entered

Appendix III: *still life/ nature morte/ Stilleben*

NHDAE: [c;u] (in art) the painting or photography of unmoving objects, such as fruit or flowers: *a still life of a bowl of pears.*

RHWDAE: [*count*], *pl.* **still lifes**. a drawing or painting of inanimate objects, as of a bowl of fruit.

OALD: **[a]** [u] the representation in painting or drawing of objects which are not living, eg fruit, flowers, etc: *I prefer landscape to still life.*
<i> [c] **(pl. still lifes)** a picture of this type.

COBUILD: **still lifes**. A **still life** is a painting or drawing of an arrangement of objects such as flowers or fruit. It also refers to this type of painting or drawing.
N-VAR

CIDE: A **still life** is a (type of) painting or drawing of an arrangement of objects that do not move, such as flowers, fruit, bowls, etc.: *We went to an exhibition of 17th century Dutch still lifes.* [c] *I find still life rather uninteresting.* [u] *He's an expert still life painter.*

LDOCE: *plural* **still lifes** *n* [c, u] a picture of an arrangement of objects, expecially flowers and fruit

W10: *n, pl* **still lifes** (1695) **1**: a picture consisting predominantly of inanimate objects **2**: the category of graphic arts concerned with inanimate subject matter

RHWCD: *n, pl.* **still lifes** **1**: a representation chiefly of inanimate objects, as a painting of a bowl of fruit.
2: the category of subject matter in which inanimate objects are represented, as in painting or photography...

DFC: *Nature morte,* tableau représentant des objets ou des animaux morts, groupés en un ensemble artistique.

PR: ◆**1°** Objets ou êtres inanimés faisant le sujet essentiel d'un tableau; genre de peinture qui s'attache à les représenter. *Peintre de nature(s) morte(s).*
◆**2°** ... Tableau dans ce genre de peinture, *«La Raie»,* célèbre nature morte *de Chardin. Nature morte au pichet, aux oranges,* se dit d'un tableau de nature morte d'après son objet principal.

LGDF: ... ein Bild, das Gegenstände, *bes* Früchte u. Blumen zeigt

RSD: ... (Malerei: Darstellung lebloser Gegenstände in künstlicher Anordnung)...

Henri Béjoint

Compound nouns in learners' dictionaries

1 Introduction

Compounds are not a popular subject for research in lexicography - unlike idioms, or phraseology in general.[1] Yet, they are important, for at least two reasons. The first is that they are in very large numbers in many languages, including English: they make up an important proportion of all lexical creations, as exhibited in English dictionaries of new words (Ayto 1996). The second and main reason is that they are, to some extent, language "in the making". They exemplify what is sometimes called "onomasiology" in the creation of lexis, and as such, they are a special challenge for the lexicographer.

The present paper will examine compound nouns - probably the largest category (Bauer 1983: 202) - rather than adjectives or verbs. After a brief look at the definition of compound nouns, I will proceed to discuss the peculiarities of their meaning, and finally examine some aspects of their definitions in the *Cambridge International Dictionary of English* (1995 - CIDE), the *Collins COBUILD English Dictionary*, second edition (1995 - COBUILD2), the *Longman Dictionary of Contemporary English*, third edition (1995 - LDOCE3), and the *Oxford Advanced Learner's Dictionary*, fifth edition (1995 - OALD5). Most examples will therefore be in English, with some additional illustrations in French.

2 Of compounds in general and compound nouns in particular

2.1 Definitions

A compound is a lexical unit composed of at least two autonomous elements (i.e. words). Several criteria for distinguishing compound nouns have been mentioned (see Tournier 1988: 63f.):

- graphic cohesion. This is difficult to apply, particularly in English, because of the variations in spelling: an English compound noun like *paper clip* can have the forms

---

1 I would like to thank Rosamund Moon for helpful comments on a draft version of this paper (her remarks are noted RM), and Philippe Thoiron for generous discussions on many of the issues.

XY, X Y, or X-Y.[2] This makes the automatic extraction of compounds particularly difficult in English.[3]

- non-compositionality. This is true in many cases, but not always. For example, *bed-settee* can be seen as the semantic addition of its two elements (Tournier 1988: 64); similarly for a large number of specialized terms.
- position of the stress: compounds are stressed as units, not on each of their elements. But in English stress position varies according to the context, and is different in British and in American English (RM).
- frequency: compounds are frequent associations. But many groupings like *I say*, etc. that are not compounds may actually be more frequent than compounds.
- lexical unity: a compound behaves like a simple word, in the sense that modifiers apply to the whole grouping rather than to one of its elements, that no other word can be inserted between the elements, etc. Again, there are many difficulties of application (see Tournier 1988: 65).

All those criteria merge into the criterion of "lexicalisation".[4] Compounds are lexicalised in the sense that they are stable in form and meaning, and used as wholes. Lexicalisation in this sense is gradable, and it is therefore difficult to isolate compounds as a clear-cut category: the frontier between proper compounds and other types of word groupings is fuzzy. Many English examples can be mentioned: *advanced learners' dictionary, apple pie, bed time, best wishes, breast cancer, busy signal, confirmed bachelor, cross-town bus, export business, football pitch, frozen food, lunch time, plastic bag, tomato juice, world war*, etc. Are they lexicalised? Are they compounds?[5]

2.2 Categories of compound nouns

Different features have been used to classify compound nouns (see Bauer 1983, Tournier 1989: 73f., etc.):

- number of elements. Many compound nouns are composed of two elements,[6] but there are also compounds with three, sometimes four elements (even more in specialized languages).[7]

---

2 Hyphenation is a clear sign of lexicalisation (see below). However, it is less frequent in American English - which prefers spaces or fusion - than in British English (RM).

3 This is one of the big difficulties of corpus-based terminology in English.

4 For a definition of lexicalisation, see Bauer (1983: 48), who mentions the potential ambiguity of the word, which is used with different meanings by different authors; Tournier (1991: 105), etc., and Béjoint (1989), where it is called "codedness"; see also Zgusta (1996: 250-1).

5 *busy signal* is not in any of the four dictionaries; *plastic bag* is in all four, but only as an example, etc. See Appendix for more examples.

6 Binary compounds are interesting in terms of "linguistic economy", because they are short enough to be readily usable even when fairly frequent, and long enough to be understandable - if they are reasonably transparent (see below).

- nature of the elements (i.e. part of speech): N + N (*egghead*), ADJ + N (*blue bell*), V + N (*daredevil*), etc.
- nature of the syntactic relation between the elements: V + N obj (*turnkey*), V + N non-obj (*peephole*), etc.
- nature of the semantic link between the elements and the compound noun as a whole. This has given rise to the well-known distinction between
  - endocentric compounds, where "the compound is a hyponym of the grammatical head", as in *beehive*, or *armchair* (see Bauer 1983: 30), and
  - exocentric compounds, where "the compound is not a hyponym of the grammatical head", as in *redskin* or *highbrow* (see Bauer 1983: 30), with
  - other sub-groups: "appositional compounds", "copulative compounds" (also called "dvandva"), etc. (see Bauer 1983: 30-31). The allocation of individual compound nouns to such categories is not always easy: is *he-goat* endocentric, exocentric, or something else?

3 Of the meaning of compound nouns

3.1 A "second level" of lexis

Derivatives and compound words together constitute a "second level" of lexis: they can only be created after their elements, their interpretation is more or less based on the interpretation of their elements, and in first-language acquisition, they are also normally acquired after the more simple words.[8]

Many compound nouns are translated into other languages by words that are also compound nouns, or derivatives. For example: English *fireman* = French *pompier* = German *Feuerwehrmann* = Spanish *bombero,* etc. English *rainbow* = French *arc-en-ciel* = German *Regenbogen* = Spanish *arco iris* = Italian *arcobaleno* = Norwegian *regnbue* = Finnish *sateenkaari* ("rain arch") = Portuguese *arco-iris* = Catalan *arc iris*, or *arc del cel*, or *arc de Sant Marti* (see also the example of *slide rule* in Boisson 1996: 535, 538-41). Of course many of these cases can be explained by the fact that the forms have been borrowed from one language to another, and there are counter-examples: *rainbow* in Polish is *tecza,* which is a simple form.[9] But many languages do seem to have a first level of simple forms

---

7 See the figures given by Kocourek for French and German terms (1982:120): compounds with 1 element: 12 to 15%, with 2 elements: 52 to 65%, with 3 elements: 24 to 28%, with 4 or more: 6 to 8%. As will be noted below, even compound nouns with two elements are sometimes shortened.

8 There are in fact many exceptions to that rule, for example when a compound has become more frequent than its elements, either in general or in a particular situation of acquisition.

9 On the whole, some languages tend to use more transparent forms than others, as has often been observed: German, for example, is more transparent generally than many languages, and English

and a second level of compounds and derivatives - and the challenge for the researcher is to find out to what conceptual frontiers this distinction corresponds.

3.2 The transparency of compound nouns

The concept of transparency is absent from most English language dictionaries of linguistics (but see Bauer 1983: 19-20). I find it useful to call "transparency" the property of a linguistic sign whose form gives a clear indication of its meaning (in that sense the contrary is opacity); I use "motivation" when the meaning can be traced from its form but only with difficulty.

Many compound nouns are more or less transparent - particularly endocentric compounds -, because they carry part or all of the form and of the meaning of their elements into the new combination. Of course, the actual transparency of a compound noun varies according to the ability of each language user to understand its elements. It is therefore difficult to say whether there is such a thing as "total transparency", because the transparency of a lexical unit cannot be evaluated out of the context in which it is used, nor independently of a particular language user with a certain linguistic competence. However, total opacity exists: compound nouns like *foolscap* or *ivory tower* are good examples. A compound noun like *hot dog* is slightly less opaque: the head is not transparent but the modifier has some kind of transparency, even out of context.[10]

Total transparency may not exist for compound nouns that have only two or three elements, because the elements can only represent part of the semantics of the whole. For example, the form *plastic bag* describes the material ("a bag which is made of plastic"), but this is not enough to define the concept, which must include the function ("a bag made of plastic which is used by shops ..."). Similarly, a *slide rule* is certainly more than "a rule which slides", etc. In many cases it is more appropriate to speak of motivation than of transparency: *afterbirth, busybody, ploughman's lunch*, etc.

Most newly-created compound nouns are transparent to some extent, for obvious reasons, but there are cases where compound nouns are deliberately created with a certain opacity, as in such euphemisms as French *technicien de surface* (instead of *balayeur*), or English *rest room* (instead of *toilet*). Compound nouns tend to lose their transparency over time (few language users can now fully interpret *charwoman*), and the evolution towards opacity may result in a single word (*gospel* is not classified as a compound noun any more).

may be more transparent than French: English *afterbirth* = French *placenta;* English *air-field* = French *aérodrome*; English *thigh-bone* = French *fémur*. Incidentally, all three of the French words are used in English as well, but in different contexts (Geoffrey Leech, personal remark).

10 Hence its placement at *hot* in OALD5? The components of a compound noun do not necessarily exhibit the same degree of transparency: one element may be more transparent than the other. This is well illustrated by eponyms, like *Parkinson's disease*, etc.

3.3 The choice of the elements

The choice of the components of compounds is a vast area that is rarely examined by linguists, probably because it goes against the sacred principle of *l'arbitraire du signe*. Yet it is an interesting area for research: what are the reasons why the particular components of a compound have been "chosen"?

Compound nouns have been described by transformational generative grammarians as the result of the deletion of an underlying verb: *wind-mill* = "the wind powers the mill"; *turnkey* = "someone turns the key"; *peephole* = "someone peeps through the hole", etc. (see Bauer 1983: 159). This may not be true of all compound nouns (*hot dog* or *hangover* could be counter-examples), yet it is useful to think of the creation of many compound nouns as the result of the reduction of a sentence (Subject + Verb + Object, etc.), and then examine which elements have been selected for the compound noun.

Take the example of *corkscrew*. The *cork* part is obvious: corkscrews "are about" corks. But why has English "chosen" *screw* if the shape (assuming that *screw* represents the shape) clearly has a secondary role in the concept (it would be a simple adjunct in the underlying sentence)? Corkscrews are still called *corkscrews* even when they have different shapes, as long as they are "instruments used for drawing corks from wine bottles" (reconstructed definition). A form like **corkpuller* would have been ideal.

Why does *screwdriver* use the verb *drive* (probably in the sense of *drive into*), when the underlying sentence contains another verb (not a single definition says "a device for driving screws (into something)")?[11] Why not call it a **screwturner*, since dictionaries define it as "a tool that is used for turning screws" (COBUILD2), "a tool for turning screws" (CIDE), "a tool ... to turn screws" (OALD5), "a tool ... that you use for turning screws" (LDOCE3), etc.? Also, why was it the DRIVE-INTO conceptual trait that was chosen, and not the PULL-OUT-OF (a **screwpuller*?)? Is a screwdriver conceived of as something with which screws can be put into place more than as something with which screws can be pulled out? Probably the constructive aspect is more important, more specific to the tool (like a door is more for closing than for opening). Are tools better defined by what they do than by what they undo? If so, why does the definition use a more general verb?[12]

The choice of the components of compound nouns raises many such questions that are important in connection with the wording of the definition of the compound, and also in terminology for the creation of terms: can it be said that some terms are "better" than others?

---

[11] The pattern exemplified by *screwdriver* ("Patient" (*screw*) + Process (*drive (into)*) + Agent (*-er*)) is used in many other terms: *fire-extinguisher, bottle-opener*, etc. If *driver* does not exist on its own with the sense used in *screwdriver*, then the status of *screwdriver* as a compound noun could be challenged.

[12] There are historical reasons for the choice of the elements of compound nouns and derivatives in some cases: French *pompier* was chosen because at the time of the creation of the form it was the use of the pump that was new (see Béjoint and Thoiron 1997: 194).

3.4 Endocentric compound nouns as "kinds of other nouns"

In some compound nouns, the element that is more "important" than the other(s) is usually called the "head": it bears the mark of number (as well as of gender in some languages) and determines the part of speech of the grouping. The head is easy to identify in compound nouns that have a noun as one of their elements, though difficult - if not impossible - for other types of compound nouns (*hangover*, etc.). In English compound nouns that have at least one noun among their elements, the head is usually the last, in French usually the first. English exceptions are compound nouns based on Latin models (N + of + N like *house of tolerance*, *bird of prey*; ADJ + N like *princess royal*, *court martial*, etc.) and others, like *passer-by*, *looker-on*, or *first cousin once removed* (examples taken from Tournier 1988: 73).

In endocentric compound nouns (endocentric compounds), the head indicates the broad category of the whole (a *red pepper* is "a kind of pepper"), and the modifier indicates the defining characteristic within that category: a *red pepper* is "a pepper that is red". Those compound nouns exhibit an IS A relation. They may be more numerous than is usually assumed: for example, compound nouns like *he-goat* or *man-servant*, though not usually classified as endocentric compounds, can be considered as exhibiting an IS A relation: a *he-goat* IS A "goat that is a he", a *man-servant* IS A "servant that is a man", etc. Similarly *jazz-rock* or *panty-hose* (classified as "copulative compounds - or dvandvas - by Bauer 1983: 203): *jazz-rock* is "rock that has something of jazz", and a *panty-hose* is a "hose that serves as panties". Even examples like *thigh-bone*, *door-knob* or *armchair*, which seem to exhibit a PART OF relation (the thigh has a bone, the door has a knob, the chair has arms), actually illustrate a subcategory of the IS A relation: a thigh bone IS A sort of bone, a *door-knob* IS A sort of knob, and an *armchair* IS A sort of chair.[13]

Words that correspond to an IS A relation can be organized in taxonomies, where simple nouns and compound nouns are typically positioned at different levels: compound nouns appear below simpler nouns. If one level is occupied by simple nouns like *cat* or *tree* (the words that are acquired first; that can be drawn, etc. See Wierzbicka 1996), the level below will be occupied by such compound nouns as *Siamese cat* or *cherry tree*. There may be a mixture of the two types on some levels: *setter* will be on the same level as *sequoia*, but also as *Siamese cat* and *cherry tree* (should we imagine that we have **setter dog* and **sequoia tree*, or *cherry* and *Siamese?*), but the compound nouns will always be below the corresponding simple forms: *red setter* under *setter*, etc. The invention, or discovery, of a sub-species of the categories designated by such compounds is likely to give rise to other, more complex, compound nouns based on the first by "piling up" modifiers: one can easily imagine a **dwarf red setter*, or a **golden giant sequoia*. Such compounds with three elements are still "binary": for example, a *golden giant sequoia* would be a "giant sequoia that is golden", rather than a "sequoia that is golden and giant". This has obvious consequences on the definitions that lexicographers have to compile.

---

[13] See Appendix for the actual genus-words used in the four dictionaries.

A *pine table* is not a **table pine*. It is a kind of table made with a special sort of wood rather than a piece of a special sort of wood to which is given a tabular form. Compound nouns are orientated,[14] and the decision to use one of the elements as head, and not the other(s), is indicative of the way we organize our linguistic representation of the variety of objects that we have to refer to by linguistic means: *jazz-rock* is "rock that has something of jazz" rather than "jazz that has something of rock". In this sense, compounds are much more interesting than simple words, because they speak of our mental categories.

3.5 The short forms of compound nouns

Some compound nouns can be reduced to one of their elements in discourse. For example, *tit* can replace *blue tit* after the first occurrence in a text, just like *bag* can replace *plastic bag* (similarly with *rest room, sea-sickness,* etc.), even though the short forms are obviously less informative than the longer forms. In such cases the two are not synonymous out of context. But some short forms have become part of *langue*, and are therefore noted as such in dictionaries[15]. The shortened form may be the modifier, which is naturally more "informative" than the head: for example, *jumbo jet* is reduced to *jumbo, Siamese cat* to *Siamese*, *cherry tree* to *cherry* (like many trees), *gospel music* to *gospel,*[16] *Parmesan cheese* to *Parmesan*, *ploughman's lunch* to *ploughman's*, *Parkinson's disease* to *Parkinson's, crossword puzzle* to *crossword,* etc. Or it may be the head that is kept: *school master* can only be reduced to *master, garden gnome* to *gnome, official receiver* to *receiver*, etc.

The rules for such reductions are complex: they are clearly linked with the "degree of informativeness" of each of the elements of the compound in the linguistic and social contexts where the form was created and is used now. A compound noun can only be shortened if the short form is clear enough, and the choice of the short form depends on the relative clarity of the two (or more) possible choices. Such compound nouns as *afterbirth, he-goat, jazz-rock, egghead, screwdriver* or *hot dog* are difficult, if not impossible, to reduce, even in precise contexts, because neither of their elements would be clear if used on their own. On the other hand, and surprisingly, a form like *Parkinson's* can be clear in many contexts, when doctors talk of diseases.[17]

---

[14] There are a few exceptions, i.e. non-orientated compound nouns: *onlooker* and *looker-on.*

[15] Some are reduced to abbreviations, like *compact disc* to *CD.*

[16] *gospel* also serves as short form for *gospel truth.* The contexts must be clear enough to disambiguate the two uses.

[17] In French, *automobile* was reduced to *auto* (though this only meant "self"), because there was no other equally important concept that was characterized by its automaticity at the time. But *vélomoteur* has never been reduced, because neither *vélo* nor *moteur* would have been informative enough on their own (*vélo*, meaning "bicycle", and *moteur*, meaning "engine", already referred to things that were well-known).

4 The definitions of compound nouns

4.1 Compound nouns that are not mentioned

As it is naturally impossible to say how many compound nouns are not mentioned in a dictionary, only a few examples will be given here: *busy signal* is not in any of the four dictionaries; *colour-blindness* is not in CIDE; *frozen food* is not in OALD5; *introductory offer* is not in OALD5 or in COBUILD2; *love triangle* is not in CIDE, LDOCE3 or OALD5 (but has a seven-line definition in COBUILD2!); *thigh-bone* is not in COBUILD2; *working hypothesis* is not in COBUILD2 or in LDOCE3, etc.[18] There are clearly two types of compound nouns that are omitted: those that were considered not to be lexicalized enough - an area of such difficulty that different answers may be acceptable in many cases; and those that were considered to be transparent enough so that their meanings could be deduced from a knowledge of their elements. The latter position is reasonable only in the context of decoding.

4.2 Compound nouns that are mentioned but not defined

Some compound nouns are simply listed towards the end of entries, but not defined. Examples are *ill-treatment* at *ill-treat* in OALD5; *colour-blindness* at *colour-blind* in OALD5, LDOCE3 and COBUILD2, etc.[19] Some are only mentioned as, or within, examples: *plastic bag* in the four dictionaries (at *bag*); *best wishes* in OALD5 (it is given a definition in CIDE). Some are just mentioned in the definition for one of their elements: *frozen food* at *frozen* for LDOCE3. This, again, is reasonable for transparent compound nouns and in decoding operations, but cases like *cross-hatching*, (not defined in OALD5), *judicial review* or *splashdown* (not defined in CIDE) could certainly have done with a definition when *museum piece*, which is fairly transparent, has a full definition in all four dictionaries.

4.3 Compound nouns that are explained by synonyms

Some compound nouns are only "explained" by a synonym (simple word or other compound). Examples are: *plastic wrap* = *cling film* (CIDE and LDOCE3), *concert-master* = *leader* (OALD5), *crosswalk* = *pedestrian crossing* (OALD5 and CIDE),

---

[18] See Appendix for more examples.

[19] Most, if not all, "-ness" compound nouns seem to be undefined, only cross-referred to the corresponding adjectives.

playschool = *playgroup* (LDOCE3 and CIDE), *landing gear* = *undercarriage* (OALD5), etc.[20]

4.4 Compound nouns that are defined

4.4.1 Compound nouns are defined in comprehension

COBUILD applies its special type of definition mainly to compound nouns that have a connotational component: *busybody* ("If you refer to someone as a busybody, you disapprove of them ..."); similarly *egghead, highbrow, killjoy, ladykiller, gospel truth, hangover*, etc. - but this is not specific to compound nouns. In the other dictionaries, most compound nouns, when they are defined at all, are defined in comprehension - a type of definition that represents their fundamentally binary character - with genus word and differentiae.

4.4.2 The genus word

The choice of the genus word is of primary importance in a definition in comprehension, particularly in learners' dictionaries, where it must be readily understandable by the dictionary users.[21]

For non-endocentric compounds, the genus word is neither more nor less difficult to choose than for simple words (an *afterbirth* is not a kind of birth, a *killjoy* is not a kind of joy, etc.): they have to be defined via a genus word that is not connected with their form: *afterbirth* is "material ...", a *killjoy* is "a person ...", a *football* (when it is not "a ball ..."), is "a game ...", a *kneecap* is "a bone ...", etc. Similarly for *splashdown, hangover, lock-up*, etc. In some cases of compound nouns formally exhibiting an IS A relation, the head is not used as genus word, either because it would be conceptually wrong: a *shooting star* is not a star, but "a meteor ..." (OALD5), "a small piece of rock or metal ..." (LDOCE3), "a line of light ..." (CIDE) or "a rock ..." (COBUILD2), or because the "head" does not represent a category that can be readily used: compound nouns like *screwdriver* or *ladykiller* cannot

---

20 A French example from PR: *tire-fesses* = *téléski*. PR then says *téléski* = "remonte-pentes pour les skieurs", and finally *remonte-pentes* = "dispositif servant à hisser les skieurs en haut d'une pente, au moyen de perches tirées par un câble".

21 See the problems caused by the misinterpretation of words used in the definitions in Götz (this volume): is a potato a vegetable in all cultures, is fuel a substance? This may be a reason for lexicographers to move their genus-words up the scale of the taxonomy, particularly in learners' dictionaries.

be defined as "a kind of driver" or "a kind of killer". They are indeed "a kind of -er", but this cannot be said in a dictionary.[22]

In some cases, the genus word is a synonym of the head, probably because the head would be obscure on its own. A *rainbow* is not defined as a kind of bow, but as "a many-coloured arch ..." (CIDE), "an arch of different colours ..." (OALD5 and COBUILD2), or as "a curve ..." (LDOCE3). Frequently - and not surprisingly - the genus word is a hyperonym of the head, or at least a more general word. This is not always easy to distinguish from the preceding case. A *fire-extinguisher* is "a cylinder ..." for COBUILD2 (is *cylinder* a hyperonym of *extinguisher*?), "a device ..." for CIDE and "a container ..." for OALD5 and LDOCE3 (those are indeed hyperonyms, though they represent very different categorizations); a *museum piece* is "an example of ..." for OALD5, and "something ..." for CIDE; a *playing-field* is "an area ..." for CIDE and for COBUILD2 and "a piece of ground ..." for LDOCE3 (though it is "a field ..." for OALD5); *hang-gliding* is "a sport ..." (OALD5 and LDOCE3) or "an activity ..." (COBUILD2; it is undefined in CIDE); a *blue tit* is "a bird ...", not "a tit ..." and a *ploughman's lunch* is "a meal ...", not "a lunch ...".

Finally, in many endocentric compounds, the head is used as the genus of the definition: a *windmill* is "a mill ..." for OALD5 (though "a building ..." for COBUILD2, LDOCE3 and CIDE); a *charwoman* is "a woman ..." for all four dictionaries; *plate glass* is "glass ..."; a *playgroup* is "a group ..."; a *playing-field* is "a field ..."; *landing-craft* is "a craft ..."; a *man-servant* is "a servant ..." (for COBUILD2, a *man-servant* is "a man"!); *Parkinson's disease* is "a disease ..." (CIDE; it is "an illness" for LDOCE3 ... and "a disorder ..." for CED); a *peephole* is "a hole ..."; a *suspension bridge* is "a bridge ...", etc. Some definitions also use the other element of the compound noun, either in addition to using the head, or not: a *kneecap* is a "bone covering the front of the knee" (OALD5; it is never defined as a cap); an *office-bearer* (or *office-holder*) is "a person who holds an office" (OALD5). One can easily imagine how far this can go: *Southern blot* could be defined as "a type of blot invented by Mr Southern"![23] This violates both common sense and one of the basic rules of defining, that the definiendum must not be used in the definiens (see Wierzbicka 1996 for a recent advocation of that rule).

In the moderate form in which this is practised in our dictionaries, however, this is not unreasonable. The question is to what category can the compound noun be attached for the definition to be clear: the better choice must be a category that is readily understandable, and a category that corresponds to the mental organization of the average speaker. A *blue tit* is defined as "a bird ..." (just like *bird of prey*) not as "a tit ..." because *bird* is a good category: it is well-known and easily identified, it has a limited number of hyponyms in non-specialist language, and is thus suitable for the average reader. In fact, it is probably the only reasonable category for *blue tit*: the blue tit is the only kind of tit that the average English speaker knows (let alone the foreign learner), and it is probably as a consequence

---

22 Few "-er compound nouns" (V + -er) seem to be defined as endocentric compounds: a *bus-driver* is a kind of driver, but a *scene-stealer* is not a kind of stealer, a *safe cracker* is not a kind of cracker, etc.

23 Such "definitions" can indeed be found in some terminological dictionaries.

conceived of not as a kind of tit but as a kind of bird. On the other hand, in cases like *suspension bridge*, the better category is clearly not the hyperonym of the whole ("a construction ..."?), but the head of the compound noun: bridges are well-known constructions, and most people will have realized that they come in different shapes. The dictionary users who consult the dictionary will be assumed to know the meaning of *bridge* already. In such cases, the formally correct definitions would be conceptually defective, and the rule can be - indeed should be - violated.

5 Conclusion

A good lexicographical treatment of compound nouns implies mentioning as many as possible (as opposed to assuming that they can be readily understood, or produced), putting them in places where they can be found quickly and easily, and giving useful explanations of their meanings. Only the latter question has been touched upon here, and our observations have been based on a limited sample of compound nouns in a limited number of dictionaries.

On the whole, the impression one gets from an observation of the definitions of compound nouns in our four learners' dictionaries is that some compound nouns are straightforward, unproblematic, easy to identify and to define: they are defined in very similar ways by all lexicographers. Others are much more difficult to categorize and explain, and give rise to all sorts of variations in their treatments and definitions, as though they stood for intermediate subcategories that are difficult to classify and characterize. What is needed is a thorough study of the different types of compound nouns, with guidelines for the best style of definition for each type. Our appendix presents our sample of compound nouns with the results of their look-up in all four dictionaries.

Compound nouns are interesting, because they are language "freshly made", in which traces of the act of creation can still be seen.[24] It is obvious that more research is needed in order to gain more insight into our categorizations and on the defining criteria that can be used in dictionaries.

---

[24] Oddly enough, they don't survive well, compared to other types of lexical creations (derivatives, shifts in meaning, etc.). See Ayto 1996.

Bibliography

The Collins English Dictionary (CED) (1979, [2]1986): Patrick Hanks (ed.). — London and Glasgow: Collins.

Collins Cobuild English Language Dictionary (COBUILD) ([1]1987): John Sinclair (ed.). — London: HarperCollins.

Longman Dictionary of Contemporary English (LDOCE) ([1]1978): Paul Procter (ed.). — Harlow: Longman.

Oxford Advanced Learners' Dictionary (OALD) ([1]1948): Albert S. Hornby (ed.). — Oxford: OUP.

Le Nouveau Petit Robert (PR) (1967, [1]1993): Josette Rey-Debove, Paul Robert (eds.). — Paris: Dictionnaires Le Robert.

Ayto, John (1996): "Lexical life expectancy - a prognostic guide". — In: J. Svartvik (ed.): Words (Stockholm: Almqvist & Wiksell International) 181-188.

Bauer, Laurie (1983): English Word-formation. — Cambridge: CUP.

Béjoint, Henri (1989): " 'Codedness' and lexicography". — In: G. James (ed.): Lexicographers and their Works (Exeter: University of Exeter Press) 1-4.

— (1993): "La définition en terminographie". — In: P.J.L. Arnaud, H. Béjoint (eds.): Aspects du vocabulaire (Lyon: Presses Universitaires de Lyon) 19-26.

Béjoint, Henri, Philippe Thoiron (1997): "Modèle relationnel, définition et dénomination". — In: Ph. Thoiron, Cl. Boisson (eds.): Autour de la dénomination (Lyon: Presses Universitaires de Lyon) 187-204.

Boisson, Claude (1996): "Les dénominations de la règle à calcul". — In: Méta 41/4, 525-566.

Cruse, D.- A. (1986): Lexical Semantics. — Cambridge: CUP.

Götz, Dieter: (this volume): "On some differences between English and German (with respect to lexicography)".

Herbst, Thomas (1996): "On the way to the perfect learners' dictionary: a first comparison of OALD5, LDOCE3, COBUILD2 and CIDE". — In: International Journal of Lexicography 9/4, 321-357.

Kocourek, Rostislav (1982): La Langue française de la technique et de la science. — Wiesbaden: Brandstetter Verlag.

Tournier, Jean (1988): Précis de lexicologie anglaise. — Paris: Nathan.

— (1991): Structures lexicales de l'anglais. — Paris: Nathan.

Wierzbicka, Anna (1996): Semantics, Primes and Universals. — Oxford: OUP.

Zgusta, Ladislav (1996): "Review of Essays on Terminology, 1995, Alain Rey". — In: Dictionaries 17, 249-251.

Appendix

- Absent (0), in example (EX), as separate entry (SE) or subentry (SUB)
- Genus-word used in the definition

	OALD5	CIDE	LDOCE3	COBUILD2
afterbirth	SE material	SE material	SE substance	0
air-field	SE area	SE area	SE place	SE area
air raid	SUB (at air) attack	0	SE attack	SE attack
armchair	SE chair	SE chair	SE chair	SE chair
bachelor's degree	EX (at bachelor)	SUB (at bachelor) degree	SE level	SE degree
bathmat	SUB (at bath)	SUB (at bath) cover	SE cloth	SE mat
beehive	SE container	SE container	SE structure	SE structure
best wishes	EX (at wishes)	EX (at wishes)	SUB (at wish)	EX (at wishes)
bird of prey	SUB (at bird) bird	SUB (at bird) bird	SE bird	SE bird
blue bell	SE plant	SE plant	SE plant	SE plants
blue tit	SUB (at blue) bird	EX (at tit)	0	SE bird
bottle-opener	SUB device	0	SE tool	SE device
busy signal	0	0	0	0
busybody	SE person	SE person	SE someone	SE If you ...
charwoman	SE woman	SE woman	SE woman	SE woman

cherry tree	SUB (at cherry) = cherry tree	EX (at cherry)	SUB (at cherry) tree	SUB (at cherry) = cherry tree
cling film	SUB (at cling) material	SE material	SE plastic	SE plastic
coffee break	SUB (at coffee) period of time	SUB (at coffee) rest	SE time	SE period of time
colour-blindness	SUB (at colour) no definition	0	SUB (at colour-blind) no definition	SUB (at colour) no definition
concert-master	SUB (at concert) = leader no definition	0	SE player	0
corkscrew	SE device	SE device	SE tool	SE device
cross-hatching	0	SE group of lines	SE lines	0
crosswalk	SE = pedestrian crossing	SE = pedestrian crossing	SE place	SE place
crossword puzzle	= crossword game	SE word game	SE word game	SUB (at crossword)
daredevil	SE person	SE person	SE someone	SUB (at dare) no definition
dessertspoon	SE spoon	SE spoon	SE spoon	SE spoon
doghouse	0	SE = kennel	0	SE building
doorknob	SE handle	SE handle	SE handle	SE handle
egghead	SE person	SE person	SE someone	SE If you ...
fire-extinguisher	SUB (at fire) container	SUB (at fire) device	SE container	SE cylinder
fireman	SE member	SUB (at firefighter) person	SE person	SE person

first cousin once removed	0	0	0	0
fog bank	0	SUB (at fog) cloud	SUB (at fog) area	SE area
fog light	SUB (at fog) light	SUB (at fog) light	SUB (at fog lamp) light	0
foolscap	SE size	SE paper	SE size	SE paper
football pitch	EX (at pitch)	EX (at pitch)	0	(at pitch)
frozen food	0	(at frozen)	in definition at frozen	(at frozen)
garden gnome	0	EX (at gnome)	EX (at gnome)	(at gnome)
gospel music	EX (at gospel)	SE = gospel music	SUB (at gospel) style	SUB (at gospel) style
gospel truth	EX (at gospel)	SE = gospel truth	SUB (at gospel) something	SUB (at gospel) If you ...
hangover	SE symptoms	SE feeling	SE headache and sickness	SE If someone ...
harbourmaster	SUB (at harbour) official	SUB (at harbour) official	SE official	SE official
he-goat	0	0	EX (at he)	0
heavy breathing	EX (at heavy)	SUB (at heavy)	SUB (at heavy breather)	SUB (at heavy)
highbrow	0	SUB (at highbrow ADJ) no definition	SE someone	SE If you ...
hot dog	SUB (at hot) sausage	SUB (at hot) sausage	SE sausage	SE roll
house of tolerance	0	0	0	0
ill-treatment	EX (at ill)	0	SUB (at ill-treat)	EX (at ill/ill-treat)

introductory offer	0	EX (at intro-ductory)	SUB (at intro-ductory) price	0
jumbo jet	SUB (at jumbo) aircraft	SUB (at jet) aircraft	SE aircraft	SUB (at jumbo) jet
kneecap	SE bone	SE bone	SE bone	SE bone
ladykiller	SUB (at lady) man	SUB (at lady) man	SE man	SE If you ...
landing gear	SUB (at landing) = undercarriage	SUB (at land) set	SE wheels and wheel support	0
landing-craft	SUB (at landing) craft	0	SE boat	SE boat
lock-up	SUB (at lock) prison	SE room	SE prison	SE = jail
looker-on	0	0	SE someone	0
love triangle	0	0	0	SE
maid-servant	0	0	SE servant	0
make-believe	SUB (at make) activity	SE believing	SE state	SE You ...
man-servant	SE servant	SE servant	SE servant	SE man
milkman	SE person	SE person	SE person	SE person
museum piece	SUB (at museum) example	SUB (at museum) something	SE piece	SE If you ...
office-bearer	SUB (at office) person	0	0	0
office-holder	SUB (at office) person	0	SE someone	SE person
official receiver	SUB (at receiver) official	SUB (at official) person	SE someone	0

panty-hose	0	SE tights	SE piece of clothing	SE tights
paper clip	SUB (at paper) piece of wire	SUB (at paper) piece of wire	SE piece of wire	SE piece of wire
Parkinson's disease	SE disease	SE disease	SE illness	0
passer-by	SE person	SUB (at pass) someone	SE someone	SE person
pedestrian crossing	SUB (at pedestrian) part	SUB (at pedestrian) place	SE place	SE place
peephole	SUB (at peep) hole	SE hole	SE hole	SE hole
pine table	0	0	EX (at pine)	EX (at pine)
plastic bag	EX (at plastic)	EX (at plastic)	EX (at plastic)	EX (at plastic)
plastic wrap	0	SUB (at plastic) = clingfilm	SE = clingfilm	EX (at plastic)
plate glass	SUB (at plate) glass	SUB (at plate) glass	SE glass	SE glass
playgroup	SE group	SE group	SE school	SE school
playing-field	SE field	SUB (at play) area	SE piece of ground	SE area
playschool	(at playgroup)	SE = playgroup	SE = playgroup	SE school
ploughman's lunch	SUB (at ploughman) meal	SE meal	SE meal	SE meal
pocket knife	SUB (at pocket) = penknife	SE = penknife	SE knife	SE knife
point of departure	SUB (at point) place or time	0	0	0
postman	SE person	SE person	SE man	SE man
princess royal	SUB (at princess) daughter	0	0	0

rainbow	SE arch	SE arch	SE curve	SE arch
red pepper	SUB (at red) fruit	SUB (at red) fruit	SE vegetable	SE pepper
red setter	SUB (at red) = Irish setter	0	0	0
rest room	SUB (at rest) toilet	SUB (at rest) room	SE room	SE toilet
school master	SE teacher	SE someone	SE teacher	SE man
screwdriver	SE tool	SE tool	SE tool	SE tool
sea-sickness	SUB (at seasick) no definition	SUB (at seasick) no definition	SUB (at seasick)	SUB (at sea) no definition
shooting star	SUB (at shoot) meteor	SUB (at shoot) line of light	SE piece of rock or metal	SE rock
Siamese cat	SUB (at Siamese) cat	SE cat	SE cat	SE cat
slide rule	SUB (at slide) instrument	SUB (at slide) device	SE instrument	SE instrument
splashdown	SE landing	EX (at splash)	SE landing	SE landing
still life	SUB (at still) representation	SUB (at still) painting or drawing	SE painting or drawing	SE painting or drawing
suspension bridge	SUB (at suspension) bridge	SUB (at suspension) bridge	SE bridge	SE bridge
tablespoon	SE spoon	SE spoon	SE spoon	SE spoon
thigh-bone	EX (at thigh)	EX (at thigh)	EX (at bone)	0
tonic water	SUB (at tonic) water	SE water	SUB (at tonic) drink	SUB (at tonic) drink
turnkey	0	0	SE = jailer	0

undercarriage	SE wheels	SE = landing gear	SE wheels	SE part
wind-mill	SE mill	SE building or structure	SE building or structure	SE building
working hypothesis	EX (at working)	SUB (at work)	0	0

Brigitta Mittmann

The treatment of collocations in OALD5, LDOCE3, COBUILD2 and CIDE

When producing texts in a foreign language, learners are likely to encounter problems when trying to find out which words typically occur together. Which verb, for example, can be used with *conclusion*? Is it possible to say *make conclusions*? Compare, for example, Dutch *een gevolgtrekking maken*. Or should it be *deduce conclusions*? (Cf. French *déduire des conclusions*). Surely not *pull conclusions* - as in German *Schlußfolgerungen ziehen*? When they face collocational problems of this kind, learners are dependent on their dictionaries for solutions. In principle, as from 1995, there is a selection of four new learners' dictionaries to choose from. Does any of these dictionaries meet the collocational needs of the EFL learners better than the others?

1 Theoretical considerations

1.1 What kind of co-occurrence of words should be included in dictionaries as a 'collocation'?

Before attempting to assess the extent and quality of the collocational information given in OALD5, LDOCE3, COBUILD2 and CIDE, a few theoretical points need to be made. The first problem that one faces when having to decide which co-occurrences of words to include in the dictionaries - and possibly to highlight as collocations - is that there is quite a broad selection of definitions of the term *collocation* itself. Some of these definitions are more useful for meeting the needs of learners than others. Purely frequency-based theories of collocation along the lines of those put forward by Sinclair (e.g. 1966: 15ff.; 1991: 115-121) or Kjellmer (1994: ix-xl) are not very helpful for this purpose, because they fail to make one vital distinction. This can be illustrated with the help of an extract from a leaflet distributed to tourists at Ely Cathedral: [1]

> The following walk-round guide draws your attention to the principal features of the Cathedral. More details may be obtained from guide-books available in the shop.

In this passage, two combinations of words have been underlined: *draw attention (to sth.)* and *obtain details*. The difference between these expressions is that the choice of verb in *obtain details* can be explained by general semantic rules of combination, whereas the choice of *draw* in *draw attention* cannot. For our EFL students the consequence of this is

---

1 *Welcome to Ely Cathedral* (Fidelity Colour Printers, Essex).

that - as long as they know what *attention, details, draw* and *obtain* mean in isolation - they could be expected to write a sentence containing *obtain details*, but would certainly not come up with the expression *draw attention.*

Draw attention is what Hausmann (1985: 118) would call a "typische, spezifische und charakteristische Zweierkombination von Wörtern", that is, a "typical, specific and characteristic combination of two words", but *obtain details* is not a combination of this kind. This distinction will be made here as well. Therefore *draw attention* will be considered a 'collocation', and *obtain details* a 'banal' or 'free' combination. It is collocations rather than banal combinations that should be included in dictionaries, since they are the ones that pose problems to learners.[2]

Other authors such as Cowie and Mackin have distinguished between co-occurrences of words of the types illustrated by *draw attention* and *obtain details* in a similar way, but with slightly different terminology (Cowie 1978: 132-137; 1989: 61-63; 1994: 3169; Cowie and Mackin 1993: xv-xvi, 478). A considerable number of the combinations found in the *BBI Combinatory Dictionary of English* would be covered by the definition of collocations used here, though this definition would not apply to what Benson, Benson and Ilson have called *grammatical collocations* (Benson/Benson/Ilson 1986: xv-xix).

1.2 The distinction between 'base' and 'collocator'

Hausmann has pointed out that the relationship between the parts of a collocation is hierarchical. He has called the one part the 'Basis', the other one the 'Kollokator', which will be translated as *base* and *collocator* here. The following list shows collocations with different kinds of structural properties. The bases are given in bold print:

violent ***storm***	Adjective + Noun
rain *lets up*	Noun (Subject) + Verb
take an ***exam***	Verb + Noun (Object)
reject *flatly*	Verb + Adverb
dead ***sure***	Adverb + Adjective
flock of ***sheep***	Noun + Noun

The first of these collocations is the combination *violent storm.* In this collocation *storm* is the base, and *violent* the collocator. The base *storm* can be defined independently of *violent*, but the collocator *violent* cannot be defined independently of the base *storm.* If German students had difficulty understanding *violent storm*, this would most certainly be because of the metaphorical and therefore somewhat unusual use of *violent*, and the entry for *violent* would be where they would look it up in their dictionaries.

So much for the understanding, or decoding of texts. When students encode texts, however, the situation is slightly different. If they wanted to express the idea *heftiger/*

---

2 For a more detailed account of the disadvantages of purely frequency-based theories of collocation, see Hausmann (1985) and Herbst (1996). The general framework of Hausmann's position is also, for example, outlined in Hausmann (1984).

gewaltiger Sturm, they would first think of *storm*, and then look for possible combinations with other words at the entry for *storm*. When we write, then, we first think of the bases and only then of suitable collocators to match them.

In short: Hausmann's distinction between *base* and *collocator* is important because the quality of a learners' dictionary as an aid to understand texts can at least partly be measured by the number of collocations that it lists at the entries for the collocators, whereas the quality of a dictionary as a means for text production can be gauged by the number of collocations given at the entries for the bases.[3]

2 Collocations in the four new learners' dictionaries

2.1 Frequency counts

Apparently, all of the four learners' dictionaries published in 1995 consider the information that they provide on collocations to be one of their most prominent assets - at least if one is to judge from the extensive treatment that they give collocations on their covers and in their front and back matter. Is this actually justified?

It would be very unwise to assess the four dictionaries on the basis of just a few entries. In order to arrive at more objective conclusions, a list of 120 collocations (cf. appendix) was compiled. These collocations were then looked up in the dictionaries, both at the entries for the collocators and for the bases. Although this number may seem small when compared to the thousands of collocations listed in the dictionaries, it should be large enough to prevent chance results. It is important to note that the list was drawn up without looking at any of the dictionaries, and is not based on any one of them. Instead, it is based partly on examples found in literature on collocations, and partly on the experience of the vocabulary needs of advanced learners of English. A summary of the results can be found in Table 1.

Table 1: Collocations in OALD5, LDOCE3, COBUILD2 and CIDE
Listed Collocations (out of a total of 120 and in approximate percentages)

Collocator			
OALD5	LDOCE3	COBUILD2	CIDE
87 (=73%)	83 (=69%)	77 (=64%)	79 (=66%)

Base			
OALD5	LDOCE3	COBUILD2	CIDE
67 (=56%)	70 (=58%)	37 (=31%)	71 (=60%)

Table 1 shows that for the entries for the collocators, the figures are similar for all four dictionaries. For about 80 out of a total of 120 combinations, all of them have either

[3] But compare the research by P. Bogaards in "Access structures of learners' dictionaries" (this volume).

provided the whole collocation in an example or definition, or mentioned the other collocational partner somewhere, or given a cross-reference from which it is possible to find the combination in question. For receptive purposes, therefore, the four dictionaries seem to be similarly useful with respect to collocations.

In contrast to this, however, the situation is very different for the entries for the bases. Here we can see that the figure for the COBUILD dictionary is significantly lower than those for the other dictionaries. While users of OALD5, LDOCE3 and CIDE can find about 70 out of the 120 collocations listed here, users of COBUILD2 can find only slightly more than half as many as they could in the others. The difference between the results for COBUILD2 and those for the others is so great that it is certain to be significant. For productive purposes, OALD5, LDOCE3 and CIDE seem to have more to offer with respect to collocations.

One of the reasons for the superiority of the collocational information given at the entries for the bases in OALD5, LDOCE3 and CIDE appears to be that they have adopted a more systematic approach than COBUILD2. It is possible to see this, for example, from the entries for the noun *rule*, where one can find far more collocations in the other three dictionaries. The collocations given in these entries are listed in table 2, together with other collocations taken from the BBI. Some of the collocations given OALD5, LDOCE3 and CIDE (but not in COBUILD2) are comparatively frequent, so that it is possible to conclude that the problem does not necessarily lie with the adoption of Sinclair's theoretical approach in the compilation of dictionaries.

Table 2: Collocations of *rule* of the type VERB+*rule* (object) and *rule* (subject)+VERB

BBI	OALD5	LDOCE3	COBUILD2	CIDE
establish rules lay down rules make (the) rules	 make rules draw up rules			
formulate a rule				
adopt a rule				
apply a rule enforce a rule				
		stick to a rule	adhere to rules	
obey a rule observe a rule	obey a rule observe a rule follow a rule			obey a rule observe a rule follow a rule play it by the rules go by the rules do things by the rules
break a rule violate a rule	break a rule	break a rule		break a rule

bend a rule	bend a rule	bend a rule		bend a rule
stretch a rule	stretch a rule	stretch a rule		stretch a rule
rescind a rule				
revoke a rule				
		rules govern sth.		

The entries for *rule* may perhaps seem rather exceptional since there is only one single verb collocator given in COBUILD2. Nevertheless, the figures for the 120 collocations studied here indicate that this example is typical in its general tendency. As a rule, COBUILD2 gives fewer of these useful building-blocks than the other dictionaries.

Table 2 contains further information. One can see that it is often possible to group collocations into broad semantic categories, depending on the different things that one can do with the objects denoted by the headwords, or that these objects themselves can do. The groups *obey-observe-follow* (etc) *rules*, or *break-violate rules* form categories of this kind. They are groups of (near-) synonymous collocations. It is here that a lot of opportunities for improving the policies of the dictionaries open up. It would often be more useful to include the most frequent collocations from different categories rather than to list many low-frequency ones from a single one. In the case of *rule*, for example, OALD5 has more to offer to the users than CIDE, since it gives them *make rules* and *draw up rules* as well.

2.2 A comparison with the earlier generation of dictionaries

A comparison of the figures for the 1995 generation of dictionaries with those of the respective earlier editions suggests that the more systematic approach to collocation of LDOCE and also, to a certain extent, OALD, has evolved over time. The list of 120 collocations (cf. appendix) was again used as a basis.

Table 3: Collocations in OALD4, LDOCE2 and COBUILD1
Listed collocations (out of a total of 120)

Collocator		
OALD4	LDOCE2	COBUILD1
68%	65%	66%

Base		
OALD4	LDOCE2	COBUILD1
53%	47%	33%

A fairly similar picture (cf. table 3) emerges from the figures for the older dictionaries. In all of the dictionaries, about the same number of collocations can be found at the entries for the collocators: just a little more than two thirds of all collocations are listed in every dictionary. At the entries for the bases, however, the outcome is more varied than in the 1995 generation. All of the percentages there are lower than the figures for the later generation of dictionaries, but they lead to the conclusion that for production purposes, OALD4 comes out top, LDOCE2 second and COBUILD1 a clear third. The tendencies of these findings are confirmed by those of Bahns (1996: 79-85), who conducted similar research on these three dictionaries, looking at 1375 collocations in all.

Quite clearly, OALD has a tradition of including collocations both at the entries of the collocators and the bases. Yet it seems that a number of improvements were made between the fourth and fifth edition, which may be explained by the introduction of large-scale corpus analysis. The difference between LDOCE2 and LDOCE3 is still greater. In the light of this gradual improvement over time it is perhaps surprising that the very first edition of the Cambridge International Dictionary of English should have a similarly good record. OALD5, LDOCE3 and CIDE seem to have a clear policy of giving information about collocations, and this seems to have worked out very well.

2.3 Differences in the presentation of collocations

So far only quantitative differences between the four dictionaries have been discussed here, but there are also considerable differences between them with respect to the way in which they present these collocations to the users.

All of the dictionaries use bold print to mark certain phrases. In principle, this is a very useful method of showing typical combinations of words, making them easy to find and identify as being typical. However, as a comparison of the entries for *conclusion* (Fig. 1) will show, there seems to be little consensus between the dictionaries on which combinations of words to highlight in this way.

Fig.1: The use of bold print in the entries for *conclusion*

OALD5

conclusion /kənˈkluːʒn/ *n* **1** [C] ~ (**that ...**) a belief or an opinion that is the result of reasoning: *a summary of the main conclusions and recommendations of the report* ○ ***I came to the conclusion*** *that he'd been lying.* ○ *What conclusions do you draw from the evidence you've heard?* ○ *I reached the inescapable/unavoidable conclusion that ...* **2** [C usu sing] the end of sth: *at the conclusion of his speech* ○ *bring sth to a speedy conclusion* ○ ***In conclusion*** (ie Lastly) *I'd like to say that ...* **3** [U] the formal and final arranging or settling of sth: *Hostilities ended with the successful conclusion of a peace treaty.* IDM **a foregone conclusion** ⇨ FOREGONE. **jump/leap to conˈclusions / to the conˈclusion that ...** to make a decision about sb/sth too quickly, before one has learned or thought about all the facts: *She was seen having lunch with him one day and everyone jumped to the wrong conclusion.*

LDOCE3

S W **con·clu·sion** /kənˈkluːʒən/ *n* **1** [C] something you decide after considering all the information you have: *These are the report's main conclusions.* | [+ **that**] *Becky came to the conclusion that he must have forgotten.* | **lead to/point to/support the conclusion (that)** *All the evidence pointed to the conclusion that he was guilty.* | **draw a conclusion** *From these facts we can draw some conclusions about how the pyramids were built.* | **jump to conclusions** (=decide that something is true too quickly, without knowing all the facts) *Don't jump to conclusions – just because they're late doesn't mean they've had an accident!* **2** [C] the end or final part of something: *I found the conclusion of his book very interesting.* **3 in conclusion** used in a piece of writing or a speech to show that you are about to finish what you are saying: *In conclusion, I would like to say how much I have enjoyed myself today.* **4** [U] the final arrangement of something such as a business deal: [+ **of**] *The conclusion of a peace treaty.* **5 be a foregone conclusion** to be certain to happen even though it has not yet officially happened: *The outcome of the battle was a foregone conclusion.*

COBUILD2

conclusion /kənkluːʒᵊn/ **conclusions** ◆◆◆◇◇

1 When you come to a **conclusion** you decide that something is true after you have thought about it carefully and have considered all the relevant facts. *Over the years I've come to the conclusion that she's a very great musician... I have tried to give some idea of how I feel – other people will no doubt draw their own conclusions.* N-COUNT: oft N that

2 The **conclusion** of something is its ending. *At the conclusion of the programme, I asked the children if they had any questions they wanted to ask me.* N-SING: also no det, usu with supp =end

3 The **conclusion** of a treaty or a business deal is the act of arranging it or agreeing it. *...the expected conclusion of a free-trade agreement between Mexico and the United States.* N-SING: usu with supp

4 You can refer to something that seems certain to happen as **a foregone conclusion**. *It was a foregone conclusion that I would end up in the same business as him... The championship result was almost a foregone conclusion.* PHRASES oft *it* v-link PHR that =certainty

5 You say '**in conclusion**' to indicate that what you are about to say is the last thing that you want to say. *In conclusion, walking is a cheap, safe, enjoyable and readily available form of exercise.* PHR with cl PRAGMATICS =to finish

6 If you say that someone **jumps to a conclusion**, you are critical of them because they decide too quickly that something is true, when they do not know all the facts. *I didn't want her to jump to the conclusion that the divorce was in any way her fault... Forgive me. I shouldn't be jumping to conclusions.* V and N inflect, oft PHR that PRAGMATICS

CIDE

con·clu·sion /kəŋˈkluː·ʒᵊn/ *n* [C] • *I found the conclusion of the film* (=the way the film ended) *rather irritating.* [C] • *Did you* **come to/reach/draw** *any conclusions* (=make any decisions) *at the meeting this morning?* [C] • *What were your conclusions* (=What did you think about the situation) *after you'd been to see the houses?* [C] • *At first I thought he was a bit shy, but I've* **come to the** *conclusion* (=decided after a lot of consideration) **that** *he's simply unfriendly!* [+ *that* clause] • *(fml)* **In conclusion** (=Finally), *I should like to say that I am deeply concerned for the future of British theatre.* • *The conclusion of the deal/treaty will make the world a safer place for all of us.* [U]

The bottom section of table 4 shows that the four dictionaries have followed entirely different policies in their use of bold type to mark syntagmatic units. These policies in themselves do not seem to be used very consistently, however, considering the differences between the entries for the collocators and the bases. On the whole, COBUILD2 only uses this means very sparingly, whereas the compilers of LDOCE3 have used bold print to identify more than two thirds of the collocations it contains. OALD5 is also fairly restrictive in its use of bold print, whereas the policy of CIDE is closer to that of LDOCE.

Table 4: Collocations in OALD5, LDOCE3, COBUILD2 and CIDE
Listed Collocations (out of a total of 120 and in approximate percentages)

	Collocator				Base			
	OALD5	LDOCE3	COBUILD2	CIDE	OALD5	LDOCE3	COBUILD2	CIDE
	87 (=73%)	83 (=69%)	77 (=64%)	79 (=66%)	67 (=56%)	70 (=58%)	37 (=31%)	71 (=60%)
Of these:								
Bold[4]	**15%**	**60%**	**4%**	**44%**	**25%**	**86%**	**16%**	**75%**
Def.	22%	24%	**64%**	20%	-	1%	16%	-
Ex.	71%	51%	87%	42%	70%	64%	92%	23%
CR	2%	-	3%	**10%**	6%	1%	3%	4%

Notes: Bold: collocation in bold print; Def: collocation in definition; Ex: collocation can be found in one of the examples; CR: cross-reference to other entry containing the collocation in question.

The second line in the bottom section of table 4 contains the figures for the definitions. It shows that although COBUILD2 exhibits certain weaknesses in its treatment of collocations, it also has exemplary features. The figures demonstrate clearly the strength of the COBUILD2 full-sentence definitions in presenting words in their typical environment. Using full sentences makes it easier to include both parts of the collocation in the definition. This means that no example is needed to illustrate that particular combination, which can save space. And in cases where an example is given, it underlines the importance and typicality of the combination in question.

The last important point of interest in this table is the comparatively large number of collocations marked CR for "cross-reference" in the column for CIDE. Most of these cross-references direct the user to so-called "Language Portraits", which are often on a different page to the entry itself. These Language Portraits usually contain further collocations, but it is quite doubtful if any user will actually look them up.

[4] These categories overlap: some collocations are given both in the definitions and the examples, etc.

3 Suggestions for improvements

Giving collocations in example sentences can take up a lot of space, which is probably the main reason why there is still so much that can be improved in this respect. It might be useful to think about other ways of providing information of this sort. The *Oxford Dictionary of Phrasal Verbs* by Cowie and Mackin and the *Langenscheidt Großwörterbuch Deutsch als Fremdsprache* have employed different ways of presentation (Fig. 2, 3). In these dictionaries, important collocations that a word enters into are given in a string between the definitions and examples.

let through [Vn ⇆ p pass, Vn.pr pass] allow (sb/sth) to pass. **O:** visitor; car; goods; defective items. **o:** immigration; customs; control-point; quality control: *A number of mistakes in the proofs were* **let through**. ○ *Most of their party were* **let through** *customs without an examination.*

let up [Vp nom] (*informal*) relax one's alertness or efforts; ease, slacken. **S:** worker, team; (bad) weather, storm; pressure, volume (of work): *Petrie's mind never* **let up** *for an instant.* SD ○ *We will never stop, or* **let up** (cf *there will be no* **let-up**), *till Tunis has been captured.* MFM

Fig. 2: *let through* and *let up* in *The Oxford Dictionary of Phrasal Verbs*

Sturm *der*; -(*e*)*s*, *Stür·me*; **1** ein sehr starker Wind ⟨ein S. kommt auf, bricht los, wütet, flaut ab, legt sich; in e-n S. geraten⟩: *Der heftige S. hat zahlreiche Bäume entwurzelt u. Dächer abgedeckt* ‖ K-: **Sturm-, -bö, -glocke, -nacht, -schaden, -signal, -tief, -warnung** ‖ -K: **Sand-, Schnee- 2 ein S. +** *Gen*; e-e starke u. oft unkontrollierte Reaktion ⟨ein S. der Begeisterung, der Entrüstung⟩: *Die Entscheidung der Regierung löste e-n S. der Entrüstung aus* -K: **Beifalls-, Protest- 3 der S.** (**auf etw.** (*Akk*)) *Mil*; ein schneller Angriff, mit dem man den Gegner überraschen will: *Die Truppen nahmen / eroberten die Stadt im S.* ‖ K-: **Sturm-, -angriff, -gepäck, -leiter 4** *nur Sg*; *Sport*; die Spieler e-r Mannschaft, die angreifen sollen ⟨im S. spielen⟩ **5 S. u. Drang** *Lit*; e-e Richtung der deutschen Literatur (in der zweiten Hälfte des 18. Jahrhunderts), die *bes* im Drama starke Gefühle u. den Wunsch nach Freiheit ausdrückte: *Die frühen Dramen von Schiller werden zum S. u. Drang gerechnet* ‖ ID **ein S. im Wasserglas** große Aufregung wegen e-r unwichtigen Sache; **S. läuten / klingeln** ungeduldig mehrere Male kurz hintereinander an j-s Tür klingeln; **gegen etw. S. laufen** heftig gegen etw. protestieren, das j-d plant

Fig. 3: *Sturm* in *Langenscheidts Großwörterbuch Deutsch als Fremdsprache*

Policies of this kind can save space and keep pressure off the examples, although it is still useful to have every collocation in an example sentence to make clear how it is used appropriately.

4 Conclusion

There is still much that can be improved about the collocational information given in the dictionaries. Nevertheless, it is possible to conclude from the data studied here that if one considers the many functions that learners' dictionaries have to fulfil, the 1995 generation of learners' dictionaries has a lot to offer with respect to collocations. All four dictionaries explain the meaning and use of many collocations at the entries for the collocators. Three out of four have an almost equally good record of providing collocations for text production. Their more systematic approach to collocations has evidently paid off, even though it could still be improved upon by reducing occasional 'plenitudes' of synonymous combinations and replacing some of these combinations with others with different meanings.

There is a large amount of collocation information in the dictionaries, though it is sometimes difficult to find. Often it would be helpful if more cross-references were used or the cross-references made more explicit. The use of bold print makes collocations more noticeable, and it might be useful to think about exploiting this means so that the most typical and frequent combinations of each semantic category are marked.

The improvement of the presentation of collocations remains one of the challenges for the next generation of monolingual learners' dictionaries. It is here that we find one of the areas where it is possible to advance one large step further on the road to the Perfect Learners' Dictionary.

Bibliography

A Dictionary of English Collocations (3 Volumes) (1994): Göran Kjellmer (ed.). — Oxford: Clarendon Press.

Collins Cobuild English Language Dictionary (COBUILD1) ([1]1987): John Sinclair (ed.). — London, Glasgow: Collins.

Langenscheidts Großwörterbuch Deutsch als Fremdsprache. Das neue einsprachige Wörterbuch für Deutschlernende (1993): Dieter Götz, Günther Haensch, Hans Wellmann (eds.). — Berlin, München: Langenscheidt.

Longman Dictionary of Contemporary English (LDOCE2) ([2]1987): Della Summers (ed.). — Harlow: Longman.

Oxford Advanced Learner's Dictionary (OALD4) ([4]1989): Anthony P. Cowie (ed.). — Oxford: OUP.

Oxford Dictionary of Phrasal Verbs (formerly Oxford Dictionary of Current Idiomatic English Vol. I) (1993): Anthony P. Cowie, Ronald Mackin (eds.). — Oxford: OUP.

The BBI Combinatory Dictionary of English. A Guide to Word Combinations (1986): Evelyn Benson, Morton Benson, Robert Ilson (eds.). — Amsterdam, Philadelphia: John Benjamins.

Bahns, Jens (1996): Kollokationen als lexikographisches Problem. Eine Analyse allgemeiner und spezieller Lernerwörterbücher des Englischen. — Tübingen: Niemeyer.

Cowie, Anthony P. (1978): "The place of illustrative material and collocations in the design of a learner's dictionary". — In: P. Strevens (ed.): In Honour of A. S. Hornby (Oxford: OUP) 127-139.

— (1989): "The language of examples in English learners' dictionaries". — In: G. James (ed.): Lexicographers and their Works (Exeter: University of Exeter) (= Exeter Linguistic Studies 14) 55-65.
— (1994): "Phraseology". — In: R. E. Asher (ed.): The Encyclopaedia of Language and Linguistics, Volume 6 (Oxford, New York: Pergamon) 3168-3171.
Hausmann, Franz Josef (1984): "Wortschatzlernen ist Kollokationslernen. Zum Lehren und Lernen französischer Wortverbindungen". — In: Praxis des Neusprachlichen Unterrichts 31, 395-406.
— (1985): "Kollokationen im deutschen Wörterbuch. Ein Beitrag zur Theorie des lexikographischen Beispiels". — In: H. Bergenholtz, J. Mugdan (eds.): Lexikographie und Grammatik (Tübingen: Niemeyer) (=Lexicographica Series Maior 3) 118-129.
Herbst, Thomas (1996): "What are collocations: sandy beaches or false teeth?". — In: English Studies 4, 379—393.
Sinclair, John (1966): "Beginning the Study of Lexis". — In: Ch. E. Bazell, J. C. Catford, M.A.K. Halliday, R. H. Robins (eds.): In Memory of J.R. Firth (London: Longman) 410-430.
— (1991): Corpus, Concordance, Collocation. — Oxford: OUP.

Appendix

List of 120 collocations looked up in the dictionaries (bases in bold print):

1. Adjective + Noun

fatal/serious/slight **accident**; sharp **bend**; weak/strong **coffee**; clear/bad/guilty **conscience**; violent/accidental **death**; lethal/fatal **dose**; high **expectations**; blond(e)/thin/sparse **hair**; strong **glasses**; strong/serious **objections**; heavy **rain**; heavy **snowfall**; weak/strong **tea**; wide **variety**

2. Verb + Noun

give **advice**; render/come to sb's **assistance**; attract/draw so's **attention** to sth.; put on/apply the **brakes**; stub out a **cigarette**; make out/write/write out a **cheque**; come to/reach/draw a **conclusion**; inspire **confidence**; sit/take/pass/sail through/fail/flunk an **exam(ination)**; comb one's **hair**; create an **impression**; turn off/switch off/turn on/switch on the **light**; purse one's **lips**; withdraw/take out/earn/raise/spend/save/borrow **money**; blow/pick one's **nose**; swear/take/administer an **oath**; wear (a) **perfume**; make/give/keep/break a **promise**; serve a **purpose**; pick up/replace the **receiver**; set/establish/break a **record**; acquire/earn/establish a **reputation**; meet **requirements**; bear **resemblance**; put up/offer **resistance**; evade/shirk **responsibility**; break/establish/lay down/obey/observe/violate **rules**; tighten a **screw**; suffer a **setback**; pick up **speed**; flick a **switch**; lay/set/clear the **table**; levy/impose/collect **taxes**; clear one's **throat**; pay a **visit**; keep/break one's **word**

3. Verb + Adverb

cry bitterly; **need** badly; **reject** flatly; **remember** distinctly/vividly; **think** hard; **watch** closely; **want** badly

4. Adverb + Adjective

fast **asleep**; sound **asleep**; sharply **defined**; stark **naked**; dead **sure**; pretty **sure**

Paul Bogaards

Access structures of learners' dictionaries

1 Introduction

Dictionaries are very rich mines of information on languages. This is not only true of big, unabridged monolingual dictionaries meant for native speakers of a given language, but also, and more and more so, of so-called learners' dictionaries, at least as far as English is concerned. As is the case with real mines, specific techniques are necessary in order to extract the riches which one knows are inside. However, whereas copper or diamond mining is done by professional engineers and specially trained workers, dictionaries belong to the public domain. This means that their handling should be as user-friendly as possible.

In order to be user-friendly, one has to know how users operate when they take the trouble to consult a dictionary. Although more and more research is being done on this topic (see e.g. Atkins 1998), not very much is known up to now about the expectations and motivations of dictionary users, nor about the ways and means they use in order to find specific types of information.

One thing that seems to be clear about the behaviour of dictionary users is that they almost never use these reference books for oral purposes, but almost exclusively in the context of reading or writing (Bogaards 1988). So it is receptive and productive use in a written context which will be taken as the background of the following discussions. And, as will be clear from the title of this paper, learners of second or foreign languages (L2) will be the special group of users to be taken into consideration.

There are a number of essential differences between receptive and productive use of (monolingual) dictionaries. As far as access is concerned,[1] these two types of use have opposite points of departure and opposite targets. Whereas receptive use is semasiological, going from form to meaning, productive use is onomasiological: it starts from a concept or a meaning which can be formulated in the mother tongue, and has as its goal some more or less equivalent form in the second language.

In this paper I will treat receptive use and productive use in two separate sections and I will discuss some problems learners may have in accessing information they know must be in the dictionary. Most examples will be taken from *Longman Dictionary of Contemporary English* (LDOCE3), *Oxford Advanced Learner's Dictionary of Current English* (OALD5), *Collins Cobuild English Dictionary* (COBUILD2) and *Cambridge International Dictionary of English* (CIDE). In both sections I will pay special attention to

---

[1] For other aspects see Bogaards 1996.

the problem of more or less fixed phrases, which constitute one of the major difficulties second language learners are confronted with (see Hausmann 1984).

2 Receptive use: from form to meaning

When reading a text, a learner may run up against lexical elements which prevent him from understanding a particular passage. Whether these elements look familiar or are totally unknown, in all cases the learner is confronted with something that presents itself as a mere form without a meaning or, at least, without a meaning that makes sense in the context. To this situation monolingual dictionaries are extremely well adapted because the main classification that is applied to the lexical materials they contain is a formal one: the alphabetical order allots a unique place to each form, and each form can, therefore, be found in a systematic and rapid way.

This simple starting point becomes more complicated because of two factors. First, not all forms are entered in the same way in the alphabetical list. Second, a search for particular information does not necessarily come to its end at the moment the relevant form has been located in the alphabetical list. Both points will be taken up hereafter.

2.1 Forms and lemmas

The first point concerns what is sometimes called the macrostructure of the dictionary. It is on the level of macrostructure that not only the total number of lemmas, but also what counts as a lemma is determined. In other words, lexicographers have to make decisions as to which forms will have lemma status and which forms will be presented in other ways or will not be presented at all. These decisions will have to be made on linguistics grounds, but when learners' dictionaries are involved, pedagogical reasons will be relevant as well.

No paper dictionary, to my knowledge, gives all forms of the recorded lexical elements in the alphabetical list: nouns are in the singular form only, verbs have only the form of the infinitive, etc. This does not cause problems as long as the user - a learner of the language - may be assumed to be able to trace all inflected forms back to their canonical forms. This will be the case with regular plurals of nouns and with regularly conjugated verbal forms, but not necessarily with forms like *mice* or *flew*. So, although they do not have lemma forms, these types of forms should have lemma status in learners' dictionaries. This is not always the case in the four learners' dictionaries we are discussing, especially not when it comes to forms like *remade, overate* or *overcame*.

Another category of forms which may cause problems is derivatives. As a consequence of the alphabetical principle, forms which are derived through the addition of a prefix are always given as lemmas on their own. Forms which have suffixes, however, are treated in different ways by the four dictionaries. LDOCE sticks to a strict alphabetical order, as does

COBUILD most of the time. The policies followed by OALD and CIDE are less straightforward: they both have subentries for *pocketful* under *pocket*, and before the next entry, *pocketbook*, breaking up the alphabetical order. It is not known whether this presentation presents any real drawbacks for the L2 reader.

The case of compounds may be slightly harder for the foreign user. As many compounds in English are written alternatively as one single word, as a hyphenated word or as two words, like in the case of *paperclip, paper-clip, paper clip*, only a strict alphabetical order can guarantee that all forms can be found easily. CIDE has a policy where compounds which are written as one single word are treated as independent entries, and compounds which are written with a hyphen or in two words are sometimes treated in the microstructure of the relevant entry of the first element, and sometimes as independent entries. As polysemous words have several entries, the user may have to look at a number of places before he will find the form he is after. A case in point are the numerous compounds with *cross: cross-channel* is given as an example under *cross [GO ACROSS]*, *cross-legged* under *cross [LIE ACROSS], cross-stitch* under the noun *cross [MARK]*, whereas *cross-eyed, cross-examine, cross-question* and a couple of others are presented as independent entries. *Crossbreed* and *crosscheck* are also independent entries, presumably because they are written as one word, but these words are written with a hyphen in several other dictionaries.

Nevertheless, despite these minor complications, one can safely assume that learners who know the alphabet are able to locate without great problems all the forms which are in a given dictionary. As was said above, however, locating the form does not always suffice: in very many cases it is necessary to go into the body of an entry in order to find out which element may lead to the semantic information that is looked for. Especially in longer entries it is therefore important that the information be organized in such a way that the users can easily find their way.

2.2 Inside the lemma

In order to simplify the task of the users, it seems wise to look at what they may know about the words they are looking up, even if this knowledge will not always be there in a very clear or explicit manner. In the first place they may be aware of the type of text they are reading and of the subject domain that is treated. Secondly, they will know in most cases whether the particular word they are looking for is a noun, a verb, an adjective or some other part of speech. Thirdly, as the context is globally understood, they will often have some rather vague idea of what the target word may mean. That is to say that, as to clues which may guide them in longer entries, dictionary users are possibly sensitive to indications of three different kinds, which I would like to call respectively *discoursal, grammatical* and *semantic*.

Discoursal indications can be of several types, which are reflected in the use of different sets of labels in the dictionaries. In the first place, a number of geographic varieties of English can be marked as such. It goes without saying that this may be useful for a reader who is looking up a familiar word form which has an unknown meaning, and who realizes that he is reading not a British but a Canadian text. The same is true for labels which specify a restricted area of use in terms of subject domains: a legal text and a paper on medicine may contain one and the same word form with very different domain-specific meanings. Labels which give indications on stylistic restrictions can be useful for the same reason. On the other hand, labels giving information on attitudes (approving, sexist, humorous, etc.) seem to be less helpful for readers who try to find their way in a long entry.

As a matter of fact, the four learners' dictionaries do not really exploit these possibilities. They only have three or less than three labels for domain-specific meanings, albeit that OALD5 uses a number of indications following the label *techn.*, such as *anatomy, computing, law*, etc. As to the stylistic labels, they distinguish five to eight different levels from *literary* or *poetic* through *spoken* and *informal* to *slang* or *taboo*; this seems a fair number. LDOCE3 marks eleven geographic varieties of English, CIDE six, OALD5 three and COBUILD2 only two, British and American. However, in none of the dictionaries do these possibly distinguishing elements seem to be used as sign posts for the users: they are in thin italics or they are, as in the case of COBUILD2, part of the normal print. Anyhow they do not catch the eye.

COBUILD2 seems to go for *grammatical* categories as guiding principles. All senses and uses of a particular form are presented in the same format, the only eye-catching elements being those of the famous extra column: N-COUNT, VERB, PHRASES, etc. It is remarkable that in the second edition of COBUILD, nominal, verbal and other uses of a given form are often grouped together, but that this is not always the case.

LDOCE3 and CIDE choose *semantic* criteria as most important sign posts. Although LDOCE3 presents nominal, verbal or adjectival uses of a given form together in entries which are marked by little superior digits, even if senses within these entries are semantically related with senses from other entries, it is the semantic clustering of senses and uses which strikes the reader immediately: short indications in capitals between black triangles are clearly meant to draw the user's attention as soon as possible to a particular place. Moreover, very long entries like *get* and *put*, but sometimes also shorter ones like *shoot* and *service*, are preceded by a menu which contains these global headings. CIDE uses what are called 'guide words' of a far more global nature. A 'guide word' is given for each entry of a given form. These entries may cover rather large numbers of senses and uses and may contain subentries devoted to other parts of speech with the same or a derived form and having a related meaning.

OALD5 does not offer any clear landmarks, except in very long entries like *get, give* or *go*, where global semantic indications precede groups of related senses. Other grammatical uses are presented as subentries preceded by a black triangle.

As no research has been done concerning the relative efficiency or helpfulness of each of these three types of guiding principles, it is difficult to judge the quality of the systems used by each of the four dictionaries.[2] Nor is it easy to determine the importance of other

---

[2] See however Bogaards 1998.

principles which are used to structure the body of longer entries. Without any further research it may be assumed that etymology, as used in dictionaries like the *Petit Robert*, would not be of great help to L2 readers. But the role frequency has to play is not that clear either. Should more frequent senses or uses be given before less frequent ones, or are there reasons to give them in the opposite order? In the first option, more advanced users should be advised not to read a long entry from the beginning, because they would have to screen many senses they already know. Maybe, they had better begin right away at the end, the second option.

2.3 Accessing multi-word expressions

As a special point I would like to mention the problem of locating multi-word expressions: collocations, fixed phrases, idioms, proverbs and the like. The four dictionaries have different policies in presenting these 'ready mades' of the language. As a matter of fact, there is no consensus on the status of many multi-word expressions. One and the same expression can be presented as a regular example of the use of one of the constituting words in one dictionary, as a fixed phrase needing only a brief explanation in another one and as a real idiom in a third one. One can only imagine the difficulties the learner may have in coming to grips with this whimsical part of the language.

But more importantly as far as access to information is concerned, the user has to choose which entry he will look at for the explanation he needs. At this point again, the four learners' dictionaries have different policies and practices. LDOCE3 and OALD5 promise to explain phrases and idioms under the first main word. This policy is followed in a stricter way by the latter dictionary than by the former one, OALD5 listing also the "main words" which are discounted in this context. Phrases which contain variable parts at the beginning may constitute a problem as to their place in the dictionary, but the solution adopted by OALD5, which consists in giving the explanation at the first constant part, does not really take into account the interests of the learners. Indeed, how can a learner who comes across a phrase like *live to tell the tale*, know that he has to look under *tell* and not under *live* because there exist in English variants like *be around to tell the tale* and *be still alive to tell the tale*?

CIDE applies the same policy. In addition, at the end of the book one can find a "Phrase Index" containing all multi-word expressions with a reference to the place where they are explained. It is to be feared, however, that this index will meet with the same fate as most other special lists and annexes in dictionaries: they are very seldom consulted. COBUILD2 has not stated any policy in its front matter and it is difficult to discover one in the dictionary as such.

Apart from the policies which are followed by dictionary makers, one should try to examine what users actually do when confronted with what may seem to them to be longer stretches of language having some peculiar meaning. Not very much is known about this matter. I have done some research where I have presented several groups of native speakers as well as learners of French and Dutch with lists of collocations and idioms, asking them to indicate the word where they would check for an explanation in the dictionary. What seems to be clear from that research is that speakers of different languages have different search strategies and that learners tend to adopt the strategies of their mother tongue when looking up multi-word expressions in the foreign language (Bogaards 1990, 1992). These results would imply that in learners' dictionaries which are meant to be used by users with very many different mother tongues, phrases and idioms should be explained in the entries of all the constituting words, or else that there should be a rigorous policy as to cross-references.

2.4 Conclusion on access in receptive use

Concluding on the receptive part of access structures in learners' dictionaries one can say that there are no big problems, neither for the learner nor for the dictionary maker, and that whatever problems there are can relatively easily be resolved. I hope to have shown that for the dictionary maker it is necessary to adopt more often and more systematically the viewpoint of the learner, even if this may lead to solutions which take rather more space. In order to make the viewpoint of learners more knowable and more explicit, there remains a lot of research to be done.

3 Productive use: from meaning to form

When learners have to produce a text in the foreign language, it is almost always the lexical material which causes the biggest problems. Learners are confronted with questions like: how do you say this in English? How can I clearly express this meaning? etc. As dictionaries, learners' dictionaries as well as most other dictionaries, are organized according to form, as we have seen in the first section of this paper; they are fundamentally not adapted to this kind of onomasiological question. Fortunately, several solutions have been proposed to overcome this problem, but as I have shown elsewhere (Bogaards 1996: 300-301) these can at best be considered to be partial: unknown lexical forms can be found in less than half of the cases, however hard a learner tries to find the words he needs. In the following sections I will briefly discuss some visual and textual remedies that can be found in different types of dictionaries.

3.1 Visual aids

One of the partial solutions to the problem of finding unknown forms in a monolingual dictionary is the use of illustrations. In a productive context illustrations can help the user to find unknown words and phrases. But this is on the express condition that the starting point is in words the learner may be assumed to know. A nice example is to be found in the "Language Portrait" *Eye, eyesight and seeing* in CIDE.

Figure 1. 'Eye, eyesight and seeing' in Cambridge International Dictionary of English (CIDE).

EYE, EYESIGHT AND SEEING

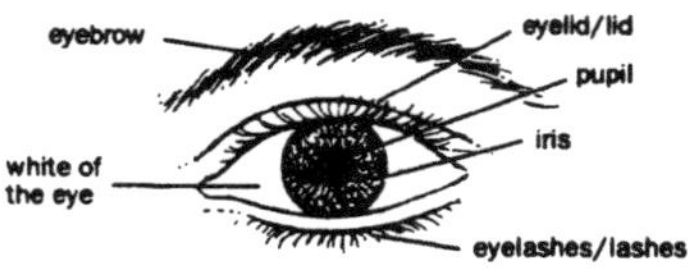

- Your ability to see is called your **eyesight**, **sight** or **vision**: *Airline pilots need to have good eyesight.* • *After his car crashed, Sam lost the sight of his left eye.* • *Sarah's over seventy and she's still got perfect vision.*
- Some common problems with eyesight: *I'm getting* **long-sighted**/*(Am also)* **far-sighted**: *I can't read a newspaper now if it's too close to me.* • *She's so* **short-sighted**/*(esp. Am)* **near-sighted** *she can't find her glasses if she takes them off.* • *Alice is* **blind**/*has* **lost her sight** *and needs a guide dog to help her.* • *Drivers may be temporarily* **blinded**/**dazzled** *by the lights of approaching cars.* • *I wear* **contact lenses** *but I always carry a spare pair of spectacles.*

look = to direct your eyes in order to see
watch = to look at something for a period of time, esp. something that is moving
see = to be aware of what is around you by using your eyes

		look	*watch*	*see*
Look **at** *all this rubbish on the floor.* *I* **can't** *see very well without my glasses.* *They all watched as I opened my presents.*	used without an object	•	•	•
I watched TV for a couple of hours. *I* **can** *see three or four empty seats.* *He says he's seen 'Jaws' ten times.*	used with an object		•	•
She sat looking through the window. *Wait a minute – I'm watching the news.* *I can't believe what I'm seeing.*	used in continuous tenses (*be seeing* is not common in this meaning)	•	•	•
Look **how** *beautifully she dances.* *Watch carefully* **where** *the ball lands.* *I can't see* **what's** *happening.*	+ *wh-* word	•	•	•
Can't you see **(that)** *he's annoyed?*	+ (*that*) clause			•
Hazel watched him open the letter. *She saw the van park outside her house.*	T + obj + infinitive without *to* (esp. referring to a completed action)*		•	•
*I like to watch people walk***ing** *past.* *We could see children play***ing** *outside.*	T + obj + v-*ing* (esp. referring to an incomplete activity)		•	•
*His parents saw him award***ed** the prize.	T + obj + v-*ed*			•

* Notice that when 'see' is used in this way in passive sentences, 'to' is required: *Someone saw Mr Kerry enter the building alone. / Mr Kerry was seen* **to** *enter the building alone.* The pattern with 'watch' is not used in the passive.

These verbs are also used in other meanings – see the dictionary.

All advanced learners know the word *eye* and whenever they want to express something concerning the eye, they find a natural point of departure in that "Language Portrait".

Unfortunately, there are not many good examples of this type to be found in the four learners' dictionaries. LDOCE3 gives one at *aircraft*, but the words given are limited to parts of the aircraft, and there is no possibility to go from there to phrases like *to change planes* or *The aircraft landed at the airport.* For French, one could imagine a learner who wants to write about the big grey animal that can pick up things with its long nose. In a dictionary which would include a table for *Les animaux* (see Figure 2), after the entry *animal* in the A to Z part of the dictionary, pictures could help him to choose the category *les mammifères*; there (see Figure 3) he would find, thanks to an illustration, the name of the animal, *éléphant*; finally he would find the word for trunk, *trompe*, which is given with the picture at the entry *éléphant* (see Figure 4).

Figure 2. 'Animals' in a French learners' dictionary.
N.B. The pictures are taken from the *Petit Larousse Illustré 1995.*

LES ANIMAUX

On distingue:

les MAMMIFÈRES* comme	le chat	le cheval
	la girafe	l'homme
les poissons* comme	le hareng	le saumon
	la truite	
les oiseaux* comme	le moineau	l'aigle
	le cygne	
les insectes* comme	la fourmi	la mouche
	le papillon	
les reptiles* comme	le serpent	le lézard
	la tortue	
les MOLLUSQUES* comme	les coquillages	la pieuvre
	l'escargot	
les BATRACIENS comme	la grenouille	la salamandre
les CRUSTACÉS comme	le crabe	la langouste
	l'écrevisse	
les vers comme	le ver de terre	la sangsue

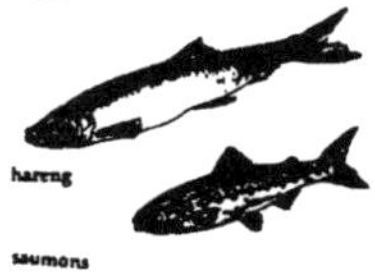

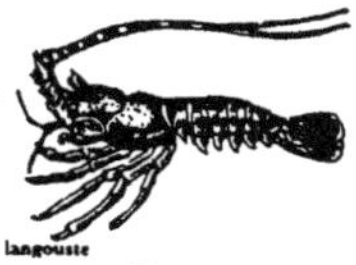

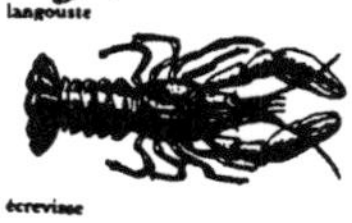

Figure 3. 'Mammals' in a French learners' dictionary (extract).
N.B. All species will be illustrated by pictures.

LES MAMMIFERES

On distingue les mammifères domestiques, pour lesquels il existe souvent quatre termes différents, ainsi qu'un verbe spécial pour le cri:

terme générique	mâle	femelle	petit	cri caractéristique
l'âne	-	l'ânesse	l'ânon	braire
le bœuf	le taureau	la vache	le veau	meugler, beugler,
			la génisse	mugir
le cheval	l'étalon	la jument	le poulain	hennir
			la pouliche	
la chèvre	le bouc	la chèvre	le chevreau	bêler
le chien*	-	la chienne	le chiot	aboyer
le chat	le matou	la chatte	le chaton	miauler
le cochon	le verrat	la truie	le goret	grogner
le mouton	le bélier	la brebis	l'agneau	bêler

et les mammifères sauvages, pour lesquels on trouve souvent trois termes:

mâle/terme générique	femelle	petit	cri caractéristique
le cerf	la biche	le faon	bramer
le chameau	la chamelle	le chamelon	-
l'éléphant	-	l'éléphanteau	barrir
le lapin	la lapine	le lapereau	couiner
le lièvre	la hase	le levraut	couiner
le lion	la lionne	le lionceau	rugir
le loup	la louve	le louveteau	hurler
l'ours	l'ourse	l'ourson	-
le rat	la rate	le raton	-
le renard	la renarde	le renardeau	aboyer
le singe	la guenon	-	-
la souris	-	le souriceau	-
le tigre	la tigresse	-	feuler

Pour les autres mammifères, il n'y a qu'un seul terme.

Remarque: Là où il n'y a pas de terme spécifique pour le mâle ou pour la femelle, on peut ajouter ces mots au nom générique: un gros rat mâle, un écureuil femelle. Si le terme pour le petit fait défaut, on dit: un petit singe, une petite baleine. S'il n'existe pas de terme pour le cri typique d'un animal, on peut dire, selon le cas: crier, pousser un cri, pousser des cris, pousser de petits cris.

Figure 4. *'Elephant' in a French learners' dictionary.*
N.B. The picture is taken from the *Petit Larousse Illustré 1995.*

It goes without saying that the use of pictures presents several drawbacks. They offer only a partial solution in that they are restricted to things that can be depicted. On the other hand it is good to realize that very many things, and even abstract things like emotions, can be evoked by pictures. Another drawback of pictures is that they are rather space consuming and that it is difficult to find pictures which are clear to learners with very different cultural backgrounds and which at the same time conserve a flavour of authenticity and 'couleur locale'.

3.2 Textual aids

Another approach to remedy the restricted access to the information in a productive context has been brought to the fore by the *Longman Language Activator*. This approach seems to be useful for more abstract words and can be taken to be more or less complementary to the one based on illustrations. If a learner wants to compose a text about a teacher who is always nicer to girls than to boys, he has to think of an English word which comes as near as possible to the concept he wants to express. Starting at *advantage* (see Figure 5), he will find a menu which gives him a choice out of four possibilities.

Figure 5. *'Advantage' in The Language Activator (extract).*

● ADVANTAGE

something that helps you to be in a better position than other people, more likely to succeed etc

1. an advantage
2. the advantages and disadvantages of a plan, system etc
3. to have an advantage over other people
4. ways of saying that something gives one person an advantage over others

4 ways of saying that something gives one person an advantage over others

give sb an advantage	**be in sb's favour/favor**
give sb the edge	**favour/favor**
be to sb's advantage	

give sb an advantage /ˌgɪv (sb) ən ədˈvɑːntɪdʒ ‖ -ˈvæn-/ [*v phrase*]
give sb an advantage over *The ex-policeman's knowledge of the law gave him an advantage over the other people training to be lawyers.* | *Its location and its lower distribution costs give the company an advantage over its competitors.* | **give sb an advantage** *The fact that Liverpool had only ten men playing for them gave the other team an advantage.*

give sb the edge /ˌgɪv (sb) ði ˈedʒ/ **to give someone a slight advantage, for example in a competition or election** [*v phrase*]
give sb the edge over *He tried to find out as much as he could about the company, believing that it would give him the edge over the other interviewees.* | **give sb the edge** *His ten years' experience of boxing will give him the edge in tomorrow's fight.*

be to sb's advantage /biː tə (sb's) ədˈvɑːntɪdʒ ‖ -ˈvæn-/ if something **is to your advantage** it will give you an advantage and put you in a better position than you were in before [*v phrase*]
I think you should accept Steve's offer to talk about your interview – it could be to your advantage. | *If you listen to the announcement about our special offers, you may hear something to your advantage.* | **be to the advantage of** *A change of government might be to the advantage of the poor.*

be in sb's favour (British) **/ favor** (American) /biː ɪn (sb's) ˈfeɪvəʳ/ **if something is in someone's favour it will give them an advantage over someone else** [*v phrase*]
The present economic situation is clearly in the Democrats' favor. | *Investors are hoping that the new system of share dealing will operate in their favour.* | **tip the balance in sb's favour** (=to give someone a slight advantage) *It will be a closely fought match but Becker's stronger service is likely to tip the balance in his favour.*

favour (British) **/ favor** (American) /ˈfeɪvəʳ/ **if a situation or conditions such as the weather favour someone, they give them an advantage over someone else** [*v* T]
The weather favours the Australians, who are used to playing in the heat. | *German negotiators denied that economic circumstances had favored their companies and given them a significant export advantage.*

If he chooses the last one, he comes to the next menu where five phrases are listed and then explained and exemplified. Reading through these possibilities, he will be able to conclude that it must be possible to say "This teacher always favours girls over boys".

As compared to the approach based on pictures, this approach requires about the same number of steps to reach the word that was needed. As it is more dependent on reading, text comprehension and logical reasoning, the task as a whole will be more demanding, but this seems to be inevitable when it comes to abstract meanings. As will be clear from the examples given, it is rather space consuming as well: the treatment of 23,000 words and phrases, grouped under 1052 key words, needs no less than 1587 pages.

3.3 Other approaches

One could think that these two approaches prove that good old bilingual lexicography was not such a bad idea, after all. As a matter of fact, bilingual dictionaries are generally much preferred by learners, even by advanced ones (see Bogaards 1988). Bilingual dictionaries do give access to specific information in a much more straightforward way; they propose direct translations, and the better ones even try to offer as much guidance to the learners as they can, discriminating between near synonyms and giving all sorts of grammatical and discoursal information. However, they don't describe the foreign language in its own right and the information given tends to be rather fragmentary.

An intermediate solution could be some form of bilingualized dictionary. The existing bilingualized dictionaries seem already to have proved their value for receptive purposes (Laufer 1994), but I have some doubts about their usefulness in a productive context. In order to give the learners access to the words they need, the *Mono-bilingual learners' dictionary. Dizionario inglese monolingue con traducenti italiani e sezione italiano-inglese* contains, at the end of the volume, a list of Italian words and English translations as a sort of index to the main dictionary (see also Martin 1985). As may be seen from Figure 6, this list looks like a bad bilingual dictionary and I am afraid it will be used in that way by many a learner, and all the more so when he is to look for the correct equivalent of words like *subito* or *stupido* in up to twenty different entries.

Figure 6. Extract of the Index in a 'Mono-bilingual learners' dictionary' of Italian.

stupidaggini drivel, rubbish
stupidamente gormlessly, idiotically
stupidità foolishness, silliness, stupidity
stupido asinine, ass, booby, brainless, clueless, dim, dope, dopey, dumb, fool, goose, gormless, half-baked, idiot, moron, moronic, scatty, soft, stupid
stupire dumbfound
stupore astonishment, stupefaction, wonderment
stupro rape
subappalto subcontract
subconscio subconscious
subcontinente subcontinent
subcosciente subconscious
subentrare take over
subire suffer, sustain, undergo
subito away, directly, forthwith, immediately, instantly, now, off, once, promptly, straight, straight away, straight off
sublimare sublimate
sublime sublime

Another attempt at bridging the gap between what is in the dictionary and what a learner can get out of it was made in a report by Augusto et al. (1995). In this report the authors elaborate a design for a bidirectional bilingual dictionary for learners of Dutch and Portuguese. The following schematic representation is given of the lemma structure (see Figure 7). What is new here is that different users may use the same entry in different ways. Figure 8 gives a tentative realization of this model for a Dutch-English dictionary of this type.

Figure 7. Pathways through an entry in a bidirectional learners' dictionary.
(From Augusto et al. 1995)

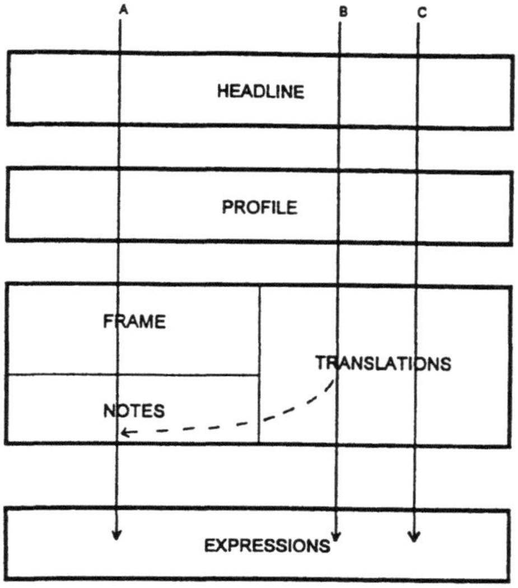

Figure 8. Example of an entry in a bidirectional learners' dictionary.
(From Augusto et al. 1995)

HEAD		ANXIOUS <adj. - bn.> [fon] <anxiously; anxiety, anxiousness>
PROF	1	[worried] bezorgd + over => [stronger; mostly predicative] ongerust + over
	2	[causing worry] angstig
	3	[=>be anxious] erg graag willen + dat
FRAME	1	s.o. is anxious about sth. s.o. has an anxious look/expression an anxious mother
	2	an anxious time an anxious question an anxious situation
	3	s.o. is anxious to do sth s.o. is anxious for s.o. else to be/do sth s.o. is anxious that s.o. else should be/do sth s.o. is anxious for sth.
NOTES	1	syn.: *worried*, *concerned*; *anxious* benadrukt de vrees van de betrokkene
TRANS	2	anxious anticipation \ bange verwachting
	3	she is anxious for her mother to be present \ zij wil erg graag dat haar moeder er bij is; he was anxious to get away \ hij stond te popelen om weg te gaan

The headline contains information on parts of speech, pronunciation and morphologically related forms. The profile enumerates the three senses of the word and gives translations. The frame presents the grammatical possibilities of each of the senses. The notes give near synonyms and discuss their meanings. The last part, 'translations', translates fixed phrases and idioms.

Learner A in figure 7 is a native speaker of Dutch who knows he needs to use the word *anxious* and who wants to verify details about its use. Learner B is again a native speaker of Dutch, but one who found the word *anxious* in a text and who wants to know what it means. His mother tongue will help him understand this meaning, but the notes may help him to obtain a finer image of its exact nuances. Learner C is a native speaker of English who wants to produce a text in Dutch. The lemma as given will help him to find the words he needs, but for details about their use he will have to look in the complementary volume. It is in that volume also that the receptive user of Dutch L2 will find what he needs.

Although the approach of Augusto et al. (1995) does not solve all problems, especially not the one of the need to consult two different volumes, what is attractive there is that the L2 words are described in the context of that language, so that a less fragmentary presentation is obtained.

3.4 The four learners' dictionaries

Up to now I have said very little in this section about the four learners' dictionaries. As a matter of fact they do not have very much to offer on this topic. As I have shown elsewhere (Bogaards 1996: 302-303), illustrations are totally absent, as in COBUILD2, or are rather scarce and treated in a somewhat haphazard manner. The rather low number of cross-references are not given in a systematic way: CIDE has the least possibilities to go from one word to the other; OALD5 and LDOCE3 are slightly more generous in offering discussions of meaning related words in their usage notes; COBUILD2 seems to be most successful in giving in a rather straightforward way a fair number of synonyms and antonyms.

3.5 Using collocations

A last subject to be treated in this section concerns again the findability of multi-word expressions. As to production, it is said that one type of these phrases, collocations, should be entered in the entries of their base, not in that of their collocator. This distinction has been elaborated by Hausmann (1979, 1984) who says that in a phrase like *célibataire endurci* the noun is the base and the adjective is the collocator. Hausmann (1979: 191-192) then goes on to say that:

> The base does not need the collocator *(endurci)* in order to be clearly defined. Matters are different for the collocator which only realizes its full meaning in combination with a base (*célibataire, pêcheur, âme*, etc.) (my translation - P.B.).

Moreover, according to Hausmann (1985: 119):

> The most important class as far as bases are concerned is the noun because it is nouns which express the things and the phenomena of this world about which we can talk. Adjectives and verbs can only be bases as far as they can be determined by adverbs (id.)

Starting from these considerations, Hausmann thinks that when producing a text, writers decide first on a base and will look only later for collocators. The conclusion he then draws seems logical and convincing: at least for productive purposes, collocations should be entered in the entry of their base, because that will be the place where users look for their preferred company.

In order to check the practical value of this distinction, I have conducted a small-scale experiment which I will report on elsewhere (Bogaards 1997). I will limit myself to the essentials of this experiment here. A list of 32 Dutch sentences containing collocations was presented to 56 Dutch learners of French. The sentences were translated except for the collocations. The subjects were asked to complete the translations or else to indicate under which word they would look for a translation. There were two conditions: 41 first year students of French had to underline a Dutch word, 15 third year students were asked to write a French word when they did not know the right translation.

The collocations had been selected according to three criteria. First, a distinction was made between collocations of nouns with adjectives and nouns with verbs. Second, the function of the words was varied: sometimes the noun had to be the base (the determined part) of the collocation, in other cases the noun had to be the collocator (the determining part). Third, the constituting words were chosen according to their frequency in Dutch as well as to the frequency of their translations in French. An example of a test item is:

> De rechter zal hem zeker een forse straf opleggen.
> Le juge ne manquera pas de lui . . . . . . sévère.
> (The judge will surely *inflict* a severe *punishment* on him.)

In this item the collocation consists of a frequent noun and an infrequent verb; the noun is the base, the verb the collocator.

The hypothesis is that for productive purposes, which have been simulated as much as possible for the Dutch learners of French who took part in the experiment, subjects look under the base, not under the collocator. This hypothesis must be rejected as will be clear from Table 1. For the first year group the percentages of choice for the base or the collocator are at chance level, for the third year group there seems to be only a slight preference for the base.

Table 1. Percentages of choices made by two groups of learners.

	First year students (N = 41)	Third year students (N = 15)
correct translations	5%	10%
incorrect or void	27%	48%
base/collocator	53/47%	62/38%
noun/adjective noun/verb	64/36% 73/27%	64/36% 67/33%
frequent/infrequent	22/78%	36/64%

In the first year group, there seems to be some preference for the noun, irrespective of its function as base or as collocator, and especially for the infrequent elements. In the third year group, who had to think of a French word which could get them nearer to the desired information, there is a lot of hesitation. A French word was written in less than half of the cases. This was due to some extent to their better knowledge of French collocations (10% correct translations as opposed to 5% for the first year group). But there were far more incorrect translations and omissions, slightly less than half of the cases involved. In many cases these subjects simply did not know where to begin, or they guessed at a translation although they had been expressly asked not to do so, maybe in order to avoid having to write a word. For the remaining cases there does not seem to be any clear preference in this group: subjects look wherever they think they might find a point of departure and mostly as a function of the words they happen to know or to think of.

Apart from these experimental data, there may be other reasons to treat collocations in the entries of all content words involved, even for productive purposes. In the first place, learners may be aware of the existence of some collocation without always being able to remember the base. So, an anglophone student might know that there exists in French an expression about something being very easy which includes the word *bonjour*. If this expression is not mentioned in the entry of that word, our student will not find it. Besides, if he knows that *easy* is *facile* in French, he will not find the expression either, because the French way of saying *easy as pie* is *simple comme bonjour*. In the same way, a Dutch learner who looks under *herbe* ('grass') in order to find the proper French equivalent for *gras maaien*, will not find what he is looking for, because in French this is translated as *tondre le gazon*. If one wants to give maximum access to the content of the dictionary, putting collocations under the base *and* the collocator seems to be a necessity, even for productive purposes.

3.6 Conclusion on access in productive use

As a conclusion for the second section of this paper one can say that helping learners in their onomasiological search is a hell of a job. Up to now no sure means have been developed, and it seems too early to judge the quality of learners' dictionaries on the basis of distinctions which may have some attractiveness on linguistic grounds but which do not stand against experimental evidence (see Zöfgen 1994: 157ff.). But although one can doubt whether such solutions will ever exist, matters are not hopeless. Much can be done to improve learners' dictionaries.

4 Conclusion

As the preceding discussions have, I hope, made clear, the notion of access structure means quite different things in a receptive or a productive context. Moreover, whereas for receptive use there is a structure which makes access possible, this is not the case for productive use. Up to now nothing of the kind of a trivial system like the alphabet has been found to get to grips with the world of concepts, notions and meanings. Nevertheless, I am sure we will have still better learners' dictionaries in the near future.

Bibliography

Longman Language Activator (1993): Della Summers (ed.). — London: Longman.

Mono-bilingual learners' dictionary. Dizionario inglese monolingue con traducenti italiani e sezione italiano-inglese (1989): P. H. Collin. — Bologna: Zanichelli.

Le Petit Robert. Dictionnaire de la langue française (1993): Josette Rey-Debove, A. Rey. —Paris: Dictionnaires Le Robert.

Petit Larousse Illustré (1995): — Paris: Larousse.

Atkins, B. T. Sue (ed.) (1998): Using Dictionaries. Studies of Dictionary Use by Language Learners and Translators. — Tübingen: Niemeyer (Lexicographica Series Maior 88).

Augusto, Celeste, Paul Bogaards, Mike Hannay, Willy Martin, Peter Jan Slagter, Fernando Venâncio, Herman Wekker, Cecile Wijne (1995): Towards a database for general translation dictionaries and bilingual learner dictionaries, with special reference to Dutch and Portuguese. — Den Haag: CLVV.

Bogaards, Paul (1988): "A propos de l'usage du dictionnaire de langue étrangère". — In: Cahiers de Lexicologie 52, 131-152.

— (1990): "Où cherche-t-on dans le dictionnaire?" — In: International Journal of Lexicography 3, 79 - 102.

— (1992): "A la recherche de collocations dans le dictionnaire de langue étrangère". — In: R. Lorenzo (ed.): Actas do XIX Congreso Internacional de Lingüistica e Filoloxia Românicas (A Coruña: Universidade de Santiago de Compostela, II) 175 - 185.

— (1996): "Dictionaries for Learners of English". — In: International Journal of Lexicography 9/4, 277 - 320.

— (1997): "Les informations collocationnelles dans le dictionnaire". — In: Revue française de linguistique appliquée 2, 31 - 42.

— (1998): "Scanning long entries in learner's dictionaries". — In: T. Fontenelle et al. (eds.): Euralex Proceedings. Papers submitted to the Eighth EURALEX International Congress on Lexicography in Liège, Belgium, Vol. II, 555 - 563.

Hausmann, Franz Josef (1979): "Un dictionnaire des collocations est-il possible?" — In: Travaux de linguistique et de littérature 17, 187 - 195.

— (1984): "Wortschatzlernen ist Kollokationslernen. Zum Lehren und Lernen französischer Wortverbindungen". — In: Praxis des Neusprachlichen Unterrichts 31, 395 - 406.

— (1985): "Kollokationen im deutschen Wörterbuch. Ein Beitrag zur Theorie des lexikographischen Beispiels". — In: H. Bergenholtz, J. Mugdan (eds.): Lexikographie und Grammatik (Tübingen: Niemeyer) (=Lexicographica Series Maior) 118 - 129.

Laufer, Batia, Linor Melamed (1994): "Monolingual, Bilingual 'Bilingualised' Dictionaries: Which are more effective, for what and for whom?" — In: W. Martin et al. (eds.): Euralex '94. Proceedings (Amsterdam: VU) 565 - 576.

Martin, Willy (1985): "Reflections on learner's dictionaries". — In: K. Hyldgaard-Jensen, A. Zettersten (eds.): Symposium on Lexicography II (Tübingen: Niemeyer) 169 - 181.

Zöfgen, Ekkehard (1994): Lernerwörterbücher in Theorie und Praxis. Ein Beitrag zur Metalexikographie mit besonderer Berücksichtigung des Französischen. — Tübingen: Niemeyer.

Kerstin Popp

Lexical units, suffixation, suffixes in OALD5, LDOCE3, COBUILD2 and CIDE

1 Introduction

Some of the most prominent innovations in the present generation of learners' dictionaries are to be found in the structure of these dictionaries – one of the most central aspects of user-friendliness. In this paper, structural advantages and disadvantages of the different policies of the four learners' dictionaries published in 1995 – OALD5, LDOCE3, COBUILD2 and CIDE – are analysed after determining which structural units in dictionaries seem to be the relevant units for an analysis of this kind. For this purpose, Cruse's (1986) concept of lexical units as the basic units in lexical semantics is applied to lexicography.

2 Polysemy and homonymy - a necessary distinction?

Whether diachronic criteria or a recognisable semantic relatedness are used to distinguish related meanings of the same form from different meanings of different forms, the distinction between polysemy and homonymy is by no means clear-cut. Lyons (1977: 551), for example, comes to the conclusion that "it is preferable to leave the theoretical status of the distinction between homonymy and polysemy unresolved."

Lexicographers frequently[1] quote statements like this and add a slightly cynical comment of the type that theoretical linguists might be in the position to tackle such problems by describing them as difficult and to leave it at that, but that lexicographers find themselves confronted with the necessity to come to clear - if arbitrary - decisions.

It seems to be a truth fairly universally acknowledged that homonyms and polysemous words have to be treated differently in dictionaries.[2] Traditionally, homonyms are dealt with in separate entries, whereas the various senses of polysemous words are supposed to be listed in one entry.

However, the four new learners' dictionaries that are discussed here present a very different picture: Only in OALD5 is a distinction between homonymy and polysemy still apparent, homonyms being covered in two or more numbered entries, whereas polysemous

---

1 See for example Bejoint (1994) or Robins (1987).
2 See for example Lyons (1995) and Schneider (1988).

words, classified as such by discernible semantic relatedness rather than according to diachronic principles, are given in one entry. In contrast, this distinction is irrelevant to the macrostructure of the other three dictionaries. LDOCE3 covers homonyms in one entry as long as they belong to the same word class and are part of the same paradigm – i.e. as long as they are what for example Lyons (1995) describes as absolute homonyms.

The entries for *bat* may serve as an example.

OALD5

bat¹ /bæt/ *n* a piece of wood with a handle, made in various sizes and shapes and used for hitting the ball in games such as cricket, baseball and PING-PONG. ⇨ picture at BASEBALL, CRICKET¹. Compare RACKET¹ 1. IDM **off one's own 'bat** (*Brit infml*) without help or encouragement from anyone else: *She made the suggestions entirely off her own bat* (ie without being asked for them). **(right) off the 'bat** (*US infml*) immediately; without delay: *He answered all their questions right off the bat.*
▶ **bat** *v* (-tt-) **1(a)** to use a bat: [V] *He bats well.* **(b)** to have a turn with a bat: [V] *Each team batted for two hours.* **2** to hit sth with a bat: [Vnp] *batting a ball (about)* [also Vn]. **'batter** *n* (*US*) (esp in baseball) a player who bats. ⇨ picture at BASEBALL.

bat² /bæt/ *n* a small animal like a mouse with wings. Bats fly at night and feed on fruit and insects. IDM **blind as a bat** ⇨ BLIND¹. **have bats in the 'belfry** (*infml*) to be crazy; to have strange ideas. **like a bat out of 'hell** (*infml*) very fast: *She dashed out of the door like a bat out of hell.*

bat³ /bæt/ *v* (-tt-) IDM **not bat an 'eyelid**; (*US*) **not bat an 'eye** (*infml*) not to show any surprise or feelings: *She listened to the sad news without batting an eyelid.*

LDOCE3

S W **bat¹** /bæt/ *n* [C]
1 ▶ **ANIMAL** ◀ a small animal like a mouse that flies around at night —see also FRUIT BAT
2 ▶ **SPORT** ◀ **a)** a long wooden stick with a special shape that is used in some sports and games: *a baseball bat* **b)** *BrE* a round flat piece of wood with a handle, used to hit a ball in TABLE TENNIS; PADDLE¹ (3) *AmE*
3 be at bat to be the person who is trying to hit the ball in a game of BASEBALL
4 do sth off your own bat *BrE informal* to do something without being told to do it: *You did all this work off your own bat?*
5 do sth right off the bat *AmE informal* to do something immediately: *I asked him to help, and he said yes right off the bat.*
6 like a bat out of hell *informal* very fast: *I drove like a bat out of hell to the hospital.*
7 old bat *spoken* an unpleasant old woman
8 have bats in the belfry *old-fashioned* to be slightly crazy —see also **as blind as a bat** (BLIND¹ (1c))

bat² *v* **batted, batting** **1** [I,T] to hit the ball with a bat in CRICKET (2) or BASEBALL **2 not bat an eye/eyelid** *informal* to not seem to be shocked, surprised, or embarrassed: *He didn't bat an eyelid when I said I was leaving.* **3 bat your eyes/eyelashes** if a woman bats her eyes, she opens and closes them quickly, especially in order to look attractive to men **4 go to bat for** *AmE informal* tohelp and support someone: *Andy really went to bat for me when I was accused of stealing that money.* **5 bat a thousand** also **bat a 1000** *AmE informal* to be very successful: *She's been batting a thousand ever since she got that new job.*

COBUILD2

bat /bæt/ **bats, batting, batted** ◆◆◆◇◇

1 A **bat** is a specially shaped piece of wood that is used for hitting the ball in cricket, baseball, rounders, or table-tennis. *...a baseball bat.* N-COUNT

2 When you **bat**, you have a turn at hitting the ball with a bat in cricket, baseball, or rounders. *Australia, put in to bat, made a cautious start.* VERB V
♦ **batting** *...his batting average... He's likely to open the batting.* N-UNCOUNT oft N n, the N

3 A **bat** is a small flying animal that looks like a mouse with leathery wings. Bats fly at night. N-COUNT

4 See also **old bat**.

5 In British English, if you say that someone **doesn't bat an eyelid** when something surprising happens or when they do something unpleasant, you are surprised or shocked because they remain calm and unemotional. The usual American expression is **doesn't bat an eye**. *When it comes to naked women on the pages of a glossy magazine, no one seems to bat an eyelid... The conspirators would have killed thousands of people without batting an eyelid.* PHRASES V inflects

6 If you **go to bat for** someone or **go in to bat for** them, you give them your support. *The old judge doesn't like the thought of no one going in to bat for the accused.* V inflects =stand up for

7 If you drive **like a bat out of hell**, you drive extremely fast; an informal expression. *He took off for Helsinki like a bat out of hell.* PHR after v

8 If someone does something **off** their **own bat**, they do it without anyone else suggesting it. *Whatever she did she did off her own bat. Whatever she did was nothing to do with me.* PHR after v

9 If something happens **right off the bat**, it happens immediately; used in American English. *He learned right off the bat that you can't count on anything in this business.* usu PHR after v

CIDE

bat STICK /bæt/ *n* [C] a specially shaped piece of wood used for hitting the ball in many games • *a baseball/cricket/rounders/table tennis bat* • *(Br and Aus infml) I didn't ask her to buy them a present – she did it* **off** *her* **own bat** (= without anyone telling or asking her to). • *(Am)* If something is done **off the bat** it is done immediately: *You can't expect to be accepted in a new town* **right/straight** *off the bat.* • See also BATSMAN. • PIC **Sports**
bat *(obj)* /bæt/ *v* **-tt-** • *He batted the ball high into the air.* [T] • *Jones will be the first to bat.* [I]
bat·ter /£ ˈbæt·əʳ, $ ˈbæṭ·ə/, **hit·ter** *n* [C] • In baseball, the batter is the person whose turn it is to hit the ball or a person who is good at this activity. • The **batter's box** is the place where the batter stands when he is trying to hit the ball. • PIC **Box**

bat ANIMAL /bæt/ *n* [C] a small flying animal with big ears and leathery wings which is active at night • *As twilight fell they could just see the bats swooping in and out from under the roof.* • *(infml dated disapproving)* A person who **has bats in the belfry** is silly and foolish with confused behaviour. See also BATS; batty. • *"Bat out of Hell"* (title of a record by Meat Loaf, 1979)

bat *obj* EYE /bæt/ *v* [T] **-tt-** (esp. of women) to open and close (your eyes) quickly several times, esp. to attract attention or admiration • *She smiled and batted her* **eyelashes** *at him.* • If you do **not bat an eyelid** you show no sign of surprise or worry when something unexpected happens: *Gail didn't bat an eyelid when Mark told her that he had crashed the car.*

OALD5 gives two entries while LDOCE3 has only one. COBUILD2 follows what they have called the "one word, one entry" approach which was already characteristic of COBUILD1, but has since been slightly modified: extreme cases of partial homonymy, such as *Polish* and *polish,* are now given in separate entries (cf. Herbst 1996). But generally, homographs regardless of part of speech, paradigm and pronunciation are included in one entry, as for example *bat* (noun) and *bat* (verb). CIDE takes the opposite approach by giving each "core meaning or sense" (viii) a separate entry, thus maximising homonymy by treating even polysemous words in several entries. In the case of *bat,* this only amounts to a traditional treatment of homonyms and results in the same number of entries as in OALD5. The difference of policies becomes more apparent in the case of *case (noun)* - as to be seen from table 1: LDOCE3 and COBUILD2 each give one entry respectively, OALD5 two, CIDE five.

	OALD5	**LDOCE3**	**COBUILD2**	**CIDE**
bat n	E, E	E	E	E, E
bat v	E, S	E		E, S
case n	E, E	E	E	E, E, E, E, E
case v	S	E		E

table 1: entries (E) and subentries including run-ons (S)

In comparison with the corresponding numbers of entries in the previous generation of learners' dictionaries - as given in table 2 -, it becomes obvious that LDOCE3 has adopted an entirely new approach, since in LDOCE2 homonyms were dealt with in separate entries.

	OALD4	**LDOCE2**	**COBUILD1**
bat n	E, E, E	E, E	E
bat v	S, E	E, E	

table 2: previous editions

It can be concluded that the distinction between homonyms and polysemous words can certainly no longer be seen as necessarily decisive for the macrostructure of learners' dictionaries, and, I would argue, justifiably so.

Why should learners be bothered with a distinction that poses problems to theoretical linguists and is in many cases intuitively unclear to native speakers? The question is which alternative structuring principle is the most user-friendly one: for learners' dictionaries, the aim should be to present a structure that is as consistent and as transparent as possible.

3 Lexical units as the basic units in lexicography

3.1 Definition

So far, it can be stated that with the exception of OALD5, entries consist of forms and varying numbers of their corresponding senses, regardless of whether these senses are related or not. Rather than entries, or some concept of a lexeme,[3] a smaller unit must be seen as the basic unit in lexicography, the lexical unit. Cruse (1986: 24) defines lexical units as:

> [...] the smallest parts which satisfy the following two criteria:
> (i) a lexical unit must be at least one semantic constituent,
> (ii) a lexical unit must be at least one word.

And he points out that:

> [...] a lexeme is a family of lexical units, a lexical unit is the union of a single sense with a lexical form, a lexical form is an abstraction from a set of word forms (or alternatively it is a family of word forms) which differ only in respect of inflections. (1986: 80)

The idea that the meaning potential of a lexeme can be split up in several senses or sememes is quite familiar,[4] but according to Lipka (1992) Cruse is the first to identify these as the meaning side of different units and to employ a specific term for these units.[5]

The crucial point to the concept of lexical units as Cruse introduces it, is of course the notion of *a single sense*. Cruse employs various methods to identify separate senses, and many others have attempted this, too. The tests developed for that aim[6] - such as coordination- or zeugma tests - might provide fascinating insights into language but are neither infallible nor widely applicable and certainly not practicable tools for dictionary-making. Furthermore, most methods give the impression that they can only be used if you already know what you are going to prove. The general picture that emerges is that there is no theoretically waterproof way to discriminate separate senses or to even find out how fine the distinction should be. The nature of language implies an indeterminate multiplicity of senses that has to be portrayed as convincingly as possible in a limited number of subdivisions of dictionary entries.

---

3 It is possible that the different macrostructures are based on differing theoretical concepts of lexemes (compare Kempson (1977), Cruse (1986), Lipka (1992), Lyons (1995)), but it seems to be far more likely that theoretical concepts of that kind are considered to be simply irrelevant for lexicographical practice.

4 Cf. Hansen et al. (1982)

5 The term lexical unit, though apt, might be considered slightly unfortunate since it has frequently been used synonymously with lexeme, lexical item or even word, i.e. referring to all conceivable kinds of units of the lexicon. (Cf. Palmer (1981), Leech (1981), Kempson (1977)). In this paper, lexical unit always refers to Cruse's definition (1986).

6 Cf. Cruse (1986), Moon (1987), Ayto (1983).

This has to be kept in mind when a comparison of the four dictionaries on an empirical basis is attempted.

3.2 Quantitative assessment

The focus of the following analysis is on the structural side of divergence in the four dictionaries, i.e. on their policies regarding the presentation of lexical units, rather than on coverage.

3.2.1 Homonyms and polysemous words

Table 3 shows the results of an investigation of a section of the four dictionaries with approximately 70 main entries and a total of 143 orthographical forms from *page* to *pancake*. The number of main entries was counted, then the number of subentries, including run-ons, and these numbers were set in relation to the total of orthographical forms covered. Next, the number of lexical units was determined. As has already been pointed out, what can be counted as different lexical units depends on the underlying notion of the term sense. For lexicographic purposes it seems to make sense to identify senses in correspondence to the classification of senses in the various dictionaries. Thus, what was counted was the number of major sense distinctions identifiable for the wordforms given. This means that for example in OALD5, where a hierarchy of senses in numbers and letters (the letters marking subsenses) is provided, only the numbered senses were counted. Also, where idioms, phrasal verbs or collocations were given the same status as the separate senses in an entry - as is the case in LDOCE3 -, they were counted as senses and therefore as lexical units of that entry. In CIDE, which lists major senses in separate entries, the number of lexical units is the same as the number of entries and subentries. This does not imply that further sense distinctions could not be found, but simply that they were not included in the broadest classification of sense divisions.

	OALD5	**LDOCE3**	**COBUILD2**	**CIDE**
number of entries	70	112	74	67
number of subentries incl. run-ons	31	28	16	32
number of orthographical forms covered	84	129	84	82
percent of total (143)	58.7%	90.2%	60.1%	57.3%
number of lexical units	134	230	151	99
average of lexical units per orthographical form	1.6	1.8	1.8	1.2

table 3: *page-pancake*: totals

It has to be pointed out again that these numbers cannot account for lexical coverage and are not meant to do so.

What is interesting is that the results for the average number of lexical units per orthographical form are surprisingly similar (table 3): 1,8 for both LDOCE3 and COBUILD2, slightly less with 1,6 for OALD5, which could be explained by the hierarchy of sense divisions mentioned above. CIDE has only 1,2 lexical units on average which is perhaps accounted for by the fact that sense divisions which are dealt with in the macrostructure of a dictionary cannot be as extensive.

However, an analysis of randomly selected homonyms and polysemous words, the results of which are presented in table 4, shows markedly different policies of the four dictionaries.

77 orthographical forms were looked at, and again, main entries, subentries including run-ons and lexical units were counted.

	OALD5	**LDOCE3**	**COBUILD2**	**CIDE**
number of entries	157	155	77	371
number of subentries incl. run-ons	30	0	0	90
number of orthographical forms covered	77	77	77	77
number of lexical units	723 (890)	1525	1129	461(720)
average of lexical units per orthographical form	9.3 (11.5)	19.8	14.7	5.9 (9.3)

table 4: *catch* 7 to *catch* 31 and others: totals

The totals indicate that LDOCE3 has by far the highest number of lexical units, followed by COBUILD2, whereas OALD5 and CIDE show distinctly lower numbers.

The numbers of entries correlate with the described policies of the dictionaries. Here it is important to note the occurrence of subentries, which are only to be found in the more semantically structured dictionaries OALD5 and CIDE - at least in presenting grammatical homonyms.

It seems difficult to account for the fewer sense distinctions in OALD5 (about 48 percent of LDOCE3), even if sub-senses are counted as well - the sum of senses and subsenses is given in brackets - the result amounts to hardly 60 percent of the lexical units in LDOCE3. With CIDE, the number in brackets presents an estimate of how many sense distinctions could be found if subsenses within entries and subentries - which are not numbered and are thus difficult to count - were included.

Some examples might serve to illustrate the differences. For the verb *catch* (table 5), LDOCE3 lists 26 separate senses or phrases. According to the front matter their policy is to show phrases which contain the word with a distinct meaning as a separate sense, and to list these in frequency order. OALD5 gives 14 senses, CIDE 7 entries and in COBUILD2 there are 22 sections to be found for the verb *catch*, which are included in altogether 31 for the orthographical form *catch*. COBUILD2's policy is to list 'meanings and uses'

(COBUILD2:x), so that different numbers can also be assigned to a different object or subject range or a phrase rather than a sense. Furthermore, these meanings and uses are ordered semantically, which can be very confusing, even though the extra column contains information suitable to help users find what they are looking for.

For the adjective *good*, OALD5 lists 21 main senses with 5 subsenses. COBUILD2 offers 16 adjective sections in the first 20 for the entry *good*, followed by phrases in sections 21 to 35. LDOCE3 has altogether 69 sections for *good*, of which numbers 3, 5 and 18-47 are phrases, and numbers 48 to 69 are contained in a special section for spoken phrases. This is certainly an extensive analysis of *good*, but even with the remarkably clear layout of LDOCE3 it does take some time to find one's way through.

CIDE has only 5 entries with the 'guide words' *very satisfactory, moral right, greeting, health* and *large amount*. Needless to say, these entries are very long and confusing, it seems that with words as versatile and frequent as the adjective *good* the system of giving core meanings in the macrostructure just breaks down.

	OALD5	**LDOCE3**	**COBUILD2**	**CIDE**
catch n	E 4	E 6	E 31	S 1; E 1
catch v	E 14	E 26		E 1; E 1; E 1; E 1; E 1; E 1; E 1
good adj	E 21(27)	E 69	E 35	E 1; E 1; E 1; E 1; E 1
good n	E 3	E 8		S 1; S 1

table 5: entries (E), subentries incl. run-ons (S) with numbers of sense dictincions

Nevertheless, it has to be pointed out that higher numbers do not necessarily imply better dictionaries. To arrive at conclusions of this kind considerable qualitative research is needed.[7]

3.2.2 Suffixations

Although they constitute lexical units in their own rights, suffixations frequently seem to be considered as not lexical enough to be included in the headwordlist. The standard argument is that it is uneconomical to define them exhaustively since their meaning is predictable by simple rules of English word formation.[8] All four dictionaries appear to follow this concept in principle, despite their otherwise very different policies where the presentation of semantically connected words is concerned.

For the purpose of this paper, the treatment of suffixations with *-ness* and *-ly* was compared, the suffixations of the adjective entries which were part of the former analysis were selected.

---

[7] Cf. for example Bogaards (1996).
[8] Cf. Stein (1985).

	OALD5	LDOCE3	COBUILD2	CIDE
number of entries	2	11	7	3
number of subentries incl. run-ons	18	3	47	32
number of mentions	6	11	0	7
number of suffixations covered	24	24	24	24
number of lexical units	38	51	65	42

table 6: *awkwardly - wildness*: totals

The results in table 6 show that LDOCE3 certainly takes the most economical approach by frequently just listing the suffixations at the end of entries, where they sometimes unfortunately give the impression of being part of the last sub-division. However, those that are considered worthy of being given entry status are dealt with thoroughly. The coverage in OALD5 is slightly more generous, but the totals give a smaller number of lexical units, assuming that mere mentionings of words with implied meanings can be counted as lexical units at all. CIDE with its policy of having subentries for separate senses manages to keep up, but what is certainly noticeable are the results for COBUILD2: here the suffixations are given as subentries in the numerous sections for meanings and uses. Thus, as can be seen in table 7, there are 4 subentries for *dully* in contrast to a mere mentioning in LDOCE3, 8 subentries for *lightly* which are distributed in 43 subdivisions of the entry for *light*.

	OALD5	LDOCE3	COBUILD2	CIDE
dully	S 1	m	S 1; S 1; S 1; S 1	S 1; S 1; S 1
lightly	S 3	E 5	S 1; S 1; S 1; S 1; S 1; S 1; S 1; S 1	S 1; S 1; S 1
goodness	E 3	E 6	E 2	S 1; S 1; E 1
kindness	S 2	E 2	S 1; E 1	S 1

table 7: entries (E), subentries incl. run-ons (S), mentions (m) with numbers of sense distinctions

Both in CIDE and in COBUILD2 the disadvantages of having sense-bound subentries becomes evident: firstly, the senses of the suffixations are spread over too many entries or subdivisions and thus can be hard to find; secondly, if there are meanings of suffixations that cannot be related to the senses of the adjective, these have to be dealt with in a separate entry, so that the same wordform can be found in entries as well as subentries with frequently insufficient crossreferences. The entries for *goodness* and *kindness*, also included in table 7, may serve as examples for this.

Altogether these results show strongly divergent ideas about the predictability of meaning from word formation rules.

3.2.3 Suffixes

The last point in this admittedly very selective analysis of the presentation of lexical units is the treatment of suffixes. Strictly speaking, suffixes are only semantic constituents, but not words and therefore not lexical units. Nevertheless, they are commonly included in the headword lists of learners' dictionaries, even if the corresponding suffixations are given in full entries.

Table 8 displays the results of a comparison of 24 suffixes.

	OALD5	LDOCE3	COBUILD2	CIDE
number of entries	23	25	14	25
number of subentries incl. run-ons	-	-	-	4
number of suffixes covered (total 24)	23	24	14	19
number of 'lexical units'	55	70	26	29

table 8: *-able* et al.

That COBUILD2 only provides 14 entries with 26 lexical units perhaps shows a different concept of the usefulness of the presentation of suffixes and cannot automatically be seen as a disadvantage. As can be seen from the entries for *-ish*, COBUILD2 seems to focus strongly on the productivity of word formation processes. What is perhaps the most central function of assigning lemma status and lexical units to suffixes in learners' dictionaries is to provide users with information about word formations such as, for example, suffixations like *tallish, smallish, tenish* etc., units that might be lexical but not lexicalised enough to appear in a dictionary.

OALD5

-ish *suff* **1** (with *ns* forming *adjs* and *ns*) of or from the specified country: ***Turkish*** ∘ ***Irish.*** **2** (with *ns* forming *adjs*) (*often derog*) of the nature of; resembling: ***childish*** ∘ ***freakish.*** **3** (with *adjs*) rather; approximately: ***reddish*** ∘ ***thirtyish.*** ▶ **-ishly** (with sense 2 forming *advs*): *foolishly.*

LDOCE3

-ish /ɪʃ/ *suffix* **1** [in nouns] the people or language of a particular country or place: *Are the British unfriendly?*| *learning to speak Turkish*|*She's Swedish.* **2** [in adjectives] of a particular place: *Spanish food* (=from Spain) **3** [in adjectives] typical of or like a particular type of person: *foolish behaviour* (=typical of a fool)|*Don't be so childish!* (=Don't behave like a child)|*snobbish* **4** [in adjectives] the ending of some adjectives that show disapproval: *selfish*|*raffish* **5** [in adjectives] rather; quite: *youngish* (=not very young, but not old either)|*tallish*| *reddish hair* **6** [in adjectives] *spoken* about; **approximately** (APPROXIMATE¹): *We'll expect you eightish.* (=at about 8 o'clock)|*He's fortyish.* (=about 40 years old)

COBUILD2

-ish /-ɪʃ/
1 **-ish** is added to adjectives to form adjectives which indicate that someone or something has a quality to a small extent. For example, if you say that something is largish, you mean it is fairly large. *She is tallish, brown-haired, and clear-skinned... With her was a youngish man in a dinner jacket. ...a tank of greenish water.* SUFFIX
2 **-ish** is added to nouns and names to form adjectives which indicate that someone or something is like a particular kind of person or thing. For example, 'childish' means like a child, or typical of a child. *She had entirely lost her girlish chubbiness. ...a man of monkish appearance. ...his affecting, Tom Petty-ish voice.* SUFFIX
3 **-ish** is added to words referring to times, dates, or ages to form words which indicate that the time or age mentioned is approximate. *I'll call you guys tomorrow. Noon-ish... The nurse was fiftyish.* SUFFIX

CIDE

-ish PLACE /-ɪʃ/ *combining form* used to form adjectives and nouns which say what country or area a person, thing or language comes from • *Spanish dancing* (=from Spain) • *Flemish lace* (=from Belgium) • *Are you English* (=from England)? • *I've always liked the Irish* (=people from Ireland). • *Do you speak Swedish* (=the language of Sweden)? • LP› **Combining forms**
-ish LIKE /-ɪʃ/ *combining form esp. disapproving* used to form adjectives which say what a person, thing or action is like • *foolish* • *mannish* • *outlandish*
-ish QUITE /-ɪʃ/ *combining form* added to adjectives to give the meaning to some degree; partly; quite • *He had a sort of reddish beard.* • *She was oldish – about 60, I'd say.* • *"Is he young?" "(Young)-ish, 40 maybe."* • *We'll start at sevenish* (= about 7 o'clock). • LP› **Approximate numbers**

In spite of the fairly extensive coverage of suffixes (including the extra pages on word formation which are provided by LDOCE3 and CIDE), explicit information about limitations or productivity of rules is hardly ever given.[9]

4 Conclusion

The concept of lexical units as the basic units in dictionaries can certainly be seen as central to lexicographic research[10] but does not lend itself easily to quantitative analyses.

The resulting figures of such comparative assessments have to be treated with caution since the policies of classifying senses in the four dictionaries are so different that it is difficult to find a comparable numerical basis.

Not every countable unit is a lexical unit, and even if one stretches the concept a bit, not every lexical unit is countable and not every countable lexical unit has to be a necessary lexical unit. And of course, the quality of presentation might be considered to be beyond countability.

Nevertheless, there are insights to be gained into the accessibility of lexical units from comparing the structuring policies of the four dictionaries.

On the level of macrostructure, it seems that the dictionaries structured according to formal rather than semantic principles come out as superior. Both COBUILD2 and LDOCE3 take a clearly polysemous approach, that of LDOCE3 seems preferable due to the additional divisions into word classes.

Generally, semantically orientated policies intend to provide the user with additional information on semantic relationships which certainly can be valuable, especially for

9 Cf. also Stein (1985)
10 In theory, lexical units are the only really relevant units for many fields of analysis – it is essential for learners to know, for example, which senses of a word have been included in a dictionary, which are most frequent, which senses correlate with which syntactic behaviour etc.

encoding purposes. For decoding purposes, however, a clear and transparent structure with fewer subentries facilitates looking up considerably. On the whole, formal structuring principles seem to be preferable since they are more consistently applicable.

What is most notable where the microstructure is concerned, is that many of the prominent innovations in the new editions already present considerable improvements with the aim to make it easier for users to find their way through often numerous sense distinctions.

The *signposts* for separate senses, and the so called *menues* for extremely long entries in LDOCE3, and COBUILD2's *superheadwords* which give broad meaning or grammatical divisions certainly are a step in the right direction. The subdivisions which are used by OALD5, for example, for extremely long verb entries, as in the case of *turn* or *do*, are comparatively rare and typographically less convincing. The fact that CIDE provides *guide words* only for entries and practically no devices to subdivide the microstructure must be seen as a considerable drawback. However, a hierarchy of senses as in OALD5 or even CIDE seems to be just what is missing in some of the longish entries with large numbers of sense distinctions in LDOCE3 or COBUILD2. The long lists in LDOCE3 could perhaps be improved by treating phrases separately from senses, although there are arguments in favour of a frequency based order. Since the subdivisions in the COBUILD2 entries are based on semantic considerations anyway, it might often be profitable to include fairly broad categorisations, thus giving a general meaning before analysing different uses.[11]

Summing up, there is certainly still room for improvement in the presentation of lexical units in all four dictionaries and I hope I have been able to point out some ways to achieve this within the different frameworks of the dictionaries. Nevertheless, it can be objectively stated that in this respect too, the new generation of learners dictionaries is definitely much closer to the perfect learners' dictionary than the previous ones.

Bibliography

Collins Cobuild English Language Dictionary (COBUILD1) ([1]1987): John Sinclair (ed.) — London, Glasgow: Collins.

Longman Dictionary of Contemporary English (LDOCE2) ([2]1987): Della Summers (ed.) — Harlow: Longman.

Oxford Advanced Learner's Dictionary (OALD4) ([4]1989): Anthony P. Cowie (ed.) — Oxford: OUP.

Ayto, John R. (1983): "On specifying meaning". — In: R.R.K. Hartmann (ed.): Lexicography: Principles and Practice (London: Acacemic Press) 89-98.

Béjoint, Henri (1994): Tradition and Innovation in Modern English Dictionaries. — Oxford: Clarendon Press.

---

[11] A defining practice which has also been employed in the valency dictionary described in Herbst (this volume).

Bogaards, Paul (1996): "Dictionaries for Learners of English". — In: International Journal of Lexicography 9/4, 277-320.
Cruse, D. A. (1986): Lexical Semantics. — Cambridge: CUP.
Hansen, Barbara, Klaus Hansen, Albrecht Neubert, Manfred Schentke (1982): Englische Lexikologie. — Leipzig: Verlag Enzyklopädie.
Herbst, Thomas (1996): "On the way to the perfect learners' dictionary: a first comparison of OALD5, LDOCE3, COBUILD2 and CIDE". — In: International Journal of Lexicography 9/4, 321-357.
Kempson, Ruth M. (1977): Semantic Theory. — Cambridge: CUP.
Leech, Geoffrey (1981): Semantics. — London: Penguin.
Lipka, Leonhard (^{2}1992): An Outline of English Lexicology. — Tübingen: Niemeyer.
Lyons, John (1977): Semantics. — Cambridge: CUP.
— (1995): Linguistic Semantics. — Cambridge: CUP.
Moon, Rosamund (1987): "Monosemous words and the dictionary". — In: A.P. Cowie (ed.): The Dictionary and the language learner (Tübingen: Niemeyer) 173-182.
Palmer, Frank R. (^{2}1981): Semantics. — Cambridge: CUP.
Robins, Robert H. (1987): "Polysemy and the Lexicographer". — In: R. Burchfield (ed.): Studies in Lexicography (Oxford: OUP) 52-75.
Schneider, Edgar W. (1988): Variabilität, Polysemie und Unschärfe der Wortbedeutung. — Tübingen: Niemeyer.
Stein, Gabriele (1985): "Word-formation in Modern English Dictionaries". — In: R. Ilson (ed.): Dictionaries, Lexicography and Language Learning (Oxford: Pergamon Press) 35-44.

Appendix

list of orthographical forms analysed:
able, act, action, as, awkward, bad, ball, bat, bit, book, boxer, break, calf, call, can, careless, case, catch, charge, chest, cold, commission, corn, correct, crazy, cut, deal, direct, down, dull, eager, ear, expire, fair, fast, foot, found, fresh, funny, good, happy, head, high, in, jam, kind, lie, light, lock, mad, mean, mess, mole, mouth, odd, pen, plant, port, position, possession, post, right, row, run, rung, shock, soft, sole, spirit, strange, strong, swallow, tap, the, thick, touch, wild

list of suffixations analysed:
awkwardly, awkwardness, carelessly, carelessness, crazily, craziness, dully, dullness, goodness, highly, kindly, kindness, lightly, lightness, madly, madness, oddly, oddness, rightly, rightness, thickly, thickness, wildly, wildness

list of suffixes analysed:
-able, -ate, -ation, -ee, -eer, -esque, - ette, -ful, -ible, -ing, -ish, -ism, -ist, -ite, -ity ,-less, -let, -like, -ly, -ness, -wise, -y

David Heath

The treatment of international varieties

1 Introduction

Writing in 1877, of the late twentieth century, Henry Sweet predicted that "... by that time England, America and Australia will be speaking mutually unintelligible languages, owing to their independent changes of pronunciation." (cf. Crystal 1995: 112). Sweet was wrong. Despite considerable variations in pronunciation, the varieties spoken in these three countries are mutually intelligible. If we extend the comparison to their spelling, grammar and morphology, we find even fewer differences between them, and those that we do find affect a limited, listable number of words. The truth of this statement will probably not be disputed, but we cannot claim that it applies to the lexicon. Yet it is essentially as a source of information about individual words that a dictionary is produced, bought and used.

The facts of the matter seem then to be clear: the accepted pronunciation standards will enable learners to understand, and be understood by, native speakers of English and other non-native speakers using one of these three varieties which is different from the one these learners are familiar with. Nor will spelling, grammar or morphology seriously impede understanding. Indeed, writing of his analysis of forty newspapers printed on the same day throughout the whole of the English-speaking world, including South-East Asia and the Caribbean, Crystal (1995: 300) says "... the exercise leaves us with the overriding impression of limited but intriguing diversity, and above all of the unifying power of the standard language." His appraisal echoes Quirk et al (1985: 18-19) "The degree of acceptance of a single standard of English throughout the world, across a multiplicity of political and social systems, is a truly remarkable phenomenon ... the uniformity is especially close in neutral or formal styles of written English on subject matter not of obviously localized interest."

We can now state the dictionary-makers' dilemma: With the exception of spelling, dictionaries are not primarily concerned with those areas in which diversity is least marked since the main demand made of a learners' dictionary is that it describe words, including many which are not neutral or formal in style and which do refer to subject matter of strong localized interest. This is a task which, in part, dictionary makers have imposed on themselves by steadily encroaching on the domain of the encyclopedia, albeit gingerly, and by exploiting corpora and research into discourse so as to be more confident about making statements about spoken language. Identifying the "facts" of the language, its diversity and usages is one thing, it is perhaps another to wish to "enrich" what began as essentially dictionaries of British English by taking account, in a number of ways, of other varieties.

Why should four British publishing houses want to cast their nets wider than British English, and how successful have they been in doing so? Up to 8 international varieties beyond Sweet's three are labelled in at least one of the four dictionaries, though only

LDOCE claims to take account of all 11. Nowhere in the front matter of any of these four dictionaries is any precise statement made about the status of the varieties. Are the dictionary-makers responding to a perceived growing influence of American English, and perhaps other varieties? CIDE (viii), for example, claims to cover "... British, American, Australian and other usages, pronunciations, spellings and grammatical patterns". Have the dictionary makers been led along this path by the use of corpora that allow them to describe more reliably usages outside Britain? Like CIDE, COBUILD refers to Australian, and interestingly Singaporean, English as important corpus sources without, however, granting these varieties any special status in its labelling policy. LDOCE claims to have considered "a wide range of English-speaking countries", but, like OALD, does not specify any beyond Britain and the United States while listing eleven national labels in its front-matter. Does providing more encyclopedic information entail reference to more varieties? Is this also true of the increased amount of pragmatic information to be retrieved from labels, illustrations, usage notes and short articles?

We see this issue from a different perspective when we consider the learners' needs. When reading they come across non-World Standard English (WSE) forms not used in the variety they are learning and also forms which have both a non-WSE and a WSE meaning. When writing they are aware that some words do not conform to the standard they are learning, for example the *travelled/traveled* and *subway* ('underpass')/*subway* ('underground railway') distinctions. I looked for a reliable source of information about those variations between varieties which learners might reasonably expect to find in their dictionary, and found what I was looking for in the *Cambridge Encyclopedia of the English Language* (CEEL). I wanted to consult an authoritative publication written for non-specialists which is, in my experience, also widely used by native speaker and non-native speaker EFL teachers. Most of the words that I discuss in this paper are taken from CEEL. I will proceed by considering in turn a small but typical and frequent sample of words illustrating variation between British and American English in spelling, pronunciation, grammar/morphology and lexis. Encyclopedic and pragmatic information lie within the scope of a paper of this kind but constraints of time and space forced me to omit them. Although no other varieties are considered systematically, my approach is justified because extending my brief would not have led to a fair comparison as the dictionaries do not have a common policy on the treatment of other varieties. This comparison, restricted as it is in scope, will nevertheless serve my purposes well. I do not want to demonstrate the putative relative strengths and weaknesses of these four outstanding dictionaries, but rather to show, from the perspective of a practising teacher in touch with learners' attitudes and needs, some pitfalls that await the dictionary-maker claiming to produce a dictionary for the advanced learner which goes beyond British English, or the "neutral" World Standard English.

Since I could not compare more than a cross-section of entries for each of the features mentioned above, I will give a brief description of my findings and finish with some general conclusions which I offer as the contribution of an experienced teacher of advanced learners.

2 The varieties behind the dictionaries

COBUILD speaks of a 70% British and 25% American English contribution and mentions Australia and Singapore as contributing 5%. CIDE claims to give equal weight to British and American English and mentions Australia. The label Australian is widely used in the dictionary, but not as systematically as the introduction suggests. LDOCE talks of British and American English without giving percentages, and of a wide coverage of other varieties. OALD refers to British and American English with no specific references to other varieties. CIDE uses six varieties labels, OALD five and LDOCE 11. COBUILD refers to varieties apart from British and American in the text, but does not list any labels. The following labels are found in at least one of the four dictionaries: British, American, Australian, Canadian, Caribbean, Indian, Irish, New Zealand, Pakistani, Scottish, South African.

I will discuss the following features: spelling, pronunciation, grammar, morphology and vocabulary (individual words and lexical units) and some encyclopedic information, including country-specific information.

2.1 Spelling

All four dictionaries discuss spelling differences in the front matter and give reliable but not identical information on the following 14 words with different spellings in British and American English:

> *aesthetic/esthetic; appal/appall; catalogue/catalog; centre/center; cheque/check; doughnut/donut; ensure/insure; honour/honor; largesse/largess; mould/mold; offence/offense; plough/plow; vice/vise.*

The treatment of these words is satisfactory in all four dictionaries although CIDE and OALD are not wholly consistent in their cross-referencing. Given that not all learners are familiar with spellings in the variety they are not learning, it is important that

(a) both forms should be cross-referenced to facilitate the understanding of unknown spellings, i.e. that variants be given at the British *and* the American spelling.

(b) where a word is polysemous or where a spelling could be misleading, as at American *check* (noun) equivalent of British *cheque*, it should be cross-referenced to the benchmark form (British *cheque*, in this case).

(c) definitions should be used to avoid ambiguity.

(d) if, as CIDE claims, another variety (Australian) is considered, the labelling must be consistent. My impression is that users of CIDE are expected to know that if no label is used, they ought to assume that Australian and British spellings concur.

2.2 Pronunciation

There is detailed discussion of pronunciation norms in all four dictionaries, including tables of transcription symbols, with comments on individual transcription symbols. The following 30 words with different pronunciations in Received Pronunciation (RP) and General American (Gen Am) were checked:

anti-; asthma; ate; capsule; clerk; clique; data; derby; erase; fracas; geyser; gooseberry; goulash; herb; leisure; lever; lieutenant; medicine; missile; nephew; nougat; progress; route; schedule; tissue; tomato; vase; wrath; z.

COBUILD includes all 30 words but only indicates both pronunciations in 23 cases, CIDE scores 30 and 26, LDOCE 30 and 29, OALD 30 and 27.

In the front matter of COBUILD the systematic variations between RP /ɑ:/and Gen Am /æ/, as in 'aunt' RP /ɑːnt/ and Gen Am /ænt/, are explained. The use of the symbol /oʊ/ for 'goat' RP (/gəʊt/ would be expected) and Gen Am requires a knowledge of phonetic transcription and phonology that can be expected of only a minority of users. Similarly, the use of the raised r in /fɜːʳ/ will surely suggest that RP has a rhotic pronunciation. CIDE uses some unfamiliar symbols, /ea/ for the vowel in RP 'hair' and /ʊɜ/ for the vowel in RP 'pure'. However, since most of the detailed information on pronunciation is given in the Language Portraits (short articles in the main body of the dictionary) it may well be overlooked. LDOCE gives /ɜ/ in the transcription table but uses /ɜː/ in the transcriptions and the unfamiliar symbol /iə/ for the vowel at the end of 'peculiar' rather than the conventional /ɪə/. OALD has the same policy as COBUILD with regard to systematic vowel variation as in RP /ɑːnt/ and Gen Am /ænt/. For the user it is essential that, where applicable, both pronunciations should be given in full and be unambiguously labelled. The use of one symbol for what are phonetically clearly distinct pronunciations, as with 'goat', should be avoided.

2.3 Grammar

The following 13 common differences between British and American English were compared:

1. verb forms: *dived/dove, sneaked/snuck, have you got/do you have?*
2. use of articles: *the River Thames/the Hudson River, half an hour/a half hour, in future/in the future, in hospital/in the hospital*;
3. number with collectives: *the government is - are/the government is;*
4. prepositions: *twenty to four/twenty of four, five past eight/five after eight, Monday to Friday/Monday through Friday, on heat/in heat, for ages/in ages*

	both forms given	British form given and labelled	American form given and labelled
COBUILD	8/13	4/13	6/13
CIDE	10/13	5/13	7/13
LDOCE	11/13	8/13	8/13
OALD	12/13	6/13	6/13

How much grammatical information do users expect to find in a dictionary? Most probably they do not expect to find grammatical information and few will consult a dictionary rather than a grammar to find it. The use that is made of any grammatical information is likely to be incidental. However, if users are looking for it in their dictionary, where would they look? Surely only under the word they are interested in. This means that in the case of words such as *team*, *orchestra*, *group* etc where there are systematic differences in the use of number between British and American English, this information should be given at every relevant word. We must not assume that learners will infer that *orchestra* and *team* behave like *family* and *group*. CIDE does label these words very systematically but only in the front matter is the user told that they can be used with a plural verb in Britain and Australia but only with a singular verb in American English. A further complicating factor is that it is becoming increasingly difficult to state unambiguously what is American usage and non-American usage in this area.

2.4 Vocabulary

Following Benson, Benson, Ilson (1986) we can postulate the following categories to distinguish words and word meanings in different varieties.

1. Words which are not part of WSE and which reflect cultural differences:
   American *Ivy League*, British *A-Levels*, Australian *billabong* (a stagnant pool)
2. Words or phrases which are used in one variety and have a synonym in another:
   British *current account*, *estate car*, American *checking account*, *station wagon*
3. Words which have one WSE meaning and at least one variety-specific meaning:
   WSE *caravan* "group of travellers in the desert" British English *caravan* "vehicle to be lived in", American *trailer*
4. Words which have a WSE meaning and a synonym in one or more of the varieties:
   WSE *undertaker* , American *mortician*
   WSE *pharmacist*, British *chemist*, American *druggist*
5. Words which have no WSE-meaning but have different meanings in two or more of the varieties:
   British *flyover* corresponds to American *overpass*
   American *flyover* corresponds to British *fly-past*
6. Some words occur in two or more varieties but are used more frequently in one than in another, or other varieties:
   British *shop*, American *store*, British *flat*, American *apartment*

I compared the treatment of the following 14 British words and usages since users will expect to be told if a word is used in one variety rather than others, even if that variety is British English, presumably the benchmark variety for all four dictionaries.

jiggery-pokery; *Jock* (= Scot); *joint* (= piece of meat); *jolly* (as in jolly good); *junction* (= American intersection); *junior school*; *kibosh* (as in to put the kibosh on something); *Kite Mark* (a symbol used on goods to indicate quality); *knock on* (used in rugby); L (meaning learner driver); *landlord* (used of a man who runs a pub); *last orders* (used in British pubs shortly before closing time); *the Law Society*; *lbw* (used in cricket)

	word or phrase included	labelled British
COBUILD	8	8
CIDE	12	9
LDOCE	11	7
OALD	10	9

These 10 culture-specific words are exponents of category 1 above:

Congress; Groundhog Day; the inner city; the Ivy League; the Law Society; lbw; a primary election; the Royal Family; solicitor; Thanksgiving Day;

	included
COBUILD	7
CIDE	7
LDOCE	7
OALD	7

These 11 words are exponents of category 2 above:

ringroad - beltway; guard's van - caboose; current account - checking account; biscuit - cookie; camp bed - cot; driving licence - driver's license; flautist - flutist; motorway - freeway; petrol - gasoline; Girl Guide/guide - Girl Scout; level crossing - grade crossing;

	Brit. word included	cross ref to Amer. word	Amer. word included	cross ref to Brit. word
COBUILD	11	8	9	6
CIDE	11 (6 = Aust.) 1 reference to Language Portrait	11	11 (2 = Aust.)	10
LDOCE	11	10	11	10
OALD	11	11	11	8

These 6 words are exponents of category 3 above:

bonnet - hood; boot - trunk; caravan - trailer; chemist/chemist's - druggist/drugstore; engine driver - engineer; holiday - vacation;

	Brit. word included	cross reference to Amer. word	Amer. word included	cross ref to Brit. word
COBUILD	5	5	5	5
CIDE	6	6	6	6
LDOCE	5	5	6	5
OALD	6	6	6	6

3 General conclusions

The prime issue here is whether lexicographers can reliably identify, and describe, a standard core English, i.e. non-variety specific English or World Standard English, and include those variants from this standard which they consider undisputed, frequent and "disponible". Linguists may argue that this may well not be feasible at any one time and that given the dynamism of English no reliable statements about a standard core English can be made, an objection that is undoubtedly valid. However, dictionaries, and especially learners' dictionaries, are regarded as absolute authorities, since they are often the most reliable systematic source of information about the language available to the learner. Hence, users should not be given the impression, an impression that is reinforced by the statements made in the advertising material put out by the publishing houses and by the front matter of the dictionaries themselves, that every non-WSE feature of several varieties is included. Indeed, a title including the word 'international', or perhaps even 'contemporary', does nothing to dispel this illusion. If a British publisher takes this putative variety-neutral English, WSE, rather than British English as the benchmark, users will be misled if such British uses as *landlord* ("a person who runs a pub") or *to put the kibosh on something* are not labelled. Present practice may confuse users; a form that is not labelled could either be one that is used in WSE or one that it is used in British English, but not necessarily in WSE.

I hope to have demonstrated that, with regard to the international varieties, learners' dictionaries can only treat spelling, pronunciation and morphology systematically and comprehensively. Even so, can they, and should they, go beyond British and American English in these three areas? Since in any one variety many words will be used in one or more senses which are distinct from WSE usage, the dictionaries ought to state quite unambiguously what their limititations are in this respect. Finally, given the influence of American English on other varieties, how many "canonical" statements can be made about the lexis of any other variety?

Bibliography

Benson, Morton, Evelyn Benson, Robert Ilson (1986): Lexicographic Description of English. — Amsterdam: John Benjamins.

Crystal, David (1995): The Cambridge Encyclopedia of the English Language. — Cambridge: CUP.

Quirk, Randolph, Sidney Greenbaum, Geoffrey Leech, Jan Svartvik (1985): A Comprehensive Grammar of the English Language. — London, New York: Longman.

John Ayto

Lexical evolution and learners' dictionaries

It is now nearly two decades since the first edition of the *Longman Dictionary of Contemporary English* was published - an event which set in train the competition between British publishers to bring out ever better and more successful ELT dictionaries, which itself produced the four dictionaries discussed at the colloquium '*The Perfect Learners' Dictionary (?)*'. In that time the vocabulary of English has undergone a lot of changes. Its expressive power has been increased by the introduction of large numbers of neologisms, reduced by the loss of some palaeologisms. Foreign learners who use a dictionary compiled in that remote period of flared trousers and Labour governments could by no means rely on it to decode every unfamiliar vocabulary item they encounter today in conversation, in reading current texts, etc.

This is not a topic that has received much serious attention. Academic criticism of learners' dictionaries these days tends to focus on other areas, such as systems of grammatical description and coverage of collocation, and treatment of vocabulary change generally gets short shrift. A sign, perhaps, of a certain disdain, in reaction to the vulgar claims of increasing size on the covers of dictionaries, and the obsession with 'amusing' neologisms in reviews of dictionaries in the popular press? But the testimony of non-native-speakers themselves on the subject of neologisms, from learners to language professionals, tends to be that it is vital for them to have access to the latest lexical developments in English. This *is* an important aspect of the role of learners' dictionaries, not least now that our tools for monitoring the lexicon are so much more sophisticated than they were twenty years ago.

The purpose of this brief survey, therefore, is to examine how the *Oxford Advanced Learner's Dictionary* (OALD), the *Longman Dictionary of Contemporary English* (LDOCE), the *Cobuild English Dictionary* (COBUILD), and the *Cambridge International English Dictionary* (CIDE) have gone about monitoring lexical evolution over the last two decades. My primary intention is not to identify the 'best' of the four dictionaries in this respect. My comparisons are mainly between successive editions of the same dictionary, rather than between different dictionaries. However, in the case of CIDE, there is no previous edition, so that is clearly not possible, and I have compared it directly with the other dictionaries.

I have based my comparison on two sections of the alphabet, *la* to *lazy* and *tall* to *telex*, which between them account for between 1.4% and 1.5% of the text of all the dictionaries. Looking at each dictionary edition alongside its successor, I have identified what the new edition adds to its predecessor, and what it omits, in terms of lexical entries and also in terms of individual senses. Apart from phrasal verbs, I have not included in my survey what might broadly be termed idiomatic phrases, although different dictionaries' ideas on what constitutes a lexical entry as opposed to an idiomatic phrase do tend to muddy the waters of comparison.

I have then gone on to examine each dictionary's new intake chronologically, in an attempt to pin down exactly how much of the new material is 'new' in the sense that it has only recently come into existence and how much of it is 'new' in the sense that it was not in the previous edition.

In the combined sections examined, OALD4 added 53 entries to OALD3 and took away 76; OALD5 added 33 entries to OALD4 and took away 73; LDOCE2 added 45 entries to LDOCE1 and took away 51; LDOCE3 added 111 entries to LDOCE2 and took away 21; COBUILD2 added 54 entries to COBUILD1 and took away 44. Extrapolated over the entire dictionary, these figures show that OALD4 added 3763 and took away 5400, an overall reduction of 1637; OALD5 added 2355 and took away 5211, an overall reduction of 2856; LDOCE2 added 3015 and took away 3434, an overal reduction of 419; LDOCE3 added 7260 and took away 1374, an overall increase of 5886; and COBUILD2 added 3763 and took away 3066, an overall increase of 697 (see Appendix: Table 1).

These dictionaries (like most other new editions of dictionaries) make great play of their additions (COBUILD2, for instance, trumpets on its jacket "more than 4000 new words and meanings"; OALD5 says it has "2,300 new words and meanings"; and LDOCE3, less explicitly, boasts of "wider coverage"). They make no overt claim to contain more words than previous editions, but that is surely the message that many readers of their blurbs will subliminally receive. However, the truth is evidently somewhat different. Three of these new editions are actually smaller in terms of lexical entries than their predecessors. One is modestly larger, and only one, LDOCE3, is much bigger.

What is the story that underlies the statistics? It is undeniable that OALD3 contained a good deal of vocabulary that was well past its sell-by date as far as the needs of foreign learners were concerned, and not surprisingly, LDOCE1's headword list was influenced by OALD3's, and took on board some of its more elderly members. Add to that the increasing availability of reliable tools for gauging frequency, and it is clear why subsequent editions have had some hard pruning to do. Golden oldies to have bitten the dust include *laager, lady of the bedchamber, lambkin, Lammas, landgrave, lazaretto, tallyman, tatterdemalion* and *Te Deum*. In the light of this wholesale clearout, it is only surprising that *lascar, tarboosh* and *taradiddle* should have survived into OALD4, and that LDOCE3 continues to this day to find space for *lampblack*. COBUILD did not start with any of this 19th-century excess baggage, but even so, there was apparently no shortage of entries in COBUILD1 whose current frequency did not justify their retention in COBUILD2 (e.g. *lady's maid, lancet, landau* and *laudanum*).

Turning to individual meanings (see Appendix: Table 2), the story is very similar. Clear-cut comparisons between editions are not nearly so easy to make as they are with lexical items, but in estimating gains and losses I have tried to eliminate phenomena such as a meaning in one edition being split into two in the next, with no additional content. Losses outweigh gains in LDOCE and COBUILD, but a significant number of these are due to a lumping policy taking over from an earlier splitting policy: for instance, in LDOCE, meanings of the verb *laugh* such as "to bring, put, drive, etc. with laughing", "to cause (oneself) to become by laughing" and "to express with a laugh" have all been subsumed in the third edition under a far more general sense of *laugh*.

So, adjusting the lexical coverage of a dictionary to meet the needs of a contemporary usership is not just a matter of shovelling in new items. As every lexicographer well knows, to reflect the changing language, some words must be let go. That is an improvement. It makes for a better, more relevant dictionary. Perhaps it would be advantageous, as well as more honest, to publicize the pruning as enthusiastically as the replenishing.

I shall now look behind the bare figures for additions, and see what sort of new words we are being presented with in these dictionaries, and in particular what their chronological profile is. There is one apparent disparity that needs to be dealt with at once: the very much larger number of new entries in LDOCE3 than in the other dictionaries. A small proportion of these can be accounted for as entries for present and past participial adjectives (e.g. *tantalizing* and *tangled*) which in LDOCE1 were indicated only by means of a code. But that aside, it would appear that, unless the sample I looked at was very unrepresentative, LDOCE3 did indeed receive a large injection of vocabulary that was not in LDOCE2. It has benefited in particular from a substantial increase in the number of compound nouns, of which examples can be seen under *land, last, law* and *tax*.

Recalling those blurbs claiming so many thousand 'new words and meanings', what is the reality that lies behind that word 'new'? To get a clearer idea of the chronological profile of the additional entries in these dictionaries, I have matched them up with the dates of their earliest recorded examples in the OED. The results can be seen in Table 3 (cf. Appendix), in terms of the percentage of new entries originating in a particular period. The results for OALD4 & 5 and LDOCE2 & 3 have been combined. The most immediately striking fact is probably that two fifths of the additions in OALD and LDOCE, and a third of those in COBUILD, are over a hundred years old (the record for the oldest, incidentally, goes to *landless* in LDOCE, which dates from the 11th century). As far as the 20th century goes, the first decade is poorly represented (by *lady's fingers, teeter-totter* and *telephone box*, as it happens). The teens do reasonably well, possibly because of a boost given to new vocabulary by World War I. There is a slight dropping off in the 20s and 30s. Then things pick up, and the 40s, 50s, and 60s are the most strongly represented decades of the century in terms of contributing additions to these dictionaries. The figures drop again for the 70s, and revive somewhat for the 80s. No items date from the 90s in this sample.

Overall, therefore, it seems this additional vocabulary may be 'new' inasmuch as it was not in previous editions, but the bulk of it is very far from being freshly minted: in OALD and LDOCE, only 11% of the new entries date from later than 1970 (in COBUILD, the figure is slightly higher).

What conclusions are we to draw from these statistics? They need to be looked at under three headings. First, the overall coverage of the dictionary. Second, its specific coverage of genuinely new vocabulary. Third, the way in which these are presented to those who use the dictionary.

Self-evidently, the date at which a word entered the language does not correlate with its contemporary currency. In this sample there are many pre-20th-century words that may have been excluded from previous editions for perfectly valid reasons - perceived unsuitablity or irrelevance, or infrequency - but which ten or twenty years on have gained in frequency (or their true frequency has been more accurately measured), or the perception of their relevance to the target usership has changed (*labia, law-maker, law-school, lamplight, tap water, tax return*, to take just a few examples). Others, to put it bluntly, will have been left out by mistake, and the mistake can now be rectified. Adequate coverage of present-day vocabulary may quite legitimately involve the addition of items that have been in existence for a long time.

As far as genuine neologisms go, are our learners' dictionaries doing a good enough job? Looking at entries coined in the 80s, if we extrapolate these percentages, we arrive at a total of 418 such items in OALD, 536 in LDOCE and 348 in COBUILD. What do these figures mean? Are they adequate or derisory? No one knows for certain how many new words come into a language each year, but a useful point of comparison may be the number of recent coinages deemed sufficiently established to be entered in OED2 and its supplements. There are 338 items (main entries, subentries, and new usages of existing entries) dated 1980 or later in OED2. To these can be added approximately 450 such items in the first two volumes of the OED Additions Series, giving a grand total of just under 800. Discounting about 17% of these as new applications of existing items, and bearing in mind the overall vastly greater scope of the OED, the figures for 80s entries in OALD, LDOCE, and COBUILD are not wildly at variance with this, which suggests that our learners' dictionaries are doing quite a good job in keeping abreast of vocabulary expansion.

Is it not, though, time for a little more honesty in the way in which all these adjustments to dictionaries' coverage are publicized? Is the dictionary-buying public, or at any rate the learners'-dictionary-buying public, not sophisticated enough to be told that revising a dictionary to meet current needs involves removing outdated or irrelevant vocabulary and introducing established items, as well as garnishing the whole with a few well-chosen recent coinages? Let us have an end to the weaselly equation of new entries with neologisms.

As I mentioned above, this sort of inter-edition comparison is not possible in the case of CIDE, so I shall conclude instead by contrasting the coverage in CIDE with that of the other three dictionaries.

It covers more or less the same waterfront. Of the additional vocabulary in OALD4 & 5 and COBUILD2, it includes about four fifths and three quarters respectively. But it does not follow LDOCE3 in its large expansion of the headword list; it has only half of LDOCE's new entries. Only 5% of words from the 80s in the other three dictionaries are not in CIDE. Over and above these, it includes several entries not in the other dictionaries. Extrapolated over the whole dictionary, there are about 2000 of these. However, their chronological distribution does not quite match that of the additional entries in the other three dictionaries: over half of them are pre-20th century, and the remainder are spread fairly evenly over the decades of this century. In the sample, there is just one term from the 80s: *televangelism*. When it comes to individual meanings, CIDE's approach to sense discrimination makes direct comparison difficult, but in this sample I was able to find only two meanings not to be found in the other dictionaries: the metaphorical use of *laager*, as in 'laager mentality', and *land* in the literal sense 'arrive', as in 'land on a square'. It would appear, from this sample, that CIDE is at least as adept at monitoring important new vocabulary coming into the language.

This is confirmed by taking a wider random sample of thirty recent introductions from across the alphabet and seeing which are included in our four dictionaries (see Table 4). In terms of sheer volume coverage of new vocabulary, LDOCE3 and CIDE do about 50% better than OALD5 and COBUILD2.

Bibliography

Collins Cobuild English Language Dictionary (COBUILD) (1987): John Sinclair (ed.). — London, Glasgow: Collins.

Longman Dictionary of Contemporary English (LDOCE) (1978): Paul Procter (ed.). — Harlow: Longman.

Longman Dictionary of Contemporary English (LDOCE2) (^{2}1987): Della Summers (ed.). — Harlow, London: Longman.

Oxford Advanced Learner's Dictionary (OALD3) (^{3}1974): Albert S. Hornby (ed.). — Oxford: OUP.

Oxford Advanced Learner's Dictionary (OALD4) (^{4}1989): Anthony P. Cowie (ed.). — Oxford: OUP.

Oxford English Dictionary (OED2) (^{2}1989): John Simpson, Edmund Weiner (eds.). — Oxford: OUP.

Oxford English Dictionary Additions Series, Volumes 1 & 2 (1993): John Simpson, Edmund Weiner (eds.). — Oxford: OUP.

Appendix

Table 1

OALD4 Additions

Lab., labia, labour-intensive, lace-up, lactation, lactose, lambswool, laminate, landform, landmass, largish, lasagna, last ditch, last minute, last rites, lat., late-comer, lateral thinking, Latin Church, laughing-stock, Law Lords, law of averages, lay into, laze about, lazy Susan, tampon, tan., tandoori, tap water, tape-recording, taramasalata, tarot, tasting, tauten, tax-deductible, tax haven, taxing, tax-man, taxonomist, taxonomy, tax return, tbsp, tea towel, tear-jerker, technical college, technical hitch, teeny-weeny, teensy-weensy, teeny-bopper, teeshirt, TEFL, telephone box, telephone number, teletext, telex (verb)

OALD4 Deletions

Labourite, lac, laconicism, lade, lading, lady of the bedchamber, lady's maid, lag (= prisoner), laic, laicize, lake dwelling, lambkin, Lammas, lamp oil, lancers, land forces, landing party, landgrave, langsyne, langur, lap (= act of lapping), lap-strap, larboard, larn, larrup, Last Day, lateen sail, lay low, lay open, lay waste, lazar, lazaretto, Lazarus, tally clerk, tally-ho, tallyman, talus, tamale, Tammany, tanner (= coin), tantalus, tap room, tapis, tapster, tare (= weed), tarpon, tatterdemalion, taw, tawse, tax collector, taximeter, teaching machine, tea dance, tea garden, tea gown, tea house, tea kettle, tearless, tea wagon, tec, techy, Te Deum, teetotum, teg, tegument, telecast, telfer

OALD5 Additions

labour force, labouring, lager lout, laid-back, lakeside, lamplit, LAN, land-based, lap-top, laser printer, later, Latino, launcher, laurel wreath, lavatorial, tape-record, tax avoidance, tax disc, tax evasion, tax-exempt, tax inspector, tax relief, tax shelter, T-bone, teacart, team-mate, teeming, tele-cottage, telephone tapping, telethon, teleworking

OALD5 Deletions

laager, labour exchange, lace into, lachrymal, lack for, lactic, ladies' man, ladle out, lady chapel, Lady Day, lagging, lake (= colour), Lake Poets, lam, lambskin, lame (verb), lampblack, lamprey, lancer, land-holder, landing-field, landing-net, landlubber, landsman, landwards, lantern-jawed, lapidary, largo, lariat, lascar, latchkey child, layover, tamarind, tamarisk, tambour, tamable, tam o'shanter, taps, tar (= sailor), taradiddle, tarantella, tarboosh, tare (= weight), tarmacadam, taro, tarsal, tarsus, tat (verb), tatting, tea strainer, tea things, tea tray, tea urn, technocracy, telegrapher, telegraphist, telegraph line, telegraph wire, telephotograph, telephotography

LDOCE2 Additions

laboured, labour-intensive, labour-saving, lady's fingers, laid-back, lakh, laminar flow, LAN, lance corporal, landmass, laparoscopy, lap-top, laser printer, lash-up, lassitude, last-minute, last post, later, lateral thinking, lavatorial, lawn mower, lawn party, layperson, laywoman, lazybones, tandoori, tape-record, tape recording, taramasalata, target (verb), tauten, tax-deductible, taxing, taxman, tax payer, tax shelter, technical college, Technicolor, teepee, teeter-totter, telegraphy, telekinesis, tele-marketing, telephone box, teletext

LDOCE2 Deletions

Labourite, lambskin, lamblike, lamming, lancers, land army, land breeze, land crab, landed interests, lapse rate, large-hearted, large-minded, larrup, laryngeal, laryngoscope, lateen sail, -latry, laugh down, laundress, lave, lavender (= coloured), lay at, tallyman, tamale, tamarisk, Tammany, tangible assets, tanning, tansy, tarboosh, tarsal (= bone), tatas, tatter, tawse, teaching machine, teacupful, teakettle, tearless, tea strainer, tea table, teatime, tea tray, tachy, Te Deum, tegument, tele, telepathist, telephony, telephotograph, telephotography, televisual

LDOCE3 Additions

labia, labour camp, labour force, labour movement, labour relations, lace-up, lactate, ladyfinger, Lady Muck, lakeside, lam, lambada, lamebrain, lamplight, lamplighter, landfill, landing charge, landless, land office, land owner, land reform, land registry, landscape architecture, landscape mode, land-scaper, laparoscope, lap belt, lap robe, larcenist, lard-ass, large-scale, largish, laser disk, last call, last hurrah, last name, last orders, last rites, late-breaking, late-night, Latino, latke, latter-day saints, laugh lines, laughter lines, launcher, laundry list, lav, lavender bag, lavender water, laver, laver bread, law court, law enforcement, law-enforcement agent, law firm, Law Lords, law maker, lawman, lawn chair, lawn sign, law school, layaway, layover, layup, tampax, tamper-evident, tamper-proof, tamper-resistant, tangled, tank top, tank up, tanned, tantalizing, Tao, Taoiseach, tapas, tape drive, tapered, tarty, tasting, tater, tattie, tattle-tale, taupe, tax avoidance, tax bracket, tax break, tax-deferred, tax disc, tax dodge, tax evasion, tax-exempt, tax exile, tax inspector, tax relief, tax return, tax year, T-ball, tbs, teacher's pet, teammate, tea shop, tea urn, techie, technicolour, techno, technophobe, teed off, teen, TEFL, tel, telecommuter, telegraph line, telegraph wire, telephone call, telephone number, telephone pole, telesales, Teletype, teletypewriter, television licence, teleworker

LDOCE3 Deletions

laager, lace into, la-di-da, lag (= prisoner), lake (= colour), lamasery, lamprey, lantern slide, lap (= action of lapping), larkspur, lay (= poem), lay brother, lay sister, laze away, tally-ho, tan (= tangent), tarn, taximeter, teach-in, technical knockout, telemeter

COBUILD2 Additions

Lab., Labour Day, labour camp, laboured, labrador, lacquered, -laden, ladybug, lam, lambast, laminate, landfill, laptop, largo, lasagne, laser disk, laser printer, Latino, launch pad, laundry list, lavatorial, lawmaker, lawman, layperson, tall tale, tapas, tarty, task-based, tasting, taupe, Taurus, tax break, tax return, tba, T-bone steak, techie, techno, technocratic, tectonic, tectonics, teen, teenaged, teepee, teething problems, Teflon, telecast, telecommuter, telecommuting, telegenic, telegraph pole, telephony, televisual, teleworker, teleworking

COBUILD2 Deletions

labial, ladder (verb), Lady Muck, lady's maid, lag (= prisoner), lam (verb), lambskin, lamplit, lancet, landau, Land-Rover, lang., languishing, lanyard, latchkey child, lattice window, laudanum, launch out, lavender water, lay (= poem), lay about, lay by, lay over, layette, lazybones, tallish, tammy, tam o'shanter, Tampax, tannery, tannic acid, tapedrive, tapir, tappet, tattooist, teachable, tearing, Teasmaid, tea strainer, teethe, telegraphic, telegraphese, teleology, Teletype

In CIDE but not in OALD5, LDOCE3, or COBUILD2

laager, laddish, la dolce vita, lady bountiful, lag (= arrest), lamington, lampstand, lamprey, land-poor, land tenure, land use, Land of the Rising Sun, larcenous, larrikin, Last Supper, law of supply and demand, lawn bowling, lay brother, lay sister, tally-ho, target language, tax allowance, taxiway, tea ball, tea strainer, teacher-training college, teakettle, teddy (= bodice), televangelism

Table 2

Individual senses

In OALD5, not in OALD3

label (noun) 2, 3, (verb) 2, lacquer 2, lactic acid 2, lad 2, 3, ladder 2, lagoon 2, lair 2, land 2a, b, c, 3b, landlady 2, languish 2, [2]lap (noun) 1, (verb), lapdog 2, large 2, [2]lark 2, last (verb) 2, 4, lather 3, lattice 2, laugh 2, launder 2, law 4, layer (verb), lay out 3, lazy 2, tally (noun), tangent 2, tangerine 2, tangle 3, [1]tap 2, tape 2b, 3, [2]taper 2, tar 2, Tarmac b, task (verb), [1]taste 4, [2]taste 4, Taurus b, taut 2, 3, tawdry 2, tea 1c, 2, 3b, teach 2, [1]tear 4, tease 2, 4, teat 2, technical 3, 4, technicality 2, Technicolor 2, technology b, telescope (verb) 2, television 2, telex b

In OALD3, not in OALD5

laborious 3, lace (verb) 2, lady 4, 7, lame 3, landed 1, 3, landmark 1, lane 3, languor 2, [2]lap (noun) 2, (verb), lapse 4, large 2, late 4, lathe 4, lay 7, layer (noun) 2, 4, (verb), tally 2, tank 2, [1]tap (noun) 2, (verb) 3, tartar 2, task (verb), tax (verb) 4, tee 2, [1]teem 1

In LDOCE3, not in LDOCE1

label 2, lace (verb) 4, 5, lad 2, 3, ladyship 2, lagoon 2, lake 2, lamp-post 2, lancet 2, land (verb) 5, landscape 4, lane 3, language 3, languid 2, large 2, lark 4, late 6, latterly 2, lattice 3, launch (verb) 2, launder 1, laundry basket 2, layer (noun) 2, 3, (verb) 2, tall 2, tank 2, [1]tap 6, [1]tape 3, [1]tar 2, tarmac 2,

[1]tart 3, task 2, task force 1, taster 2, tasty 3, teal 2, [2]tear 8, [1]tease 3, [2]tease 2, technical 5, technician 2, technology 2, tee off 2, 3, [2]telegraph 2, telephone 4

In LDOCE1, not in LDOCE3

labour (noun) 4, (verb) 2, lace (noun) 3, lad 2, laity 2, lame 3, laminate (verb) 1, 4, land (noun) 2, [1]lap 2, [3]lap 3, lapse (noun) 4, 5, (verb) 2, lard (verb) 1, lash (noun) 4, 5, late 3, 4, 6, laugh (verb) 2, 3, 4, 5, laughable 1, laughter 2, laurel 2, lavatory 3, law 6, lawful 3, lax 3, 5, lay 4, 7, 9, layer (noun) 3, 4, (verb) 2, [1]tally 4, tambour 2, 3, tamp 2, [1]tan 3, tangerine 3, [2]tap 1, 2, [1]tar 2, [2]tart 2, task force 2, [2]taste 6, tea 1, tea garden 1, tease 2, 3, [1]telegraph 3, [2]telephone 2, 3, [2]telescope 2, televise 2

In COBUILD2, not in COBUILD1

labyrinth 2, lace 5, 6, laden 2, lame duck 2, Laotian 3, lard 2, latch onto 2, 3, late 2, lately 2, layer 3, tally 3, tangential 2, tango 2, target 4, tarnish 3, taste 6, taster 2, taut 2, tawdry 2, tear 3, telegraph 3

In COBUILD1, not in COBUILD2

lacking 3, lacquer 2, lag 2, lamb 4, land 3, 7, landlord 2, language 2, 3.1, 3.2, large 6, late 7, latitude 2, latter 3, laughingly 2, law 6, law and order 2, lazy 4, lay 1.5, 1.6, 1.7, 6.4, 6.7, 8, lay down 2, 5, lay into 2, lay up 2, tangle 1.4, tap 7, 9, tapestry 2, tattered 2, tattoo 1.2, tax 5, tea 1.2, team 3, tease out 1, technical 1.3, technically 2, 3, technology 2, teem 2, telepathic 2, telescope 2, 3

Table 3

Chronological breakdown of new entries

	OALD4 & 5	LDOCE2 & 3	COBUILD2
pre-1900	41%	41,5	33
1900	1	2	-
1910	8	7	5
1920	7,5	5	-
1930	4,5	5	14,5
1940	8	10	8
1950	10,5	8	10,5
1960	9	10,5	10,5
1970	3,5	5	6
1980	7,5	6	10,5

Table 4

	OALD5	LDOCE3	COBUILD2	CIDE
AIDS	+	+	+	+
backslash	-	+	-	-
boardsailing	-	-	-	-
boot (up)	+	+	-	+
brill (*adj*)	+	+	+	+
camcorder	+	+	+	+
computerate	-	-	+	-
contra (*n*)	-	-	-	-
DAT	-	+	+	+
download	+	+	+	+
e-mail	+	+	+	+

foodie	-	+	+	+
freebase	-	-	-	+
-gram	-	+	+	+
heterosexist	-	-	-	+
kissogram	-	+	-	+
legionella	-	-	-	-
microlight	+	+	-	+
microwavable	-	+	-	+
MIDI	-	-	-	+
palimony	-	+	+	-
perestroika	+	+	+	+
Rambo	-	-	-	+
spreadsheet	+	+	+	+
trial (*v*)	-	+	-	+
veejay	-	+	-	-
Walkman	+	+	+	+
wysiwyg	+	+	-	+
yomp	+	-	-	-
yuppie	+	+	+	+

Klaus-Dieter Barnickel

Political correctness in learners' dictionaries

Introduction

The subject of political correctness in learners' dictionaries is certainly not one that is most relevant to lexicography. It is, however, both important and interesting: Important, as it is one of the chief developments in recent years impinging on the borderline between society and language, interesting, as it can demonstrate the ways in which learners' dictionaries react to new developments in language and society.

We will not go into details on the rise and development of political correctness (PC) as a social phenomenon, which interestingly arose in the seventies at about the same time as - with the publication of LDOCE1 - new concepts of learners' dictionaries were being developed. The discussion has been and is still characterized by two opposing views: one takes the subject very seriously; its adherents attempt to change attitudes by first changing the language and linguistic items. This is shown in lists like the one published by the Ontario Women's Directorate in the Internet. Here is just a short excerpt of (non-inclusive = politically incorrect vs inclusive = politically correct) words (*Ontario Women's Directorate*, p.4):

NON-INCLUSIVE	INCLUSIVE
actress	*actor*
alderman	*municipal councillor*
ballerina	*ballet dancer*
barmaid	*bartender*
businessman	*business executive*
call girl	*prostitute*
career girl, career woman	*executive, manager, professional*
cameraman, cameramen	*camera operator, camera crew*
cleaning lady	*cleaner*
clergyman	*cleric, member of the clergy*
comedienne	*comedian, comic*
craftsman	*artisan*

The other view is highly critical of this and shows itself in ironic or even satirical publications which contain substitution forms, too, but all of them of course suggested with irony or even satire (all examples from Beard/Cerf 1993).

dead	*terminally inconvenienced*
promiscuous	*sexually active*
physically disabled	*physically challenged*

having a missing limb	*orthopedically impaired*
spendthrift	*negative saver*
dishonest	*morally different*
ex-girl-/boyfriend	*insignificant other*

This study will deal with the following aspects:

1. comments on PC itself, in introductions, usage notes or dictionary entries,
2. inclusion or exclusion of words that are felt by many people to be politically correct or incorrect,
3. characterisation of PC in the entries of these words by labelling or other means,
4. politically correct or incorrect language in the definitions, text examples and illustrations,
5. reaction to PC in older editions and development of LDs with respect to PC.

Comments on the subject and labels used

At the outset one has to say that none of the dictionaries has a relevant label or even a hint at PC in their introductions or user's manuals. What all new editions do have, though, are the entries at *political correct(ness):*

OALD5	(sometimes derogatory) the principle of avoiding language or behaviour that may offend particular groups of people: an excessive display of or belief in this
LDOCE3	only adj: language, behaviour and attitudes that are politically correct are regarded as right and acceptable because they are careful to avoid offending women, black people, disabled people etc:
COBUILD2	is behaviour and beliefs that reflect the attitudes and language that are typical of people who hold left-wing or liberal views; often used showing disapproval
CIDE	If someone is politically correct (abbreviation PC) they believe that language and actions which could be offensive to others, esp. those relating to sex and race, should be avoided. A word or expression which is politically correct is used instead of another word or expression to avoid being offensive: Some people think that 'fireman' is a sexist term, and prefer the politically correct term 'firefighter'.

As can be seen, both OALD5 and COBUILD2 share the somewhat critical attitude of many people on this subject. Only LDOCE3 gives a practical and concrete definition and only CIDE gives an example.

Survey of politically (in)correct words

In none of the learners' dictionaries is there a hint at the term PC itself in any of the entries. The use of this expression as a label is restricted to the older edition of LDOCE3 at *politically correct*: "It is not politically correct anymore to say handicapped." Usage labels for PC are: *derogatory, offensive* and in LDOCE3 very often *politeness*. None has a common description for sexist, racist and other discriminating words. The label *sexist* can only be found in OALD5 where it is characterised as "unfair or patronizing attitude towards a person of the opposite sex" and includes words such as *career girl, dolly bird, looker*. It is, however, never mentioned in the entries of the words analysed below.

It is more or less left to chance if students will come across and learn more about this phenomenon of the English language. In OALD5 it is the entry at *gender* where they can find a survey of the gender-related words:

Note: When writing or speaking English it is important to use language that includes both men and women equally. The following notes give help with doing this.

The human race

Man and **mankind** have traditionally been used to mean 'all men and women'. Many people consider the use of these terms discriminating against women and prefer to use **humanity, the human race, human beings** or **people**.

Jobs

The suffix **-ess** in names of occupations such as **actress, authoress** and **hostess** show that the person doing the job is a woman. Many people now use the same word for both sexes because it is unnecessary to make a distinction between men and women doing the same job: **actor, author, host**.

It is also usually possible to use a neutral word like **assistant, worker, person** or **officer** instead of man/woman in the names of jobs.

salesman/saleswoman	= *sales assistant*
headmaster/headmistress	= *headteacher*
policeman/policewoman	= *police officer*
fireman/firewoman	= *fire-fighter*
chairman/chairwoman	= *chairperson* or *chair*

Many people prefer these alternatives since most jobs are now open to both sexes. They are very common in newspapers, on television and radio and in official writing, in both British and American English.

When talking about jobs that are traditionally done by the other sex, some people say: **a male secretary/nurse/model**. Or they say: **a woman doctor/barrister/driver** (NOT **female**). Many people, especially women, feel it is offensive to mention a person's sex unnecessarily in this way.

Pronouns

Everybody, everyone, anybody, anyone, somebody, someone, etc are usually followed by the plural pronouns **they, them**, and **their**: *Does everybody know what they want? - Somebody's left their coat here. - I hope nobody's forgotten to bring their passport with them.*

You can also use **he or she**, **his or her**, or **him or her**, especially in more formal speech or writing: *Everyone knows what's best for him or herself.*

In writing you can also use **he/she** or **(s)he**: *If in doubt, ask your doctor. He/she can give you more information.*

Alternatively, the sentence can be rephrased, using a plural noun. Instead of saying: *A baby cries when he or she is tired,* you can say *Babies cry when they are tired.*

This note is hinted at at the end of the entries of *man*, *mankind*, *business-*, *chairman* (but not *spokesman*). But there is no cross-reference at *fireman*, *headmaster*, *policeman*, *salesman*, where we do not even find the suggested entry *sales assistant*. This, of course, minimizes the chances for students to get a proper insight into PC related problems.

In LDOCE3 students can find the relevant information at *man:*

USAGE NOTE: MAN

Politeness

Many people no longer use **man** to mean 'men and women in general' because it gives the impression that women are not included. They prefer to use **humans** or **human beings**: *abilities found in humans* (rather than in 'man'). Also you might see: *every disease known to human kind* rather than *every disease known to man/ mankind.*

Generally you use the word **person** when it is not important to say whether you are talking about a man or a woman: *Sandy's a really nice person. / unemployed people.*

It is also advisable not to use words that contain **man** in the names of jobs, because this seems to mean that only men do that job or that the person is a man. So say that someone is a **chairperson,** rather than a **chairman,** especially when it is a woman. Similarly it is better to say: **spokesperson, businesspeople**, or **salesperson.**

Sometimes you do not need to use **-man, -woman**, or **-person** in the names of jobs at all. For example, people are more likely to say **firefighter** than **fireman, police officer** than **policeman,** and in British English, **headteacher** or **head** instead of **headmaster** or **headmistress.**

Here the treatment of sexist language is even more deficient: apart from usage problems of *-man, -woman, -person* there is no hint at the other related items mentioned in OALD5 and CIDE. Cross-references to the usage note are only at *mankind* and *human*, not at *human-*

kind, businessman, chairman, spokesman or any of the other cases mentioned, so whether a student gets any information on the usage of these words, is left to chance even more.

In accordance with its general policy, COBUILD2 has no special usage note but a relevant remark in individual entries. Consequently it is likely to be more careful and consistent than the other learners' dictionaries. And in fact there is a relevant comment in all the words analysed, even at *authoress* and *developed*, where the other dictionaries lack any characterisation. Exceptions are *handicapped* and the combinations with *-man* (*business-, chair-, spokes-, headmaster, -mistress* and *fireman*, where at least there is a cross-reference to *firefighter*).

CIDE is the most detailed and elaborate of the four learners' dictionaries. It has a whole page of various items in this field, including the question of pronouns after *someone* etc. and more stylistic problems such as the order of words in *women* and *men*. But here, too, we can see the strange phenomenon of highlighting words as to *man, man-made, camerawoman, authoress, male nurse* as *sexist* without a cross-reference in the respective entries.

USING LANGUAGE THAT IS NOT SEXIST

Sometimes the use of particular words can support unfair or untrue attitudes to a particular sex, usually women. For example using the pronoun *he* to refer to a doctor, when you do not know if they are male or female, might support the belief that it is not normal for women to be doctors. Many people speaking or writing English today prefer to avoid using language that is sexist. This modern *non-sexist* use of language is sometimes called *inclusive language*.

Old-fashioned sexist language	Modern non-sexist language
Male pronouns *he*, *his* and *him* are used even though the sex of the person is not known.	You can often avoid unnecessary male pronouns by using the plural pronouns *they, them*, etc. instead. Male pronouns can also be replaced by combinations like *she or he*, *him or her*, *her or his*. Sometimes a pronoun can be avoided completely.
"Someone's on the phone." "What does **he** *want?"*	*"Someone's on the phone" "What do* **they** *want?"*
The television viewer hardly ever leaves **his** *chair.*	*Television viewers hardly ever leave* **their** *chairs.*
A gardener is usually proud of **his** *garden.*	*A gardener is usually proud of* **his or her** *garden.*
A child needs to feel that **he** *is liked by* **his** *friends.*	*A child needs to feel liked by friends.*
Words formed from 'man' are used when referring to people generally. (But notice that many words like *manager* or *manufacture* are not connected with 'man' at all.)	Use other words when referring to both men and women.
Man/mankind *is polluting the Earth.*	**People** *are/* **Humanity** *is/* **Humankind** *is polluting ...*
Man *is not the only animal that uses tools.*	**Human beings** *are not the only animal ...*

No **man** *has ever climbed this mountain before.* *Who's* **manning** *the office?* *This is the largest* **man-made** *lake in Europe.*	**No one** *has ever climbed this mountain before.* *Who's* **staffing/ running** *the office?* *This is the largest* **artificial** *lake in Europe.*
Many jobs or activities are strongly connected with a particular sex.	Use expressions or pronouns that do not support sexist assumptions.
The teacher must not be late for **his** *class.* *A manager has a duty towards* **his** *workers.* *The fall in prices is great news for* **housewives**. *A* **mother** *should never leave a baby alone in the house.* **He** *might hurt* **himself**.	*Teachers must not be late for* **their** *classes.* *A manager has a duty towards* **his or her** *workers.* *The fall in prices is great news for* **consumers/shoppers**. **Parents** *should never leave babies alone in the house.* **They** *might hurt* **themselves**.
Job names are used which refer unnecessarily to the sex of the person.	Use job names that apply equally to women and men.
We're meeting a group of **businessmen**. *The* **chairman** *cannot vote.* *Jane is a* **camerawoman**. *She's a very talented* **authoress/lady writer**. *John is training as a* **male nurse**. *workman; salesman/saleslady; airline stewardess*	*... a group of* **businesspeople/executives**. *The* **chairperson/chair** *cannot vote.* *Jane is a* **camera operator**. *She's a very talented* **author/writer**. *John is training as a* **nurse**. *worker; sales representative/agent; flight attendant*
Male words are almost always put before female words in common combinations.	Do not use one order of words more often than the other.
men and women; brothers or sisters; husbands and wives; his and her; he or she; him and her	
The words used for men and women in the same situation are not equal. For example the title *Miss* tells you that the woman is not married, but *Mr* applies to married and unmarried men.	Use equal male and female terms.
Ted and Angela are **man** *and* **wife**. *I have three* **girls** *and two* **men** *working for me.*	*Ted and Angela are* **wife** *and* **husband**. *I have three* **women** *and two* **men** *working for me.*
Mr *Lewis and* **Miss** *Masters.*	**Ms** *Masters and* **Mr** *Lewis.*

If we take a closer look at the entries of the words mentioned in these usage notes, we are confronted with a still more confusing picture: *Man*, for example, in the sense of 'human being', 'the human race' is "old-fashioned" for LDOCE3, even "offensive" for CIDE, in

COBUILD2 people just "dislike" this use and in OALD5 students have to go back hundreds of pages to *gender* to find that "this use discriminates against women".

At *mankind,* OALD5 has the following note at "gender": "as this term might be considered biased against women the use should be avoided." COBUILD2 says that "some people dislike this use" (the same as with man), and LDOCE3 and CIDE are satisfied to refer to the relevant usage notes.

All four learners' dictionaries treat *chair, chairman, chairwoman* and *chairperson* side by side; LDOCE3 has no cross-reference to the usage note. In COBUILD2 both examples for *chair* and *chairperson* are female: "She is the chair of the Defense Advisory Committee on Women in the Military." "She's the chairperson of the safety committee." In CIDE all four words are treated together in one entry to show their equivalence.

Housewife is compared to *house-husband* in OALD5 whereas LDOCE3 refers it to *homemaker*; COBUILD2 contains no such alternatives and CIDE has an entry at *homemaker* with the following obviously PC example: "I was earning more money than Ian, so we agreed that he would be the homemaker when Mary was born."

At *everyone* OALD5 gives just a reference to gender, but no examples with plural pronoun. LDOCE3 has the following usage note at *each*:

> "**Each** and **every** may be followed by a plural pronoun, especially when you are talking about both males and females: *Each girl must make up her own mind. Each person must make up their own mind.* It sounds a little formal to say: *Each person must make up his or her own mind.* and it is considered sexist to use *he* unless you are only talking about men or boys."

COBUILD2 gives the example "Everyone in the street was shocked when they heard the news." without a comment and so does CIDE.

At *Ms* both OALD5 and LDOCE3 state that "Some women prefer the title Ms to Mrs or Miss", the latter even in a politeness note at *Mr*. For COBUILD2 it is "used, especially in written English" and CIDE simply has "title used before the family name or full name of a woman". And it is only COBUILD2 which has a restriction of *authoress*: "Some female writers object to this word, preferring to be called authors."

Surprisingly none of the learners' dictionaries makes any remark on a whole number of words which are considered by many people as sexist or which are so controversial in PC discussion: this is - to mention only a few examples: *postman* is still "the person (or even man) whose job is to collect and deliver letters" (with the exception of CIDE which has *postman, postwoman* and *letter carrier* in the same entry). *Dustman* is simply "the person whose job is to remove waste from dustbins" (where again CIDE alone has a hint at Br fml *refuse collector*). *Milkman* is "someone who delivers milk to houses each morning". *Fireman* is even restricted to "a man whose job is to stop fires burning". However, all learners' dictionaries with the exception of OALD5 have a reference to *firefighter*. Interestingly enough neither OALD5 nor LDOCE3 or COBUILD2 see any problems in the usage of *cleaning lady,* which is missing altogether in CIDE, which, however, allows for the following example sentence: "Chris has an evening job as an office cleaner."

A closer look at racist words shows that it is only LDOCE3 which has a politeness usage note at *Negro* and cross-references at *black* and *coloured*: "People of African origin usually prefer to be called *black*, or in the US, often *African-American*. In the UK the term Afro-Caribbean is often used."

A *negro* is qualified as "sometimes offensive" in OALD5, for COBUILD2 it is "an old-fashioned word which some people find offensive" and CIDE has a label *dated* and the remark: " 'Negro' is now considered offensive by many people and words such as 'Black' and 'African American' are used instead." Similar restrictions are given for *black*, where surprisingly CIDE has no entry for the meaning [people] at all, only for the meaning [bad] which reads "some people avoid using black to mean bad, as it might offend black people."

A rare coincidence can be found at *coloured*, where all four learners' dictionaries have a similar qualification as the one found in OALD5: "dated, often offensive". OALD5 and LDOCE3 see no restriction in the usage of *Indian*: for COBUILD2 this is an "old-fashioned use" and CIDE is the only dictionary which gives the alternative *Native American*: "This is considered offensive by many people."

There is no such item in any of our learners' dictionaries for physically discriminating words, but again there is no obvious lack of characterisation in individual entries. At *disability* OALD5 says: "many people now feel these words are offensive and prefer to use expressions with *disabled* and *disability*." CIDE gives the restriction *dated* whereas LDOCE3 and COBUILD2 treat it as a neutral word. At *cripple* all four dictionaries agree on "offensive", an agreement which is more or less also true of *lunatic* (which is even *taboo* for CIDE). *Fat* is criticized in OALD5 as "not polite" and LDOCE3 has the usage note: "If you want to be polite about someone, do not say that they are *fat*. (A little) *overweight* or just *large* is a more polite way of saying the same thing." There is no such restriction in either COBUILD2 or CIDE.

Here again there are surprisingly many words which are not seen as impolite or offensive, such as *deaf*, *bald* or *near-sighted*, which is only "an old-fashioned word" in COBUILD2, or *retarded* which is "old-fashioned" in COBUILD2 and "dated" in CIDE. And in none of the learners' dictionaries do we find PC alternatives such as *mentally challenged* or *differently abled*.

If we look at socially discriminating words we get the same picture. It is only in LDOCE3 that *underdeveloped* has a cross-reference to *developing country* and in COBUILD2 we can find the following qualification: "Some people dislike this term and prefer to use developing." Even more astonishing is the fact that for *old* one has to go back to the older edition of LDOCE3, where the following usage note is to be found: "when speaking of people, elderly is a polite way of saying old."

To sum up we can say that all the learners' dictionaries have done their homework, some more, some less, but all of them meet just the basic demands (entry for *politically correct*, usage note on sexist words and labelling the more frequent and obvious examples) without additional exercises or decorations (labels or other ways of marking and cross-references at the bulk of sexist words). If we have to name a top pupil it is certainly CIDE, which not only has the most elaborate usage note, but also most labels in entries. Let us try and find if this is corroborated by other basic items of a dictionary, namely definitions and examples.

Definitions and example sentences

Definitions are quite obviously politically correct in all of the learners' dictionaries. A definition such as the following from the OALD1 at *negro* would be unthinkable today: "[...] with woolly hair, thick lips and a flat nose." In all cases the definitions refer neutrally to persons/someone/people who they treat in a sexually neutral way.

Cowie (1995) analysed about 500 entries in OALD3 and OALD4 for the use of sexually biased pronouns in example sentences and found that there was a striking progress in OALD4 to avoid these. Our own comparison covers the entries *fab* - *fall* (ca. 150 entries each) (The survey does not contain examples with *I*, which normally have the same frequency as female. *We* is included in plurals. Besides there are quite a few neutral sentences like: "the unpleasant reality lurking behind that facade of respectability" in every learners' dictionary.)

Example sentences in learner's dictionaries (*fab* to *fall*)

OALD5			**LDOCE3**			**COBUILD2**			**CIDE**		
female	male	plural	female	male	plural	female	male	plural	female	male	plural
37	38	33	46	58	45	30	80	50	65	70	60

OALD5 has an equal share of female and male examples. Its policy is clearly to give both a female and a male example in each individual entry:

> "[...] a facetious young man." "She kept making facetious remarks."

There remain a few examples which could be criticised as sexist by some people:

> "She only looks young because she's had a face-lift"; "She signed the letter in good faith, not realising its implications." "[...] a faithless friend/wife/ally." "The President has proved he is fallible after all."

LDOCE3 gives fewer examples with female pronouns and also has clearly more examples with an obvious sexist tendency:

> "McManus is facing the biggest challenge of his career." "The boss is a hard man - hard but fair." "She keeps trying all these faddy diets." "Over the years her beauty had faded a little." "She fell down in a faint."

On the other hand we get the impression that women are mostly the "good" and men the "bad guys":

> "She has an amazing facility for mental arithmetic." "She obviously knows what she's doing - the facts speak for themselves." "She has a great faculty for absorbing information." "He refused to help me, despite the fact that I asked him several times." "Harry's ambitious plans ended in failure." "The woman who sold me the car claimed she had acted in good faith." "The old law wasn't fair to women."

COBUILD2 has far more male than female examples, which also often show traditional attitudes:

> "She had a beautiful face." "He had worked on the factory floor for 16 years." "For once, the artist's fertile imagination failed him." "She was like a princess in a fairy tale." "She insisted that she had remained faithful to her husband." "Almost without exception these women fall victim to exploitation."

But of course it is doubtful if there is any sexual bias in the following example:

> "Prince Charles has again fallen from his horse."

CIDE has almost equal numbers between the sexes. Like OALD5, if there is more than one example, the editors try hard to make one male, the other female:

> "Was your wife faithful during your marriage?" "He was faithful to his wife throughout their 30-year marriage."

Some examples show a change in roles:

> "She's gone out to get a packet of fags." "She works in a factory."

And not only strong men, too:

> "He faints at the sight of blood."

What is more, most examples try to be very PC and some of them even refer to the discussion:

> "There is no fairness in paying female workers a third less than male workers." "He offered to do all the washing up if I did all the cooking, which seemed like a fair deal."

Development of learners' dictionaries with respect to PC

As outlined in the introduction, another interesting aspect is the development of PC in the various editions of the learners' dictionaries. In the following tables I have compiled the entries for the words already analysed in the new editions. We will be dealing with OALD4 (1989), LDOCE2 (1987) and COBUILD1 (1987) as the editions of the 80s and OALD3

(1974), LDOCE1 (1978) as the 70s-edition and finally OALD2 (1963) as the only edition of the 60s.

OALD4 has a similar usage note at *man* as the new edition: "Man can be used, in a similar way to mankind, to mean 'all men and women'. Many people consider this biased against women and avoid it by using *humanity, the human race* or *humans, human beings, people.*" Likewise a usage note at *chairman* says that "To avoid sexual bias and unnecessary repetition *-person* can be used: *chairperson, spokesperson, business person. Chair* is increasingly used to mean *chairman* or *chairwoman.*" At *everybody* we can find the following note: "Traditionally, if the sex of the person is unknown, the masculine pronouns *he, him, his* have been used to refer to both females and males [...] Many people today consider this shows sexual bias and try to avoid it. The preferred way, especially in speech, is to use *they, them* or *their* with a singular neutral meaning."

LDOCE2 has usage notes both on sexist and racist words (at *person* and *black*), which, however, are not as elaborate as in LDOCE3; it highlights the problem of combinations with *-man* at *chairman*, and even has a politeness remark at *fat*. It points out at *everybody* that it is "[...] often followed by a plural pronoun, except in very formal speech and writing", which is obviously more a stylistic than a sociolinguistic problem to the editors. *Ms* is "a title for a woman who does not wish to call herself either Mrs or Miss". *Negro* has the label *tech or not polite* and a usage note: "Black is the word preferred by many black people. *Coloured* and, especially, *Negro* are now considered by many black people to be offensive."

The first edition of COBUILD even points out in its introduction: "We regularly refer to the indefinite pronouns such as *someone* by the words *they, them, their,* because *he* and *she* are restricted to male and female referents respectively. We have abandoned the convention whereby *he* was held to refer to both men and women [...] it is a very sensitive matter for those who have pointed out the built-in sexism of English." In its entry, however, the usage of *man* is not restricted: "You can refer to human beings in general as *man.*" *Negro* is "a fairly old-fashioned word that some people find offensive." Although COBUILD1 is well aware of sexist language, which is proved by the introduction, the entries themselves are less PC than the 80s edition of the other learners' dictionaries.

A closer look at the 70s editions shows that the first edition of LDOCE has no gender usage note, but is more sensitive as far as race is concerned; it has a first tentative remark on the use of plurals after *someone* etc.: "[...] often followed by a plural pronoun, except in very formal speech and writing." *Has everyone finished their drinks/his or her drink* (fml)? There is no remark at *man*, however at *chairman* "person in charge of a meeting": "She's one of our best [...] chairmen." And it contains an entry for *chairperson* and *chairwoman*: "a female chairman". Unlike in OALD5 we can find an entry for *Ms*: "title for a woman who does not wish to call herself either Mrs or Miss" and a label at *negro*: "*tech or not polite* black person". All this taken together makes this new dictionary a lot more PC than OALD3, which admittedly was four years earlier.

OALD3 states that *chairman* "is a person presiding at a meeting" and *businessman* is even "a man who is engaged in buying and selling etc.". *Negro* is neutrally "[...] member of the black-skinned races [...]" and *cripple* "a person who cannot use his body properly". It is only at *lunatic asylum* that we find the restriction: "*mental home* and *-institution* are the names in present-day use".

As can be seen, there is a clear cut between the 70s and the 80s editions, which is not surprising as the PC discussion started in the 70s and we must concede at least half a decade before this shows in dictionaries. Here we can find the first usage notes on this problem (both in OALD and LDOCE at *man*) and here is the first time that COBUILD remarks on the sexism of the English language in its introduction. If we go further down in lexicographic history, we can see that LDOCE shows at least traces of PC language and consciousness as early as the 1978 edition, whereas OALD in this respect is almost identical with the 1963-edition, which was still a politically incorrect paradise.

Example sentences in older editions of learner's dictionaries (fab to fall)

	OALD			LDOCE			COBUILD		
	female	male	plural	female	male	plural	female	male	plural
80s	33	41	20	36	33	23	30	51	22
70s	15	61	18	10	40	21			

The examples confirm the findings in the definitions: A clear-cut breach is evident in the 80s editions with strikingly more female pronouns than in the earlier editions. And again it is COBUILD which is apparently more male biased.

OALD4: compared with the previous edition, a more equal distribution between male and female forms can be found: "He fell on his knees and begged for mercy." "The toddler tried to walk but kept falling down." "She fell over and broke her leg." A reversion of roles can be seen in the following examples: "He plays the piano with surprising facility." "For eight years she was in fact spying for the enemy."

LDOCE2 shows a fair division of male and female examples: "I'm sure she'll do as she promised; I've got great faith in her." "He still has great talent, but he has lost faith in himself." As in OALD5, a reversion of male/female roles is made apparent in: "She possesses fabulous wealth." "Everyone admired the way she faced out the opposition in the debate." "When we faced her with all the evidence, she admitted the crime." "She works in a car factory."

In COBUILD1 female forms are under-represented. If they are used, women are seen rather negatively: "She faced criminal charges for deceiving the State." "She felt she could never show her face in town again." "She failed in her attempt to swim to France." The following example is interesting: "If an examiner fails you in a test or examination, he or she decides that you have not reached the standard that is required."

OALD3 manifests a general tendency to use more male than female examples, which show traditional role models: "She is looking for a husband but hasn't found her ideal yet." "Her face is her fortune: said of a woman who has beauty, but no dowry or talents." "He succeeded in spite of great danger." "The faceless men who have power in commerce and industry." Equal distribution of male/female examples is still the exception: "His hopes faded." "All memory of her childhood faded from her mind."

LDOCE1 is still characterised by a strong bias towards examples with men: "His facility with languages is surprising." They even invade female provinces such as: "His desire for black hats is only a passing fad." Sometimes, however, there are traces of PC views as in: "Officially he is in charge, but in fact his secretary does all the work." "That the rich get richer and the poor poorer is a fact of life."

Illustrations

Another interesting point in our discussion are illustrations, where one might expect editors not to be as sensitive and careful as with text examples. Of course, this analysis can only be carried out in OALD5 and LDOCE3, where illustrations can be found. Here, too, LDOCE3 seems to be the more careful of the two, because we can see a fair number of different races in various pictures (e.g. *at physical contact*) and also an equal share of jobs between men and women. One might ask, however, if the picture at *kitchen* does not stick to the old role model as the man is creatively preparing the meal while the woman's privilege is the cleaning and washing up.

Idioms

One of the surprising results of this investigation was the fact that obviously collocations and idioms seem to have evinced the attention of PC watchers. Without objection it is still *no-man's land, to a man, man-to-man, the man in the street, man about town* or *three-man panel*. Children still walk in *Indian* and not in *Native American file*, and in some departments there are still *too many chiefs and not enough Indians* (and not *Native Americans*). And we still do *not know some people from Adam* (and not from *Eve*). This obviously still goes *for every man Jack* (and not *for every woman Joan*) and - be honest, who thinks of a woman when they refer to people *living the life of Riley*?

Bibliography

Collins Cobuild English Language Dictionary ([1]1987): John Sinclair (ed.) – London, Glasgow: Collins.
Longman Dictionary of Contemporary English ([1]1978): Paul Procter (ed.) – Harlow: Longman.
Longman Dictionary of Contemporary English ([2]1987): Della Summers (ed.) – Harlow: Longman.
Oxford Advanced Learner's Dictionary of Current English ([3]1974): Albert S. Hornby (ed.) – Oxford: OUP.
Oxford Advanced Learner's Dictionary of Current English ([4]1989): Anthony P. Cowie (ed.) – Oxford: OUP.
The Advanced Learner's Dictionary of Current English ([2]1963): Albert S. Hornby (ed.) – London: OUP.

Beard, Henry, Christopher Cerf (1993): The Official Politically Correct Dictionary and Handbook. - New York: Villard Books.
Cowie, Anthony P. (1995): "The Learner's Dictionary in a Changing Cultural Perspective". - In: B. B. Kachru, H. Kahane (eds.): Cultures, Ideologies and the Dictionary (Tübingen: Niemeyer) 283-295.
Whitcut, Janet (1984): "Sexism in Dictionaries". - In: R.R.K. Hartmann (ed.): LEXeter '83 Proceedings: Papers from the International Conference on Lexicography at Exeter, 1983 (Tübingen: Niemeyer) 141-144.
Ontario Women's Directorate: Words that count women in. - http:// info- sys.home. vix/ com/ men/ pc/extracts/ontario.html.

André Moulin

The advanced learners' dictionary: syntax cum semantics

1 The advanced learner: an ID card

The theme proposed for our present symposium is a perfect example of the kind of syntactico-semantic puzzle any EFL learner has to solve when decoding complex noun phrases. Indeed, he might, quite innocently, wonder whether we have come here to talk about a perfect dictionary or about a dictionary which is meant for the perfect learner.

I imagine we all interpreted the title in the former sense, although a few words about the latter one might be in order. The point I want to make is that, working in widely varying contexts with students from very different backgrounds, we all have our own, local, implicit or explicit, definition of the concept of the advanced learner and, why not, of the perfect advanced learner, i.e. of the kind of motivation, language mastery, prior experience of dictionary use that type of learner should have acquired in order to make the most of the particular brand of dictionary we are now dealing with.

When I hear the words 'advanced learner', I immediately think of my own flock: first- and second-year, francophone Belgian undergraduates, doing a four-year degree in Germanic languages and literatures, i.e. studying in parallel both the language and the literature of two Germanic languages (English and German or English and Dutch). After graduation, some of them find a job in industry or commerce, but the majority traditionally become FL teachers in secondary education. I have explained in Moulin (1993) the problems posed by the gaps and weaknesses in these undergraduates' prior linguistic education, and will not bother you with the details. A few remarks concerning their needs are however relevant to our present discussion.

There is a broad consensus among our department's staff members that the aim we pursue is to teach students how to decode and encode oral and written, literary and non-literary discourse, in other words, that one of our main tasks is to help them develop to a very advanced degree the four basic skills.

My own approach is currently as follows. As far as first-year students are concerned, my two chief priorities in the context of our present discussion are filling the wide gaps in their mastery of syntax and developing and vitalizing their very limited vocabulary. The majority of the lectures are therefore devoted to a systematic examination of the main points of English syntax (use of the articles, tenses, modals, relative pronouns, etc). To enrich their general vocabulary the students also have to use *Word-Routes*, the CUP English-French thematic lexicon. The dictionary on their reading list is a bilingual one. To those who have not already got *Harrap's Shorter*, we recommend buying either *Le Robert & Collins Senior* or the *Oxford Hachette.* Attempts to introduce learners' dictionaries at this stage have, on the whole, been unsuccessful, because of problems we shall discuss below.

In my second-year courses, I very much lay the emphasis on the 'grammar of words': problems such as the countability potential of nouns or syntactic - mainly verbal - patterns. Although I am not teaching a course in linguistics, I consider that, given the level to be reached by my students and the job they are preparing for, it is indispensable for them to approach grammar not in a purely descriptive but in a heuristic, reasoned, argumentative way. The patterns in question are therefore examined, analysed with the help of the necessary theoretical apparatus and illustrated by numerous example sentences culled from different sources. These sentences are in turn manipulated in various exercises. The students thus not only have to understand the mechanics of the patterns but are also expected to memorize their most frequent exponents and to learn how to use them in context.

2 The imperfect teacher's predicament

My problem as a teacher is twofold: (a) adopting an approach which covers this whole range of needs - understanding, memorizing and applying correctly these syntactic, semantic and pragmatic characteristics - and (b) finding, or devising, tools which help me to implement this approach - and this is where my troubles begin.

When they first start learning foreign languages, children or adolescents - to say nothing of their parents - instinctively purchase bilingual dictionaries. The latter have become current consumption goods and you find some of them in many large stores. Clearly, it is now common knowledge or even popular wisdom that to learn a foreign language you need a good bilingual dictionary. This success is not attributable to efficient marketing only. The main reason is that the man in the street sees foreign language learning in terms of mastering a large number of words, and, as he instinctively uses his mother tongue as a reference, the bilingual dictionary is obviously the perfect grimoire, the book of magic formulas which will enable him to cross the border into the marvellous land of multilingualism.

Typically, these adolescents turn to their bilingual dictionary mainly for decoding tasks. Being provided with a mother tongue equivalent of the unknown word they have looked up gives them a feeling that they really understand it, that they know what it means. As far as encoding tasks are concerned - writing short dialogues or compositions - many FL teachers encourage beginners or even intermediate learners to simply re-use ready-made chunks of language which they have come across in their coursebooks and learned to manipulate: producing these little texts looks more like assembling in their own fashion familiar Lego blocks than like really putting their own thoughts into words. If these learners suddenly feel like expressing an original idea, it will most likely occur to them in their mother tongue and they will, to the great displeasure of some teachers, seek advice from a bilingual dictionary.

As this has become something of a reflex, I never try to discourage my own advanced learners from doing so. The problem is rather to teach them how to make the most of the incredible fund of information available in bilingual dictionaries (part of speech, field and style labels, etc). Incidentally, the problem is briefly mentioned in Atkins and Varantola

(1997: 16 ff.). Admittedly, in the experiment these two authors describe, the testees are practising yet another, very specific skill - translating - but we all know that, whatever the task they are confronted with, dictionary users have a sometimes rather irrational and often very idiosyncratic way of selecting and using their lexicographic tools. What we may not know so well is to what extent encoding tasks, even when assigned to advanced users, continue to be conceived of as translating tasks. When reading my students' essays, I very often come across wording which suggests that the whole conceptualization job has been done in French. Part of the difficulty thus consists in convincing them that they should try harder to think in English and in demonstrating to them the advantages of using for a number of tasks not bilingual but learners' dictionaries, to say nothing of thesauri, synonym finders, etc. Although these students are in their late teens or in their early twenties, the presence of illustrations, tables, encyclopedic information - the kind they need for decoding tasks - often proves to be an excellent argument to persuade them to use such dictionaries at all. Once this has become instinctive, half the battle is won and one can start teaching them to exploit the full potential of the tool. Personally, I must confess that the only way I have found of achieving this is to place learners' dictionaries on the list of works to be used in class and at home.

3 Matching grammar handbooks and learners' dictionaries: the case of ergativity

The problem confronting me in this course for second-year students is consistency - finding a grammar handbook which tackles patterns in a way which is both scientifically and didactically satisfactory, and a dictionary which provides the corresponding information for individual items and preferably does so within the same conceptual and terminological framework. I have tried various types of combination but have so far been unable to find one which really fits the bill. There are plenty of good grammar books or learners' dictionaries around, but the difficulty is that they do not seem to be aimed at the same audience.

Now, I have no a priori ideas as to what constitutes an acceptable grammatical explanation, except that, as I suggested above, it must not be a mere prescriptive, simplistic recipe, but has to address the learner's faculty of reasoning and take into account his level of linguistic awareness. It must therefore strike a balance between two poles: be clear and comprehensible but do justice to the complexity of the phenomenon it is meant to clarify. Given the dual approach I have adopted, what the grammar book says should not only be compatible with what the grammatical part of the dictionary says but also aim at the same level of complexity. There is for instance little point in asking the grammar to deal in some depth with a phenomenon such as ergativity, if the dictionary used in conjunction provides no indications concerning this problem and strictly limits itself to the admittedly neat and uncontroversial distinction between transitive and intransitive verbs or verb uses.

This takes us to the particular grammatical point I wish to discuss a bit more in detail - ergativity. I grant this is not a particularly easy topic. There is considerable disagreement among linguists concerning the term's coverage and more particularly concerning its relevance to English grammar.[1] This may be the reason why, even though they deal with the phenomenon in some way or other, many grammarians do not use the term, which often makes it difficult for those who consult their works to locate the relevant explanations. This is for instance the case with Huddleston (1984). With Quirk et al's *Comprehensive* (1985), the problem is different: most of the relevant aspects are examined and cross-referenced, but under separate headings.[2] Besides, the grammar, quite understandably, stops short of suggesting that there may be a direct relationship between a verb's semantic structure and its syntactic potential. To get that type of explanation, we have to turn to semanticists such as Levin or Dixon, which is what we shall presently do.

To put it in a nutshell, Levin (1995: 53 ff.) starts from the premise that any verb denotes an action, state or process involving one or more participants called *arguments* of the verb. A speaker who knows the meaning of the verb knows the number and type of arguments it requires and also the manner in which these arguments can be realized syntactically, i.e. the ways in which the verb can be used in a sentence.

If we take for instance the verb *break*, we notice that it has both a transitive and an intransitve use:

John broke the vase. The vase broke.

The two uses share a common core of meaning - both describe a change of state in a certain physical object - but the sentences differ in meaning: in the former example, the cause of the breaking is explicitly mentioned. Consequently, the transitive and intransitive uses of *break* are referred to as the causative and non-causative uses of the verb, respectively. The causative use of *break* involves two participants, whereas the intransitive involves only one. The argument that denotes the participant that brings about the action is referred to as the *agent*, whereas the term *patient* is generally used to refer to the argument that undergoes the change in question. Besides, the causative/inchoative alternation represented by these examples is not idiosyncratic to *break*: it relates transitive and intransitive uses across a large set of change-of-state verbs such as *shatter, crack, open, melt, etc.*

Levin also explains that two types of lexical semantic representation are possible for a verb like *break*. Some researchers, including Fillmore, propose that the arguments-taking

---

1 For a detailed discussion see R. M. W. Dixon (1994). The latter namely objects to the use of the term 'ergative' as a descriptive label for the 'subject type' in a construction such as *The officier marched the soldiers*.

2 Within Chapter 16, which is about the complementation of verbs and adjectives, Section 16.19 (III) deals with intransitive verbs which can also be transitive, "but where the semantic connection between subject and verb is different in the two cases" (p.1169). The user is also referred to the section entitled *Semantic roles of clause elements* (p.740 ff.) which deals with such notions as the *agentive, affected* and *recipient* roles played by the subject. Section 10.21 examines the subject's role as *external causer*, *instrument* and *affected*. In Appendix I, which is about word-formation, Section I.42 (p.1556) briefly deals with morphological problems (*sad* > *sadden*) and Section I.54 (p.1564) deals with the conversion of intransitive to transitive verbs and vice versa.

properties of a verb be represented by a list of semantic roles, labels that identify the arguments of a verb according to the semantic relations they bear to the verb:

Causative *break*: (agent, patient)
Non-causative *break*: (patient)

Others decompose the meaning of the verb by introducing a set of primitive predicates. This is the method applied to the causative alternation in Levin and Rappaport Hovav (1995: 79ff.). These authors argue that in an alternation like *Pat broke the window/the window broke*, the transitive use has roughly the meaning 'cause to V-intransitive'. A verb like *break* on both its transitive and intransitive uses has a complex semantic representation involving the predicate cause. This is basically different from a verb like *laugh*. This leads us to two very different semantic representations:

break: [[*x* DO-SOMETHING] CAUSE [*y* BECOME *BROKEN*]]
laugh: [*x LAUGH*]

In 1991, R.M.W. Dixon published *A New Approach to English Grammar, On Semantic Principles* whose aim was "to put forward a semantically oriented framework for grammatical analysis" (p.XIV). The idea is thus to group words together in a natural way into large classes that have a common meaning element. These are referred to as *semantic types*: verbs such as *begin, start, finish* are called the BEGINNING type; etc. Dixon also sees the problem in terms of semantic roles and of their relation to syntactic relations. As far as verbs are concerned, they are grouped as one semantic type because they require the same set of participant roles: for instance, all GIVING verbs require a donor, a gift and a recipient, as in *John gave a bouquet to Mary*. If we turn to syntax, the problem is to see how the roles of each type, at the semantic level, are mapped onto syntactic relations, at the grammatical level. For ATTENTION verbs, for instance the perceiver is grammatical subject and the impression is marked as object.

Dixon's semantic grammar also has a very interesting chapter, entitled: "*What sells slowly, but wears well?* Promotion to Subject". Among other things this chapter explains clearly the difference between passive and promotion to subject: *The woolens were washed well* is different from *The wooolens washed well*, where *well* refers to the washable qualities of the clothes. It also analyses the circumstances under which promotion to subject is possible, e.g. when there is some marker of success, the marker being an adverb, the negative particle, a modal, etc. as in *The middle house won't let*.

Now, what precedes represents only a small fraction of the argumentation developed by Levin & Rappaport Hovav and Dixon. I am in no way suggesting that the monographs or studies quoted are fit reading for the advanced learners I am talking about. The point I want to make is simply that it is possible to extract from these highly specialized studies a few quintessential elements which will help the students in question to better understand the problem and as a consequence make better use of the indications provided by dictionaries. These essential points are, in my opinion, the following:

1. The fact that a verb's meaning can be viewed in terms of identifiable and countable arguments;
2. The fact that, for one and the same verb, some of these arguments are not always present, and the way in which their presence or absence influences the verb's syntactic behaviour;
3. The theoretical possibility of grouping verbs into syntactic categories which rest on a similar semantic makeup and the difficulties this is bound to entail when it comes to defining either semantic roles or semantic primitives and to finding a satisfactory semantic superordinate term to identify a particular category. But, as I said above, developing our students' linguistic awareness and thus giving them some idea of the challenges linguistic inquiry has to meet is part of our job and will also give to their mastery of the foreign language an indispensable analytical dimension.

To round up our brief theoretical examination of the subject, I would like to allude to an article published in 1989 by T. Fontenelle and J. Vanandroye which showed that it was possible to retrieve ergative verbs from the LDOCE database by using three different types of clues: the simultaneous presence of several grammatical codes (e.g. T1+I0; T1+L9; etc); the presence in the definitions of words such as *cause to, allow, help, make*, etc; morphological clues such as derivatives ending in *-ate, -en, -(i)fy*.

If we now turn to learners' dictionaries, it is obvious that this approach can also be applied - visually, not electronically this time - to the paper version of most of them. If you take e.g. the *Oxford Advanced Learner's Encyclopedic* (1992), the simultaneous presence of codes **Tn** and **In** or the presence in the definition of the bracketed phrase *cause to* is a clear indication of ergative potential. The CIDE also distinguishes between transitive and intransitive senses and uses the same bracketed *cause to* formula. Naturally, these clues are simply indicative of an ergative potential: not all verbs ending in *-ify* are ergatives (*codify, simplify* are not). As a consequence, if ergative verb senses are not labelled as such, the user has to decide for himself whether or not this is the case. This means he has to look at the definitions, examples, etc. in order to collect all the possible clues. Unfortunately, the latter are not always easy to interpret. In fact, the way in which the explanations are provided may suggest to the user that the transitive and intransitive uses are two different senses.

Take for instance the CIDE explanation for *boil down* in its figurative sense:

- To **boil down** information, or to **boil** information **down**, is to reduce it, usually so that it contains only its most important parts: *The journalist boiled down his lengthy report to just a few paragraphs.*
- To **boil down to** something is to be the reason for it: *The problem all boils down to a lack of money.*

Now, does this mean that there are two verbs, *boil down* and *boil down to*, the one being transitive and the other intransitive? In COBUILD2, these two uses are presented as two facets of the same sense, and *boil down to* is labelled as an ergative phrasal verb.

The same problem arises with the 1995 edition of the OALD: ergative potentiality is usually suggested either by the definition or by the examples. Here are two examples:

fasten: (b) ~ **sth (up)** to close or join sth: [Vnp] *Fasten up your coat.*
(c) to become closed or attached: [Vp] *This dress fastens up at the back.*

intensify: to become or make sth become stronger or more concentrated: [V] *Her anger intensified.*
[Vn] *The terrorists have intensified their bombing campaign.*

One might wonder why the same potential is presented as one sense in the case of *intensify* and as two in the case of *fasten*. It seems to me that using the V-ERG (or any equivalent) label would greatly simplify the task of both lexicographers and users and give the latter a more accurate idea of a verb's different senses.

The first dictionary to systematically label ergative verb senses was indeed COBUILD1. This first edition (1987) gave the following explanation (p. 1620-1):

> **V-ERG** In this dictionary V-ERG is used in the grammar notes beside entries to describe verbs which are both transitive (V+O) and intransitive (V) in the same meaning. They are described as V-ERG because there is restriction on the type of subject which can be used with the intransitive verb. With V-ERGS, the object of the transitive verb can be used as the subject of the intransitive verb. For example 'peas' is the object of the transitive verb 'freeze' in *You can freeze peas* and is the subject of the intransitive verb in *Peas freeze well.* Other examples are **open** and **boil.** E.g. *We couldn't **open** the window... The window **opened** easily... He had **boiled** the kettle... The kettle **boiled**.* Some verbs are described as V OR V-ERG. Verbs described in this way have a transitive and intransitive use in the same way as the examples shown above and, in addition, they have an intransitive use with a subject which is different from the object of the transitive verb. An example is **sail.** E.g. *He **sailed** the boat towards Dover... The boat **sailed** towards Dover... He **sailed** towards Dover.*

This explanation seems to me to have both strong and weak points. On the one hand it stresses the semantic and syntactic relationship between the transitive and intransitive uses of the verb and the constraints influencing the choice of subject in the intransitive variant. What it does not say, however, is that in the *freeze* example, the presence of the adjunct (or of some other marker of difficulty) is obligatory: **Peas freeze* is, to my knowledge, unacceptable to most native speakers. If one looks at the dictionary entry for *freeze* (sense 2), one notices that the label V-ERG is followed by another indication saying: IF V THEN USU + A, which means that the adjunct is usually considered to be necessary. But, of course, this does not tell us what type of adjunct.

Suddenly, this academic year, the matching miracle seemed to happen. In 1995 Harper-Collins had published the *Collins Cobuild English Dicitonary* (New Edition). In 1996, the *Collins Cobuild Grammar Patterns 1: Verbs* came out. As the grammar uses the same conceptual framework, the same grammatical patterns and labels as the dictionary and systematically refers the user to the latter's definitions, I thought I had at last found the perfect grammatico-lexical couple. Besides, the grammar in question deals in great detail with several types of verbs I wanted to examine closely with my students, not only ergative verbs, but also link verbs, reciprocal and ergative-reciprocal verbs.

I therefore asked my second-year students to purchase it together with the dictionary. The idea was to read and discuss in class passages from the grammar which the students had prepared at home. They thus had to look up in the dictionary the verb senses mentioned in the passages in question and make sure they understood the examples cited in the grammar and in the dictionary to illustrate these senses. As the grammar is an incredibly rich and terribly complex collection of patterns, I shall limit my very tentative observations to the chapter concerning ergative verbs.

1. If we use the classification of codes proposed in T. Herbst (1996), we notice that the COBUILD codes have undergone an important modification. Whereas COBUILD1 had codes of the type V+O, V+C, V+O+O, in which the letters refer mainly to syntactic functions, COBUILD2 has adopted for verbs a two-tier system in which the main label (V-ERG, V-LINK, etc.) is complemented by sub-codes like V, Vn, Vprep/adv, Vn prep/adv. in which the letters represent parts of speech. The grammar, however, examines each of these sub-codes from the point of view of the structural combination they may present and thus introduces tables with syntactic labels. Here is such a table (p.478):

V

	Verb group	
Subject	**Verb**	**Adjunct (optional)**
The pattern	altered	
My spirits	lifted	
That meeting	will reconvene	in two weeks

Vn

	Verb group	**noun group**	**Adjunct**
Subject	**Verb**	**Object**	**(optional)**
All creatures	alter	their environment	a little
Some motorists	blast	their horns	in support
Sunlight	can lift	the spirits	
Ministers	will reconvene	their meeting	today

Now, the introduction to the dictionary (p. xxix) clearly explains that as far as ergative verbs are concerned "the noun group that is the subject in the **V** pattern refers to the same kind of thing as the noun group **n** in the **Vn** pattern". This is also often confirmed by the examples provided under the entry for any verb sense bearing the V-ERG label. In other words, if the learner uses the dictionary and the grammar in conjunction, he knows:

- that he is dealing with an ergative verb;
- what kind of surface/part-of-speech patterns this verbs fits into;
- what the syntactic functions are inside the pattern;
- what kinds of nouns are used in this pattern for the verb in question.

It seems to me that this is already much more than what is available in many other reference works.

2. One of the grammar's merits is certainly that it describes complex phenomena in simple language and avoids any surfeit of specialized jargon: its explanations are therefore accessible to learners with little or no linguistic preparation. Unfortunately, this sometimes leads the grammarian to coin his own terminology and his choices are, to my mind, sometimes unfelicitous. So the traditional *patient* of ergative verbs ('The vase' in *The vase broke*) becomes the *doer* whereas the *agent* becomes the *causer* ('John', in *John broke the vase*).

The vase broke gets the following, rather questionable, comment: "When the 'causer' is inanimate, it may be the immediate cause of the action". An example such as *Raspberries freeze well* gets the following explanation (p.475): "The 'causer' may provide the conditions in which a natural process takes place". This compares rather unfavourably with Dixon's explanation mentioned above or with the *Comprehensive's* comment that "the adverbial imputes a characteristic to the referent of the subject" (p.744). Besides, the explanation provided by the *Cobuild Patterns* fails to mention the compulsory presence of a difficulty marker.

Comparing *The vase broke, John broke the vase* and *The vase was broken,* the grammar says:

> The third example is the passive of the second example. We said above that in the first example, you may understand that the vase broke by itself or that someone caused the vase to break, whilst in the second example, you must understand that John caused the vase to break. In the third example, you understand that the vase did not break by itself, but do not know who caused the breakage. The Subjects of the first and the third examples are the same, but the meanings are different. (p.476).

Now, Levin would probably object to such an explanation on the ground that vases do not, as a rule, break by themselves and would argue that in *The vase broke* the breakage is understood to have been brought about by an external but unmentioned cause. Besides, the user's attention might have been drawn to the ambiguity of a sentence like *The vase was broken* in which the agent (in the syntactic and semantic sense) is not mentioned.

3. Many of the semantic categories under which the verbs are grouped do not quite satisfy me either. On the whole, they seem to me to be too broad. Take again the *break* group (p. 480), which contains "verbs concerned with something breaking or being damaged". It divides into two sub-groups. The first sub-group gathers such verbs as *break, erode, hang, suffocate* and *warp* in some of their senses. When one checks in the dictionary the senses involved, one has some difficulty in seeing how they can be placed in the same semantic category (whose common denominator is thus the idea of *breaking* or *being damaged*). It is for instance difficult to link *break* ("when an object breaks or when you break it, it suddenly separates into two or more pieces, often because it has been dropped or hit") and *suffocate* ("If someone suffocates or is suffocated, they die because there is no air for them to breathe"). The second sub-group goes from *blow* (a fuse or tyre) to *tear*. The reason why it was necessary to divide the group into two sub-groups escapes me, all the more since some verbs such as *break* and *tear* appear, albeit in different senses, in both sub-groups. When one peruses the dictionary entries for these two words, one notices that the lexicographers have deemed it necessary to distinguish a separate sense for *break* (break 2) when the latter applies to a part of your body. Perhaps this was thought necessary because this particular sense of the verb also has a nominal derivative (*It has caused a bad break to Gabriella's leg*). *Tear* also seems to appear in the two sub-groups because two senses have been distinguished in the dictionary: *tear 2.1* ("If you tear paper, cloth, or another material, or if it tears, you pull it into two pieces or you pull it so that a hole appears in it") and *tear 2.4* ("If you tear one of your muscles [...]"). Here again, it seems that the presence of the word in two sub-groups is made necessary by the entry's sense division. Now, the question is: is this

sense division really necessary? This is of course a matter of policy (see for the *break* example the differences between COBUILD1 and COBUILD2). One might argue that the multiplication of senses may help the user make fine distinctions and associate (as in the case of *a break*) a noun with a specific verb sense from which it is derived. On the other hand, one may feel that some of these fine distinctions are not very useful, increase the difficulty of having semantically consistent tables and thus lead to the multiplication of the latter.

Now, to sum up my tentative assessment of the grammar, I would thus say that although - or perhaps because - it is a trove of patterns and pattern combinations, I found it very difficult to use as a teaching tool - which, admittedly, is not what it is meant to be in the first place. I have also suggested how some of the explanations it provided left me somehow unsatisfied because their phrasing was vague or because they remained purely descriptive without attempting the kind of integrative elucidation provided by the semanticists. As far as COBUILD2 is concerned, one may agree or disagree with its definition of key technical concepts such as ergative or ergative link verbs, but one has to admit that the dictionary presents a self-consistent, extremely detailed, clear and very accessible picture of English verbal behaviour. It certainly goes a long way towards meeting the needs of the type of students I have been talking about.

4. As a matter of fact, I asked these students at the end of the academic year to give me their own assessment of the approach we had adopted. They did not particularly relish the continual toing-and-froing between the grammar and the dictionary in order to locate in the dictionary the ergative senses mentioned in the grammar and found some of the tables too comprehensive and too varied to allow any memorizing. On the other hand, they had quite a few positive comments to make about the fact that the issue of ergativity had been examined from different, complementary viewpoints. While they underlined the identificatory and mnemonic value of the definitional and morphological clues, they said they had also enjoyed discussing the way in which semantic and syntactic elements interacted in ergative verbs. The examination of English examples inevitably led to comparisons with their mother-tongue counterparts: in French, the equivalent of *to cook, cuire* is also both transitive and intransitive; *to break* is either *briser* or *se briser*. This comparison with the mother tongue did not, as one might have feared, trigger the old reflex of seeking refuge in the safe haven of bilingual lexicography. It rather led to interesting considerations on the respective advantages and drawbacks of the two types of tools. The students also pointed up the interest of the chapter from Dixon's semantic grammar concerning the constraints on promotion to subject. They found it offered an ideal blend of stimulating observations and practical recommendations. These are of course only short-term, subjective user judgments. The future may tell us to what extent this experiment has contributed to these learners' overall progress.

4 Conclusions

1. The approach I am advocating clearly implies a close cooperation between grammarians and lexicographers specializing in learners' dictionaries and a large measure of agreement concerning a number of crucial points: the nature of the grammar's conceptual framework, the nature and degree of complexity of the explanations to be provided by either type of partner, the precise definition of the key concepts, etc.

2. Although every teacher should decide for himself how far he can take his own students along the path of linguistic theory in order to help them improve their mastery of the various skills, I think there is a real need for grammar books which discuss issues such as transitivity, ergativity, reciprocity, etc. from the specific point of view of very advanced foreign learners and help them not only to understand but also to memorize the behavioral patterns of verbs, nouns, etc. I really think that approaching the problem at once from the angles of morphology, syntax and semantics makes it easier for learners not only to understand but also to classify, taxonomize and finally remember and use competently the various patterns.

3. To meet the grammatical needs of this type of advanced learner, a learners' dictionary should, in my opinion, provide concerning the syntactic potential of verbs, nouns and adjectives information which is much more detailed than what we now have in most existing dictionaries. I know that the 1978 *Longman Dictionary of Contemporary English,* which is one of the dictionaries which went furthest in that direction, was criticized on the ground that its grammatical codes were so complicated that students never used them. Perhaps the LDOCE was simply ahead of its time. Two years ago, I read with my students the introduction to Cowie & Mackin (1975), which also associates syntactic patterns (where the letters have no mnemonic value) with collocational indications. Some of these students, now in their last year, tell me that they now instinctively turn to this dictionary and to the patterns' explanation whenever the need arises.

4. While I very much hope that the dictionaries of the year 2000 will all feature detailed grammatico-semantic codes, I also wish to underline the necessity of taking into account the learners' overall needs and their consulting habits. As far as the macrostructure is concerned, the advanced and detailed information I am asking for should not be a pretext to eliminate any form of illustration or encyclopedic wisdom - the only exception I can think of being the traditional appendix about ranks in the Armed Forces. Clearly, even very advanced learners find colour illustrations, cultural information, etc. extremely attractive and very useful. After all, they use their dictionary not only for encoding but also for decoding tasks such as reading newspaper articles, novels and short stories, which is why this encyclopedic aspect of learners' dictionaries is highly valued by our literary colleagues. The ongoing multimedia revolution and multiplication of electronic dictionaries should encourage publishers to devise tools in which these various dimensions are harmoniously integrated. As far as the microstructure is concerned, accessibility should be the governing principle. As the user looking for a word is normally thinking in terms of sense and meaning, semantic considerations (such as embodied in guide words, for instance) should preside over the design of entries. This also implies that etymological and historical truth should be taken

into account. Multiplying entries, for instance, not only disorientates the user but often misinforms him concerning the origin, evolution and parentage of the words defined.

Bibliography

Cambridge Word Routes. Anglais-Français. - Lexique thématique de l'anglais courant (1994): Elizabeth Walter (ed.): . — Cambridge: CUP.

Collins Robert French-English English-French Dictionary (^{3}1993): Beryl T.S.Atkins, Alain Duval, Rosemary C. Milne (eds.). — Glasgow: HarperCollins.

Collins Cobuild English Language Dictionary (1987): John Sinclair (ed.). — London, Glasgow: Collins.

Collins Cobuild English Grammar (1990): John Sinclair (ed.). — London, Glasgow: Collins.

Collins Cobuild Grammar Patterns 1: Verbs (1996): John Sinclair (ed.). — London: HarperCollins.

Harrap's New Shorter French and English Dictionary (1986): Peter H. Collin (ed.). — London: Harrap.

Le Nouveau Petit Robert (1993): Josette Rey-Debove, Robert Paul (eds.). — Paris: Dictionnaires Le Robert.

Longman Dictionary of Contemporary English (1978): Paul Procter (ed.). — Harlow: Longman.

Longman Dictionary of English Language and Culture (1992): Della Summers (ed.). — Harlow: Longman.

Oxford Dictionary of Current Idiomatic English: Volume 1: Verbs with Prepositions and Particles (1975): Anthony Cowie, Ronald Mackin (eds.). — London: OUP.

Oxford Advanced Learner's Encyclopedic Dictionary (1992): Jonathan Crowther (ed.). — Oxford: OUP.

The Oxford Hachette French Dictionary (1994): Marie-Hélène Corréard, Valérie Grundy (eds.). — Oxford: OUP.

Atkins, Beryl T.S., Krista Varantola (1997): "Monitoring Dictionary Use". — In: International Journal of Lexicography 10/1, 1-45.

Dixon, Robert M.W (1991): A New Approach to English Grammar, on Semantic Principles. — Oxford: OUP.

— (1994): "Ergativity". — Cambridge: CUP (=Cambridge Studies in Linguistics 69).

Dirven, René (ed.) (1987): Fillmore's Case Grammar. — Heidelberg: Groos.

Fontenelle, Thierry,(1996): "Structural Regularities vs. Definition Patterns: A Riposte to Boguraev". — In: ITL, Review of Applied Linguistics 113/114, 321—334.

Fontenelle, Thierry, Jocelyne Vanandroye (1989): "Retrieving Ergative Verbs From a Lexical Database. Dictionaries". — In: Dictionaries, Journal of the Dictionary Society of North America 11, 11-39.

Herbst, Thomas (1996): "On the way to the perfect learners' dictionary: a first comparison of OALD5, LDOCE3, COBUILD2 and CIDE". — In: International Journal of Lexicography 9/4, 321-357.

Huddleston, Rodney D. (1984): Introduction to the Grammar of English (=Cambridge Textbooks in Linguistics). — Cambridge: CUP.

Levin, Beth (1995): "Approaches to Lexical Semantic Representation". — In: D. Walker, A. Zampolli, N. Calzolari (eds): Automating the Lexicon (Oxford: OUP, 413.

Levin, Beth, Malka Rappaport Hovav (1995): Unaccusativity: At the Syntax-Lexical Semantics Interface. — Cambridge, Massachusetts: the MIT Press (=Linguistic Inquiry Monograph Twenty-Six).

Moulin, André (1993): "What Grammar? Teaching EFL Grammar at University Level.". — In: Interface, Journal of Applied Linguistics 7/2, 71-90.

Quirk, Randolph, Sidney Greenbaum, Geoffrey Leech, Jan Svartvik (1985): A Comprehensive Grammar of the English Language. — London, New York: Longman.

Gisela Böhner

Classroom experience with the new dictionaries: OALD5, LDOCE3, COBUILD2, CIDE

Two years ago I asked a pupil why he did not use his dictionary more regularly and more frequently because by doing this he could improve his written English. He answered: "Much too time-consuming. I just take a word I think fit and let the teacher sort it out."

This brought me - not for the first time - to the question: is there anything wrong with our dictionaries and/or with the way we teach how to use them?

For those who are not familiar with the Bavarian system of education let me briefly introduce the school I work at: the school is a traditional grammar school, a *mathematisch-naturwissenschaftliches Gymnasium*, situated in a rather rural area of Northern Bavaria with about 1200 pupils ranging from 10-19 years. Languages are core subjects and the pupils start with English as their first foreign language right from the very beginning, so they have had at least 7 years of English by the time they leave after the Abitur.

From the 11th form on - after 5 years of English - the pupils are allowed to use a monolingual dictionary for their tests. The Bavarian Government, that is the Bavarian Department of Education, has strict guidelines as to which dictionaries are allowed in Bavarian schools, right down to the ISBN-number, so at the moment in school we can only gain experience with two types of the new dictionaries: the OALD and LDOCE in different editions, normally OALD4 and OALD5 and LDOCE1 and LDOCE2.

For this paper I decided to prepare a kind of questionnaire together with my pupils that was based on their experience, on their experience with these two dictionaries. For a test of all four dictionaries I decided on an exercise with my advanced-level course.

The questionnaire:

There were to be three groups of participants, according to their experience and practice with the dictionary:

Group 1 : taken from the 11th form (107 participants) with little or hardly any practice with the monolingual dictionary.

Group 2 : foundation courses (dt. '*Grundkurse*'), (86 participants), years 12 and 13. For most of the pupils, but not for all of them, English is important for their final exam. So some of them just do time and are not really interested in learning more than they already know, for them it is enough to just scrape through, they are not really motivated.

Group 3 : advanced-level courses (dt. '*Leistungskurse*'), (78 participants), years 12 and 13, are the pupils majoring in English, finishing school with a written exam after 9 years of English.

Altogether there were 271 participants.

After discussions in classes and courses, with colleagues and studies in literature concerned with lexicology, we - some of my pupils and I - formulated statements and questions concerning the pupils' usage of dictionaries in tests, in school and at home (here we included the bilingual dictionary), and as a second part the pupils were asked to give their criteria for an ideal dictionary. To get really honest results the pupils did not have to give their names on the questionnaires.

To cut a long story short: the results were anything but surprising at least not for me and my colleagues. They confirmed everything we had always suspected:

During the test I use my monolingual dictionary to find out...

Chart 1
I use my monolingual dictionary to...[1]

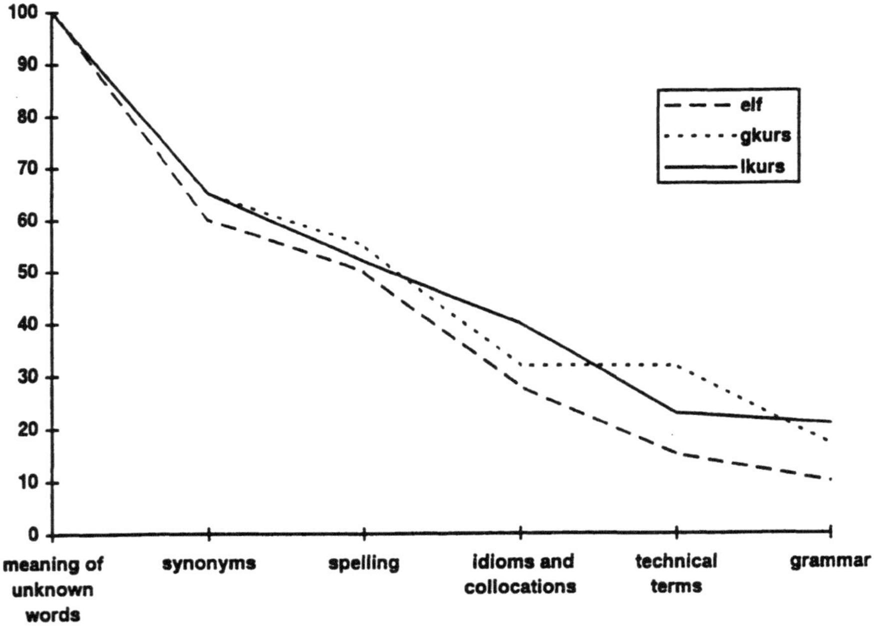

All three levels agreed with 100% that they used the dictionary to find out the meaning of unknown words, between 60-65% use it to find synonyms, better vocabulary for their compositions etc, between 50-55% check the spelling with it, with regard to idioms and collocations the curves start to separate, first differences can be seen: 40% at advanced-level indicate that advanced-level student probably recognize idioms more easily and are better trained to look for and use correct collocations, whereas the 11th grade (28% use their dictionary in this respect) do not have enough experience to use their dictionary on idioms.

1 abr. elf = 11th grade; gkurs = foundation courses; lkurs = advanced-level

An interesting fact may be that the foundation courses regard their dictionaries rather as reference books when it comes to looking up and understanding technical terms like alliteration or fable etc. 32% probably use the dictionary to answer questions on stylistic devices etc. The 11th grade has with 15% not yet discovered this value of their dictionary. Only 10% of the 11th grade and 17% from foundation courses use their dictionaries to sort out questions of grammar, whereas 21% of the advanced-level pupils try to profit from the grammatical sections. Less than 10% of all pupils look up differences in register or BrE and AmE. These figures seem to prove that lack of experience and practice prevents, especially the 11th grade, from making the most of their dictionary. As far as the foundation courses are concerned it could be a mixture of either lack of practice but also lack of motivation. With regard to level of styles or differences of American and British English, less than 10% used their dictionaries in these areas.

Bavarian school tests at this level normally consist of a text, comprehension questions, a composition (comment etc.) and a translation English into German. To confirm the results of the first statement we added a second statement.

During the test I always use my dictionary to...

Table 1

	understand and translate the text	answer the questions	write the composition
11th	97%	59%	57%
gkurs	100%	83%	62%
lkurs	100%	73%	48%

All three levels used it nearly 100% for the translation and the comprehension (ties in with 100% unknown meaning), 83% of the foundation courses, a rather high number I cannot really explain, use it to answer the comprehension questions compared to 73% of the advanced-level pupils. Again the figures show that the 11th grade do not yet make the most of their dictionaries - only 59% use it to answer the questions, and also only 57% to write their composition. Here, too, foundation course pupils seem to make most of their dictionary with 62%, whereas advanced-level pupils with 48% seem to have the vocabulary at their fingertips.

Things are different at home where pupils can use the bilingual dictionary. The statement ran:

At home I use my dictionary to find out...

Table 2

	bilingual		monolingual	
	meaning of an unknown word	spelling	vocabulary and synonyms	grammatical information
11th	100%	52%	43%	14%
gkurs	94%	54%	58%	22%
lkurs	92%	43%	62%	16%

92% to 100% use their bilingual dictionary to find out the meaning, between 43% and 54% use it to check the spelling.

The monolingual dictionary was supposedly used by 62% to 43% of the pupils to find synonyms and vocabulary.

Grammatical information was a good deal less sought after in the monolingual dictionary, between 22% and 14%.

These are not really satisfying results: for instance, let us take the case that a student looks up the meaning of *to avoid* in his/her bilingual dictionary, in all cases she/he will get the meaning correctly but what about the information that *avoid* is followed by a gerund?

To find out the amount of time the pupils use their dictionary we included the statement:

I use my dictionary not more than 15 minutes a week

Table 3

	monolingual not more than 15 min	bilingual about 15 min a week
11th	73%	75%
gkurs	93%	88%
lkurs	67% (11% 15'+)	76% (15% 15'+)

73% of the 11th grade and 93% of the foundation course pupils use their monolingual dictionaries not more than 15 minutes a week. The same applies for the bilingual one:

between 75 and 88%. The figures for the advanced-level are slightly better, because here some pupils use it more that 15 minutes: 15% the bilingual one, the monolingual 11%.

I consider these results rather depressing: how can pupils get practice and experience if they use their dictionaries so little?

In the second part of the questionnaire we asked pupils:

Which aspects of your dictionary keep you from using it regularly and frequently?

Chart 2

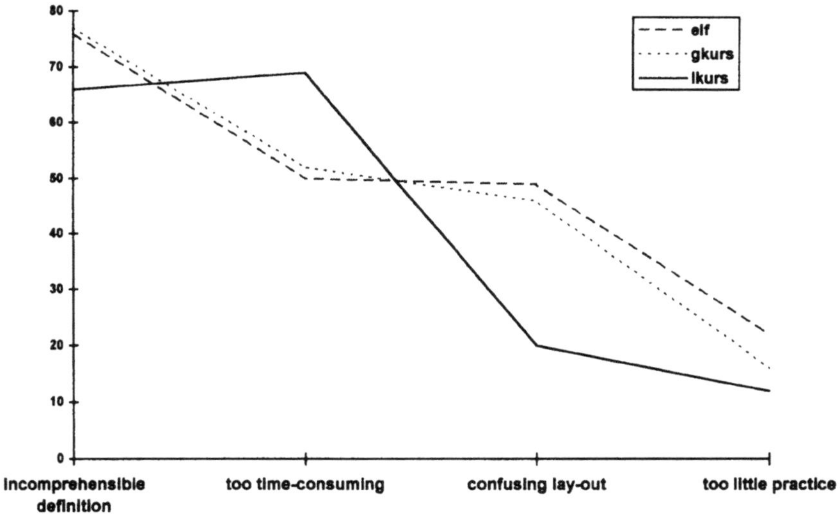

Here the results of the 11th grade and the foundation course were very similar, as you can see from the more or less parallel curves. The worst that could happen was obviously that an unknown word was explained with more unknown words or a substantive with the verb or vice versa. This fact was criticized by 77% of 11th and gkurs pupils, but only 66% of the advanced-level pupils said this stopped them from using it. They seem to be under greater time-pressure than the other two levels, because 69% said that it took too long to find out the correct meaning, compared to 50% and 52% 11th and gkurs respectively.

With regard to speed and time-pressure we compared the results of the question:

What happens if you have to read through a very long entry?

Table 4

	stop reading when just right	break off without having got the information wanted
11th	75%	13%
gkurs	73%	15%
lkurs	70%	28%

Between 75% and 70% stop reading when they think the answer is about right. Between 13% and 15% of the 11th grade and the foundation course respectively do not read to the end, but break off – a clear sign of time-pressure: 28% of the advanced-level pupils do the same.

With regard to the lay-out, that is the structure of single entries the practice of the advanced-level student showed clearly that 80% could handle their dictionaries quite well, whereas the other two levels (49% to 46%) said the lay-out was one reason they did not use their dictionary regularly and frequently. Only 12% of the advanced-level and 16% of the foundation course pupils blamed their teachers and said that they had not had enough practice and guidance on how to use a dictionary. The 11th grade with 22% are at an early stage of becoming familiar with their dictionaries, though only 22% thought that they did not have enough practice.

I do not want to leave out some of the more curious answers given to this question: why not use it...: 9 pupils admitted to being too lazy to use it, some argued that a CD was much faster and more fun. They were joined by 15 who thought the monolingual dictionary was altogether too heavy to use! The three pupils of the foundation course who thought a monolingual dictionary was altogether unnecessary and a waste of money should be mentioned here, too.

The last part of the survey was concerned with finding the criteria for an ideal dictionary.

Your ideal dictionary should have...

Chart 3

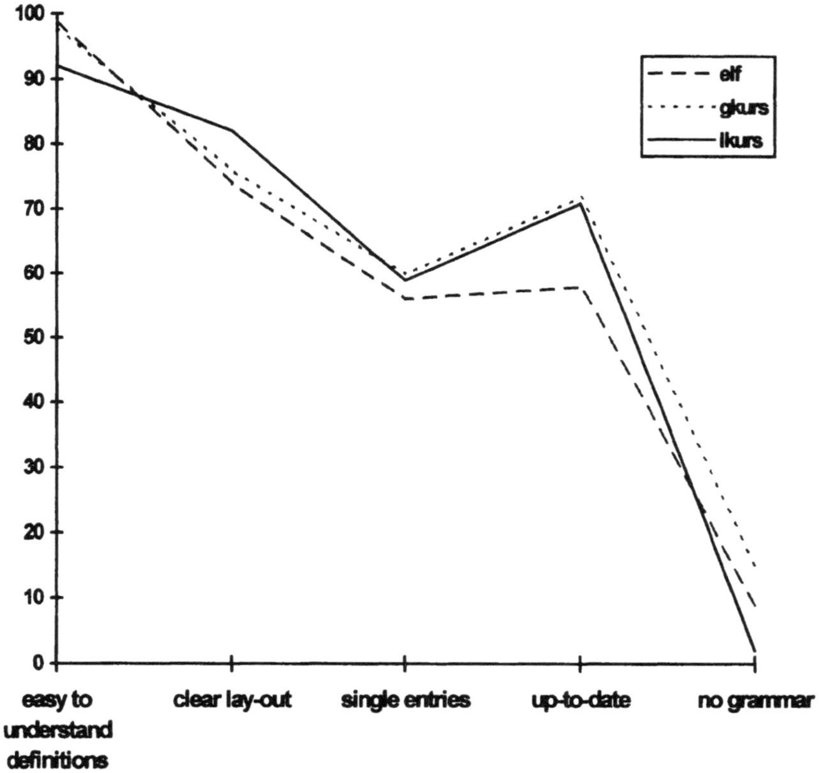

Easy to see that easy-to-understand, clear and short definitions had top priority with all levels. Although the advanced-level courses had stated that the lay-out did not really keep them from using their dictionaries, now 82% think that a clear, well-structured lay-out makes a dictionary ideal. 60% of all three levels agree that they prefer single entries for each meaning of a word to block entries with numbers. Between 72% and 58% think only a very modern, very up-to-date dictionary is ideal.

As a surprise came the result that although they hardly use the grammatical section of their dictionaries, they do not want to miss it in a dictionary. Especially the advanced courses regard the grammar information as a kind of insurance, in case it is needed. Only 2% of this level think a dictionary is ideal without it. The foundation course seems to be more realistic: 15% could do without it.

Among other criteria mentioned were: the demand for more pictures, the use of colour in the lay-out, a thumb index especially to make a dictionary fast, tuning it so to speak. One suggested an Internetlink via cellular telephone or satellite dish! A cynic's conclusion could be: the pupils' ideal dictionary is light, lean, cheap and German-English/English-German!

As at the moment only two of the new dictionaries can be used in Bavarian schools a test of all four dictionaries could only be superficial and cursory. Gathering material for a project on urban legends and internetlore, I came across a book that contained quite a collection of these stories (Brunvand 1988) and one of them seemed suitable for a test because of its headline's ambiguity: the inhabitant of an asylum had escaped into a laundry, had raped two of the washers there and fled. A newspaper had printed this story and had given the article the very ambiguous headline: *Nut screws washers and bolts*. This gave me the idea: why not test the dictionaries with this headline?[2] The headline was ambiguous enough for the pupils not to guess the meaning immediately and their task was to decipher the headline with the help of these four dictionaries and after having done this they were asked to give the dictionaries marks for:

a. easy-to-understand-definitions
b. clear lay-out
c. the speed they could be used with. That is where could the definitions be found quickest, i.e. under time pressure.

With regard to definitions LDOCE3 came first: the best and easiest to understand. OALD5 was a good second, the pupils thought some of the definitions a bit too complex. With regard to lay-out the pupils were very impressed by CIDE with its guide word system in frames if there is more than one core meaning, something they had never seen before and they suggested colouring the frames to give the dictionary even more structure. The short definitions in CIDE were also very welcome, they liked the defining vocabulary as they liked the one from LDOCE3. The pupils thought both dictionaries LDOCE3 and CIDE were very suitable for quick finding, the OALD5 was again a good second with regard to speed. As they are used to the lay-out of the OALD5 now, having worked with it for nearly 1,5 years, this does not come as a surprise, but the pupils still thought that there was room for improvement. They dislike especially the enumeration within the running text. For them COBUILD2 was very confusing, very strange and as they do not consider grammatical information important in a dictionary, they thought that the margin with the grammatical abreviations was wasted and confusing. From their point of view they could not understand the structure of entries.

So the pupils' message to publishers and editors is clear: they want definitions which are short and simple and easy to understand and they want the lay-out as structured and graphically clear as possible. But what is the pupils' message to us teachers? As the survey shows pupils are mainly concerned with the meaning of words when using their dictionary, so first of all we should help them to find what they are looking for. One way to do this

---

2 I want to point out that the test was by no means representative, it was not scientific and surely not objective.

could be intensive and frequent work with the defining vocabulary of the dictionaries, in order to make pupils familiar with them and thus taking them their fear of hard to understand definitions. If the definitions prove no longer an obstacle, time pressure will decrease and pupils will be able to make further use of their dictionaries, because the new dictionaries are too good and too comprehensive to be only used for looking up the meaning of words. With less pressure the pupils might even get into the habit of checking grammatical problems with the help of their dictionary, although with regard to grammar we teachers would perhaps first have to sharpen our pupils' *mistake awareness* (dt. Fehlerbewußtsein). In the forefield of this study I checked two tests (lkurs and 11th) carefully. Which mistakes could have been avoided if the pupils had used their dictionaries properly? It turned out that about 30% of the mistakes could have been avoided,[3] if the pupils had used their dictionaries to their best advantage. When asked most of the pupils said that they had not known that there was something wrong with this construction, so they had not looked it up. Furthermore, they claimed that time pressure had prevented a prolonged study of doubtful constructions.

But how to sharpen *mistake awareness*? How to work with the defining vocabulary? How to train pupils to get the most of their dictionaries? Here are many rewarding projects waiting for us teachers in the future.

Bibliography

Brunvand, Jan Harold (1988): The Mexican Pet: More "New" Urban Legends & Some Old Favourites. — New York/London: Norton Paperback.

Heath, David et al. (1989): Dictionary Techniques. Praktische Arbeit mit dem DCE. Lehrerhandreichungen. — München: Langenscheidt/Longman.

---

3 As quoted in: Heath, David et al. (1989): *Dictionary Techniques. Praktische Arbeit mit dem DCE. Lehrerhandreichungen.* - München: Langenscheidt/Longman, p.2.

Burkhard Dammann

Teachers' demands on learners' dictionaries

Before I come to the point of my paper I should like to mention some of the parameters of my professional work. Like Dr. Böhner, I teach English at a Bavarian *Gymnasium*, which means we have to follow the guidelines of a specific curriculum within the complex framework of the German educational system. We have teaching experience at all levels of secondary education, but we cannot speak for any teacher outside our domain, although we may assume that, on the whole, our aims, wishes and problems are not much different from those in other *Länder*.

Dr. Böhner has pointed out some problems in her practical work with students at the upper school level. It should be quite clear at the beginning of this paper that that is the group of learners I have in mind when talking about teachers' demands. It is not the beginners who are quite satisfied with a dictionary that fulfills basic needs only nor is it the large body of students at the university who, for all we know, might never feel tempted to use learners' or monolingual dictionaries at all. I do, of course, include teachers among the users of this type of dictionary.

Teachers have to put different demands on dictionaries than students - for various reasons. Apart from pursuing their own individual interests and aims, teachers have to adhere to certain administrative regulations. What does the Bavarian curriculum (for English at the *Gymnasium*, upper school level) say on monolingual dictionaries? Not much, since it is mainly concerned with aims and not with methodology, i.e. we are told what to teach and not how to do it. Thus it is entirely up to the teachers when and how often they use textbooks or reference books on grammar or dictionaries and how they tell their students the best way to cope with helpful material. At the upper school level, students are allowed to use monolingual dictionaries at almost all kinds of tests, including the *Abitur*. Since the monolingual dictionary is the only help admitted, it is given some space in the curriculum, albeit rather small, scattered over several pages. The following is a fairly comprehensive list of what the curriculum says when referring to monolingual dictionaries:

- (terms:) collocation, register, style, idiomatic expression, use of language, context restriction
- (advice to students when to use their dictionaries:) revise, activate knowledge, identify mistakes, improve style, recognise collocations
- (as regards style and usage students should:) observe appropriate register and tone in spoken and written English; make use of clear and concise expressions; avoid breaks in style; adapt style and register to context (i.e. the relevant communicative situation).

In short, students should be encouraged to make use of all the help they can find in a monolingual dictionary.

Bearing that in mind, what do teachers want? I cannot refer to a statistically reliable survey but I hope I have collected enough ideas to paint a fairly representative picture.

- Definitions - adapted to the learners' needs: When I asked the Bavarian teacher trainers what should be improved in learners' dictionaries, one of them wrote down "Definitions as simple as in the LDOCE 2 but more precise". Is that improbability in a nutshell? A recent book review was happy that Oxford had "at last broken its user-unfriendly tradition of the unlimited defining vocabulary". I must confess that I was a little shocked when they did (in OALD 5). Let me explain. I realise that there is a large number of students who find coping with a dictionary very hard (see Böhner, this volume), and many of them are quite happy with dictionaries that strive to make definitions easy to understand. But: we teach in contexts, and in the last three years before the leaving exams our contexts are authentic texts of a very wide variety - from the Sun of Stratford to *The Sun* of the London docklands, so to speak. The more restricted the defining vocabulary is, the more remote it seems to the language of the text the student is working on. To my mind, that is a very important point. Learning a language is a time-consuming business - so why should dictionaries offer fast food? - I do not wish to go any deeper into this, however. Wars have been fought over this question. Anyway, do corpus-based dictionaries not offer hope for a fair compromise?
- Examples - clear and concise: If, for reasons just given, the definition has to be kept fairly simple, then it is the examples which can help to give the touch of authenticity. Ever so often students find that the wording of the example is very similar to that in the text they are studying. Quite apart from giving them the meaning of the word they have been looking for, it helps them to understand that words, like most people, feel better in neighbourhoods they are acquainted with.
- Number of entries/neologisms: this is probably one of the most difficult questions. A good learners' dictionary should be one volume only, and it should not be too bulky - all the new dictionaries are only just acceptable as regards size or simply too large. Consequently, the number of headwords to be found in a dictionary should not be the main selling factor. Teachers and other amateur reviewers of new publications look for words like 'Zulu' or 'zyzygy' to test quantity. The LDOCE finalised that quest years ago: 'zzz' is the definite last entry. I wonder whether any of our students even dreams of looking up a 'word' like that. I have to confess dictionary reviews can make delightful reading. Is it not rather satisfactory that 'bimbo', 'couch potato', 'glitterati' and 'gobsmacked' have found their way into most of the new dictionaries? One reviewer misses 'mousetrap cheese', however. Nowhere to be found. My guess is that it is either what it seems to say it is or I personally would not want to know. Do we have to demand that words like 'baguette' be included or other free-floating internationalised words? For purposes at school leave something for the teacher to find out, please (even if he then accuses the dictionary makers of not being with it)!

- Collocations (idiomatic expressions, phrasal verbs): this "fuzzy region of phraseology", to use Professor Cowie's words, presents one of the biggest problems for the learners of English - the more information a student can find in a dictionary on this topic the better.
- Labels to denote varieties, register, style, attitude, restrictions, grammar ....: this demand is an absolute must - if not directly for the students, then for the poor teacher to enlighten his pupils about all the niceties connected with what is called 'intercultural learning' or 'cross-cultural understanding' (including PC) today. Grammar labels, to my mind, have always been more of a favourite with teachers than with students - which is well-supported by what Dr. Böhner found out. But: this symposium seems to have shown (special thanks to Prof. Aarts!) that no learners' dictionary should go without clear grammar labels!
- Information on frequency.
- Information on pronunciation, stress.
- Usage notes (Notes on usage): unanimous verdict: very useful.
- Illustrations (if possible in colour - colour values!).
- Systematic cross-references (cf. various statements at this Symposium about collocations!).
- Symbols (easily identifiable).
- Introduction: usable for classroom purposes.
- Abbreviations/acronyms: more - and in alphabetical order (i.e. not in appendix).

The following items were mentioned by various teachers but would definitely make the dictionaries too bulky or too expensive: (short) etymology, thesaurus, update sheets, CD-ROM with sound examples.

Finally, two demands that were listed by several teachers (who should really know better):

- special pages with grammatical/linguistic features
- (more) information on "intercultural knowledge".

These two items have been put separately for a specific reason that marks the main difference between users at the school and the university levels. Pupils at Bavarian schools are allowed to use a monolingual dictionary in most tests at the upper school level, including the leaving exams, the *Abitur*. They have to show that they have mastered all the basic aspects of the English grammar, that they have learned something in the wide field of cultural studies, that they know how to analyse a literary text. So explicit grammar pages (giving detailed information on rules) in dictionaries present a problem; so do special lists of words (and all bilingual explanations!). Nothing on 'false friends' and how to form an adverb and where to place it in the sentence, please. Nor should dictionaries contain detailed information on fields like education or the mass media, for example. Thus most information of encyclopaedic character is ruled out. All this might help to explain why only two learners' dictionaries have been admitted in Bavaria so far.

Do the teachers have reason to grumble? Hardly. The history of monolingual learners' dictionaries, especially in recent years, has shown that enormous improvements have been made. If there is one lesson I have learned at this Symposium it is that we teachers must make much more use of the new type of corpus-based dictionary!

II. Learners' dictionaries – other dictionaries

Franz Josef Hausmann

Semiotaxis and learners' dictionaries

Did you make your own bed this morning? Probably not: if you are troubled about how to make a bed, ask the dictionary. Dictionaries know everything about everything. For instance CIDE:

> When someone **makes the bed**, they put sheets and covers, or a DUVET on the bed, and/or make these smooth so that the bed is comfortable to sleep in.

Where, in which dictionary entry do we find this definition? Answer: in the entry *bed* [FURNITURE]. And I think this is a good lexicographical policy.

But what about the entry *make?* Does the dictionary have to define *make the bed* in the entry *make*? This is a case of SEMIOTAXIS (Hausmann 1997). It is a SEMIOTACTIC problem. Semiotaxis tells us to what extent words may be defined without context. Obviously there is a great difference in the definability of words. Many words don't need any linguistic context to be defined. *Bed* is such a word: "a large rectangular piece of furniture, often with four legs, which is used for sleeping on" (CIDE). We may call the word *bed* semiotactically 'autonomous', or 'independent'. We can test the autonomy of words by reversing the lemma-definition order. What are the words defined by the following definitions:

OALD5	
a place where people are kept as a punishment for crimes they have committed or while waiting for trial	prison
the ability to accept delay, annoyance or suffering without complaining	patience
the natural state of rest in which the eyes are closed	sleep
unable to see	blind

Obviously, too, *make* in *make the bed* is not autonomous, but dependent on the context. You can't define this *make* without referring to the bed. Another example: you can define *water* without context, but you can't define *hard* in the sense of "containing a lot of LIME (= a chemical substance) which prevents soap from cleaning" without referring to water. The autonomous words and senses are on the side of the open-choice-principle, the non-autonomous words and senses are on the side of the idiom-principle (Sinclair 1987). Therefore the autonomous words can be learnt by a foreigner without context. *Bed* = *Bett* = *lit*. The non-autonomous words have to be learnt in context.

We may now return to the initial question. Where to define *make the bed*, in the article *bed*, in the article *make* or in both? There are several lines of argument one could take:

1. *Make the bed* realises a sense of *make* (sense 40 in LDOCE which lists 45 senses). It is part of the polysemy of *make* and needs defining in the article *make*.

2. The sense of *make* in *make the bed* is entirely dependent on the sense of *bed*, which is autonomous. Senses of dependent words should be defined nearest to the autonomous words they depend on. So define *make the bed* nearest to the definition of *bed.* Only autonomous words and senses should be defined in their alphabetical place. For the other it suffices to quote them and to cross-reference to the article of the autonomous partner (*bed*).

MAKE: .... make the → bed

Let's turn to the reality of treatment in our dictionaries. CIDE and COBUILD2 do not mention *make the bed* under *make*. The other dictionaries (OALD5, LDOCE3) define *make the bed* twice under *bed* and under *make*. COBUILD is remarkable for having dropped *make the bed* in the article *make*.

	OALD5	LDOCE	COBUILD	CIDE
make	1(c) to arrange a *bed* so that it is ready for use	13. to tidy (a bed that has just been slept in) by straightening the sheets, pulling over the cover, etc. (LDOCE2) 40. *make the bed* (to pull the sheets and covers over a bed so that it is tidy after someone has slept in it) (LDOCE3)	15. if you *make* the bed, you prepare it so that it is neat and tidy and ready for someone to sleep in (COBUILD1) see make 1.7 (used in large number of expressions...) (COBUILD2)	Ø
bed	1(a) *make the beds* (i.e. arrange them so that they are ready for sleeping in)	1. *make the bed* (= make it ready for sleeping in) (LDOCE2) 1. (= tidy the bed covers) (LDOCE3)	14. when you *make* the *bed*, you neatly arrange the sheets and covers of a bed so that it is ready to sleep in. (COBUILD2)	see p.1

I consider double definition as in LDOCE3 a waste of space. Neither could one say that CIDE is a semiotaxis-oriented dictionary, because, in the case of *hard water*, CIDE, like all other dictionaries, quotes and defines only under *hard.* None of our four dictionaries quotes or defines *hard water* under *water*, while semiotactic analysis requires quoting and defining of *hard water* where *water* is defined. In the article *hard* it suffices to cross-reference to water.

HARD: .... hard → water

Dictionaries should mirror the reality of language and they should respond to principles of economy. Semiotaxis to me seems able to give clear answers to certain questions a lexicographer is faced with. Eliminating all defining of dependent words and senses in the articles of these words may seem to many too revolutionary a method to adopt in learners' dictionaries. But even in this case semiotaxis leads to a fundamental principle which is far from being realised in all cases. This principle means that in the case of non-autonomous words and senses definition must come *after* the context and not *before*. The context must be placed left of the definition and not right.

Take the case of *knotty* in the collocation *a knotty problem*. Obviously *knotty* is non-autonomous. The definition "complicated and difficult to solve" doesn't lead to the word except in rather difficult crossword puzzles. Therefore dictionaries should place the definition *after* the context and not *before*. There should be right-side definition and not left-side definition. Do our dictionaries adopt this philosophy? The situation is as follows:

knotty: (+/- means presence or absence of the collocation in the article *problem*)

OALD5 Def.+cont.	**LDOCE2** Def.+cont.	**COBUILD1/2** Def.+cont.	**CIDE**
1. full of knots *wood, hair* 2. complex and difficult to solve [+] *problem* *question*	1. (of wood) containing knots 2. full of difficulties [-] *problem*	1. *problem* [-] complicated and difficult to solve problems 2. *wood* has a lot of small hard areas on it where branches once grew	(of a problem or difficulty) complicated and difficult to solve *question* [-] *problem*
	LDOCE3		
	1. difficult to solve [-] *problem* 2. *wood...*		

In this case only COBUILD and CIDE are semiotactically correct with their right-side definition. Unfortunately this is by no means a general rule. See the case of *confirmed bachelor* in the article *confirmed.*

confirmed:

<table>
<tr><th>OALD5</th><th>LDOCE2</th><th>COBUILD1/2</th><th>CIDE</th></tr>
<tr>
<td rowspan="3">firmly established in a particular habit or state

[+] bachelor (a single..)
drunkard/gambler</td>
<td>firmly settled in a particular way of life or way of thinking

bachelor [-]</td>
<td>someone who has a particular habit, attitude, or belief that they are very unlikely to change

non-smoker [-]</td>
<td rowspan="3">having had a particular habit or way of life for a long time so that change seems unlikely

bachelor [+]
sports fanatic
whisky drinker</td>
</tr>
<tr><td>LDOCE3</td><td>COBUILD2</td></tr>
<tr>
<td>bachelor [+]
alcoholic
vegetarian etc.

someone who seems completely happy with the way of life they have chosen</td>
<td>bachelor [-]
atheist [-]</td>
</tr>
</table>

Neither OALD nor COBUILD nor CIDE nor LDOCE2 take into consideration the dependent character of *confirmed.* They do left-side definition. Unlike these LDOCE3 shifted to a semiotactically correct description. See also *make* 40/13 in LDOCE3/LDOCE2 (see table 1). And this is confirmed by the treatment of *meet* in the sense of *to meet the deadline*.

meet:

OALD5	LDOCE2	COBUILD1/2	CIDE
7. to do, fulfil or satisfy what is required *requirements* *conditions* *deadline* [+] 8. to pay sth *cost*	10. to satisfy (a need, demand, etc.) *expectations* *demand* 11. to pay *debts* **LDOCE3** 9. *demand* *need* *requirement* to satisfy a 10. *aim* *goal* *target* [+] to achieve an... 11. *debts* *costs* *expenses* to pay ~... (deadline [+])	6. a need, requirement or condition 9. of a sufficient quantity or quality to fulfil its needs, requirements 7. *problem* *challenge* deal satisfactorily with it 10. *crisis* *challenge* *deadline* [+] 8. cost... *cost, repayments*	[FULFIL] to fulfil, satisfy or achieve *demands* *needs* *requirements* *conditions* *obligations* *deadline* *target* also: pay

I think there is need for a strong theory of semiotaxis. We have to distinguish what we may call *autosemantic words* from *synsemantic* ones. This is important for language learning and is important for lexicography. Because when we do bad left-side definition, we suggest the lexicon to be compositional. But it isn't. The lexicon is essentially idiomatic. Therefore most of the dictionary definitions must be good right-side definitions.

A note on confusions

There is some confusion about collocations.

First confusion: The linguistic term *collocation* has at least two senses:

a) The *Sinclairian* sense (Sinclair 1987)
   synonym: co-occurrence
b) Mel'čuk/Benson/Hausmann - sense (Mel'čuk 1998, Benson 1997)

I only talk about b) and so does Brigitta Mittmann (this volume).

Let's take an example: How can you say in English: make new shoes comfortable. Which is the right word? Le "mot propre"?

G	einlaufen (Schuhe ~)
F	briser ses chaussures
E	break in new shoes

Where do we find the collocation in our monolingual dictionaries?

	Collocator	Base
COBUILD	+	∅
LDOCE	+	∅
CIDE	+	∅
OALD	∅	∅
BBI (Benson 1997)	-	+

Someone who is in search of the right word *break in* can't find it in the first four dictionaries. *Break in shoes* is a hidden collocation. In BBI however they can find it in the entry *shoe*. The question we may ask is: How many hidden collocations are in our learners' dictionaries?

Second confusion: Bogaards (this volume) asked students where they open the monolingual dictionary, in the article *infliger* or in the article *peine*?

Infliger	une peine
Collocator	Base
break in	shoes

But that question does not make sense.

For productive purposes students in search of *break in* or *infliger* cannot open the dictionary with the article *break in*. There cannot be 38 % of collocator's articles openers because this is hidden for the production purpose searcher in a monolingual dictionary.

Conclusion: Bogaards' tests are not valid for my search theories. They don't meet the theory.

Bibliography

Benson, Morton, Evelyn Benson, Robert Ilson (1997): The BBI Dictionary of English Word Combinations. Revised edition. — Amsterdam: Benjamins.

Hausmann, Franz Josef (1997): "Semiotaxis und Wörterbuch". — In: K.-P. Konerding, A. Lehr (eds.): Linguistische Theorie und lexikographische Praxis (Tübingen: Niemeyer) (= Lexicographica Series Maior 82) 171-179.

Mel'čuk, Igor (1998): "Collocations and Lexical Functions". — In: A. P. Cowie (ed.): Phraseology. Theory, Analysis and Applications (Oxford: Claredon Press), 23-53.

Sinclair, John (1987): "Collocation: A Progress Report". — In: R. Steel, T. Threadgold (eds.): Language Topics (Amsterdam: Benjamins) 319-331.

Jonathan Crowther

Encyclopedic learners' dictionaries

A discussion of encyclopedic learners' dictionaries (ELDs) should properly begin with an examination of the term itself. And before we look at ELDs we should perhaps ask ourselves what we understand by the term *encyclopedic dictionary*, especially since, in Britain at least, the publication of encyclopedic dictionaries as such appears to be a fairly recent phenomenon, whereas dictionaries and encyclopedias have been around for many years. The publishers Hutchinson published their *Encyclopedic Dictionary* in 1991, describing it as 'a synthesis [...] both a dictionary and a concise encyclopedia'. In the same year Oxford University Press issued the *Oxford Encyclopedic English Dictionary* as an 'innovative all-in-one reference book [...] combining a description of the English language with facts about the world'. And Chambers in 1994 published their *Encyclopedic Dictionary*, calling it 'two essential reference books in one', with a 'complete and unique integration of language and culture' (a significant phrase). The suggestion that these well-known publishers of reference books were breaking new ground with these compendium volumes might seem strange to the dictionary-reading public in the USA and Europe (especially France and Germany) where the practice of including encyclopedic material in general dictionaries is long-established and the expected norm. Indeed the historical tradition of British lexicography seems to have been broadly in favour of including encyclopedic material or at least the encyclopedic treatment of certain entries up to and including the 18th century. Johnson's dictionary of 1755 was not untypical in this regard. Thereafter in Britain there was something of a divergence as vocabulary itself and the scientific study of language grew, and 'pure' encyclopedias included more and more factual information about the world while dictionaries became increasingly concerned with the analysis of lexical words and their meaning. The *Oxford English Dictionary*, and the other smaller Oxford dictionaries that followed it, such as the *Concise Oxford Dictionary*, were conceived strictly as language dictionaries, and their example has influenced British lexicography for much of the present century, whereas in the USA, France and Germany the tradition of producing all-purpose single- and multi-volume dictionaries has continued largely unchanged (with the exception of Webster's *Third New International Dictionary* (1961), which controversially omitted the non-lexical supplements of its earlier editions, apparently as a way of keeping the size of the dictionary within manageable limits). *Collins English Dictionary*, first published in 1979 under the editorial directorship of the American Lawrence Urdang, took a notable step towards bridging the Atlantic divide by incorporating a large amount of 'international encyclopedic material – biographies of famous people and accounts of important cities, regions, and countries', though it stopped short of describing itself as an encyclopedic dictionary, and has not done so in subsequent editions either.

This development is probably very welcome to the average intelligent layperson in Britain, who likes the idea of being able to look up most of what he or she needs to know about words (whether or not they begin with a capital letter) within a single pair of covers rather than having to hunt in a variety of different volumes. The distinction between lexical words and non-lexical (or encyclopedic) words bothers the ordinary dictionary user far less than it does the professional lexicographer or linguist, and there is no reason why it should. They are all part of language, after all. It is in any case impossible to separate linguistic information and encyclopedic and cultural information into watertight compartments. Every lexicographer brings to his or her task a set of personal perceptions and preconceptions about the world which to a greater or lesser extent will colour what he or she writes, however neutral he or she consciously tries to be. To describe a mouse as a small rodent, as many dictionaries do, implies that the definition-writer has in mind a prototypical rodent which is bigger than a mouse, though bigger by how much is uncertain. Corpus evidence tells us that mice are often described as 'little' or 'tiny', not because the rodents in question are particularly undersized as mice go, but because in our culture 'mouseness' and smallness are associated. In other cultures it may be quite different for all I know: perhaps their verminousness or their squeakiness or even their furriness is regarded as a more prominent feature of the mouse stereotype. Another area where encyclopedic information is often apparent in lexical dictionaries is the regular inclusion of adjectives derived from proper names, such as *Rabelaisian*, *Kafkaesque* and *Micawberish*. These can only be properly defined in the context of the names from which they are formed, and not to include those names as headwords may be regarded as perverse to say the least. So it seems a natural, if not inevitable, progression for dictionaries to extend their coverage to include a range of encyclopedic and cultural material.

Doing so is not without its attendant problems however, as those of us who have been involved in the business of adapting existing dictionaries in this way have found. The first and most obvious problem is making the selection of material to include. Even a large encyclopedic dictionary (whatever 'large' means in the context of such works of reference) can only cover a tiny fraction of the totality of world knowledge. Some idea of the target readership and its likely needs is clearly desirable, but identifying these in a way that can establish helpful guidelines for the compiler is extraordinarily difficult. Then there is the question of the defining style itself. It seems that no one method is best for defining all entry words, and that a mixture of styles is needed, with encyclopedic material usually dealt with in a more discursive or 'natural' style than that used for defining lexical words (though this may be less true in the case of EFL dictionaries where the trend is increasingly towards a greater use of 'non-lexicographese' throughout). This mixture of styles can look especially uncomfortable where encyclopedic information is added to existing lexical entries, reinforcing the notion sometimes expressed that ELDs are something of a hybrid. Likewise the omission of grammatical and other linguistic information from encyclopedic entries when it is given for lexical entries might on the face of it look odd. Labelling *Freudian* as an adjective is uncontroversial but most lexicographers would presumably have misgivings about labelling *Freud* as a noun. 'Proper noun' would perhaps be acceptable, but no standard label would be appropriate for, say, a book or song title. However, such problems probably exercise lexicographers more than their readers and they need represent no serious impediment to the further development of encyclopedic dictionaries. What is strikingly missing from most dictionaries in general, including encyclopedic dictionaries for native speakers, is connotative meaning. As Sidney Landau (1989) has written, "dictionaries deal only with certain kinds of meaning and ignore other kinds no less important, and we must not suppose that associated meanings cease to exist because dictionaries fail to note them." This omis sion may be because connotative or associative or affective or emotive meaning (the range of overlapping variants is particularly significant) is far more difficult to pin down than denotative meaning, but the attempt to do so is a central aim of the encyclopedic dictionaries for foreign learners of English which have so far been published. As Penny Stock (one of the team that produced the *Longman Dictionary of English Language and Culture*) pointed out in a talk she gave at the Euralex Conference in Tampere, Finland in 1992, it is precisely the associative or connotative meaning of discourse, together with its cultural allusions, that can cause the most problems for non-native users of a language. "Lexicographers", she said, "should change their notion of what constitutes meaning in terms of dictionary definitions [... and] definitions should include encyclopedic material determined by the stereotype of a lexical item. [...] They should include explicit information on the stereotype in addition to the factual information that must also be given [...] they should include information on cultural associations for lexical items; and [...] they should include words such as *glass slipper* and *Wimbledon* which are often excluded from dictionary headword lists but which are present in texts and need to be understood just as much as *cat* and *vegetable*." Fighting talk indeed.

If this is true for native-speaker dictionaries, it is arguably even more true for learners' dictionaries. As Zgusta (1989) has observed, "since language is embedded in culture, cultural data are important to the learner not only for steering his linguistic behavior but frequently for choosing the correct lexical equivalent. Such cultural information can be understood in a broad way, so that it can pertain to political and administrative realities of the country or countries whose language is being learned, and so on. Undoubtedly, a good part of this information is of encyclopedic character; be this as it may, it belongs to what the learner has to learn." Béjoint (1981) has made a similar point: "To understand a lexeme completely, non-native speakers have two additional problems that are not faced by native speakers. Sometimes, the concept or entity itself is unknown to them (culture-specific words). In such cases, the dictionary-maker cannot be content with providing a limited definition, as for other words, or as in dictionaries for native speakers. He must give information about the objects, institutions, etc., themselves, and this will require an encyclopedic type of definition. Sometimes the denotative meaning of a lexeme is fairly well-known internationally, but a particular connotation is specific to one national culture (e.g. *pumpkin* in the USA). [...] For such words, foreign students, even at a fairly advanced level, need to be given information about the connotative value." The supply of such information has long been a feature of ELT course-books and supplementary materials, in which the language is taught in the context of aspects of the life and culture of Britain, America and other English-speaking countries, so the emergence of the encyclopedic learners' dictionary can be seen as a natural, even predictable, development (though it is perhaps worth adding the caveat given by David Heath and Thomas Herbst in their review of ELDs in *Fremdspra-*

chen Lehren und Lernen (1994) that non-mastery of a language should not be equated with ignorance of its related culture).

In looking more closely at published ELDs, I shall confine myself largely to the *Longman Dictionary of English Language and Culture* (LDELC) and the *Oxford Advanced Learner's Encyclopedic Dictionary* (OALED), both published in 1992. The *BBC English Dictionary*, published by HarperCollins, also in 1992, describes itself as "equally suitable for native and non-native speakers of English", but is not, I suggest, truly an encyclopedic learners' dictionary so much as a dictionary for what it calls "citizens of the world", adult listeners to the BBC World Service, restricting its encyclopedic coverage to people and places worldwide that feature regularly in news coverage, and with little or no connotative information. Likewise Room: *An A to Z of British Life* (OUP 1990) and Paul: *A Guide to the English-Speaking World* (Longman 1975) are essentially small encyclopedias, containing no purely lexical material. I do not intend, and it would be quite wrong of me here, to make a comparative assessment of LDELC and OALED, beyond mentioning the rationale behind OALED and some of the problems we encountered in producing it, while noting how the two dictionaries have dealt differently with some of these. I am sure that most of you are reasonably familiar with them both and have your own ideas about their respective merits. The single most difficult decision in preparing OALED was determining the criteria for selection. It is easy enough to assume that the deciding factor as regards the inclusion policy for encyclopedic learners' dictionaries should be whether the information – linguistic or cultural or both – is likely to be useful to the foreign language learner (provided the level at which the dictionary is aimed is clearly delineated). It is another matter altogether to decide what the user is actually likely to need or find useful. For OALED our market research had indicated the need for a learners' dictionary at a slightly higher level than OALD, containing not only additional lexical vocabulary appropriate for this level, but also wider reference coverage generally. This we interpreted as meaning factual information, such as literary, historical, geographical, biographical and other entries, together with a large number of longer 'articles' on broader aspects of British and American life (such as Government and the Law) and 'mini-notes' explaining the particular connotations certain words have for English-speaking people in addition to their basic dictionary meanings. There were thus various degrees of 'encyclopedicity' in the finished book. It was also decided to make the individual encyclopedic entries global in scope but to restrict the articles and the mini-notes to British and American life. The editorial policy for LDELC appears to have been broadly similar (though the numbers of different entry types vary considerably). The encyclopedic entries in LDELC are weighted rather more in favour of British and American subject matter than those in OALED. There are fewer special articles (called 'features') in LDELC than in OALED but many more 'culture notes' (the Longman equivalent of mini-notes). In retrospect I am not sure of the wisdom of making the encyclopedic entries global in scope. David Heath and Thomas Herbst, in their review already referred to, make the point that a German student would probably not look up *Gorbachev* or *Plato* in an encyclopedic learners' dictionary for its factual content (since this information would be more readily accessible and more fully treated in a German encyclopedia), though he or she might want information on the English spelling and pronunciation of such names, or enlightenment on the British tabloid press nickname *Gorby*. The question however must remain: is the provision of such relatively limited information sufficient justification for including in such a dictionary a large number (but still a tiny fraction of the total number) of proper names from around the world? I am really not sure. I also feel that there is a somewhat grey area, or at least a certain overlap, between expanded entries with added encyclopedic content (which may include connotative information) and culture (or mini-) notes, and even with the 'usage notes' which both dictionaries contain and which occasionally contain cultural as well as linguistic information. This overlap may be inevitable, and, again, probably bothers the lexicographer more than the dictionary user, but more rigour in differentiating the criteria for each should probably be applied. At the same time it is fair to say that cultural information cannot always be related to a single dictionary entry-word but is about choices, conscious or inbred and unconscious, and social background. An article on employment inevitably and rightly includes reference to unemployment and social attitudes to it, as well as other related aspics of the topic. The use of special articles and notes in encyclopedic learners' dictionaries is an indication that a traditional A-Z dictionary layout is inadequate for the satisfactory presentation of much cultural information. Notes and articles are needed to draw ideas together and tease out comparative significance. Overlap with individual A-Z entries is therefore inevitable, and indeed necessary for maximum accessibility of information.

Once editorial policy on encyclopedic coverage has been decided, the dictionary editor can and should consult specialists in making a choice from each of the various subject fields to be covered and in identifying the salient facts to be mentioned in each entry (though specialists may not know what cultural items learners are most likely to need and their opinions need to be balanced where possible by research among ELT teachers and their students). Far more problematical is the selection process for and content of the culture-specific items to be included. There are few if any recognized specialists in this area, and it is not always easy for lexicographers on their own to identify what is specific to their own culture. (We also need to recognize that learners above a certain age do have a basis of general knowledge and are not ignorant just because their English is not fluent.) Corpus evidence is perhaps less plentiful or helpful here than for the literal meanings and usage of words. The risk of including idiosyncratic personal attitudes and opinions, or of perpetuating dated stereotypes, is considerable. That words and phrases carry for native speakers special connotations with which non-native speakers may be unfamiliar is obvious, but how is the lexicographer to determine the extent to which a given connotation is accepted within the culture, and how widely does such a connotation have to have been accepted for it to warrant inclusion in a dictionary for learners? These are difficult questions to answer without a panel of informants of different ages, social background and so on to consult on each and every point, which may not be a practical publishing possibility. In these days of the soundbite and the spin-doctor, cultural allusions may also be widely recognized for a short time before fading from view and therefore importance. We hear a great deal in Britain today about *sleaze* and *sovereignty* (nothing to do with Her Majesty), but how long will their special cultural connotations be current? There is the added problem that students of English in other parts of the world may well be less familiar with British culture than those in western Europe, where there is perhaps less danger of cross-cultural misunderstanding. So a culture note on an aspect, say, of youth culture in Britain which is valuable to a Japanese student may strike a German or a French student as so obvious as not to be worth stating. In our desire, for practical publishing reasons, to make such a dictionary suitable for all EFL markets, we run the risk of saying too much for some and too little for others.

I must briefly mention the matter of the limited defining vocabulary. LDELC, based as it is on the text of LDOCE2, uses the same defining vocabulary, which is listed in full at the back of both dictionaries. Although a defining vocabulary was introduced for the first time in the fifth edition of OALD, OALED was based on the previous (fourth) edition which used no such vocabulary so that the language of entries (including mini-notes and special articles) is on the face of it more 'difficult'. It was however my experience when working on OALED that encyclopedic material of all kinds requires by its very nature an additional layer of vocabulary over and above that needed for defining lexical words, if explanations are to be clear and precise and not overloaded with internal glosses. It would be interesting to know whether a comparative analysis has been done of the words in small capitals in 'definitions' in LDELC and LDOCE2. I should also like to know of any research that has been done into the reaction of learners' dictionary users to variations of typeface or other internal conventions (such as asterisks indicating cross-references) within definitions.

Encyclopedias probably date more quickly than dictionaries and encyclopedic learners' dictionaries more quickly than their lexical equivalents. This puts publishers under added pressure to produce regular updated editions, and this in turn may have a strong bearing on editorial policy. LDELC clearly has a wider coverage of popular and youth culture than does OALED, which gives correspondingly more space overall to what for want of a better term could be called 'high' culture. This may reflect the slightly different target markets for which the two books are intended, but it raises the interesting question to what extent young students using an ELD will consult it for information on current pop stars, films, television programmes and the like, how far they will feel frustrated if they fail to find their latest interests and heroes included, and what their reasons for looking them up were in the first place. Further research is needed into which types of encyclopedic entries students (and teachers) most often consult and why. Which, if any, are consulted as part of a language production exercise and not solely for receptive or comprehension purposes? I suspect that the success of such a dictionary has at least as much to do with its general accessibility and readability, and this is partly a matter of design and of keeping the amount of information presented within reasonable limits. In other words the risk of 'information overload', even for quite advanced students, should not be underestimated. Other factors outside the purely editorial aspects of the dictionary include size, portability and above all price.

So are encyclopedic learners' dictionaries here to stay? Does encyclopedic and cultural information have a place in the perfect learners' dictionary, and if so would this apply also to dictionaries pitched at other levels of learner ability? Other questions also need to be asked. How much information needs to be given in encyclopedic entries? What kind of proper noun entries are really worth including? What should the cultural scope of encyclopedic information be? Heath and Herbst register a strong plea for the development of specifically bilingual ELDs for individual markets so that the differences between the 'home' and target cultures could be more thoroughly addressed. Whether this will come about I cannot say. The publication of electronic multimedia versions of ELDs is another obvious possibility, with the advantage of their being able to incorporate many more visual images, sound, video and so on. Whatever the future holds, I think more research is needed on the use to which the existing ELDs are put and how students react to their various design features.

(I am grateful to Martin Stark, whose MA dissertation for the University of Exeter 'Encyclopedic Learners' Dictionaries: A Study of their Design Features from the User Perspective' (1996) helped me, especially in its bibliography, with certain aspects of this talk.)

Bibliography

BBC English Dictionary (1993): John Sinclair (ed.). — London & Glasgow: HarperCollins.

Collins Dictionary of the English Language (1979): Laurence Urdang (ed.). — London & Glasgow: Collins.

The Concise Oxford Dictionary of Current English ([9]1995): Della Thompson (ed.). — Oxford: Clarendon Press

Longman Dictionary of English Language and Culture (1992): Della Summers (ed.). — Harlow: Longman.

Oxford Advanced Learner's Dictionary of Current English, Encyclopedic Edition (1989, 1992): Jonathan Crowther (ed.). — Oxford: OUP.

Webster's Third New International Dictionary (1961): Philip Babcock Gove (ed.). — Springfield (Mass.): Merriam.

Béjoint, Henri (1981): "The foreign student's use of monolingual dictionaries: A study of language needs and reference skills". — In: Applied Linguistics 2/3, 207-222.

Heath, David, Thomas Herbst (1994): "Enzyklopädische Lernerwörterbücher". — In: Fremdsprachen Lehren und Lernen 23, 149-163.

Landau, Sidney I. (1989): Dictionaries. The Art and Craft of Lexicography. — Cambridge: CUP.

Stock, Penny (1992): "The Cultural Dimension in Defining". — In: Tommola et al. (eds.): Euralex '92 Proceedings: Papers Submitted to the 5th Euralex International Congress on Lexicography (Tampere: Euralex), 113-120.

Zgusta, Ladislav (1989): "Idle Thoughts of an Idle fellow; or, Vaticinations on the Learners' Dictionary". In: M. Tickoo (ed.): Learners' Dictionaries: State of the Art (Singapore: SEAMO Regional Language Centre) (=Anthology Series 23), 1-9.

Dieter Götz

On some differences between English and German (with respect to lexicography)

The following are some observations on English and German (and on learners' dictionaries) that you make while you actually write dictionaries.

1 Dictionaries of German will be 'less complete'

Among the words that are not found in Langenscheidt's *Großwörterbuch Deutsch als Fremdsprache* (GWDaF) are e.g. *Applikation, arid, humid.* Words like these are called *Fremdwörter* in German, i.e. alien or foreign words. Lexicographically, this means that they are traditionally relegated to special dictionaries, and pragmatically, that they are part of a fringe vocabulary of specialised languages, in this case of medicine and of meteorology and geography. In contrast to that, the English word forms *application, arid, humid* occur not exclusively in medical or meteorological texts but also in "normal, everyday" language, and lexicographers catch them, so to say, with their frequency nets. These and many other words of Latin or Greek origin are well established in the vocabulary of English, much better established than in the vocabulary of German. This is also shown by the fact that, in English, many have become polysemous. Thus *illuminate*, apart from its technical meanings, also means 'explain' or 'provide an example', whereas German *illuminieren* is very rare and restricted to technical usage.

Users will therefore be likely to find a greater number of technical terms in English dictionaries than in German dictionaries, and therefore German dictionaries will appear less complete or less useful: *tonsillitis, laryngitis, oesophagus* will occur in English learners' dictionaries but *Tonsillitis* etc. will have no entry in a German learners' dictionary. English dictionaries automatically cover (at least a large part of) technical language vocabulary.

In order to remedy this deficiency you would have to develop a special procedure for a German dictionary. You would want to do a frequency analysis for sub-corpora of, say, medical texts, then to determine frequency bands. After that you would have to determine how important medical texts are to your dictionary. Suppose you had six frequency bands for the general language part, then you could equate your highest medical frequency band with the medium (or higher, or lower) general frequency band, thereby establishing a degree of coverage for medical language. You would, of course, also have to decide about what degree is to be assigned to what kind of sub-corpus. That is to say, you would have to factorise sub-corpora. Since there is quite a number of these aliens you might wish to deal with them very quickly in just one or two lines.

The real point of this may be that lexicographical strategies developed for English need not necessarily be suitable for other languages. Perhaps you are ill-advised when you follow British lexicography too closely.

There are 17 words of the type *Applikation* on page 1-8 in the *Duden Fremdwörterbuch: Abakus, Abandon, Abbreviation, Abdomen, aberrant, Ablution, Abolition, Abundanz, abyssal, Adduktion, adhärent, Admission, Admonition, adoleszent, Adoration, adult* (and hundreds within A - D). To repeat: these words are words that do occur in German texts. Yet these words do not appear in a German learners' dictionary. Their English counterparts, however, are all to be found, at least as word forms, in an English learners' dictionary.

2 Compounds and N+N-phrases

English has got quite a number of compounds, and German has got even more. You have to be very liberal with compounds in a German learners' dictionary, even with self-explanatory compounds, for several reasons.

First, there is a large number of things that are expressed by compounds, such as *Schlafanzug, Lampenschirm*. Second, the learner needs to know whether the first part of a compound has a singular form, like *Kopfkissen* or a plural form like *Kinderbett* or an *s*-form, like *Versicherungspolice*. And finally, English often has a phrase where German has a compound. Thus, *EXport BUsiness* (with double or level stress) is a phrase, and therefore it is not found in a learners' dictionary. Some learners' dictionaries do not list *world war*: grammatically speaking, *world war* is simply a kind of war, as is *cold war* or *Gulf war*, and is therefore no candidate for lemmatising. Perhaps these phrases escape the lexicographer's attention, since *export business* and *world war* are orthographically two words each and do not occur in word lists as done by computer. *Exportgeschäft, Exportunternehmen, Weltkrieg*, on the other hand, are single-word units, and are, as such, obvious items for a dictionary. Not lemmatising them implies a conscious act of suppression. Neither LDOCE nor COBUILD care about *tomato juice*, but the GWDaF mentions *Tomatensaft*. This is because the modifier *Tomaten-* is a plural form, different from the *Apfel-* in *Apfelsaft*, different again from the shortened *Himbeer-* in *Himbeersaft*. So in order to express the world around you, a German dictionary has to list quite a number of words where English has none because naming takes place at phrase level and not at word level. One may, however, argue that the business of a dictionary is to tell you what things are called in a language, no matter whether you use a phrase or a word. Lexicographically, confining yourself to word level is perhaps no good policy (even if it can be justified linguistically). At any rate, a German dictionary has to list a large number of compounds (if only for reasons of morphology) and thus has to deal with more words (and things) than its English counterpart.

3 Lexicalisation

Lexicalisation, or rather, a higher degree of lexicalisation, may well be a general trait of German. In English, you can *paint a landscape, paint a wall, paint a vase with flowers.* The semantic distinction between the various occurrences of *paint* is either left to the general context or to syntax. In German, word formation steps in and provides altogether four different lexical items: *malen, anmalen, bemalen, aufmalen.* These four items have to be listed, even if they show some kind of overlap. Note that the meaning 'paint something on something' can be expressed with *etwas auf etwas malen, etwas mit etwas bemalen, etwas auf etwas aufmalen.* The word form *paint* is semantically and syntactically more flexible than *malen.* Since in German there is a vast number of verbs that allow prefixing with *ab-, an-, auf-, be-* (down to *zer-*), this means that a German dictionary is inherently more repetitive than an English one. It has to deal various times with, so to speak, the fact of painting and with the morphology of one and the same form – and therefore needs more space than its English counterpart.

Also, word formation forces a German learners' dictionary into explicitly dealing with affixes. There are roughly 370 verbs with *ab-* in the GWDaF, which calls for comprehensive treatment. Foreign learners will want to know whether *ab*-verbs are separable or not. In case you do not want to repeat the fact of separability for each of these 370 verbs, you have to develop a cross reference system.

More or less the same applies to verbal compounds. In English, birds fly away and you would not lemmatise *fly away.* But since what they do in German is *wegfliegen* or 'awayfly', you have to lemmatise these verbal compounds, and again there is the difference between phrase level in English (verb plus adverb) and word level in German. Lemmatising e.g. *herüberschwimmen* means that you have to lemmatise an expression like 'swim across towards us'. In the GWDaF verb compounds with *her-* and *herab-* ... *herzu-* require 12 entries with information on word formation, with roughly 220 verbs in these entries, and another 230 normal entries for individual verbs.

(The present spelling reform in German will complicate matters even further. From August 1998 on we will still have separable verbs written together, such as *wegfliegen* and also separable verbs written separately, such as *auseinander gehen.* The latter look like phrases but need special treatment since they are in no way different from the other verb compounds.)

In all, German word formation, being as it is, presents you with considerable problems of space, makes it necessary to be explicitly metalinguistic and leads to cumbersome problems of referencing.

4 German, metalinguistically

Again, space. German as a metalanguage is a bit unwieldy and relatively long-winded. If you translate English into German, you need more letters. If you translate something like *a tax of a fixed amount* into German as *eine Steuer von festgesetzter Höhe* you have 18 letters vs. 30 letters. If 40,000 entries in German need each 10 letters more than 40,000 English entries, this means a disadvantage of 400,000 letters or some 8,000 lines, which corresponds to more than one hundred columns or some 50 pages. It is easy to imagine what that means if you adopt the COBUILD style of definition. You would have to render *if one person agrees with another or if two people agree* by *wenn eine Person mit einer anderen übereinstimmt oder wenn zwei Personen miteinander übereinstimmen...* (46 letters vs. 87 letters). Your dictionary is going to be a very fat volume for very fat wallets. There are some who suggest that the GWDaF take over the COBUILD style plus the extra column – which shows you how naive academic metalexicography can be.

This longwindedness tempts German dictionaries into using abbreviations and other shortening devices even if that implies a lower degree of reader-friendliness. The discrepancy in space between German and English metalanguage is also an important point for future dictionaries of the bilingualised kind (i.e. bridge dictionaries, see below). An English version of the GWDaF would be feasible and even slimmer than the original, a German version of an English learners' dictionary would have to be very selective in order to retain about the same size.

German as a metalanguage was called "a bit unwieldy" above. This is partly due to gender in German. English dictionaries make extensive use of series of nouns, such as *an event or activity; a book, film or story; a slight problem or difficulty; a person or an animal.* These can appear in subject or object position, they can also be postmodified by *wh*-clauses. But note that e.g. *an event or activity* expands, because of gender, into *ein Ereignis oder eine Handlung,* plus preposition it would be e.g. *während eines Ereignisses oder einer Handlung*, and postmodification needs alternatives like *das/die; in dem/der.* A series like *an idea, plan, or thought* does usually not work in German. You can solve these difficulties by sometimes using the plural, or by using still more abbreviations like *etc.,* or by using very general nouns.

Unfortunately, many of these general nouns sound stilted or pompous and not natural in German. English speakers do not object to saying that *a cup* is *a small container* or that *a shed* is *a small building*, but *eine Tasse* is not *ein kleiner Behälter* nor would *ein Schuppen* be called *ein kleines Gebäude.* There are some pragmatic differences between German and English in the area of hyponymy and hyperonymy that might be worth following up. When explaining *spoon* English dictionaries use *implement, tool, utensil.* The *genus proximum* of *Löffel* is, of course, *Besteck (cutlery)*, but this is too rare to be of much use. There is nothing in between *Besteck* and the most general noun *Gegenstand.* Your only choice is something like 'an object with which you eat soup', and this sounds more than clumsy, not only in German. It is possible that this "hyperonymic awkwardness" is due to the attitude towards dictionaries in German-speaking countries. Dictionaries are consulted for spelling problems, but hardly anybody cares about what they say on shades of meaning or on the "right word". There might, in German-speaking countries, be less exposure to, and less familiarity with, dictionaries than in France or Great Britain.

5 High-frequency explanatory words in English

One of the meanings of *to charge* is explained in learners' dictionaries with the help of *ask*, for instance, *ask someone to pay the amount* etc. This looks easy and it need not be criticised. However, for an intermediate German learner of English, the item *ask* is exclusively connected with *fragen*, i.e. 'ask a question'. Most users will understand *ask someone to pay the amount* as 'ask someone whether they will/can/might pay the amount' etc. Of course, they may then abandon this reading and hit on the correct meaning.

It is not only "intermediate" learners that are affected by puzzles like these, but also advanced learners. In Raymond Chandler's *The Lady in the Lake* detective Marlowe reports *(I) asked to see Mr Derace Kingsley.* German university students of English usually translate *Ich fragte, ob...*, about eight out of ten, and two out of ten use *verlangen*. If you ask the latter why they will tell you that this kind of guy is not the kind that asks you a question. They will not tell you that *ask somebody to do something* usually requires *verlangen* or *wollen.* Hellmuth Karasek's translation even has *Ich bat darum, Mr Kingsley sprechen zu dürfen,* i.e. 'I asked (her) whether I might see Mr Kingsley'. As if Marlowe had said "May I see Mr Kingsley, please."

This is perhaps not a minor point. For decades, frequency counts have been made for English, and have always yielded high-ranking verbs like *ask, see, break, miss, tell, meet*, verbs that recommend themselves for definition vocabularies, because of their frequency.

When working at how to explain words in the GWDaF I thought I might simply translate the defining vocabulary of LDOCE. But I soon found that *ask* splits up into *fragen, bitten, befehlen*, or that *miss* splits up into *fehlen, versäumen, verfehlen, verpassen, nicht treffen, nicht schaffen ... zu*, and that *break* splits up into *brechen, zerbrechen, bersten, reißen, zerreißen, zerbersten.* At first sight these splittings-up do not appear remarkable, since lexical divergence is common when you look at two or more languages, and German verbs are polysemous, too. But note that *ask* is strictly speaking not a polysemous verb. The different meanings are tied up with different structures, such as *ask + N + wh-CL (I asked her what time it was); ask + N + to-INF (They asked him to leave); ask + N + for N (They asked me for a penny); ask + about (I asked about his health).* It is the word form, or lemma, *ask* that is common, not the verb *ask.* Perhaps some explanations in English learners' dictionaries are "simple" only when you disregard valency.

With verbs like *break* the case is different. *Break* is a kind of general verb, and hyperonymous to e.g. *burst, snap, shatter, split*, which are more subject-specific or object-specific than *break* is. But note that the German verbs into which *break* splits up (*reißen, bersten*) are not hyponymous to *brechen.* You can explain *snap* and *burst* using *break*, without being cumbersome or inelegant. But in German, if a rope or a string *snaps*, what they do is *snap* – and you have to use something like 'becomes two parts', since the general verb *kaputtgehen* is too colloquial for dictionary use. *Choose* can be used for explaining e.g. *decide, select, elect, pick, vote* (in COBUILD), but none of the usual German equivalents to *choose*, such as *wählen, entscheiden, aussuchen, auswählen* is as general or hyperonymic as *choose*.

For dictionary makers of English all this means that *ask*-type verbs and *break*-type verbs will provide explanations that sound natural and easy (sometimes deceptively so), whereas dictionary makers of German often have to turn to cumbersome paraphrases. It may, of course, also mean that even if a defining vocabulary of about 2,000 words makes sense for the lexicography of English, this is not necessarily the case for the lexicography of German. You might need more.

6 Getting meaning across to the learner

If you look up *quaint* in an English-German dictionary you will learn that it "means" 'kurios, merkwürdig, drollig, malerisch, gemütlich, altmodisch'. This, however, is nothing but a motley collection of contextually bound translation equivalents, and it will never lead you to the meaning of *quaint*, namely 'attractive, especially when considered strange or old-fashioned'. Monolinguals describe their language from within, as it were. *Choose* does not mean 'wählen', as bilinguals and the outside German view suggest, but usually 'decide in favour of'. A *field* is an area of grass or any other arable piece of land, definitely not a *Feld*, a piece of information that you will not find in most bilingual dictionaries. It is necessary for the intermediate/advanced learner to be given this kind of information.

One might say that this is precisely what English learners' dictionaries do. Of course they do, but the information is also well-hidden. If you explain *fierce* by 'fierce conditions are very intense, great or strong' you forget that, for an intermediate German learner of English, *condition* does not mean 'state' but 'prerequisite' or 'if-ness'. For such a learner 'the condition of sharing a friendly relationship' does not lead to *friendship/Freundschaft* but perhaps to something like 'the condition under which you share with friendly relatives', i.e. to nonsense. A *fife* is a small pipe-shaped instrument, true, but a German will think of a small saxophone, associating pipe with smoking-pipe (and only with smoking-pipe). If you say that *fuel* is a material, you lead them astray because *Material* is something solid. They would not even understand what you tell them about *potatoes:* 'a roundish root vegetable with a thin brown or yellowish skin' because they will equate *vegetable* with *Gemüse* and a *potato* (in German) is not a kind of *Gemüse*. So maybe they think it is a kind of anomalous carrot or a celery. This is definitely nothing for which lexicographers of English should be blamed. They are certainly not responsible for the fact that German dictionary users equate *ask* and *fragen, choose* and *wählen, miss* and *vermissen, place* and *Platz* (not to mention all other false friends). Perhaps there is a connection between these difficulties in decoding and the deplorable under-use of dictionaries that is reported by Böhner (this volume).

7 The perfect learners' dictionary

The question then is how dictionaries should communicate their information to (intermediate/advanced) users. There may be two solutions that do not exclude each other.

It must be plainly stated that CIDE, COBUILD2, LDOCE3 and OALD5 present their language – English – in a way other dictionaries of other languages can only dream of. Though they call themselves "learners' dictionaries" they are in fact superior linguistic enterprises, unrivalled by other dictionaries in the English-speaking world. (Probably they present more information than the average learner needs.) We should bear in mind that these dictionaries are also, in most cases, the only "authorities" students can turn to after leaving school, that they are the only bases for individual progress. As it is, the didactic implications of these dictionaries have not yet been fully appreciated.

Learners must be systematically taught how to use these dictionaries. However, teaching the use of these dictionaries is not just a matter of one or two lessons or 45 or 90 minutes (as anyone who teaches English at university level knows). It should be an integral and substantial part of the syllabus. We need systematic material that makes sure that explanations are fully understood. Learners must know what it means if a word is labelled *techn* or *formal*. We need grammars that are geared to these dictionaries and lead towards understanding e.g. [C], [U],[C; U], *look ↔ up* or *look 'up*, complementation, entries dealing with *dis-*, *-ment*, in fact all that grammar that learners think is absent from 'the easy English'. This might be a possible way of really benefiting from the learners' dictionaries.

Another solution is to bilingualise monolingual dictionaries and produce bridge versions. In such a dictionary the metalanguage is the learner's native language, which ensures that most of the information will be readily understood. For example:

ask... **1** *ask someone something* bedeutet, daß man jemanden etwas fragt, eine Auskunft will. *"How many languages can you speak?" he asked. A young man asked if we were students...* 'fragte, ob wir Studenten seien'. *I asked him what he wanted ...* 'Ich fragte ihn, was er wolle' ... *He asked me my name ...* 'Er wollte wissen, wie ich heiße'. **2** *ask somebody to do something* bedeutet: man sagt jemandem, daß man will oder verlangt, daß er etwas tun soll: *He asked me to tell him where I had been...* 'Er wollte von mir wissen, wo ich gewesen war'. **3** *ask someone* (zusammen mit der Nennung eines Ortes) bedeutet, daß man jemanden dorthin einlädt: *I asked her to the party.* **4** ... **5** ... [Morphology and grammar codes neglected; based on COBUILD1]

This kind of dictionary would be very user-friendly and readily accessible, it would also describe English "from within" (see above), it would serve as a kind of bridge towards the larger monolinguals. It would, of course, have some drawbacks, too. For reasons mentioned earlier, bilingualising any of the English monolinguals (OALD, LDOCE, CIDE, COBUILD) would mean expanding them to about 2,000 - 2,700 pages, which again would mean a prohibitively high price. Bridging therefore implies selection and it would render the dictionary, from the point of view of vocabulary, less useful.

There is also a commercial drawback. Bridge dictionaries of English, being directed, would come in different versions (German, French, Italian etc.) and would sell on a smaller scale.

Publishers would probably be not overly enthusiastic about them. Nevertheless, this type of dictionary might be the ideal foundation for the later use of the more advanced dictionaries.

The idea of a bridge dictionary is particularly attractive if we consider those languages that are typically taught as second or third foreign languages, i.e. German or Spanish. The number of learners who might be able to use a German monolingual at school will be fairly low. Learners at universities, who do German from scratch, will hardly be able to use a German monolingual until their fourth year. That is to say that the market in many countries, such as the Unites States, is very limited indeed. (And what "market" means in terms of research funds for a dictionary, is obvious.) Also, such a monolingual cannot create a demand: for many users it is like a box of tools that will not open. What I suggest, therefore, is that one should have German, or French, or Spanish monolinguals and derive bilingual bridge versions from them in order to make all the "valuable" information accessible.

It is easy to see that the expression "a perfect learners' dictionary" might be ambiguous. But in fact the reading 'a dictionary for the perfect learner' does not make much sense. There is no single perfect learner. You may be an ideal and successful learner after three years of English, or after six years, or after nine years. At each stage you will need new and different material.

It is (assuming that the demand of English will increase still further) foreseeable that somehow the learners' dictionaries will split up into different versions. What we have now are perfect tools for very advanced learners, but what we might also need are, perhaps somewhat unexpectedly, more modest dictionaries that bridge the gap between the obnoxious three hundred page bilingual and the advanced products of 1995.

Bibliography

Collins Cobuild English Language Dictionary (COBUILD) (1987): John Sinclair (ed.). — London, Glasgow: Collins.

Duden Fremdwörterbuch (^{6}1997): Werner Scholze-Stubenrecht (ed.). – Mannheim: Duden.

Großwörterbuch Deutsch als Fremdsprache. Das neue einsprachige Wörterbuch für Deutschlernende (GWDaF) (1993): Dieter Götz, Günther Haensch, Hans Wellmann (eds.). – Berlin, München: Langenscheidt.

Thomas Herbst

Designing an English Valency Dictionary: combining linguistic theory and user-friendliness

1 The project of an English valency dictionary

Accuracy of description and easy accessibility of the information to the user are the two main aims any dictionary is likely to pursue. As all lexicographers and users of dictionaries know, it is sometimes difficult to satisfy both criteria equally well. Accuracy and user friendliness thus need to be considered the poles between which the design of a dictionary will have to find its place.

Although this conflict exists for any type of dictionary and, after all, is the reason why lexicography is more of an art than a science, it may be particularly strong in the case of dictionaries which have a very clear and pronounced theoretical basis. One such case is presented by valency dictionaries, which are closely related to a particular theory of syntax, namely the valency model developed within the wider framework of dependency grammar.

One such project is the English Valency Dictionary that was compiled at the Universities of Erlangen-Nürnberg, Reading and Augsburg with David Heath, Ian Roe, Dieter Götz and myself as editors. The dictionary provides detailed syntactic and semantic valency descriptions of some 500 verbs, 500 adjectives and 300 nouns of English.[1]

Valency dictionaries are highly specialised dictionaries aiming to provide an extensive account of the formal, semantic and lexical or collocational aspects of the complementation structures of words. They can serve three main functions:

- the function of making a contribution to descriptive linguistics since they cover an aspect of the grammatical behaviour of lexical items in great detail,
- the function of a production dictionary for foreign learners of a language by enabling them to use the appropriate constructions in language production and

---

[1] At the present stage, a manuscript has been completed which is being prepared for publication. Plans and first drafts were developed from the mid-eighties on by David Heath and myself. Several years later, Ian Roe from the University of Reading and, a few years after that, Dieter Götz in Augsburg joined the editorial team. In 1994 Michael Klotz joined the project as chief lexicographer, and later Kerstin Popp and Brigitta Mittmann - all working at the Lehrstuhl für Englische Sprachwissenschaft at the Institut für Anglistik und Amerikanistik of the University of Erlangen-Nürnberg, where the organizational centre of the project is located, as well as Heike Hänlein at the University of Augsburg. For outlines of the project see Herbst (1987), Klotz (1997), Herbst/Klotz (1998).

- the function of what could be called a marking dictionary for non-native teachers by enabling them to check whether something a student has written is acceptable in the language or not.

Such dictionaries have existed for languages other than English for quite some time, and they differ considerably with respect to which of these functions they attribute most importance to. There are several for German - starting with Helbig and Schenkel's 1968 *Wörterbuch zur Valenz und Distribution deutscher Verben* - but also, some of them contrastive, for many other languages such as French (Busse/Dubost 1983), Spanish, Romanian, Polish, Japanese, but not for English. This may be due to the fact that the general English leaners' dictionaries, since the introduction of the verb patterns by Hornby in OALD, have included formal complementation patterns. Furthermore a number of specialised phrasal verb dictionaries (such as ODCIE) address one of the central areas of verb complementation in English and thus cover part of the valency problems. Thus while we cannot make any great claims as to the general idea of writing a valency dictionary as such, the project of compiling a valency dictionary for English may have been subject to two conditions specific to English:

- Firstly, English so far seems to be the only language for which large-scale corpora such as the British National Corpus or the COBUILD corpus are available for such an enterprise. Having direct access to the Bank of English in Birmingham with its 320 million words from Erlangen, Reading and Augsburg was an enormous advantage in many respects.
- Secondly, the extremely high standard of English lexicography puts special demands on any new project, both with respect to the information provided and the aspect of user-friendliness[2], which was the subject of many papers of this conference. Since we target as our prime user group advanced students and foreign teachers of English, it seemed important to us to present the information in a very accessible, i.e. non-technical form.

In this special situation finding a balance between theoretical rigour and accuracy on the one hand and intelligibility and accessibility of the information on the other was of prime importance. It is the purpose of this paper to outline this project and in particular to discuss some of the decisions that had to be taken in the process of designing and compiling the dictionary.

---

[2] Cf. Cowie (1987).

2 Valency as a lexicographical problem

2.1 Valency as a problem in language production and language assessment

The first point to make about the English Valency Dictionary project described here is that - despite the remarkably high standard of the general learners' dictionaries discussed in this volume - there is still a need for a special valency dictionary of English. One main overall function of these general learners' dictionaries is error prevention since they aim at enabling the foreign user of the language to avoid errors both in the perception and the production of language. As far as production is concerned, one key area of potential errors is that of complementation - or valency -, as has been shown in many studies. At a slightly more sophisticated level of competence - referring to the marking dictionary function identified above -, an experiment carried out at the University of Erlangen/Nürnberg in spring 1997 confirmed that this also applies with respect to the ability to assess whether a particular complementation pattern is acceptable with a particular word. The results of the experiment provide a clear indication of the need for a new dictionary in this field.

96 students of English, 58 of them beginners and 38 about to take finals, most of them studying to be teachers, were given 40 example sentences taken from the Birmingham Bank of English contained in the valency dictionary. They were asked to assess the corresponding valency patterns as "correct", "probably correct (but not sure)", "probably incorrect" and "incorrect". 11 sentences were manipulated so that they contained a valency error. The degree to which errors were not suspected is remarkable. If, for instance, only 9% of the students were definite, i.e. said "incorrect" in the case of *will announce to purchase* or 46% for *pretended not recognizing me*, this does not signal a particularly high degree of error spotting competence.

What is even more remarkable is that of the 29 sentences directly taken from the Bank of English, 11 gave rise to suspicions with more than 50% of the students questioned. With 6 of them more than 50% said they were sure or almost sure the valency pattern used was wrong.

Sentences containing valency errors [11 out of 40]	Error not suspected		definite about error
	58 beginners	38 advanced	96 students
30 [...] will announce to purchase [...]	64%	55%	9%
27 [...] try to decorate floors and windows in the same neutral colours [...]	72%	47%	16%
37 [...] multiply 5 with itself [...]	69%	42%	18%
3 [...] preserve the site of greater damage [...]	36%	16%	23%
35 [...] planned linking up with FIAT [...]	26%	37%	24%
34 [...] learn being more open [...]	19%	32%	27%
6 [...] pressing to a public inquiry [...]	29%	16%	29%
19 [...] were clearly regarded important [...]	21%	26%	37%

31 [...] avoid to make mistakes [...]	29%	11%	39%
11 [...] pretended not recognizing me [...]	21%	29%	46%
26 [...] tried finding her [...]	9%	16%	51%

Sentences without valency errors [29 out of 40]	Error suspected		definitely or probably an error
Error suspected by more than 50%:	58 beginners	38 advanced	96 students
1 Don't pretend to ignorance.	97%	100%	92%
39 [...] the storm-force wind prevented one even walking	84%	95%	77%
20 [...] report of the special conference [...]	88%	76%	74%
28 [...] would require they treat members equally [...]	84%	87%	69%
15 Hospitals [...] are trying to protect against [...]	69%	63%	57%
22 [...] Hugh went to see about her [...]	72%	58%	52%
14 [...] protect certain home industries against competition [...]	72%	29%	44%
9 I [...] pretend surprise.	59%	45%	41%
16 [...] inclined to quarrel over pointless things [...]	66%	39%	40%
40 [...] share in looking after the children [...]	60%	55%	39%
12 [...] have pronounced vehemently against concessions	52%	68%	38%
38 [...] raced each other to the door.	60%	55%	35%

2.2 Valency as a problem for lexicography

This type of error is quite obviously a key problem in terms of performance (i.e. the production of language) and competence (where it is particularly important with respect to the assessment of learner language). Since valency structures are dependent on individual words and since grammars can only deal with the phenomenon in a very general - and hence rather unsatisfactory - way by establishing all the valency patterns of a language and providing lists of examples the place for this kind of information is the dictionary.

This was recognized in foreign language lexicography at least as far back as 1899 when Henry Sweet demanded that "a throughly useful dictionary [...] ought to give full information about those grammatical constructions which characterize individual words" (1899: 139). Of course this insight is reflected in many dictionaries. In particular, the verb patterns contained in Hornby's OALD and their counterparts in other EFL dictionaries are important devices with respect to this particular problem. Despite the great improvements in the presentation and the coverage of valency information in the general learners' dictionaries which are the subject of this volume,[3] it is perfectly clear that the amount of detail that can be provided in such dictionaries which address many other needs as well is limited. It is thus perfectly natural that general learners' dictionaries should contain only such patterns that are considered important or frequent because they are of prime importance with respect to language production. Nevertheless the differences in coverage between the four latest editions revealed by Klotz (this volume) is somewhat surprising. Furthermore, general learners' dictionaries tend to focus on the formal aspect of complementation while providing relatively little information on the semantic and collocational ranges of the patterns indicated.

2.3 Theory and practice

There are two aspects in which a valency dictionary may prove superior to the treatment of valency phenomena in general dictionaries: by focussing on one area of description

- a valency dictionary is able to cover that area in much more detail,
- a valency dictionary can be based consistently on one particular model of linguistic description.

It has to be said, however, that while any valency dictionary will be strongly linked with a syntactic model, valency theory, as with other dictionaries, there will always be areas of conflict between theoretical principles and insights and possibilities of presentation in a dictionary. As a consequence, lexicographical decisions had to be taken in order to establish the balance between linguistic accuracy and appropriateness and such lexicographical principles as intelligibility to the user.

In section 3 some of the key elements of the particular version of valency theory on which the English Valency Dictionary is based will be described briefly[4], while section 4 presents an outline of the way they were realized or modified in the actual dictionary entries.

---

3 Cf. Herbst (1984), Lemmens/Wekker (1986), Bogaards (1996).

4 See also Herbst (1988) and Herbst/ Roe (1996).

3 Valency theory

3.1 The application of valency theory to English

The theoretical background to the dictionary is provided by valency theory - a theory that - as a result of a rather remarkable combination of work in foreign language lexicography and theoretical linguistics - has become the most established model of complementation in Germany over the last thirty years or so.[5] Nevertheless, it has to be said that the theory has so far been applied to English on a rather modest scale - for instance in the work of Emons (1974), Allerton (1982) and Matthews (1981).[6] This can in no way be compared with the attention that Anglo-American theories have received in Germany, of course, but this may say more about linguistic dominance than the value of the theory.

3.2 Valency theory and traditional approaches to sentence analysis

3.2.1 Types of complement

Valency theory, which would not claim to have the same theoretical scope as, for instance, transformational grammar, and which is relatively agnostic as to the wider theoretical framework in which it is to be used, presents in a number of important ways an attractive alternative to the more established ways of dealing with complementation. Since it devotes a considerable amount of attention to the distinction between elements in a sentence that are specific to a particular word and those that are not, the theory is particularly attractive to lexicography.

On the other hand, it would be wrong to create the impression that the valency approach to complementation is radically different from, say, the approach taken in the *Comprehensive Grammar of the English Language* (1985) or what, from a valency point of view, can be seen as a superior version of that approach, the model employed by Aarts and Aarts in *English Syntactic Structures* (1982/1988). On the contrary, they share some very important basic assumptions:

The distinction that is crucial to valency theory is that between complements - or *actants* in Tesnière's (1959) terminology - and adjuncts or peripheral elements, as Matthews (1981) calls them, Tesnière's *circonstants*. It is the complements that are part of the valency of a verb. Thus in a sentence such as

---

[5] Cf. Helbig (1992) or Herbst/Heath/Dederding (1980).

[6] Cf. also Buysschaerts (1982), Herbst (1983).

[1A] *Following Ben Nicholson's first visit* to St. Ives, he painted a number of landscapes and paintings of Porthmeor beach.[7]

he and *a number of landscapes and paintings of Porthmeor beach* are classified as complements of the verb *paint*, which thus has a valency of 2, whereas *following Ben Nicholson's first visit to St. Ives* is a freely addible adjunct, which does not form part of the valency of the verb.

The distinction between complements and adjuncts is reflected in the classifications of CGEL or Aarts and Aarts in that the subordinate clause in [1A] would be classified as an optional adverbial in CGEL, which is not part of the complementation pattern. Terminologically, Aarts and Aarts come closer to the valency approach in that they do not, like CGEL, distinguish between obligatory adverbials and optional adverbials but between adverbials and complements - where the definition of adverbial corresponds to that of adjunct or peripheral element in valency theory and - with one exception - that of complement to that of complement in valency theory.

	Following Ben Nicholson's first visit to St. Ives	**he**	**painted**	**a number of land-scapes and paintings of Porthmeor beach.**
valency theory	adjunct	complement		complement
CGEL	optional adverbial	subject		direct object
Aarts/Aarts	adverbial	subject		complement: direct object

Secondly, although valency theory over the years has developed a large number of criteria and syntactic tests to establish the distinction between complements and adjuncts, the overall success of such attempts seems doubtful. In practice there is perhaps little difference with respect to the actual patterns identified between a valency and, say, the CGEL approach to complementation.

3.2.2 Degrees of optionality

One important difference between a valency approach and the treatment of complementation in CGEL concerns the identification of the elements that carry valency or complementation. This is related to the distinction that is made in valency theory with

[7] The examples used in this section are mostly taken from the following works: Tom Cross (1994): The Shining Sands. Artists in Newlyn and St Ives, 1880-1930. — Tiverton/ Cambridge: Westcountry Books/ The Lotterworth Press; Tom Cross (1995): Painting the Warmth of the Sun. St Ives Artists, 1939-1975. — Tiverton/ Cambridge: Westcountry Books/ The Lotterworth Press; Mel Gooding (1994): Patrick Heron. — London: Phaidon Press.

respect to what I would like to call the degree of optionality of complements, which, in various modifications, plays a part in all valency accounts. Based on a classification made by Allerton (1982), it seems appropriate to distinguish between three types of complements:

Firstly, obligatory complements, i.e. complements which cannot be deleted if a word, or a particular sense of a word, are to be used in an acceptable sentence, such as *Newlyn* and *at the western end of Mount's Bay* in

[2] Newlyn lies at the western end of Mount's bay.

Secondly, optional complements, which need not be realised if the verb is to be used in an acceptable sentence:

[3A] In November 1958 he resigned as London correspondent to the magazine, privately determined never again to write criticism.

[3B] Heron had made it a condition [...] that he would write only when he felt his primary commitment, to painting, was satisfied.

Thus *criticism* is an optional complement as is *a number of landscapes and paintings of Porthmeor beach* in [1A], since its presence is not essential for the verb *paint* to be used in an acceptable sentence:

[1B] He was positively encouraging to Patrick, allowing him to paint in the afternoons.

Whereas [1B] and [3B] are perfectly self-sufficient sentences, in other instances the use of a word without one of its complements is subject to special conditions, as Allerton (1975) has pointed out. Comparing sentences such as

[4A] Heron was never to forget the impressions of the light and landscapes of West Penwith.

[4B] We must not forget that the artist is also an ordinary man.

[4C] How could I possibly forget?

or

[5A] Would Heron try to discover within himself a gift for non-figurative painting?

[5B] He ought to try.

[4C] and [5B] only seem acceptable in contexts where it is clear what the referent of the complement that is not realised syntactically is. Such complements thus form a third type, which can be termed contextually optional complements.[8]

---

[8] For a discussion of these complement classes see Herbst/ Roe (1996).

This way of looking at these syntactic phenomena is different from the CGEL account in two ways: Firstly, in valency theory the various occurrences of *paint, write, forget* and *try* are seen as two different uses of the same verb, whereas according to CGEL, where no distinction between obligatory and optional complements is made, they each represent two different verbs which are related by a word formation process, as is pointed out under the heading of "change of secondary word class" in Appendix I (Herbst/ Klotz 1998). Valency theory in general would take the lexical unit in the sense described by Cruse (1986) as the basis of a valency description.

3.2.3 Prepositional complements

The second area where valency and the CGEL or Aarts/Aarts approach differ with respect to the units they identify as carrying valency is of even more importance to lexicography. It is exemplified by sentences such as

[6] She drew on these memories in her sculpture.
[7] No less than forty-four artists were showing their work to the public.

Here, CGEL would analyse *draw on* and *show to* as complex lexical items termed prepositional verbs, whereas valency theory identifies a complement type prepositional complement, by which is meant a prepositional phrase that has complement status. As indicated in CGEL, there are indeed arguments for both analyses.[9] On balance, we tend to think it highly preferable to treat the occurrences of *write* with a noun phrase in [3C], with a prepositional phrase with *about* in [3D], *of* in [3E], *to* in [3F] and a *that*-clause in [3G] as instances of the same lexical unit *write*.

[3C] It was in *Arts* in March 1956 that Heron wrote the celebrated article that recorded the first collective showing in London of the post-war New York School.
[3D] Heron continued to write about Braque.
[3E] He could write of Braque now with a certain detachement.
[3F] Zennor, he wrote to Middleton Murry and Katherine Mansfield in the spring of 1916, 'is a most beautiful place: a tiny granite village'.
[3G] He wrote that he had found himself 'compelled to refrain from jettisoning the figurative function entirely'.

This can, of course, only be done if a complement type prepositional complement is regognised and in fact it was the "emancipation" of prepositional phrases to the same

[9] Cf. Herbst/ Klotz (1998)

complement status as that of casemarked noun phrases that played a very important role in the early phases of German valency grammar.

Lexicographically, this has important repercussions. It is difficult to see why both COBUILD2 and LDOCE3 should deal with *decide on* in a sub-entry of *decide* thus splitting it off from *decide to do* and *decide that*. It is even more difficult to see the rationale behind depriving *decide against* and *decide in favour of* of that status.[10]

COBUILD2

decide /dɪsaɪd/ **decides, deciding, decided** ◆◆◆◆◆

1 If you **decide** to do something, you choose to do it, usually after you have thought carefully about the other possibilities. *She decided to do a secretarial course... He has decided that he doesn't want to embarrass the movement and will therefore step down... The house needed totally rebuilding, so we decided against buying it... Its outcome will decide whether Russia's economy can be reformed at all... Think about it very carefully before you decide.*
VERB =make up one's mind; V to-inf; V that; V against/in favour of n/-ing; V wh; V

2 If a person or group of people **decides** something, they choose what something should be like or how a particular problem should be solved. *She was still young, he said, and that would be taken into account when deciding her sentence... This is an issue that should be decided by local and metropolitan government.*
VERB; V n

3 If an event or fact **decides** something, it makes it certain that a particular choice will be made or that there will be a particular result. *The goal that decided the match came just before the interval... The results will decide if he will win a place at a good university... Luck is certainly not the only deciding factor, but it does play an exceptionally large role.*
VERB =settle; V n; V wh; V-ing

4 If you **decide** that something is true, you form that opinion about it after considering the facts. *He decided Franklin must be suffering from a bad cold... For a long time I couldn't decide whether the original settlers were insane or just stupid.*
VERB; V that; V wh

5 If something **decides** you to do something, it is the reason that causes you to choose to do it. *The banning of his English play decided him to write something about censorship... What decided him was a cynical question: 'If I fail, I'll be no worse off than I am now, will I?'*
VERB; V n to-inf; V n; Also V n that, V n against/in favour of n/-ing

decide on. If you **decide on** something or **decide upon** something, you choose it from two or more possibilities. *After leaving university, Therese decided on a career in publishing.*
PHRASAL VERB =settle for; V P n

LDOCE3

S1 W1 **de·cide** /dɪˈsaɪd/ *v* **1** [I,T] to make a choice or judgment about something, especially after a period of not knowing what to do or in a way that ends disagreement: **decide to do sth** *Tina's decided to go to Prague for her holidays.* | **decide that** *It was eventually decided that four London hospitals should be closed.* | **decide who/what/how etc** *I can't decide what to do.* | **decide whether/if** *Women now have greater freedom to decide whether or not to get married.* | [+ **between**] *I'm trying to decide between the green and the blue for the bathroom.* | **decide sth** *I'm eighteen now —I have a right to decide my own future.* | **decide for yourself** (=make your own choice or judgment, without asking anyone else to do it for you) *You must decide for yourself whether to leave college.* —see also DECISION (1) **2** [T] to be the reason for someone making a particular judgment or choice: **decide sb to do sth** *What was it that finally decided you to give up your job?* | **deciding factor** (=a very strong reason that forces you to make a particular decision) *Money should not be the deciding factor over who runs a TV station.* **3** [T] if an event, action etc decides something, it influences events so that one particular result will happen: *A goal in the last minute decided the match.* | **the deciding vote** (=the person who has the deciding vote makes the final decision, because all the other votes are equally divided) **4 decide in favour of/decide against** **a)** to choose or not choose someone or something: *After long discussion they decided in favour of the younger candidate.* **b)** if a judge or JURY (1) decides in favour of someone or against someone, they say in court that someone is guilty or not guilty: *The jury decided in favour of the plaintiff.*

decide on sth *phr v* [T] to choose one thing from many possible choices: *Have you decided on a date for your wedding?*

Summing up, it can be said that establishing prepositional complements in this sense and treating patterns where optional complements are realised syntactically as instances of the same lexical units as those where they are not results in a considerably smaller number of lexical units identified.

[10] Busse (1998) reveals quite a number of inconsistencies of this kind in the new learners' dictionaries.

3.2.4 The status of the subject

A third major difference between the valency approach and the complementation approach is described in CGEL note 16.18 as "valèncy [...] includes the subject of the clause, which is excluded (unless extraposed) from complementation" and this is the one exception where the definition of the term complement by Aarts and Aarts (1982/1988) does not coincide with ours.

Subjects present a highly intricate theoretical issue. Valency grammarians usually classify the subject as an obligatory complement on the grounds that it cannot be deleted. This is quite obviously not true if one considers passive sentences such as

[1C] They are painted in a variety of methods.

Of course, there still is a subject but it is not realised by the same complement as the subject in [1A] or [1B].

This discrepancy can be resolved by distinguishing between structural necessity and valency necessity. The fact that active declarative main clauses need a subject is part of structural necessity; whether a complement is obligatory or optional can only be resolved by considering active and passive uses of that verb. In other words, I would advocate a kind of intermediate position between canonical valency theory and the traditional subject-predicate-distinction in that I would consider the latter to be relevant at the level of structure but not of valency.

	Following Ben Nicholson's first visit to St. Ives	**he**	**painted**	**a number of land-scapes and paintings of Porthmeor beach.**
STRUCTURE	ADJUNCT	SUBJECT	PREDICATE	
VALENCY	ADJUNCT	OPTIONAL COMPLEMENT	PREDICATOR	OPTIONAL COMPLEMENT

Complements are to be seen as part of the lexical valency structure of a verb. Since their degree of optionality depends on whether they can function as subject, the formal specification of a complement class must in my view entail information on whether the complement can occur as the subject of an active clause, as the subject of a passive clause, or whether it cannot occur as a subject at all.

A very obvious justification for including subjects in an account of complementation is, of course, that they can take different forms and that this is just as much dependent on the individual verb as the different forms elements such as objects can take. However, it has to be emphasized that this is a rather theoretical statement to make.

4 Lexicographical considerations

4.1 Components of a valency description

On the basis of the considerations outlined above, the ideal valency description should contain the following types of information:

- whether a complement can occur as subject in active or passive clauses
- which (morphological) form it has
- which semantic role or semantic function it expresses or
- which lexical items can realise this complement and, finally,
- whether it is obligatory, optional or contextually optional.

4.2 User-friendliness and linguistic analysis

These demands are in obvious contrast to the ideas of accessibility of information and user-friendliness. As was pointed out before, while we imagine the users of the English Valency Dictionary to have a higher linguistic competence of English than the average users of a general learners' dictionary, we do not expect them to have any advanced knowledge of linguistic theory or valency theory, in particular.

In fact, from a lexicographical perspective, certainly for a linguist coming from the English learners' dictionary background, neither the German valency dictionaries nor the valency models developed for English seem to offer obvious models for a lexicographical description. Thus, it must be seen as one of the great disadvantages of the Helbig/Schenkel dictionary that its entries appear rather technical and as such do not particularly appeal to non-linguist users who are not accustomed to dealing with features such as '+ Hum'.

Helbig/Schenkel (1968)

vorschlagen

I. vorschlagen$_{2+(1)=3}$
II. vorschlagen → Sn, Sa/$\text{NS}_{\text{daß, w}}$, Inf, (Sd)

III. Sn →	1. Hum (*Der Versammlungsleiter* schlägt eine Pause vor.)
	2. Abstr (als Hum) (*Die Regierung* schlägt eine Friedenskonferenz vor.)
Sa →	1. Hum (Wir schlagen *den Kollegen* für eine Auszeichnung vor.)
	2. Abstr (als Hum) (Wir schlagen *den Betrieb* für eine Auszeichnung vor.)
	3. Abstr (Wir schlagen *einen Kompromiß* vor.)
	4. Act (Wir schlagen *Fußballspielen* vor.)
NS →	Act (Der Lehrer schlägt vor, *daß nicht geraucht wird / wer ausgezeichnet werden soll.*)
Inf →	Act (Der Lehrer schlägt vor, *die Sache zu vertagen.*)
Sd →	1. Hum (Er schlägt *seinem Freund* einen Büchertausch vor.)
	2. Abstr (als Hum) (Die Kommission schlägt *dem Betrieb* eine Plankorrektur vor.)

We have tried to avoid abstract labels of that kind. Similarly, formulae such as 1 (+ 1) = 2 are of more value to linguists than to users who consult the dictionary in order to find out how to use a particular word. The Helbig/Schenkel or Schumacher (1986) approach, however, seems to make it relatively easy for the specialist linguist to retrieve information, whereas the information relevant to the general user is not immediately interpretible. In the English Valency Dictionary we have adopted the opposite policy: to enable the general user to get at the information relatively easily whilst putting the expert linguist in a position to arrive at the relevant conclusions in a more theoretical framework somewhat indirectly.

This is reflected in the central features of the valency dictionary: the general layout, the way that semantic information is provided and the kind of complement classes established.

The complement classes established by Emons (1974), which are strictly based on the principle of commutation, do not lend themselves easily to a general lexicographical application, let alone the technical categories employed in his model.

Emons (1974: 177-178)

believe 12

S12[P12 + E1[NOM1/ES1] + E2[NOM2/ES2[*that*]]]

(1) *I believe that story.*

(2) *I believe that you come.*

believe 13

S13[P13 + E1[NOM1/ES1] + E3[NOM3[*in*]/IK3[*in* + *-ing*]/ES3[*in*]]]

(1) *I believe in the bible.*

(2) *I believe in going to the doctor.*

believe 125

S125[P125 + E1[NOM1/ES1] + E2[NOM2/ES2] + E5[NOM5/IK5[*to*]/ES5]]

(1) *I believe him a coward.*

(2) *I believe him to be a coward.*

Similarly, Allerton's (1982) distinction between objects and objoids, which reflects the ability of a complement to occur as the subject of a passive clause and is thus central to a valency account as we see it, employs terminology that would make the dictionary too difficult to use for anybody not familiar with the theory. This applies especially to subcategories such as 'Match objoids' etc.

Allerton (1982: 148)

accuse "explicit attributing of bad action or motive to someone"
1. subject "performer"
2. object "affected (*or* major mental focus)"
[3. *of*-prepositional objoid "(minor) mental focus"]
e.g. Charles accused Oliver [of the crime]

In fact, even the term object is problematical. It is by no means as straightforward as one might think since even closely related approaches such as CGEL and *English Syntactic Structures* use it in a different way in that passivization is seen as a defining criterion by the latter and a prototypical criterion by the former. Thus, *a nice house* in

[14] They had a nice house.

would be classified as an object in CGEL and as a predicator complement by Aarts and Aarts. However, if passivization is not a defining criterion for objects and if information about the semantic role of a complement is given in a different place in the description, there is at least no need for the term object in a valency description.

Irrespective of terminology, we came to the conclusion that a description of the complements of verbs based on their ability of occurring as subjects would result in a rather complex presentation. All the more so, since restrictions on passivization, as studies such as the ones by Stein (1979) and Svartvik (1966) have shown, sometimes are not simply a matter of the complement class but can be dependent on a variety of lexical, contextual or semantic factors which would be very difficult to grasp in the first place and impossible to present in a comprehensible form in the second. Distinguishing between complements that can function as subjects in passive clauses and those that cannot would in many cases have resulted in a duplication of the number of patterns for a particular verb as well as in the need to make use of more sophisticated symbols while still not providing information that is wholly reliable.

Thus in the English Valency Dictionary we have opted for a presentation where cases in which only the passive is possible or where the passive is very frequent are indicated; furthermore we have taken care to include passive examples where this seemed appropriate and, apart from that, we think that general restrictions on the passive should be deducible through the sense distinctions made. Thus while the passive has by no means been ignored, it is certainly one area where the account of word complementation as presented in the dictionary gives priority to userfriendliness over theoretical accuracy in that it does not attempt to give a totally systematic account of passivization and the range of possible subjects.

4.3 Description of complement classes in the dictionary

Although from a theoretical point of view the question of whether formal or functional categories should be used in an account of complementation is debatable, for a valency dictionary formal categories seem to present a more immediate starting point. Interestingly enough, this insight is also reflected in the pattern systems of COBUILD2 and LDOCE3, which in the previous editions did use the term object, but, like OALD4/5, now use pattern representations based purely on formal categories.

In the English Valency Dictionary symbols such as N (for noun phrase), ADJ (for adjective phrase), to-INF (for a *to*-infinitive) and so on are used, which, of course, must be seen as standing for the corresponding phrases or clauses.

As can be seen from the model entries for *propose* and *vote* (section 6), the entries as envisaged at the present stage of the project consist of two columns. The left-hand column lists all patterns of a word, the right-hand column gives examples for each pattern and subpattern which are taken directly from the Bank of English.

The left-hand column reflects the principles of valency theory in that it is divided up into blocks of monovalent, divalent, trivalent and tetravalent complementation. These are separated by slim lines. Thus the quantitative valency of a word is not taken as a prime structuring criterion as in the Helbig/Schenkel dictionary but can be derived from the number of such pattern blocks.

4.4 Obligatory and optional complements in the dictionary

The same line is taken with respect to the distinction between obligatory, optional or contextually optional complements. It would of course have been possible to indicate the two types of optionality by different kinds of bracketing, such as round brackets for optional and square brackets for contextually optional complements. However, as with the possibility of occurrence as a passive subject, this would have resulted in increasing the number of patterns - because a complement can be optional in one sense and obligatory in another. Furthermore, brackets do not exactly contribute to easy interpretability of the formulae; apart from the fact that the significance of the different types of brackets might not have been clear to all users.

For this reason, only one type of bracket is used in the dictionary, and that rather sparsely. In the main pattern block, the fact that a word has an obligatory valency of 1 and an optional valency of 2 is indicated by the fact that both the monovalent and the divalent patterns are listed in the left-hand column, related, however, through references to the same note after the examples. Again, we think that the practical information - how can this word be used? - is immediately accessible in this form, whereas the slightly more sophisticated question of whether a complement is obligatory or optional can be answered by checking whether the pattern without the respective complement occurs for the same sense as well, in which case it is optional, or not, in which case it is obligatory.

4.5 Structure of entries

The point at which this dictionary perhaps makes the most radical break with traditional dictionaries is the fact that it is not organized according to senses. Although, as pointed out above, valency structures must be seen as properties of lexical units rather than those of lexical items, the layout of the valency dictionary takes lexical items as its basis. There are several reasons for this:

Firstly, a dictionary focussing on syntactic features of words should perhaps give most prominence to those features. We feel that listing all patterns of a word in one column facilitates the looking-up process considerably. Organizing entries according to senses would have meant

- that users wanting to find out whether a particular pattern exists would have had to check all senses and
- that many patterns would have had to be listed more than once.

Secondly, semantic information is dealt with in a rather flexible way in this dictionary. The types of information included are:

- obviously, an indication of the sense of a word in a particular valency structure
- an indication of the range of a particular complement, i.e. the general semantic, lexical or collocational restrictions of a particular complement as well as
- an indication of the differences in meaning between different patterns such as *talk about* and *talk on*.

I am sure there is no need to outline here why both a feature approach or a kind of case grammar approach appeared unsuitable for this enterprise - both as far as the general intelligibility of the notions applied and their descriptive adequacy is concerned. The analyses soon revealed that in some cases the semantic side of complements could be described in terms of hyperonyms, always allowing for some sort of prototypicality, whereas in other cases it seemed necessary to provide much more specific information in terms of explicitly listed collocations, for example.

Thus, we decided that the semantic component of the valency dictionary should be based on the principle of flexibility. As far as sense descriptions are concerned, the policy adopted in the English Valency Dictionary is to afford the luxury of not stating the obvious.

Although senses that only occur in one pattern are often indicated through glosses, the most important place where semantic information is given is the note block, which is placed underneath the examples. If there is more than one note, these are numbered A, B etc. Thus three senses were distinguished for the verb *propose*, which are described in notes A to C. A reference to the corresponding note is given after every example and the notes contain indicators in which patterns a particular sense occurs so that semantic-syntactic cross-referencing is possible in both directions.

If a note is mainly to indicate a sense distinction, it consists simply of a short indication of the relevant sense in the form of a synonym or a short paraphrase, as in the case of *ask*, where the three senses 'inquire', 'request' and 'invite' are given. The purpose of such short indications is to enable the user to identify the appropriate sense, not, of course, to provide a full definition as one would in a general learners' dictionary. In the case of nouns or adjectives, which often have many senses that are not relevant in terms of a valency description, the note may simply indicate the sense relevant to the examples given without making an attempt to cover all facades of meaning of that word.

Information on the meaning aspects of the complements is usually given in the notes in the form of prototypical sentences, generally indicating the range of a complement by the use of hyperonyms, often followed by a paraphrase, as in note A of *propose* (Cf. section 6).

> If a person proposes or proposes to a member of the opposite sex, they ask them to marry them.

Where such general labels did not seem appropriate, lists of collocations similar to those in ODCIE are used:

> A person can wear
> (i) clothes, a particular colour, jewellery, glasses, makeup,
> (ii) a particular expression such as a smile,
> (iii) their hair in a particular way.

In other cases, patterns are contrasted in the notes. This is the case with *try*:

> *try* can mean 'attempt':
> (i) Someone can try something they want to do or achieve.
> (ii) Someone can try to do something or try doing something. Note that the infinitive only occurs in this sense: *a person tries to do something* always means that they attempt to do it; in informal language one can also say *try and do something*. The *ing*-form is also frequently used in this sense, although traditional descriptions sometimes claim that it only occurs in sense B.

Thus these notes fulfill a variety of different functions. We see the flexibility applied in the notes as a strength - we are convinced that no abstract consistent labelling system is able to grasp the enormous complexity of semantic and lexical relations at work in semantic valency. Apart from the fact that we hope that the description given will provide a suitable basis for linguistic research of a more theoretical kind, the use of non-technical everyday terms in the notes and their slightly ad hoc character seem the only option open to a dictionary aiming at the kind of users we have in mind.

5 Contradictions between theory and practice

Work on the English Valency Dictionary, as no doubt work on many other dictionaries before it, has shown the difficulties of putting linguistic insights into lexicographical practice. Not only do the demands of user-friendliness, which have to be rated very highly in a dictionary aimed at a wider user group than that of fellow-linguists, impose obvious limits upon the kind of formalisms and categories employed. It is equally true that the thorough research into the syntactic patterns of individual words bring to surface an enormous amount of detail, which even a lexicographical (let alone a grammatical) description is not able to represent in any useful way.

This is why in the English Valency Dictionary many compromises had to be made, where the scientific precision of syntactic research had to be overruled by the arts-character of lexicography. Nevertheless, the editors hope that these compromises - both as far as the translation of principles and categories of valency theory into a dictionary format and the flexibility with respect to the semantic information provided is concerned - were the right ones to satisfy the needs of the language learner and the language teacher for whose needs this valency dictionary is designed.

6 Model entries

vote

verb

Patterns:

1.	**+ 0**	*People have refused to go and* ***vote****.* → A *It is a democratic right not only to* ***vote*** *but to seek election.* → A *They would* ***vote*** *in a General Election.* → A
2.	**+ N**	*Naturally, we hope they are patriotic people who* ***vote*** *Conservative.* → A *They intended to* ***vote*** *Thatcher.* → A
3.	**+ to-INF**	*The United Nations Security Council has* ***voted*** *to give Iraq six weeks to withdraw from Kuwait or face being forced out.*→ A *Only 39% **voted** to stay in.* → A *Gore is a Vietnam veteran, and he* ***voted*** *to authorize the use of force in the Persian Gulf.* → B
4.	**+ (that)-CL**	*I* ***vote*** *that we all go to Holland.* → B *I* ***vote*** *we eat now.* → B
5.	**+ against N/V-ing** **against**	*We did not* ***vote*** *against the introduction of the Emergency Powers Act.* → A *45 MPs* ***voted*** *against the Government.* → A *One club president, who did not want to be named, said most of the Townsville clubs would* ***vote*** *against joining the new competition.* → A *A majority of the 18 MEPs abstained on the question of extending the range of issues on which the Council of Ministers can be decide by majority vote, in defiance of Downing Street demands that they should* ***vote*** *against.* → A
6.	**+ by N**	*There have been only three instances since 1923 in which a member has been granted the right to* ***vote*** *by proxy.* → A *On many issues, member states already* ***vote*** *by majority.* → A
7.	**+ for N/V-ing** ***<frequent>***	*Who did you* ***vote*** *for?* → B *He urged French Communists to* ***vote*** *for Mitterand.* → A *The member declared that on no account would he* ***vote*** *for the Government's proposal.* → A *The councillors have defied the law by refusing to* ***vote*** *for setting a level for the government's new local authority tax.*→ A *Many unions found it hard not to* ***vote*** *for keeping the clause.* → A
8.	**+ in favour of N/V-ing** **in favour**	*If the French were to* ***vote*** *in favour of Maastricht, the financial collapse that followed the Danish no vote could be substantially reversed.* → A *The fund's constitution required 75 percent of committee members* ***vote*** *in favour of winding up.* → *A* *Twenty-nine per cent said they would* ***vote*** *in favour.* → A *Some right-wing Euro-sceptic MEPs will vote against changes, but most Tories will abstain or* ***vote*** *in favour.* → A

9.	**+ on N/V-ing** **on wh-CL** **on wh to-INF**	*The House of Commons had ist first opportunity to discuss and **vote** on the White Paper.* → A *We will **vote** on it.* → A *Shareholders will **vote** on putting both men on the board at the annual meeting next month.* → A *First of all, we should **vote** on whether we're going to have a referendum.* → A *The bank workers are to **vote** on whether to strike and the postal workers may go out in June.* → A *MEPs will **vote** on whether to accept or reject the revised draft at the end of this month.* → A *The Chamber of Deputies will **vote** on whether to start impeachment proceedings against him.* → A
10.	**+ yes/no**	*63% of the people **voted** yes in the recent referendum.* → A
11.	**+ N + N**	*The union **voted** itself larger welfare benefits.* → C *She was **voted** Most Promising Actress by the London theatre critics.* → D
12.	**+ N + for N**	*The sums involved amounted to 8% of the monies Parliament **voted** for the upkeep of the armed forces.* → C
13.	**+ N + to N**	*The government has just **voted** another nine million pounds to the defence budget.* → C
14.	**+ N + ADV**	*No one ever wanted to **vote** you out of office.* → A *Thirteen men were **voted** onto the executive committee.* → A

Notes on meaning:

A (i) **People can vote on a particular proposal or issue**, ie. try to arrive at a majority decision on it

(ii) **A person supporting can vote**
(a) for a proposal,
(b) in favour of a proposal or just **vote in favour**
(c) to do something or
(d) yes,
a person opposing can vote
(a) against a proposal or a person or just **vote against**
(b) no,
ie. cast their vote that way; if **an institution such as a parliament** votes a particular way, a decision is taken.

(iii) In an election, esp. in a political context, **a person can vote**
(a) Democrat, Conservative, S.P.D., Green etc., i.e. for a political party
(b) Koek, Banerjee, Blair, etc., i.e. for a particular candidate
(c) for a particular candidate such as Kohl or a party such as the S.N.P.,
ie. cast their vote for them.
(*used in patterns 1, 2, 3, 5, 6, 7, 8, 9, 10 and 14*)

B *vote* can also mean 'suggest'; e.g. in the phrase ***I or we vote that something should be done***; an informal use
(*used in patterns 3 and 4*)

C In formal language, *vote* can also mean 'allocate money to an institution'

An organization such as a government or a trade union can vote money

(i) for a particular purpose

(ii) to an institution or an account.

(used in patterns 11, 12 and 13)

D **A group, esp. a jury, can vote a person man/woman of the year etc.**, ie. award them a specifictitle, often in a competition.

(used in pattern 11)

Idiomatic phrasal verbs:

+ down ↔ N — *That will allow them to* ***vote down*** *the entire report without being identified as anti-women. (= defeat by a vote)*

+ in ↔ N — *Not surprisingly he was* ***voted in***. (= elected as a member of Parliament)

+ out ↔ N — *This was a safe Labour seat: he would never be* ***voted out***. (= lose the seat)

+ through ↔ N — *The proposal was instantly* ***voted through*** *with two to one in favour. (= forced through in a vote).*

propose *verb*

Patterns:

1. + 0	*In her only published interview with the press she laughed off suggestions that Bertie had had to* ***propose*** *three times.*→ A
2. + N	*Tony Benn's bill* ***proposes*** *confiscation of all Crown lands, property and buildings in return for a lump sum.* → B *It was heralded in 1975 by the publication of Modern Painting and the Northern Romantic tradition by Robert Rosenblum, a seminal study which convincingly* ***proposed*** *an alternative reading to the history of modern art.* → B *The Chancellor Mr Major has instead* ***proposed*** *a less ambitious scheme restricted to a so called hard ECU currency.* → B *The issue is an urgent one, because according to the constitution it is the president who will* ***propose*** *a candidate for Prime Minister to the National Assembly, which meets on Tuesday.* → B *He and his colleagues in generative grammar have naturally concentrated on areas of grammar where abstract principles can be* ***proposed****, and have simply ignored areas where the prospects of finding such principles look poor.* → C *Christopher Wren (1657)* ***proposed*** *an elaborate theory of an elliptical corona .* → C *This is particularly important if a speaker has* ***proposed*** *a toast because the audience may forget to applaud as it sits down again afterwards asked everyone to raise their glasses* (= call for a toast to be drunk)
3. + to-INF	*So what I* ***propose*** *to do is just generally have a look at inflation this morning.* → B *Mr Bush has also* ***proposed*** *to get rid of American nuclear shells in Europe* → B *The BCF is* ***proposing*** *to house its coaching staff at the velodrome* → B *Such critics might, for example, argue that the data which Chomsky* ***proposes*** *to explain with the Binding Principle is better accounted for using some other principle of UG.* → C
4. + V-ing	*This went down badly with the traditionalist parties, which had* ***proposed*** *holding immediate elections in the refugee camps.* → B *President Gorbachev also* ***proposed*** *giving the Soviet Republics a greater say in decision making at a national level.* → B

5.	**+ (that) -CL**	*The Report **proposed** that local authorities, together with the police, should be given a clear statutory responsibility* → B *He would also be **proposing** that they hold joint peace rallies in areas affected by violence.* → B *At the European Community Foreign Ministers' Council today the EC Commission President Jacques Delors **proposed** that a draft charter for an all-European energy community to include the Soviet Union be put up for approval at the coming CSCE summit in Paris.* → B *He did not **propose** she join him.* → B *Oppenheim **proposed** that message dreams are most easily explained as literary embellishments of dreams experienced at an incubation site.* → C
6.	**+ to N**	*Were you **proposed** to (or did you propose) in an unusual setting?* → A
7.	**+ N to-INF**	*Freud felt that inferiority was not as central a theme as Adler **proposed** it to be, but still believed it to be a childhood response to "injuries" to our self-esteem.* → C
8.	**+ N + as N**	*Therefore Warnock **proposed** the fourteen day limit as a convenient legal point.* → B
9.	**+ N/V-ing + to N**	*Listen, I'm going to **propose** something to you.* → B *The Secretary said he will **propose** to the Soviet Foreign Minister Mr Eduard Shevardnadze setting up a working group on deterrents* → B

Notes on meaning:

A If a person proposes or proposes to a member of the opposite sex, they ask them to marry them.(*used in patterns 1 and 6*).

B *Propose* can mean 'suggest' .
A person can propose
(i) **something to someone**
(ii) **to do or doing something**
(iii) **that something should be done.**
Note that *they etc. propose to do or propose doing* can mean 'plan' rather than 'suggest' if the action to be carried out is the sole decision of the person proposing it.
(*used in patterns 2, 3, 4, 5, 8 and 9*).

C *Propose* can mean 'claim'.
A scientist or philosopher can propose
(i) **a theory**
(ii) **that something is the case.**
(*used in patterns 2, 3, 5 and 7*).

Bibliography

Oxford Advanced Learner's Dictionary (OALD4) (⁴1989): Anthony P. Cowie (ed.). — Oxford: OUP.

Oxford Dictionary of English Idioms (ODCIE) (1983/1993): Anthony P. Cowie, Ronald Mackin, Isabel R. MacCaig (eds). — Oxford: OUP.

Wörterbuch zur Valenz und Distribution deutscher Verben (1968, ²1973): Gerhard Helbig, Wolfgang Schenkel. — Leipzig: Enzyklopädie.

Aarts, Jan, Flor Aarts (1982/1988): English Syntactic Structures. — New York, Leyden: Prentice Hall/Martinus Nijnhoff.

Allerton, D.J. (1975): "Deletion and proform reduction". — In: Journal of Linguistics 11, 213—238.

— (1982): Valency and the English verb. — London, New York: Academic Press.

Bogaards, Paul (1996): "Dictionaries for Learners of English". — In: International Journal of Lexicography 9/4, 277-320.

Busse, Ulrich (1998): "English Learners' Dictionaries and Their Treatment of Phrasal Verbs". — In: A. Zetterston, V. H. Pedersen, J. E. Mogensen (eds.): Symposium on Lexicography VIII. Proceedings of the Eighth International Symposium on Lexicography May 2-4, 1996, at the University of Copenhagen (Tübingen: Niemeyer), 111-134.

Busse, Winfried, Jean-Pierre Dubost (²1983): Französisches Verblexikon. Die Konstruktion der Verben im Französischen. — Stuttgart: Klett.

Buysschaert, Joost (1982): Criteria for the classification of English adverbials. — Brussel:AWLsK..

Cowie, Anthony (1987): The Dictionary and the Language Learner. — Tübingen: Niemeyer.

Cruse, D. A. (1986): Lexical Semantics. — Cambridge: CUP.

Emons, Rudolf (1974): Valenzen englischer Prädikatsverben. — Tübingen: Niemeyer.

— (1978): Valenzgrammatik für das Englische. Eine Einführung. — Tübingen: Niemeyer.

Helbig, Gerhard (1992): Probleme der Valenz- und Kasustheorie. — Tübingen: Niemeyer.

Herbst, Thomas, David Heath, Hans-Martin Dedering (1980): Grimm's grandchildren. Current topics in German linguistics. — London: Longman.

Herbst, Thomas (1983): Untersuchungen zur Valenzz englischer Adjektive und ihrer Nominalisierung. —Tübingen: Narr.

— (1984): "Bemerkungen zu den Patternsystemen des Advanced Learner's Dictionary and das Dictionary of contemporary English". —In: D. Götz, T. Herbst (eds.): Theoretische und praktische Probleme der Lexikographie (München: Hueber) 139-165.

— (1987):"A Proposal for a Valency Dictionary of English". — In: R. F. Ilson (ed.): A Spectrum of Lexicography (Amsterdam, Philadelphia: John Benjamins) 29-47.

— (1988): "A valency model for nouns in English". — In: Journal of Linguistics 24/2, 265-301.

Herbst, Thomas, Ian Roe (1996): "How obligatory is obligatory?". — In: English Studies 77/2, 179-199.

Herbst, Thomas, Michael Klotz (1998): "A valency dictionary of English - a project report". — In: A. Zettersten, V. H. Pedersen, J. E. Mogensen (eds.): Symposium on Lexicography VIII. Eighth Symposium on Lexicography May 2-4, 1996, at the University of Copenhagen (Tübingen Niemeyer) 65-91.

Klotz, Michael (1997): "Ein Valenzwörterbuch englischer Verben, Adjektive und Substantive - Vorstellung eines Projektes". — In: Zeitschrift für angewandte Linguistik 27, 93-111.

— (this volume): "Word complementation in English learners' dictionaries- A quantitative study of CIDE; COBUID2, LDOCE3 and OALD5".

Lemmens, Marcel, Herman Wekker (1986): Grammar in English learners' dictionaries. — Tübingen: Niemeyer.

Matthews, Peter .H. (1981): Syntax. — Cambridge: CUP.

Quirk, Randolph, Sidney Greenbaum, Geoffrey Leech, Jan Svartvik (1985): A Comprehensive Grammar of the English Language. — London: Longman.

Schumacher, Helmut (1986): Verben in Feldern. Valenzwörterbuch zur Syntax und Semantik deutscher Verben. — Berlin: de Gruyter.

Stein, Gabriele (1979): Studies in the Function of the Passive. — Tübingen: Narr.
Svartvik, Jan (1966): On Voice in the English Verb. — The Hague: Mouton.
Sweet, Henry (1899/1964): The practical study of languages: a guide for teachers and learners. — London: OUP.
Tesnière, Lucien (1959): Éléments de syntaxe structurale. — Paris: Klienksieck.

III. Dictionaries – corpora – perspectives

Della Summers

Coverage of spoken English in relation to learners' dictionaries, especially the Longman Dictionary of Contemporary English

When conceptualizing new dictionaries for learners of English, we begin with the assumption that learners *want* to know and learn about natural spoken language. We assume that they want to understand spoken English in order to converse with their own age group if they visit the UK or the US; that they want to communicate with other non-native speakers of English using English as a modern lingua franca as they travel round the world; or that they want to be able to use spoken English in their adult life, whether by giving a paper at a conference in English or by taking part in business meetings or telephone calls.

The teacher's perspective may be somewhat different. Teachers may have doubts about the value of including spoken language in a dictionary. They may think - with some justification - that spoken language is disjointed, less precise, and above all grammatically imperfect when compared with written English. The bulk of the exams that are taken by students of English in countries around the world still concentrate on written English. The advantages of the written form of English in terms of its permanence and the availability of students' scripts for marking at a later point or a different place are obvious. On the other hand, there is an increasing trend for papers on spoken English to be included as part of the examinations in most countries.

The language presented in many English textbooks as normal English conversation is not really very natural or typical of ordinary spoken communication. Unusual grammatical patterns may be included, and often repeated to make a point in a way that tends not to happen in speech. We at Longman Dictionaries have been sensitized through working for several years with corpuses of naturally occurring spoken language, and it therefore seems very apparent to us when conversations are "made up". We understand that this is done to teach a language point in what is supposed to be a lively and natural context, but this often does not ring true. This is probably because the starting point for writers of such textbooks is usually a syllabus. In the case of dictionaries, there is no syllabus; it is the language itself that is being presented. Yet even with dictionaries that claim to be corpus-based, we often find the same type of forced, unconvincing language as in textbooks. This is most apparent in example sentences.

1 Spoken language in dictionary examples

Take this example for *folly* from the latest edition of the *Oxford Advanced Learner's Dictionary* (OALD5):

It's utter folly to go swimming in this weather.

What makes this example seem improbable is that *folly* is a very unusual word, more typical of rhetorical speech than the casual context of going swimming. There are only 15 instances of the word *folly* on the 10-million word spoken corpus of the British National Corpus; one is about a pub called the Folly, 3 or 4 are about Folly Farm, and several about a horse called Folly. In fact there are no instances of *folly* in this meaning on the British spoken corpus at all.[1] Yet the example above seems to be a spoken example.

Spoken language is obviously heavily reliant on the context for its meaning. It is therefore especially difficult to make up examples in dictionaries without real concordance lines. When this is done, the example writer is forced to supply the context in just one sentence and this can again bring about an unnatural scenario, as here, under the verb headword *fool*:

I was only fooling when I said I'd lost your keys.

Even the example from the *Longman Dictionary of Contemporary English*, which is much more closely based on spoken corpora, is clearly modified from any authentic conversation, although it is more representative of how the phrase is used in that the use is shown in bold as a preformed language chunk:

> **3 sb is just fooling** *spoken* used to say that someone is not serious and is only pretending that something is true: *Don't pay any attention to Henry. He's just fooling.*

2 Corpus resources

Reliable linguistic data for spoken language has long been the holy grail of lexicographers. In order to create corpora that reflect the norms of language use, considerable thought and study have gone into the design and composition of the corpora used by Longman. In the case of the spoken component of the British National Corpus,[2] the corpus was split into two equal halves: the Demographic part and the Context-governed part. The 5-million-word Context-governed part was recorded in 4 basic contexts, as recommended to us by one of our advisers, Professor Douglas Biber of the University of Northern Arizona. These were Education, Business, Institutional, and Leisure, as shown in this graph:

---

1 Nor any instances of *folly* in this meaning on the 5-million-word Longman American Spoken Corpus.

2 The British National Corpus was created by a consortium of Oxford University Press, Longman Group Limited, Chambers, the University of Lancaster, the British Library, and Oxford University Computing Service, with subsidies from the British government. Longman was responsible for designing and collecting the 10-million-word spoken component.

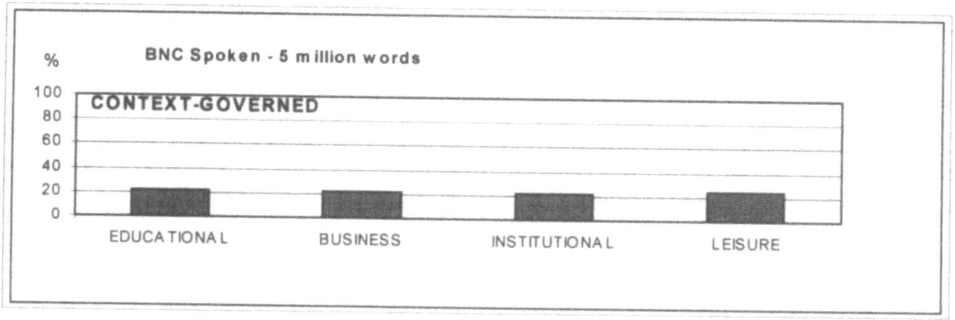

This involved recording in all types of contexts, from primary schools through to business meetings.

The other 5 million words were based on demographic principles using market research techniques.

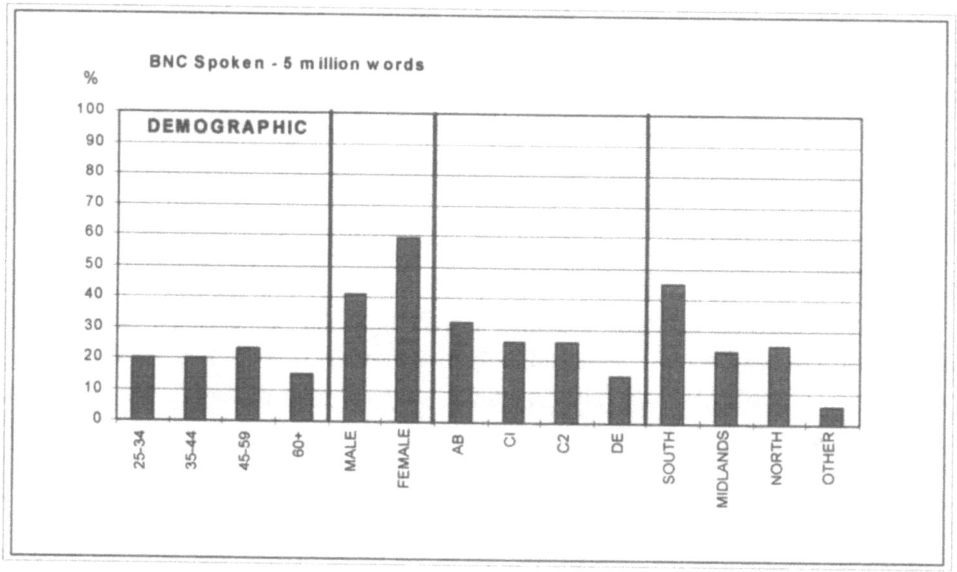

The definitions of the socio-economic categories are:

A	Higher managerial, administrative or professional
B	Intermediate managerial, administrative or professional
C1	Supervisory or clerical, and junior managerial, administrative or professional
C2	Skilled manual workers
D	Semi and unskilled manual workers

Our volunteers recorded all that was said around them in their daily lives, using unobtrusive Walkman tape recorders to get spoken data covering a wide range of speech acts and social levels. All parts of the United Kingdom are represented in the BNC Spoken Corpus.

Here is the makeup of the Longman American Spoken Corpus, a 5 million-word corpus gathered on our behalf by the University of Santa Barbara, using demographic principles based on the most recent US census figures to determine the corpus design:

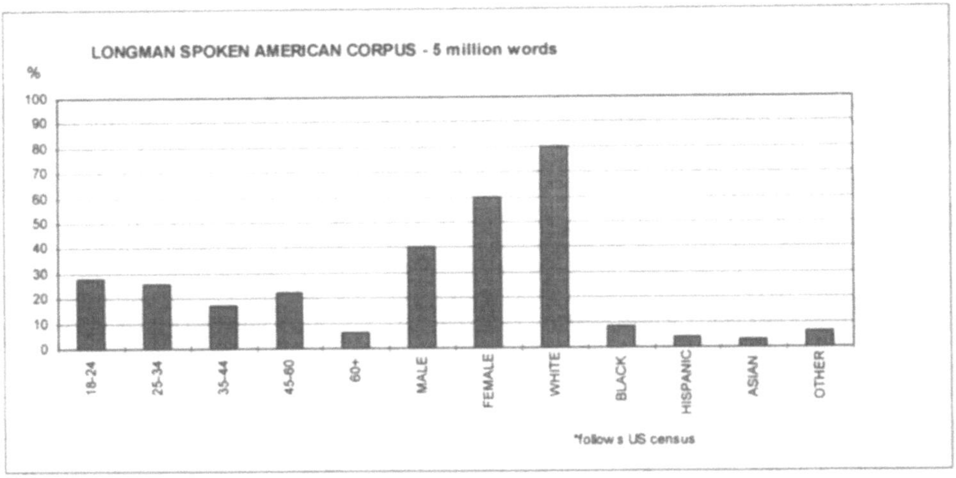

The use of the corpus affects all areas of dictionary-making from decisions on which words to include to examples, but here is a short extract from the raw data, the actual taped conversation. The speakers are Emma and Kelly, two 15-year-old girls from the Midlands:

Emma: She made [*erm*]... Heather a birthday cake the other day and, I, I've got to say actually this cake was pretty good but like she had to take it to school! I mean, the girl is **sad**! If you're gonna take a birthday cake to school, I mean, that is **sad**, isn't it?

Kelly: My brain's just died!

Emma: But that is very, very **sad**! But like [*erm*], she took it to school, and Scott was giving us a lift to school so she didn't have to walk and she's in the car and she's going if this gets, if this gets all smashed up, Scott, I hope you realise I'm blaming you! And she was serious!

This use of *sad* is quite well attested on the British spoken corpus and also on the American spoken corpus (as in *somebody had really really sad hair*), and is now quite a common informal term in casual speech. These are the entries from LDOCE and the Collins COBUILD Dictionary:[3]

---

[3] This use of *sad* is not included in the *Oxford Advanced Learner's Dictionary.*

5 ▶ BORING ◀ *spoken slang* used to say that someone or something is boring and unfashionable: *I think Carole's a bit of a sad name. Oh, sorry, is your mum called Carole?*| ***sad bastard*** *Get a life, you sad bastard.*

LDOCE3

4 If you describe someone as **sad**, you do not have any respect for them and think their behaviour or ideas are ridiculous; an informal use... *sad old bikers and youngsters who think that Jim Morrison is God.*	ADJ-GRADED: usu ADJ n = pathetic

COBUILD2

Both these entries are creditable attempts at defining and exemplifying a lexical item which presents considerable difficulties for the lexicographer. The LDOCE definition concentrates on the unfashionable aspect, which is generally borne out by our British and American corpuses. The COBUILD definition concentrates on the value judgment aspect. The LDOCE example is taken direct from our spoken corpus, and rings true. The inclusion of the lexical unit *sad bastard* is also a true reflection of the word's use. Although the COBUILD example is clearly real, it relies heavily on the reader knowing who Jim Morrison is. Interestingly, the synonym in the side column, *pathetic*, is one case where this device works, since *pathetic* is a pretty close synonym of *sad*, although notice that it would not be possible to substitute it in the sad hair example mentioned above.

Another interesting point is the use of the *spoken* label in LDOCE. This label is used to mean "more frequent in speech than writing", with the register information being given in the *slang* label. COBUILD does not label, except to say it is informal. Of course, any word that can be said can be written down, but nonetheless we would defend *sad* being labelled *spoken* because it is typical of spoken language whether or not it can be found in journalism, which often attempts to replicate the feel and vocabulary of informal speech.

3 Spoken phrases

In LDOCE, we see the documentation of the phraseology - so typical of spoken English - as a real innovation. Special spoken phrase boxes are used to highlight this important phenomenon of English. The entry for the verb *like* includes more than 20 fixed expressions identified through analysis of the spoken corpora, such as:

10 c) if you like used to suggest one possible way of describing something or someone: *This experience was, if you like, a door that opened up a whole new world.*

11 whatever/anything etc you like especially BrE whatever you want: *Which play shall we go to see? Oh, whichever you like.* | *Come and stay with us for as long as you like.*

13 b) **how would you like it if?** used to ask someone how they would feel if something bad happened to them instead of to you or someone else: *How would you like it if you got home to find you'd been burgled?*

17 I'd like to think/believe (that) a) used to say that you wish or hope that something is true, when you are not sure that it is: *I'd like to believe that one day he'll be well enough to lead a normal life.* **b)** used to say that you think you do something well, especially when you do not want to make yourself seem better than other people: *I'd like to think that my work is as good as anybody's here.*

Although these are obviously not new expressions, it is interesting to note that some of the other dictionaries do not give them special prominence, and sometimes do not include them at all, yet they are all well attested on the spoken corpora, as in the concordance lines below from the British National Corpus for *if you like* and *I would like to think that*:

And I think the local touch **if you like** of the principal beat officer...
[It] was the posh part of the flats **if you like**.
[It] was meant as a bit of sympathy **if you like**, you know.
Yes, we took on board robotic technology **if you like**, to reduce costs.

We can see from the header records on the corpus (not shown above) that *if you like* in sense 10 c), where the speakers are hesitantly describing something in a new way, is used mainly in the context-governed part of the spoken corpus, in lectures, and this ties in with the notion of a lecture as a type of language much like positional academic writing.

These sample concordance lines show the type of language data that lies behind the inclusion of ***if you like*** as a spoken phrase (LDOCE sense 17)

And **I would like to think that** other companies in the industry...
And **I would like to think that** everybody in, on this committee...
I would like to think that inspite of all the pressure, we can still find time to talk.
What **I would like to think** is that we have put together an action plan that will succeed...

4 Frequency and word choice

Another reason for including spoken language in dictionaries is of course to distinguish for students of English when spoken language is not appropriate. The comparative statistics between frequency in spoken and frequency in written English can very much guide the lexicographer's work, as we see here:

Frequencies of alone, on your/her own and by yourself in spoken and written English.

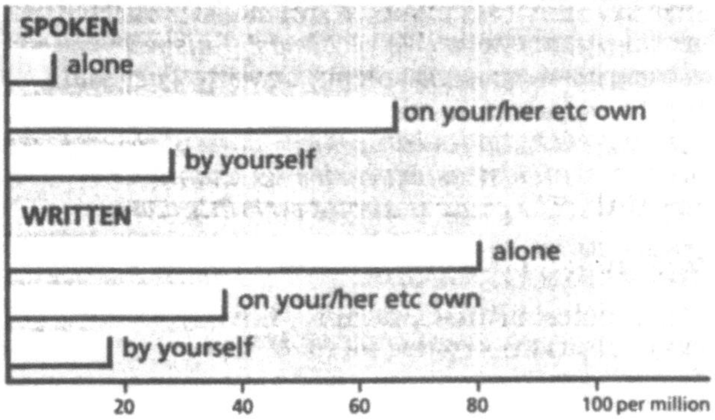

Based on the British National Corpus and the Longman Lancaster Corpus

In spoken English it is more usual to say **on your own** or **by yourself** rather than **alone**. In written or more formal English **alone** is more common.

USAGE NOTE: ALONE

Word choice: **alone, on your own, by yourself, lonely, lonesome, lone, solitary**

If you are **alone** or, less formally, **on your own/by yourself** that just means that no one else is with you, and is neither good nor bad: *I just wanted to stay at home alone/by myself.* With verbs of action, **on your own** and **by yourself** often suggest that no-one is helping you: *I want to swim alone* (=with no one else there). | *I want to swim on my own/by myself* (=either with nobody else there or with other people there but not helping).

If you are **lonely** or **lonesome** (*AmE*) you are unhappy because you are alone: *I feel lonely living away from home/a lonely old man.* Places etc can be **lonely** or **lonesome** if they make people feel lonely: *a lonesome little town on the prairie.* Things that you do can also be **lonely**: *a lonely journey/job/life etc.* **Lonely** is never an adverb but **alone** often is: *She travelled alone* (NOT lonely).

A **lone** or **solitary** person or thing is simply the only one in a place, and therefore might seem a little lonely: *a lone figure in the middle of the square* (=it is the only one there). In spoken English, you are more likely to talk about: *a figure on its own in the middle of the square.* Sometimes **solitary** can suggest that you choose to be alone: *She is a very solitary person.* (LDOCE3)

This allows us to provide students with good reliable information that may indeed only confirm what their teacher has told them, but we find that students like information presented in this graphic way; it makes a point to the student that they remember, and is reinforced by a usage note here which shows the nuances of meaning that we have discovered from the corpus. Note the much simpler pedagogic examples, which are presented in this way to underline the differences in words with similar meanings. The intention is that the inclusion of this type of information, clearly stating the relative infrequency of the English word *alone* in spoken English in a dictionary, will persuade students that *on your own* really is the correct, normal lexical item, and is preferable to using the slightly overformal word *alone*, which may prevent them from reverting to cognates such as *allein* in German through their realization that there are many words to express the idea of being alone in English, each of which has a slightly different meaning or connotation.

Rosamund Moon

Needles and haystacks, idioms and corpora: Gaining insights into idioms, using corpus analysis

Someone once commented at a conference on corpora and lexicography that using corpora to get information about the sorts of item that he was interested in was "like looking for a needle in a haystack". He was something of a corpus sceptic, but his comparison points to an unavoidable and self-evident truth about corpora. Corpora tell you a lot about what recurs, what is common, and what is typical, and on the basis of this, it is possible for lexicographers and other linguists to make robust statements about the central aspects of a language. But corpora do not tell you about marginal features, rare items, and untypical patterns - except to provide evidence that they **are** marginal, rare, or untypical. Other information in such cases is not so robust. Furthermore, the best corpus tools in the world can be compared to metal detectors, infra-red imaging, or even prosaic magnets, usable on the largest of haystacks; however, if the haystack contains no needle, it will not be found.

Idiomatic locutions - *spill the beans, play with fire, under someone's thumb, black and blue,* and indeed *looking for a needle in a haystack* - fall into the category of marginal items. The main part of this paper looks at what corpora **do** tell us about items like these: the last part looks at how this is reflected in dictionaries.

Up until about 1990, the corpora in general use in lexicography and research into English lexicology varied in size between a few hundred thousand words and around 20 million words (There were a few larger corpora in use in language engineering work.) Corpora in these ranges contained very few instances of the majority of idioms. In Moon (1998: 60ff.), I set out figures based on observations of idiom frequency in an 18 million word corpus, the Oxford Hector Pilot corpus (see further below). The advent of much larger corpora such as the 100 million word British National Corpus or the (now) 323 million word Bank of English mean that statistically idioms and idiom-like items are more likely to show up, although there may still not be enough evidence to describe them adequately. This point must be emphasized: 10 instances of a technical term such as a disease or flower name may be enough evidence to describe its linguistic behaviour fully, and further examples might add nothing of interest. But idioms are inherently complicated: they have their own internal grammars, their own connotations and pragmatic functions, and they very often have fluid, contextually-determined meaning. 10 instances may suggest some tendencies which 10 more may corroborate or confound, but only larger numbers of tokens can confirm. To study idioms satisfactorily, very large corpora are needed. It is only now that very large corpora are available, that satisfactory studies of the patterning associated with idioms and their uses in discourse begin to be viable.

To explore this in more detail, let us take up the case of *looking for a needle in a haystack*. In the 18 million word Oxford Hector Pilot Corpus, there were 2 tokens. Both were in the form of the comparison *like looking for a needle in a haystack*, but the occurrence of 2 events or instances is no better than random chance, and so little weight can be attached to this level of evidence. All we can say is that the item has been observed and in that particular form.

The Bank of English is nearly 20 times larger than the Oxford Hector Pilot Corpus, and so could be expected to provide a fuller picture of the expression. A search for the lemma *look** within 5 words of the lemma *needle**, itself within 5 words of the lemma *haystack** yields 24 matches (see Appendix, Figure 1). The lexicogrammatical patterning of the expression here is fairly clear. 10 tokens realize the comparison *like looking for a needle in a haystack*; an 11th has a variation or exploitation *like looking for a needle in several haystacks*, in order to emphasize. A further 6 realize comparison in different forms, signalling this with words such as *akin, comparable*, and *analogous*; another, a heading, makes the comparison through implicature and through cohesion with the following text. This leaves 6 lines - 3 in infinitive form (twice after a deontic modalizer, once in a statement of purpose), two finite examples as metaphors implying comparison, and the final token a direct comparison involving a different sense of *look*: *looks like a needle in a haystack*. Note that there are no negative or passive examples. Just as the formal patterning is clear, so too is the semantic and discoursal usage. The comparison intrinsic in metaphorical language is usually overt here, and this expression has the function of evaluating a task, activity, or endeavour mentioned in the co-text.

But there is more: the search has been too simplistic, because it was over-refined. A further search, this time just for the lemma *needle** and within 5 words of *haystack** yields a total of 80 matches, and a selection of these is shown in Figure 2 (see Appendix). (There is a further instance with *several bails of hay* rather than *haystack*, and 4 with *like looking for a needle*, with ellipsis of or substitution for *haystack*.). While the pattern *like looking [...]* is still the strongest pattern, there are many tokens which have broad synonyms for *look for* instead, such as *search, hunt*, and even *find*. Several tokens transform the expression adjectivally, as *in a needle in a haystack situation*.

These variations are too numerous and extensive to be dismissed as manipulations or exploitations, even taking their originating texts and genres into account (see further below). Note that the overall picture even here confirms that the expression is used discoursally in explicit or implied comparisons and in evaluations, and grammatically in positive, active structures. Note also that although 85 tokens sounds like a substantial body of evidence from which to reach fairly robust conclusions about the behaviour of the expression, this is still a relatively infrequent lexical item, at around 1 per 4 million words of The Bank of English. Other, single-word, items at this frequency level include *etiology, disequilibrium, granddaddy, hollowness, igneous, methylated, samphire, strychnine, timorous, ungentlemanly*, and *zydeco*: many of these are quite restricted words in terms of register or subject field.

What, unequivocally, corpora tell us about idioms and idiom-like expressions is that they are relatively infrequent, that their forms are often unstable and often manipulated lexically, and that their importance as discoursal devices is as clearly seen in massed corpus evidence as in discrete and complete texts. These are the general traits which can be observed, and which I shall summarize below. Beyond this, is a mass of detail relating to the individual cases of individual expressions, such as the one already discussed.

Research into frequency aspects of fixed expressions demonstrates that the majority are rare. For example, with respect to the 18 million words of the Oxford Hector Pilot Corpus, over 70% of a set of nearly 7,000 expressions occur less than once per million words, and just over half of these occur with frequencies no better than random chance. Looking more particularly at idioms such as *spill the beans* and *call the shots*, 85% occur less than once per million, and 47% with frequencies no better than random chance. 84% of proverbs (*you can't have your cake and eat it, live and let live*) and 91% of similes (*as white as a sheet, as clear as day*) were found with negligible or random frequencies, and almost all of the rest occurred less than once per million. The *Collins Cobuild Dictionary of Idioms* (1995) included over 4000 idioms, proverbs, and similes, and was written with The Bank of English, then totalling 211 million words. This much larger corpus confirmed the tendencies showing up in the smaller corpus. Clearly, only the better-attested expressions were treated in this dictionary - and their frequencies were recorded in terms of bands -, but even here frequencies are still low. The highest band comprises around 750 items, around one-sixth of the dictionary headphrases, each with at least 1 token per 2 million corpus words. The next two bands comprise respectively 750 items occurring 3-5 times per 10 million words and 1500 items occurring 1-3 times per 10 million words. The remaining idioms have frequencies of less than 1 in 10 million words, and some have only a handful of lines to prove their existence or currency in English. These kinds of frequency trends are confirmed by other corpus-based research: see Moon (1998: 64ff.) for accounts of this.

Corpora also provide evidence of other aspects of idioms. There are many discussions in the literature, especially psycholinguistic literature, of the potential ambiguity of idioms: see, for example, Gibbs (1986), Popiel and McRae (1988), and Cronk et al. (1993), and a general overview in Titone and Connine (1994). While strings such as *spill the beans* and *call the shots* are theoretically ambiguous, in reality, or rather in the reality of corpus text and context, they are not: few or no examples of literal uses of these precise strings are ever found. The 323 million word Bank of English contains 91 instances of *let the cat out of the bag/the cat is out of the bag*, 241 of *(skate) on thin ice*, and 109 of *beat about/around the bush*. In all cases, all instances are idiomatic in meaning, and none literal. Even where there is substantial evidence of literal meaning (for example, 181 literal instances of *in/into hot water*, and 178 idiomatic), no instances are ambiguous between literal and idiomatic meanings when context and collocation are taken into account: in this case *dip, dissolve, soak, wash*, together with the inanimacy of the affected, distinguish the literal from the idiomatic uses, where the affected is animate and collocating words include *be, find oneself, get*, and *land*.

Similarly, discussions in the literature deal with syntactic aspects such as transformation potential, passivization, inflectability, and so on. Large corpora can demonstrate the truth or otherwise of hypotheses. For example, idioms such as *kick the bucket* and *blow one's top* are considered one-place predicates (Newmeyer 1974: 329f.; see also Nunberg et al. 1994: 516ff.), and therefore not passivizable, unlike *spill the beans* and *pull someone's leg*, which are two-place predicates. Corpus evidence supports these hypotheses, but shows that in many cases, although a handful of passive tokens are found, the overwhelming tendency is for the expressions to be active. The following table shows numbers of active and passive tokens for a few expressions: note that *break the ice* and *give someone the cold shoulder* have lexical "passives" in the forms *the ice breaks* and *get the cold shoulder*.

Idiom	active	passive
bite the dust	145	0
bury the hatchet	110	9
call the shots	387	5
face the music	193	0
pull someone's leg	99	15
spill the beans	193	4
break the ice	159	3
(the ice breaks	---	7)
give someone the cold shoulder	60	4
(get the cold shoulder	---	27)

We can therefore begin to build up a picture of preferred patterns and structures: tendencies rather than rules, in keeping with other corpus-driven work (see, for example, Francis 1993).

We have already seen evidence of the variability or instability of forms of the expression *looking for a needle in a haystack*. Many idioms and idiom-like expressions are completely frozen in form, apart from conventional inflection of component verbs, although it is worth pointing out that even here there may be restrictions on person, gender, number, tense, and aspect: for example, *they were kicking the bucket* seems ill-formed, and men rather than women *blow their tops* or *pull people's legs* according to the corpus: thus demonstrating an even greater degree of fixedness.[1] However, corpora show that a large number of other expressions are flexible and variable: see Moon (1998: 120ff.) for detail, discussion, and exemplification. Such variation may consist of simply a variant word as in *sugar/sweeten/sugarcoat the pill* or *burn one's boats/bridges*, or more extensive exploitation of the underlying metaphorical conceit or schema as in *sit on the fence/be on the fence/get off the fence*, etc. In more extreme cases there are idiom clusters, relating to a single conceit or schema, but with little fixed lexis. In the following two clusters, all the forms listed are found in corpus evidence, and there are no fixed lexical words at all.

fan the fire of something
fan the fires of something
fan the flames (of something)
add fuel to the fire
add fuel to the flame
add fuel to the flames

---

[1] See Fraser (1970) for discussions of rankings and degrees of frozenness.

fuel the fire
fuel the fires
fuel the flame
fuel the flames (of something)

wash one's dirty linen/laundry in public (mainly British)
air one's dirty laundry/linen in public (mainly American)
do one's dirty washing in public (mainly British)
wash/air one's dirty linen/laundry
wash/air one's linen/laundry in public
launder one's dirty washing (mainly British)
dirty laundry/linen/washing

Although conventionally canonical forms are given as *fan the flames* or *add fuel to the fire*, or *wash/air one's dirty linen in public,* the corpus realizations show that to imply that there **are** canonical forms and that these are **fixed** forms would be misleading and wrong.

All this raises a very important question for lexicography: if the lexis is variable and unstable, what is the citation form? Where one particular phraseology is commonest, it can be identified and selected as the headphrase or citation form in a dictionary. But how can its lack of fixedness be shown, and contrasted with more invariant or frozen items?

Corpora also provide more refined information about distributions of idioms, showing that many items are particularly associated with certain genres or situations. This can be seen even in relatively unbalanced corpora such as The Bank of English. *Looking for a needle in a haystack* is a case in point. It is particularly associated with written and scripted oral sources, rather than conversation. There is only 1 token in the 20 million words of unscripted conversation, and the large majority of tokens come from such sources as *New Scientist*, the *Times*, fiction and non-fiction, and transcripts from the semi-scripted BBC World Service. This suggests that the expression is relatively high-level or formal, or associated with high-level registers. Moreover, the commonest topics which it is used about are science and technology (including the only token in conversation). Many of the instances are comparing, crudely, some aspect of scientific research to *looking for a needle in a haystack*, or are saying that achieving a goal or making a discovery is tantamount to *finding a needle in a haystack*, as in:

Collecting the samples involves trudging through rainforest for days at a time. From then on it's a lengthy process. Isolating the active factor is **like looking for a needle in a haystack.** (*She* Magazine)

The documents are not comprehensively indexed, so retrieving any of the 23 million pieces of paper stored there makes **looking for a needle in a haystack** seem easy. (*Times*)

A: But there's been no progress made in finding viruses for the more common types of leukaemia.
B: No erm that's true. Sometimes it **is** er **a needle in a haystack.** (Conversation)

> **Technology: Toxin test finds needle in the haystack**
> By Brett Wright, Melbourne
> Just when you thought it was safe to eat a hamburger, researchers in the US have developed an analytical technique they claim is so sensitive it can measure the effect on your DNA of eating one piece of cooked meat. Adapted from a technique normally used to date rocks, the new method will help toxicologists studying the impact on living cells of potential toxins and carcinogens at extremely low doses. (*New Scientist*)

The following example extends and exploits the metaphor:

> Searching for Higgs particles at these high energies will demand the greatest ingenuity from experimenters. One of the clearest ways in which a Higgs particle may manifest itself is through its decay back into two Z particles, which can in turn each decay into a lepton and its antiparticle. So the Higgs particle would produce a characteristic 'signature' of two lepton-antilepton pairs. A plot of the number of times such events happen against the total mass energy of the two pairs would reveal a peak corresponding to the mass of the unseen Higgs particle. However, experimenters will be **searching** among the debris from many competing processes for the proverbial **needle in a haystack** - indeed, only in 10 billion collisions is calculated to produce an observable Higgs particle. So physicists are already developing the technology they will need to be able to sift rapidly through the **'hay'** in order to find the **'needles'**. (*New Scientist*)

The expression has become a stock comparison in writing about science and technology.

A small-scale investigation of The Bank of English, involving a dozen or so expressions, reveals a number of such specializations:

strong in journalism:

beg the question (mainly British 'serious' journalism)
bite off more than you can chew (mainly British)
bite the dust
bury the hatchet
call the shots
face the music
give/get the cold shoulder
let the cat out of the bag
sit/be on the fence, get off the fence
spill the beans (mainly British)

strong in conversation:

pull someone's leg

strong in fiction:

beat about the bush (mainly British?)
hold your horses (mainly in dialogue)
spill the beans

strong in non-fiction:
beg the question (mainly British)
break the ice
sit/be on the fence, get off the fence

This kind of specialization of idiom use points to an emerging stylistics of idioms, "phraseo-stylistics" to use Gläser's term (1986), which must deal with individual expressions.

More generally, both The Bank of English and the Oxford Hector Pilot Corpus show that idioms tend to be commonest in journalistic writing. Contrary to intuition, idioms tend to be less common in unscripted or authentic conversation than might be expected. They are certainly often informal and certainly salient, but their density in conversational modes and genres is lower than in some others (Moon 1998, 72ff.). This is in contrast with other kinds of phraseological unit which are very common in conversational and other forms of spoken English: see, for example, Pawley and Syder (1983); Aijmer (1996) who provides detailed discussion. Such units include conventions and the routine formulae of interactions such as rituals of thanking and greeting on the one hand, formulae for emphasizing and downtoning on the other. They also include specialized phraseological frames, such as

I'm (just) curious to know (that...)
it's nice to know (that...)
it would be interesting to know (that...)
it's important to know (that...)
that's useful to know
I'm glad to hear (that...)
it's nice to hear (that...)
it'll be interesting to hear (that...)

and so on: compositional but semi-fossilized devices used, in this case, to organize the information - transfer structure of interactions. Devices and frames like these are very common in conversation, and the patterns are very different from those which can be observed in written data.

It is worth pointing out here that the vintage of a corpus is important: usages and distributions change over time, often very short periods of time, and there are fashions involved. When The Bank of English was updated and expanded from 211 million words to 323 million in the summer of 1996, I discovered that a number of Americanisms, idioms found previously only in the subcorpora of American texts, were now showing up unequivocally in British English. These included *crash and burn, cover the waterfront, beat the bushes, cut to the chase, (live) high on the hog, a knock-down drag-out fight,* and *push the envelope*, as well as the traditionally American variants *blow one's own horn* (British *blow one's own trumpet*) and *not see the forest for the trees* (British *not see the wood for the trees*). Some of these expressions were mainly used in British English with reference to American topics, a kind of code-switching, but others were more firmly or widely established. The trend was for the expression to be found in ephemeral sources such as magazines and journalism, more prone to quick influence and more in need of showing that they were attuned to the Zeitgeist. Culture and the media in general and cybertexts are the carriers here.

One final aspect of idioms and corpus-based research should be mentioned. We saw earlier that *looking for a needle in a haystack* was typically used in evaluations, often after *be* or a word signalling comparison, where the writer/speaker is describing the difficulty of a task. Not only are these classifiable as evaluations in terms of structure and meaning, but the very expression itself carries a connotation of evaluation, assessing positively the activity and effort involved, and not always connoting that the difficulty is so great as to make the activity pointless. (Compare *labour of love*, which also designates hard work and effort, but in British English at least sometimes connotes the pointlessness of the exercise.) What corpora show up is the regularity of evaluative orientations: idioms are used as graphic ways of conveying an opinion. The semantic - discoursal schema associated with an individual idiom involves typical topic and context of use and typical text function. It also involves the culturally-determined interpretation, assessment, and evaluation of the denoted activity as part of the schema: since this is culturally determined and intrinsic to the lexical selection itself, common to the lexicons of both writer/speaker and reader/hearer, it is likely to be accepted as read rather than negotiated. The following examples show idioms in evaluations:[2]

> In the same month another **lame duck**, Rolls Royce, was nationalized when it threatened to go bankrupt, thus completing the reversal of the initial government strategy. (non-fiction)

> From its humble beginnings 40 years ago, consumer electronics in Japan is now a $35 billion-a-year business. This is just **the icing on the cake**. Counting all the components and industrial equipment that Japanese electronics companies make as well, they are now generating between them an annual $200 billion of sales - almost as much as the whole of the American electronics industry. (The *Economist*)

> They **are sitting on the fence** and refusing to commit themselves on whether they would support the extension. They certainly have no need or wish to help Mr. Singh out of his predicament. (transcriptions of BBC World Service)

To summarize, therefore, the state of the art with respect to corpus-based research into idioms in English: corpora provide evidence of the frequencies, distributions, and currencies of idioms; of their genre preferences; their conventions of syntactic and collocational behaviour; their formal instability and variability; and their conventions of discoursal behaviour and connotations. Only very large corpora can provide such information with any degree of robustness (for many items), and the picture emerging from corpora is, I consider, leading towards new models of idioms and phraseological or

---

2 See, for example, Fernando (1996: 153ff.); Moon (1992); Moon (1998: 215ff.), for further discussion of the functions of idioms in discourse and the evaluations they contain.

semantic units in general, into which many of the traditional ideas can be incorporated but adjusted to accord with the data. Are idioms just needles in corpus haystacks? I prefer to see them as the straws, the individual wisps, that constitute the haystacks: and straws in the wind of developing models of English lexis and the English lexicon, as evidenced in corpora.

In the final section of this paper, I want to look at idiom coverage in dictionaries. The first point to be made is that idioms in learners' dictionaries tend to be neglected, squeezed into the ends of entries with minimal attention. This is scarcely surprising, given their infrequency and given that they are often considered suitable for receptive use only, not productive. But this does not mean that learners (and translators, the other group of users of monolingual learners' dictionaries) do not face considerable problems with idioms. In **decoding** there are problems associated with recognizing idioms as idioms or non-compositional units - particularly acute when the idiom form varies from the notional canonical form - and with understanding their overt and connoted meanings, which may be key to understanding a whole passage. In **encoding**, there are problems associated with replicating the typical and the acceptable lexicogrammatical patterning and avoiding ill-formedness - difficult since the 'rules' have not been properly and completely identified and described at all, let alone recorded in dictionaries - as well as replicating typical connotation and discoursal function. In recoding, there may be problems of interference, false friends, and inappropriately or inadvertently formed calques.

The lexicographical problems are immense. They include problems of placement and indexing (in paper dictionaries); problems of assessing the canonical form and conveying variability; problems of showing syntactic behaviour and collocations; problems of conveying evaluations and connotations; and problems of conveying phonological and intonational information. In bilingual dictionaries, there are problems of translation - whether to give glosses in the target language, or whether to give (crude) idiomatic equivalents, which may well not match up perfectly.

These problems can be seen in entries for looking for a needle in a *haystack* in various dictionaries. Figure 3 (see Appendix) compares the host entries from the 4 learners' dictionaries: *needle* in the case of OALD5, CIDE, and LDOCE3, *haystack* for COBUILD2 (this variation in placement is itself problematic). COBUILD2, CIDE, and LDOCE3 all agree that the dominant pattern, to be shown in the definition, is *like looking for a needle in a haystack*; however, COBUILD2 and CIDE use font changes to indicate that *a needle in a haystack* is the fixed part, and *like looking for* [...] a collocation: whether learners fully appreciate this subtlety is of course moot. OALD5 shows the dominant pattern in an example. COBUILD2, CIDE, and LDOCE3 all imply in their definition wording that this expression is used to evaluate ("used to say", "if you say that [...] you mean that"); in contrast, OALD5's definition implies that a needle in a haystack **is** a thing that is almost impossible to find, in the same way that a cat **is** a feline mammal. Only LDOCE3 suggests that the expression is restricted in register, only OALD5 indicates intonational pattern for encoding, and only OALD5 adds an example. None indicates directly anything syntactic, other than the class IDM in OALD5, and PHRASE in COBUILD2. COBUILD2 and CIDE alone imply that this expression semantically is to do with "trying" to find something, part of an activity, rather than a completed event: This is supported by current Bank of English corpus evidence. Interestingly, none of the dictionaries implies anything positive about the activity and search, and all stress the semantic component of the impossibility or unlikelihood of finding the thing in question, although many Bank of English tokens have an altogether more positive flavour. Finally, in a verbosity comparison, OALD5 and CIDE both have 39 words, COBUILD2 32 words, and LDOCE3 19 words: OALD5 and CIDE have the same number of words, but OALD5 fits in an example and label, whereas CIDE is all definition.

These entries as a whole are not bad, given space limitations, but equally they could be better. Inevitably, specialized dictionaries of idioms have more space to deal with this expression more fully, and figure 4 (see Appendix) shows extracts from 3 learners' dictionaries of idioms. CCDI (unlike its sister COBUILD2) and LDEI embed the expression under needle: so effectively does ODCIE, although here it is in a continuous alphabetically ordered series, sandwiched between *need/require no introduction* and *needless to say*, and prefaced by the parenthetical *(look for)* and non-alphabetized *a*, which may obscure it positionally. CCDI and ODCIE have considerably longer entries than LDEI. CCDI explicitly refers to variations and exploitations; ODCIE exemplifies variations, explicitly mentions the variants of *haystack*, and shows the optionality of *look like*; and LDEI gives *searching* as an alternative to *looking*. All the dictionaries give examples. ODCIE glosses the expression as if it were an ordinary verb, that is with a traditional infinitive definition which does not indicate defectiveness, but the others define it as the non-finite *like looking [...]*: the structure in 2 of the 4 examples in ODCIE. CCDI gives frequency indication, LDEI gives a syntax gloss. Note that CCDI was written with a corpus as basis, and ODCIE a corpus-like collection of authentic citations. [3] All these dictionary entries give a more rounded description of the expression than the general learners' dictionaries - but could anyone, except for very expert linguists, really encode from them? Perhaps this is a question which should not be asked here and at this point.

Figure 5 (see Appendix) shows entries for the expression from a bilingual English - French dictionary (CR), together with entries for the parallel and equivalent French expression taken from a French monolingual general dictionary (MR) and a French monolingual dictionary of idioms (DEL). DEL gives a more authoritative and historical picture of the expression *chercher une aiguille dans une botte de foin*, and indicates variations. Both MR and DEL gloss it as an infinitive, the traditional format for verb definitions. The French side of CR gives a variant in French, and gives the English equivalent as an infinitive translation; the English side adds *fig* to indicate metaphoricality. Both sides translate as infinitives. I do not know, in the absence of a French corpus, whether the French is typically found as a finite verb or as a non-finite verb (the citations in DEL do not rule the former out, but do not support it either). The corpus evidence for English suggests that it is at least possible that the French expression may be more complicated than the dictionary entries suggest.

---

[3] A second, corpus-based, edition of LDEI was published in 1998.

Where there is no direct lexical equivalent, bilingual dictionaries can be even more misleading. Here, for example, are the translations offered by CR for two comparatively common English idioms. * indicates that while the expression is not "part of standard language", it is used "by all educated speakers in a relaxed situation" although not in "a formal essay or letter, or on an occasion when the speaker wishes to impress". (I would suggest that this last point is debatable, since idioms are often used discoursally and rhetorically at points where the speaker is most definitely trying to impress and develop an effect). ** gives a stronger warning against use, saying that the "expression is used by some but not all educated speakers in a very relaxed situation".

> **to rock the boat*** jouer les trouble-fête, semer le trouble *or* la perturbation; **don't rock the boat*** ne compromets pas les choses, ne fais pas l'empêcheur de danser en rond*

> **to spill the beans*** *(gen)* vendre la mèche (*about* à propos de); (*under interrogation*) se mettre à table**; parler

While these equivalents and paraphrases may be helpful for L1 French speakers in decoding the English expressions, they will not, in spite of the usage warnings, really help L1 English speakers wanting to encode into French, as there is not enough information about context and connotation.

The practical solution for the learners' dictionaries may well be to play down idioms, to prioritize a few common ones, and to ignore others, on the grounds that it is too difficult and space-consuming to deal fully with these expressions. Yet this is only a partial solution. These are important items in terms of discourse, even if they are minor items in the lexicon. Somewhere the problems must be faced. The different dictionary entries between them show a variety of strategies which could be synthesized into a perfect description of *looking for a needle in a haystack*, and a descriptive frame for such expressions in general. But without a corpus to provide the basis for the description, there is a great danger that important features will be missed.

The perfect learners' dictionary would take this into account. It would demonstrate form and patterning, genre and context, and evaluation and pragmatics. Not least, it would have a search engine or placement praxis which would make *looking for a needle in a haystack* not at all like looking for needle in a haystack. In this way, we could begin to make progress, descriptively, lexicographically, and pedagogically.

Endnote

The author, as the editor of CCDI, one of the editors of the first edition of COBUILD, and a contributor and consultant to the second edition of COBUILD, hereby acknowledges responsibility for the lexical description and lexicographical decision-making in those titles.

Corpus data is drawn from The Bank of English corpus created by COBUILD at the HarperCollins Publishers and the University of Birmingham.

Bibliography

Collins Robert French Dictionary (CR) (³1993): Beryl T. Atkins (ed.). — London, Glasgow: HarperCollins.
Collins Cobuild Dictionary of Idioms (CCDI) (1995): Rosamund Moon (ed.). — London, Glasgow: HarperCollins.
Dictionnaire des Expressions et Locutions (DEL) (1988): Alain Rey, Sophie Chantreau (ed.). — Paris: Robert.
Le Micro-Robert (MR) (1988): Alain Rey, Paul Robert (ed.). — Paris: Robert
Longman Dictionary of English Idioms (LDEI) (1979): Thomas Hill Long (ed.). — London: Longman.
Oxford Dictionary of English Idioms (ODCIE) (1983/1993): Anthony P. Cowie, Ronald Mackin, Isabel R. MacCaig (eds.). — Oxford: OUP.

Aijmer, Karin (1996): Conversational Routines in English: Convention and Creativity. — London: Longman.
Cronk, Brian C., Susan D. Lima, Wendy A. Schweigert (1993): "Idioms in sentences: effects of frequency, literalness, and familiarity". — In: Journal of Psycholinguistic Research 22/1, 59-82.
Fernando, Chitra (1996): Idioms and Idiomaticity. — Oxford: OUP.
Francis, Gill (1993): "A corpus-driven approach to grammar". — In: M. Baker, G. Francis, E. Tognini-Bonelli (eds.): Text and Technology: in Honour of John Sinclair (Philadelphia, Amsterdam: John Benjamins) 137-156.
Fraser, Bruce (1970): "Idioms within a transformational grammar". — In: Foundations of Language 6/1, 22-42.
Gibbs, Raymond W. (1986): "Skating on thin ice: literal meaning and understanding idioms in conversation". — In: Discourse Processes 9, 17-30.
Gläser, Rosemarie (1986): "A plea for phraseo-stylistics". — In: D. Kastovsky., A. Szwedek (eds.): Linguistics across Historical and Geographical Boundaries 1 (Berlin, New York, Amsterdam: Mouton) (=Linguistic Theory and Historical Linguistics) 41-52.
Moon, Rosamund E. (1992): "Textual aspects of fixed expressions in learners' dictionaries". — In: P. Arnaud, H. Béjoint (eds.): Vocabulary and Applied Linguistics (London: Macmillan) 13-27.
— (1998): Fixed Expressions and Idioms in English: A Corpus-based Approach. — Oxford: OUP.
Newmeyer, Frederick J. (1974): "The regularity of idiom behavior". — In: Lingua 34, 327-342.
Nunberg, Geoffrey, Ivan A. Sag, Thomas Wasow (1994): "Idioms". — In: Language 70/3, 491-538.
Pawley Andrew, Frances H. Syder (1983): "Two puzzles for linguistic theory; nativelike selection and nativelike fluency". — In: J. C. Richards, R. W. Schmidt (eds.): Language and Communication (London: Longman) 191-225.
Popiel, Stephen J., Ken McRae (1988): "The figurative and literal senses of idioms, or all idioms are not used equally". — In: Journal of Psycholinguistic Research 17/6, 475-487.
Titone, Debra A., Cynthia M. Connine (1994): "Descriptive norms for 171 idiomatic expressions: familiarity, compositionality, predictability, and literality". — In: Metaphor and Symbolic Activity 9/4, 247-70.

Appendix

Figure 1

```
          vessel - a task akin to looking for a needle in a haystack in Asia's busy waters, which have changed little since
              job, comparable with looking for a needle in a haystack. <p> Some people are going to be missed in routine
        the active factor is like looking for a needle in a haystack. For instance, there's a seed used as a household
          first have to look for that particular needle in a haystack well-stacked against blacks. <p> The area of advocacy
 'ell it's really analogous to looking for a needle in a haystack, except that our approach has been to burn down the
   if we can use the analogy of looking for a needle in a haystack, effectively we burn down the haystack. Which means we
 just moved away. So it's like looking for a needle in a haystack # it's almost impossible to find # REP: The UN
          ecosystems respond. <h> Looking for needles with a Haystack </h> <b> By KURT KLEINER </b> <bl> WASHINGTON DC </bl>
              manual screening as 'looking for a needle in a haystack". On average, only between 3 and 5 smears out of every
      similar signals. 'It's like looking for a needle in a haystack when the haystack contains many other things that
          today as a--a target that looks like a needle in a haystack, a mobile missile launcher which, precisely because it'
    <f> at those mountains. Like looking for a needle in a haystack! With ten hours to do it in!" He turned to Lovelock. '
     find it." <p> It'll be like looking for a needle in a haystack," Sabrina said. <p> And if you look long and hard
 to London. Sin City. So we're looking for a needle in a haystack.' And in a haystack of needles, just to complicate
        an honourable judge. Like looking for a needle in a haystack," Klaus muttered to himself, 'but if you find one,
     defines 'serendipity # It's looking for a needle in a haystack and discovering the farmer's daughter. We discovered
     this area that will be like looking for a needle in a haystack ! We're working on the case, too, without much luck."
    attacking the Scuds is like looking for a needle in a haystack," he said. We need to attack their command and control
     of paper stored there makes looking for a needle in a haystack seem easy. But Abbey has no plans to transfer the
 ie said. <p> It would be like looking for a needle in a haystack." <p> Mr Phillips said the burglary at his London
             Catching him is like looking for a needle in a haystack." <p> The park's owners have threatened to sue Joerg
             is rather like looking for a needle in several haystacks. The latest American work concentrates on limb
           Harrier to look for the proverbial needle in the haystack. <p> Insp Felix Grayson told The Sunday Mail yesterday
     <o> You've always got to look for the needles in the haystack." <p> It was only then that he noticed something. <p>
```

Figure 2

```
          vessel - a task akin to looking for a needle in a haystack in Asia's busy waters, which have changed little since
      is so new that the proverbial search for a needle in a haystack doesn't even begin to compare to the problem facing
         unmapped, to go at. Stanley's heroic needle-in- a-haystack job took two years. In November 1871 he found the
             job, comparable with looking for a needle in a haystack. <p> Some people are going to be missed in routine
         ALDRED BILL Gath reckons he can find a needle in a haystack just by focusing his mind on the object. <p> He also
       I wore that tie I would 'stand out like a needle in a haystack". On another occasion, when asked by my mother if I
           in Australia # it could be a bit of a needle in a haystack situation." <p> Prof Kaldor's co-researchers were
             equivalent to finding the proverbial needle-in-a-haystack, bolsters proof of a primordial comet reservoir just
      be slightly less difficult than finding a needle in a haystack; the surgeon has no idea which side to investigate or
           the active factor is like looking for a needle in a haystack. For instance, there's a seed used as a household
           first have to look for that particular needle in a haystack well-stacked against blacks. <p> The area of advocacy
      prospect than the proverbial search for a needle in a haystack # declared The Lancet late last year, only to conclude
        No erm that's true. Sometimes it is er a needle in a haystack. <M01> The viral theory might also explain the higher
     Well it's really analogous to looking for a needle in a haystack, except that our approach has been to burn down the
        if we can use the analogy of looking for a needle in a haystack, effectively we burn down the haystack. Which means we
     just moved away. So it's like looking for a needle in a haystack # it's almost impossible to find # REP: The UN
     message. <p> IN CONFRONTING this formidable needle-in-a-haystack challenge, astronomers suggested certain special
     many competing processes for the proverbial needle in a haystack - indeed, only in 10 billion collisions is calculated
            a bomb in a suitcase makes finding a needle in a haystack look simple. In the four years since Pan Am flight 103
          blocks of DNA. 'It becomes a molecular needle-in-a-haystack puzzle," says Sklar. <p> The resolvases do not attack
          ecosystems respond. <h> Looking for needles with a Haystack </h> <b> By KURT KLEINER </b> <bl> WASHINGTON DC </bl>
              manual screening as 'looking for a needle in a haystack". On average, only between 3 and 5 smears out of every
        similar signals. 'It's like looking for a needle in a haystack when the haystack contains many other things that
          today as a--a target that looks like a needle in a haystack, a mobile missile launcher which, precisely because it'
        easy if it were only as easy as finding a needle in a haystack. <p> Milhollin: Well, yes, it's small. You can pick it
         Not only did I want to drop Greenfield's needle-in-a-haystack nonsense. I wanted to drop it all. I had no desire to
       <f> at those mountains. Like looking for a needle in a haystack! With ten hours to do it in!" He turned to Lovelock. '
        find it." <p> It'll be like looking for a needle in a haystack," Sabrina said. <p> And if you look long and hard
     small business you say? Difficult. Bit of a needle in a haystack. Still, it used to be a pretty threadbare haystack in
     the northern part of the state." <p> It's a needle in a haystack," Andrews said. 'No one ever mapped the locations of
     to London. Sin City. So we're looking for a needle in a haystack.' And in a haystack of needles, just to complicate
        a sex killer in the general population is needle-in-a-haystack time. The sorry truth is that the police are not very
       to find the place, but it's the proverbial needle in a haystack, isn't it? They could bring in the military and the
          an honourable judge. Like looking for a needle in a haystack," Klaus muttered to himself, 'but if you find one,
     in hesitant German. Evidently the phrase 'a needle in a haystack" had not occurred to him; but he spoke sorrowfully of
            narrow sizes is like &hellip; well, a needle in a haystack. Shoe manufacturers, please note.) However,
        defines 'serendipity # It's looking for a needle in a haystack and discovering the farmer's daughter. We discovered
         Chameleon." It sounds like hunting for a needle in a haystack," Frank remarked, 'but if we should come across either
        this area that will be like looking for a needle in a haystack ! We're working on the case, too, without much luck."
        attacking the Scuds is like looking for a needle in a haystack," he said. We need to attack their command and control
          by Drake and others were dogged by this needle-in-a-haystack problem. Advances in electronics and computer
     of need ladder of success moving experience needle in a haystack point with pride ripe old age sadder but wiser
          therapeutic way within an organism, the needle-in-a-haystack process of searching for new drug compounds has
        but the intrinsic difficulty of finding a needle in a haystack, which it can do little about. <p> The F-117a's
         in a battle that is like searching for a needle in a haystack. Sometimes to find the needle, you need to burn the
        of paper stored there makes looking for a needle in a haystack seem easy. But Abbey has no plans to transfer the
               a suitable match makes finding a needle in a haystack seem a simple task, as the Deacons were soon to
```

Figure 3

LDOCE3

nee·dle[1] /ˈniːdl/ *n* [C]
1 ▶ SEWING ◀ a) a small thin piece of steel, with a point at one end and a hole in the other, used for sewing: *a needle and thread* **b)** a KNITTING NEEDLE
2 ▶ DRUGS ◀ a very thin, pointed steel tube at the end of a SYRINGE, which is pushed into your skin to put a drug or medicine into your body or to take out blood
3 ▶ POINTING ◀ a long thin piece of metal on a scientific instrument, that moves backwards and forwards and points to numbers or directions
4 ▶ FROM A TREE ◀ a small needle-shaped leaf, especially from a PINE tree: *pine needles*
5 ▶ FOR PLAYING RECORDS ◀ the very small, pointed part in a RECORD PLAYER that picks up sound from the records; STYLUS (1)
6 like looking for a needle in a haystack *informal* used to say that something is almost impossible to find
7 a needle match *BrE* a game in which both teams are determined to win because they do not like each other
needle[2] *v* [T] *informal* to deliberately annoy someone by continuously making unkind remarks or stupid jokes: *She's always needling me about my accent.*

OALD5

needle /ˈniːdl/ *n* **1** [C] a small thin piece of polished steel with a point at one end and a hole for thread at the other, used in sewing: *the eye of a needle* ○ *She threaded the needle expertly.* See also PINS AND NEEDLES. **2** [C] a long thin piece of plastic, metal, polished wood, etc without a hole but with a pointed end or a hook: *ˈknitting needles* ○ *a ˈcrochet needle.* **3** [C] a thin, usu metal, POINTER(1) in an instrument for measuring, etc: *the speedometer needle* ○ *The compass needle swung round.* **4** [C] a pointed hollow end of a SYRINGE: *disposable needles for injecting drugs.* ⇨ picture at INJECTION. **5** [C] a thing like a needle(1) in shape, appearance or use, eg the thin pointed leaf of a PINE[1] tree or a pointed rock: *dead pine needles.* ⇨ picture at PINE[1]. **6** [C] a STYLUS used in playing records. **7** [U] (*infml*) anger or hostility, esp in situations where people are rivals: *A certain amount of needle has crept into* (ie gradually appeared in) *this game.* ○ *a needle game/match* (ie one in which the competitors are very fierce rivals). IDM **a needle in a ˈhaystack** a thing that is almost impossible to find because it is hidden among many other things: *Searching for one man in this big city is like looking for a needle in a haystack.* **sharp as a needle** ⇨ SHARP.
▶ **needle** *v* (*infml*) to provoke or annoy sb, esp with words: [Vn] *I could see that my questions were needling him.*

CIDE

need·le SEWING TOOL /ˈniː·dl̩/ *n* [C] a thin metal pin, used in sewing, which is pointed at one end and has a hole called an EYE at the other end for thread, or a longer stick, without a hole, which is used with another stick of the same type to KNIT • *a needle and cotton/***thread** • *Here, your eyes are better than mine – could you* **thread** (= put thread through) *this needle for me?* • *What size* **knitting** *needles did you use for that sweater?* • If you say that trying to find something is like looking for **a needle in a haystack**, you mean that it is impossible or extremely difficult to find, esp. because the area you have to search is too large. • See also NEEDLEWORK. • PIC⟩ **Handicraft, Pins and needles**
need·le MEDICAL TOOL /ˈniː·dl̩/, **hyp·o·der·mic need·le** *n* [C] the long hollow pointed part of a HYPODERMIC which goes under the skin when giving an INJECTION (= putting a drug into the body through the skin) • *Each needle is sterile and is disposed of after use to prevent the spread of infection.* • *I used to be terrified of* **the** *needle/(Am and Aus infml)* **getting needles** (= being INJECTED) *when I was a kid.* • A **needle bank** is a place where people who use (esp. illegal) drugs can go to exchange their old, dirty or used needles for new clean ones. • PIC⟩ **Pins and needles**
need·le POINTER /ˈniː·dl̩/ *n* [C] on a compass or measuring device, the thin moving part which points in a particular direction or points to a particular measurement • *The needle on a compass always points to magnetic north.* • PIC⟩ **Pins and needles**
need·le LEAF /ˈniː·dl̩/ *n* [C] a long thin stiff leaf of a FIR tree • *We want a Christmas tree that won't drop its needles all over the carpet.* • *Pine needles covered the ground under the trees.* • PIC⟩ **Pins and needles**
need·le MUSIC /ˈniː·dl̩/, **sty·lus** *n* [C] *infml* the part of a **record player** (= a machine on which records are played), which touches the record as it turns round and which is made of a hard material, such as a DIAMOND • *It sounds like the needle on your record player needs to be replaced.*
need·le *obj* ANNOY /ˈniː·dl̩/ *v* [T] *infml* to annoy (someone), esp. by repeated criticism • *As always, after he had been with his mother for a couple of days, she had begun to needle him.*

COBUILD2

haystack /heɪstæk/ **haystacks**
1 A **haystack** is a large, firmly-built pile of hay, often covered with a straw roof to protect it, which is left in the field until it is needed. N-COUNT
2 If you are trying to find something and say that it is like looking for **a needle in a haystack**, you mean that you are very unlikely indeed to find it. PHRASE

Figure 4

CCDI

needle

like looking for a needle in a haystack

◄

If you say that trying to find something is **like looking for a needle in a haystack**, you mean that it is extremely difficult or even impossible to find it.

Police have told Mrs Barrow that searching for the dog will be like looking for a needle in a haystack. She agrees that once a greyhound has disappeared, the chances of recovering the animal are slim.

□ People often extend or vary this expression. For example, if you say that looking for something is **like looking for a needle in several haystacks**, you are emphasizing that you are very unlikely indeed to find it.

Finding a gene amongst the hundreds of thousands of genes contained on a chromosome is rather like looking for a needle in several haystacks.

Then of course we've got to find the antibody that we want, and that's the problem with the new technology. It's really like the needle in the haystack. We've got to go through the haystack, straw by straw, pulling out the needle.

ODCIE

(look for) a needle in a haystack etc (look for) sb/sth almost impossible to find, to distinguish or isolate from the crowd or mass which contains him/it **n:** **haystack**, ⚠ **bundle of hay**, (old use) **bottle of hay** □ *Somewhere along that waterfront there might be somebody who knew her. I walked till the straps chafed raw places on my legs, and hardly felt them, but it was like* ***looking for a needle in a bundle of hay****, of course.* RFW □ *There is an excusable feeling that trying to find any practical benefit from SALT* (US-Soviet Strategic Arms Limitation Talks), *or other set-piece conferences, is like peering through the wrong end of telescope in search of* ***a needle*** *that is not* ***in the haystack****.* L □ (NONCE) (a novel) *'The Odessa File' looks likely to pull off a very similar coup. The plot concerns* ***another needle*** *lost* ***in another haystack*** *and our young hero has to find it before the balloon (or in this case a rocket) goes up.* L □ (NONCE) *All I could do was to go on searching, alone, at random, like a man approaching* ***a haystack*** *with a piece of cotton in his pocket, ready to thread* ***the*** *first* ***needle*** *he finds with it.* CON

LDEI

NEEDLE

(as) sharp as a needle see at SHARP

get° the (dead) needle *sl* **a.** to become angry or annoyed (with someone): *he's got the dead needle to you because you've been talking about him* [V: usu. foll. by *to* + Ⓟ] **b. give° ① the needle** to annoy (someone) or make (someone) angry: *his refusal to admit his mistakes gives me the needle* [V] <Probably referring to the pain and annoyance caused by sticking one's finger with a sewing needle

like looking/searching for a needle in a haystack very difficult or almost impossible to find: *trying to find one small boy in the large crowds at the football match was like looking for a needle in a haystack* [Adj 1]

a 'needle match *not fml* a game of sport or a competition in which the opponents are very eager to defeat each other, esp. because of bad feelings between them: *Their captain, centre-half John Deering, said yesterday: 'This is no joke. Both teams are keen to win,... A few of the lads have had private wagers with opposing players, so that it makes it more of a needle match.'* (*Daily Mirror* 11 May 74) [N 3]

Figure 5

DEL

AIGUILLE, *n. f.*

De fil en aiguille → FIL.

Vx. ***Pourvu (garni, fourni) de fil et d'aiguille,*** « pourvu de tout le nécessaire » (dans Montaigne, I, 35).

Chercher une aiguille dans une botte (un tas,...) de foin, « chercher une chose presque introuvable ».

Vous lui avez dit de vous trouver une femme dans Paris [...]. Autant valait chercher une aiguille dans une charretée de foin que de chercher dans Paris une femme soupçonnée d'aller au bois de Vincennes, et dont le signalement ressemblait à celui de toutes les jolies femmes de Paris. (BALZAC, *Splendeurs et Misères des courtisanes*, éd. de 1845, t. I, p. 320.)

Il y avait un office des réfugiés. Mais tu parles qu'ils étaient un peu débordés. [...] le surlendemain, je tombe nez à nez avec une infirmière de la maison d'Orléans. L'aiguille dans la botte de foin. (L. ARAGON, *Blanche ou l'Oubli*, p. 171.)

Vx. ***Ne pas savoir faire un point d'aiguille,*** se disait d'une fille ignorante du fainéante.

Raisonner (discourir, disputer) sur des pointes d'aiguille → POINTE.

Passer par le trou d'une aiguille → TROU.

MR

aiguille [egɥij] n. f. **1.** Fine tige d'acier pointue à une extrémité et percée à l'autre d'un trou ⇒ **chas** où passe le fil. *Enfiler une aiguille. Aiguille à coudre, à repriser.* — Loc. *Chercher une aiguille dans une botte de foin,* chercher une chose impossible à trouver. DE FIL EN AIGUILLE : en passant d'un sujet de conversation à l'autre. **2.** *Aiguille à tricoter,* tige de métal ou de matière plastique pour faire du tricot. **3.** Tige métallique effilée des chirurgiens servant aux injections, aux sutures. **4.** Tige métallique terminée en pointe qui sert à indiquer une mesure, etc. *Les aiguilles d'une pendule. L'aiguille aimantée d'une boussole.* **5.** Portion de rail mobile servant à opérer les changements de voie. ⇒ **aiguillage ; aiguiller.**

CR

needle ['ni:dl] **1** **n** **a** *(most senses)* **aiguille** *f.* **knitting/darning** *etc* **~** aiguille à tricoter/à repriser *etc;* **record-player ~** saphir *m* de tourne-disque; **gramophone ~** aiguille de phonographe; *(Bot)* **pine ~** aiguille de pin; *(fig)* **to look for a ~ in a haystack** chercher une aiguille dans une botte de foin; *(Drugs sl)* **to be on the ~** être héroïnomane, se shooter‡ à l'héroïne; *see* **pin, sharp** *etc.*

b *(Brit fig)* **he gives me the ~‡** *(tease)* il me charrie‡; *(annoy)* il me tape sur les nerfs* *or* sur le système*; **to get the ~‡** se ficher en boule‡.

2 **vt** **a** (*) *(annoy)* asticoter, agacer; *(sting)* piquer *or* toucher au vif; *(nag)* harceler. **she was ~d into replying sharply** touchée au vif *or* agacée elle a répondu avec brusquerie.

b *(US)* **to ~ a drink‡** corser une boisson.

3 **comp** ▸**needle book, needle case** porte-aiguilles *m inv*

CR

f *(loc)* **~ des crosses à qn*** to try and pick a fight with sb; **~ fortune** to seek one's fortune; **~ des histoires à qn** to try to make trouble for sb; **~ midi à quatorze heures** to complicate the issue, look for complications; **~ noise à qn** to pick a quarrel with sb; **~ la petite bête** to split hairs; **~ une aiguille dans une botte** *ou* **meule de foin** to look for a needle in a haystack; **~ des poux dans la tête de qn** to try and make trouble for sb; **~ querelle à qn** to pick a quarrel with sb; **~ son salut dans la fuite** to seek *ou* take refuge in flight; **cherchez la femme!** cherchez la femme!

Jan Svartvik

Corpora and dictionaries

1 In search of a collocation

In preparing my paper for this Erlangen rendez-vous I did two things, both of which will no doubt cheer up our friends in the publishing line to hear: first, I bought all four learners' dictionaries to be discussed at the colloquium; second, I read the "How to use the dictionary" part in each dictionary, something lexicographers claim to be most atypical of the run-of-the-mill dictionary-user.

As I am typing this sentence, I start worrying – a phenomenon that is a characteristic of us users of English who happened to be born in the expanding circle – especially on occasions like this when speaking to an audience made up of the cream of EFL lexicography. My particular worry is now: can I actually use *run-of-the-mill* as a modifier of a human noun head like *dictionary-user?*

To find the truth, I push the button to link me up with the hard disk version of our biggest English-Swedish bilingual dictionary: true enough, my suspicions are confirmed - the one example provided has an abstract, inanimate head: *a run-of-the-mill performance.*

I then press another button to check a monolingual work available on CD-ROM, *The Random House Dictionary,* but can still see no light at the end of the tunnel: it gives the definition "merely average; commonplace; mediocre: *just a plain, run-of-the-mill house; a run-of-the-mill performance*".

So I turn to manual searches of the 1995 editions of the four British learners' dictionaries which are in focus at this colloquium. In the *Longman Dictionary of Contemporary English* I find, in strict alphabetical order, *run-of-the-mill* with the explanation "not special or interesting in any way; ordinary: *a run-of-the-mill performance*". At this point I start wondering whether *run-of-the-mill performance* is some kind of high-frequency collocation, or could there be some other explanation?

In the *Cambridge International Dictionary of English* I eventually discover the example: "It's just a run-of-the-mill (= not special) war film."

The *Oxford Advanced Learner's Dictionary* says "often derog, not special; ordinary: a run-of-the-mill detective story."

By now, mentally preparing myself to try and find a "safe" alternative expression, I finally turn to *Collins Cobuild English Dictionary*, which says: "person or thing is very ordinary, with no special or interesting features; used showing disapproval. *I was just a very average run-of-the-mill kind of student... For many they clearly represent an alternative to run-of-the-mill estate cars.* " At last, COBUILD gives the answer I am looking for: *run-of-the-mill* has indeed been used with a human noun (even if *kind of student* is not a crystal clear human head). But how can I be absolutely certain that this single example is not one of the freaks that are bound to end up in any 200-million-word corpus? Of course, I should trust the professional *Sprachgefühl* of the lexicographer in charge, but I do find the basis for a usage decision still worryingly fragile. I really want to know more about the general use and frequency of this expression.

Consequently I seek advice from a corpus. As expected, the size of the Brown and Lancaster-Oslo/Bergen corpora, our two standard electronic workhorses, is inadequate for a lexical enquiry of this type. The 100-million word British National Corpus (BNC), however, should be more helpful, and I can fortunately access it via a link to the GramTime project at Växjö University. The BNC gives the total number of occurrences as 53, almost a third of which turn out to have a human head noun. As a bonus, extracting the examples and ordering them in a concordance format on the screen takes less time than looking up one example in the printed dictionaries. Here are the animate noun heads in the BNC:

run-of-the-mill artist
run-of-the-mill brothers and sisters
run-of-the-mill composer
run-of-the-mill customers
run-of-the-mill duffers
run-of-the-mill managers
run-of-the-mill millionaire
run-of-the-mill MPs
run-of-the-mill person
run-of-the-mill players
run-of-the-mill senator
run-of-the-mill student
run-of-the-mill waitress

My particular problem has now been satisfactorily solved, but this procedure can hardly be a general solution of the collocation worries that affect students in the expanding circle of English. I suspect publishers are not prepared to expand EFL dictionaries much further beyond the present 1900-odd pages to take care of less frequent collocations. Nor can we expect the run-of-the-mill EFL student to acquire (let alone install!) the British National Corpus, or have an electronic link-up to Oxford. But what should be a realistic possibility is for dictionary-makers to supply, as an option, a reasonably large and representative corpus on CD-ROM to accompany the printed dictionary.

2 Today's EFL dictionaries

The *run-of-the-mill* example illustrates just one kind of service an advanced EFL student might reasonably expect from a good usage dictionary, but a single hit is of course no guarantee to make that dictionary a "best buy". What it does suggest is that

- large corpora have become obligatory lexicographical tools for dictionary-makers, and
- dictionary-users might have to supplement dictionary look-up with actual corpus access.

There is no doubt that English dictionaries, especially EFL ones, have improved enormously over the last decade or so. I suggest there are four main reasons for this development:

- widespread global demand for English to make EFL publishing economically attractive;
- keener national and international competition among publishers;
- greater awareness of EFL students' needs;
- increased use of corpus resources.

Reading dictionary publishers' blurbs which stress their heavy reliance on corpora - now enjoying an upmarket status they certainly did not have in the sixties when the first electronic corpora were being compiled - makes you wonder how A.S. Hornby and Michael West managed at all to produce their epoch-making works. Lexicographers have long had a solid reputation for energetically "checking" other dictionaries and, now, the new practices of also checking real texts have no doubt had a salutary effect. Instead of asking themselves "What is there in dictionary X for me?" lexicographers now seem to reformulate the question as "How can available data improve my description?"

The field of English language teaching is now in the fortunate situation of having several very good monolingual dictionaries at its disposal. (The situation for bilingual dictionaries is less clear, and we are looking forward to the time when good use can be made of the bilingual corpora.) But *good* does have a comparative *better* and a superlative *best*, a word which actually figures in the theme of this colloquium. So what is still missing? What should we expect from tomorrow's dictionaries?

3 How are dictionaries actually used?

I would like to discuss some general EFL needs such as "What is involved in knowing a word?", taking Paul Nation's classification as a starting-point (see Table 1, from Nation 1990: 31).

Table 1. Knowing a word

"R" stands for receptive use, i.e. listening and reading, and "P" for productive use, i.e. speaking and writing. The classification is according to four general criteria: form, position, function and meaning.

Form	
Spoken form	R What does the word sound like?
	P How is the word pronounced?
Written form	R What does the word look like?
	P How is the word written and spelled?
Position	
Grammatical patterns	R In what patterns does the word occur?
	P In what patterns must we use the word?
Collocations	R What words or types of words can be expected before or after the word?
	P What words or types of words must we use with this word?
Function	
Frequency	R How common is the word?
	P How often should the word be used?
Appropriateness	R Where would we expect to meet this word?
	P Where can this word be used?
Meaning	
Concept	R What does the word mean?
	P What word should be used to express this meaning?
Associations	R What other words does this word make us think of?
	P What other words could we use instead of this one?

Studies of actual use of teaching materials indicate that what most EFL students use their dictionaries for is to find out about meaning, spelling and pronunciation, in that order (MacFarquhar & Richards 1983, Nation 1990: 135, Summers 1988: 114). I have nothing to say about spelling, where monolingual dictionaries are well equipped (particularly now when syllabification is regularly included), but let us look at how well the other two needs - meaning and pronunciation - are met in EFL dictionaries.

4 Meaning in dictionaries

Speaking of conceptual meaning, I find the rather negative view of bilingual dictionaries - an attitude which is not uncommon among writers on lexicography - unfair, if not incorrect. The majority of EFL students actually prefer bilingual dictionaries, and there are good reasons for it. Here are three:

- Monolingual definitions, not just of words denoting abstraction, tend to be circumlocutory and often unhelpful. To choose a very concrete word as an example: in a monolingual dictionary it takes some 50 words to define the two meanings of the English word *radiator* - and there is of course still no guarantee that the meanings will be clear to the EFL student. By contrast, a bilingual English-Swedish dictionary can achieve this by giving the two corresponding Swedish words: *värmeelement* and *radiator*.
- A bilingual dictionary is useful for both reception and production, whereas monolingual dictionaries have a weak spot when it comes to production. To be fair, there are on-going efforts to remedy this, such as the launching of the *Longman Language Activator*.
- Finally, and perhaps most importantly: there is an intrinsic value in knowing what word in your mother-tongue corresponds to an English word. I believe this is true in general, not just in a translation situation, in that there is a mnemonic value in linking an L2 word to an L1 word. There are studies to show that there is interaction between the lexicons of the two languages in one user (Channell 1988: 86).

It is clear that words in one language, and their translation equivalents in the other (when such exist), are related in the brain in a nonrandom way, much as a word and its synonym in the same language may be connected in an associational network (Albert & Obler 1978: 246).

5 Pronunciation in dictionaries

Pronunciation is usually handled well in EFL dictionaries, particularly in those where IPA transcriptions of both British and American, the two major standards, are given side by side (a most welcome development!). While it is my experience that most advanced foreign users master and even appreciate IPA transcriptions, native users seem to be adamantly opposed to them. As a result, dictionaries for domestic consumption often resort to printing, at the bottom of the page, a "key" which is space-consuming, probably rarely consulted and also pretty useless.

Still, even a sound phonetic transcription like IPA is hardly considered a particularly good read by all, and will remain an intriguing mystery to too many EFL students. This is where the modern speaking computer can offer a quite dramatic improvement. In my machine I now have the *Random House Webster Unabridged Dictionary* on one CD-ROM. After almost instant lexical look-up of a word that occurs in a text I am working on, I can click on the transcription and actually hear the pronunciation of the looked-up word - repeatedly if needed. Even a close friend of IPA has to admit that no phonetic script can beat the actual sound. Since electronic dictionary look-up requires so little energy and time -compared to walking over to a shelf, locating and checking a printed dictionary - he new technique actually enhances dictionary use. It is only thanks to the new technique that I learnt, only a short time ago, that a nautical word, *buoy*, which is most familiar to me in print, meaning

> a distinctively shaped and marked float, sometimes carrying a signal or signals, anchored to mark a channel, anchorage, navigational hazard, etc., or to provide a mooring place away from the shore

and pronounced /bɒɪ/ in Britain also has a very different American pronunciation /'buːɪ/, which is unpredictable from the British pronunciation. If we look at global English there are today actually a number of native varieties, not just the standard British and American. They differ quite clearly in spoken but not in written mode. It would therefore be possible, and interesting, to include one preferred spoken variety (British, Australian, etc.) - or several - in the dictionary voice output component.

6 Spoken English in dictionaries

One traditional weakness of dictionaries is that the spoken language is inadequately represented, but this is clearly changing in corpus-based dictionaries. One of the typical features of spoken English is the use of a range of "discourse items": responses like *yes* and *no,* softeners like *you see* and *you know,* initiators like *now* and *well.* In the London-Lund Corpus they are more common than prepositions, adverbs, conjunctions and adjectives. To take one example: the word *well* is probably unique in that its use as a discourse item - as in *well, what do you think about so and so?* - is more or less restricted to the spoken language. It is in fact the fourteenth most common word in the corpus - more frequent than core words like *but, this, they, think.* Any lexicographer working with a spoken corpus is bound to think twice before discarding it with a simple but pretty useless label such as "interjection". It is in cases like *well* that our four dictionaries under scrutiny show striking variations in their treatment.

At Lund University we have made a special study of spoken English corpora, an exercise that, for one thing, has made us more aware of the importance of intonation. Since this is a text-bound rather than a word-bound linguistic feature, word-ordered dictionaries can hardly be expected to handle intonation in general. There are, however, certain lexical items that seem to carry intonation, for example (see Altenberg 1990 and further references there):

> we discussed the matter BR\IEFLY |
> BR\/IEFLY | there is nothing more I can D\O about it |

In the first example, *briefly* is a manner adverb and normally has clause-final position and nuclear prominence with a falling tone. In the second example, *briefly* is a style disjunct, typically placed in clause-initial position and in a separate tone unit, usually with a falling-rising tone. The interesting thing is that the different positions and intonations are accompanied by different meanings: according to the OALD5 'for a short time' and 'in a few words'; according to the CIDE 'for a short time' and 'using few words' respectively. Two dictionaries give additional information: for the second example, COBUILD2 gives 'sentence adverb', and COBUILD has the extra margin label 'ADV with cl'. For the learner, it would be useful to have information also about the typical intonation of such sentence adverbs. *Briefly* is not an isolated phenomenon but represents a class, including *frankly, simply, literally, personally, clearly, naturally, superficially, technically, ironically, happily, hopefully* (see Altenberg 1990: 180, Quirk et al 1985: 568), as in this sentence introduced by what has been called 'viewpoint subjuncts':

> *Morally*, *politically*, and *economically*, it is urgent that the government should act more effectively.

It would be a help for students to have such suprasegmental information in spoken form in a dictionary, where they are more likely to look for the word than anywhere else.

7 Grammar in dictionaries

I will now go on to discuss some other aspects of EFL dictionaries based on other parts of Table 1.

First grammatical patterns, particularly their productive aspect: "In what patterns must we use the word?" It is an interesting point since it brings up the question of the relation between lexis and grammar.

We have seen an increase of grammatical information going into learners' dictionaries ever since Hornby started the admirable practice of indicating the words' grammatical constructions in the *Advanced Learner's Dictionary* (which for that very reason became an early favourite of mine). I still believe this is an important aspect in evaluating EFL dictionaries. There is little value in knowing words unless we can make sentences with them. Of course there is the grammar book, which traditionally gives this kind of information. However, it often fails on two counts:

- First, a grammar can, and should, state the types of constructions in the language, but it cannot give such information for all the words in the language. Most lists of words that are assigned to a particular grammatical pattern are non-exhaustive.
- Second, not only do grammars leak, they also lack a generally adopted and accepted form of organisation, whereas a dictionary has the alphabetical one - an unbeatable order. Since we start to build sentences with words rather than abstract grammatical structures, it is natural to give grammatical information in the dictionary. Yet we also need grammars: a dictionary cannot replace the grammar when it comes to stating the structural properties of the language: word order, inflections, etc. Ideally there should be a closer link between a dictionary and a grammar than we have seen so far. Like Andrew Pawley I believe "that structural linguistics and lexicography have both been harmed by their long intellectual and institutional apartheid" (Pawley 1996: 206).

In talking about dictionaries we nowadays have to make a distinction between traditional paper dictionaries and new electronic dictionaries. The search engine of an electronic dictionary such as the CD-ROM versions of *Random House Webster Unabridged Dictionary* or the *Oxford English Dictionary* is superior to manual search in two respects: it permits faster lookup and, most important, it enables the user to find all occurrences of a word or a phrase under all lexical entries in the dictionary. For example, the infinitive construction with the verb *want*, as in

He didn't want his name to appear in the newspapers.
I don't want there to be any misunderstanding.

is a construction type where a Swedish speaker, with high predictability, is likely to go completely wrong for contrastive reasons (the corresponding Swedish verb having a finite clause construction: *Han ville inte att hans namn skulle ...*). By searching for *want to* etc. (techniques called "filtered headword search" and "full text search") the student can get all the examples with these combinations appearing under different head-words. (In practice, of course, there is a big problem with a search of a large data-base generating a surfeit of examples - most of them irrelevant!) That is to say, the electronic dictionary is not just a paper dictionary wrapped up in a machine, but adds a new dimension in offering information which is not practically available in a printed dictionary.

8 Collocations revisited

According to Table 1, productive collocations refer to the question "What words or types of words must we use with this word?". I have already given an example at the outset of my paper but, since this is an area where a corpus can prove particularly useful - and not only to non-native speakers - let me give one more. Dwight Bolinger has a table that shows acceptable and unacceptable collocations of the adjectives *good*, *strong* and *high* with the nouns *likelihood*, *probability*, *possibility* and *chance*. (See Table 2 from Bolinger 1975: 103.)

Table 2. "Nouns stereotyped with particular adjectives"

good likelihood	strong likelihood	*high likelihood
*good probability	strong probability	high probability
good possibility	strong possibility	*high possibility
good chance	*strong chance	*high chance

To compare these data, presumably intuitively-based, with those in a corpus I checked the twelve word combinations in the British National Corpus and got these frequencies:

348	good chance
41	high probability
13	strong chance
12	high chance
8	strong likelihood
7	strong probability
5	high likelihood
4	strong possibility
4	good possibility
1	high possibility
1	good likelihood
1	good probability

This search shows that all twelve combinations actually occur in the 100-million-word corpus, whereas Bolinger accepts 7 and rejects 5. However, of the latter *good probability* and *high possibility* occur only once in the corpus, but *high likelihood* occurs 5 times, *high chance* 12 times, and *strong chance* 13 times. Without a closer analysis of language variety, text type and grammatical construction, such frequency information from a large mixed corpus is, of course, of limited lexicographical value. However, I believe that, to most people in need of information about collocability, this type of data would be welcome. Also, even if some examples of such "nouns stereotyped with particular adjectives" might be found in a dictionary, the search will be exhausting, unsystematic and lack frequencies.

9 Word frequencies

Word frequencies are often used to determine the ordering of meanings in dictionaries, and actual figures are also beginning to appear with word-entries. It is only with the arrival of corpora that we have a substantial basis for making statements about frequency. Still, some caution is called for here: corpus-based word frequencies are directly related to the types of text that make up that corpus. For example, since spoken language is underrepresented in standard corpora (such as the BNC and the Bank of English) a fact like the high-frequent use of *well* in spoken discourse (mentioned above) may well "disappear" in a megacorpus dominated by written texts.

Here is frequency information supplied by COBUILD:

WORD FREQUENCY BANDS
(based on *Collins COBUILD2 English Dictionary*, p. xiii)

- Frequency band 1: c. 700 words
  the, and, of... (grammar words)
  like, go, paper, return... (very frequent vocabulary items)
- Frequency band 2: c. 1200 words
  argue, bridge, danger, female, sea...

The words in the top two bands (totalling some 1900 words) account for approximately 75 per cent of all English usage.

- Frequency band 3: c. 1500 words
  aggressive, medicine, tactic...
- Frequency band 4: c. 3200 words
  accuracy, duration, miserable, puzzle...
- Frequency band 5: c. 8100 words
  abundant, crossroads, fearless ...

The total number of words in these bands is just under 15,000, and the dictionary states: "The words in the five frequency bands are of immense importance to learners because they make up 95% of all spoken and written English." I am not a firm believer in frequency as an overriding factor in course and materials design, but it is undoubtedly an important one for the early stages of learning. The English words which make up the remaining 5 % of a text are of course so numerous that they cannot be listed. Nor can they be predicted since they will vary very much depending on text type, and a good portion of the words in a text will be hapax legomena. The 95% figure is interesting in that it is the level that has been found to be critical for second language learners' comprehension of unsimplified texts. Also, the figure of around 15,000 words is likely to be the vocabulary of English-speaking students (see Nation 1990: 189f.).

This kind of frequency information is useful for teachers and materials writers, and can offer a glimmer of hope to students who constantly hear about the enormously rich vocabulary of English compared to that of their L1.

10 Summing-up

The Perfect Learners' Dictionary might include the following package:

- The printed book – which I now find difficult to see entirely replaced by the electronic dictionary – but of course supplemented by a CD-ROM version.
- A dictionary well co-ordinated with a grammar, where the grammar may also be available in electronic form and accessible via direct links between dictionary and grammar.
- Access to corpora for specific searches, such as collocations, where a dictionary can never be adequate in view of the prohibitive page space and look-up time required.
- Pronunciation offered by direct voice output, either just the preferred variety or several varieties.
- A toolbox in the word-processing package – preferably with links to the dictionary and grammar as mentioned – including a spelling-checker and a thesaurus. I believe most people find the spelling-checker useful – especially because it also does welcome service as a typing-checker – but the thesaurus is of limited use in its present form. Getting suggestions of a host of synonyms or pseudo-synonyms is useful only if you know what these words actually mean and how they are used. The situation would be improved if each suggested item carried a link to enable immediate look-up in a monolingual or bilingual dictionary or a concordance. For example, looking up the word *situation* from the previous sentence I get *circumstances, predicament, condition, case, plight, state*. Clearly none of them can replace *situation* in this context. But this is a decision I can make only because of my previous experience of these suggested replacements – the list is of little help to the less advanced student, i.e. the person who most needs help.
- The grammar-checkers which are provided with the word-processing packages have to be dramatically improved if they are to be of any use at all. For example, having spent a good portion of my postgraduate life on a study of the passive to discover that it is highly frequent in scientific texts, I do not like being told, again and again, by some anonymous grammatical Silicon Valley guru, that I am using too many passives. There seems to be a huge gap in the quality between these grammar-checkers and the parsers used by computational linguists (this is a tip for Bill Gates).

However, this Perfect Learners' Dictionary that I have outlined will be an unwieldy, possibly even unmanageable tool, and probably not a Perfect Dictionary for the Learner as much as a Dictionary for the Perfect Learner.

11 Acknowledgement

I want to thank Bengt Altenberg, Lund University, and Hans Lindquist, Växjö University, for helpful comments on a draft version of this article.

Bibliography

Longman Language Activator (1993): Della Summers (ed.) — Harlow: Longman.
Oxford English Dictionary on CD-Rom (1989) — Oxford: OUP.
Random House Webster's Unabridged Dictionary (1993) — New York: Random House.

Albert, Martin L., K. Obler (1978): The Bilingual Brain. — New York: Academic Press.
Altenberg, Bengt (1990): "Spoken English and the Dictionary". — In: J. Svartvik (ed.): The London-Lund Corpus of Spoken English. Description and Research (Lund: Lund University Press) 177-191.
Bolinger, Dwight (^{2}1975): Aspects of Language. — New York: Harcourt Brace Jovanovich.
Channell, Joanna (1988): "Psycholinguistic Considerations in the Study of L2 Vocabulary Acquisition". — In: R. Carter, M. McCarthy (eds.): Vocabulary and Language Teaching (London: Longman) 83-96.
MacFarquhar, P., J. C. Richards (1983): "On Dictionaries and definitions". — In: RELC Journal 14, 111-124.
Nation, Paul (1990): Teaching and Learning Vocabulary. — New York: Heinle & Heinle.
Pawley, Andrew (1996): "Grammarian's Lexicon, Lexicographer's Lexicon: Worlds Apart". — In: J. Svartvik (ed.): Words (Stockholm: Almqvist & Wiksell International) 89-211.
Quirk, Randolph, Sidney Greenbaum, Geoffrey Leech, Jan Svartvik (1985): A Comprehensive Grammar of the English Language. — London, New York: Longman.
Summers, Della (1988): "The Role of Dictionaries in Language Learning". — In: R. Carter, M. McCarthy (eds.): Vocabulary and Language Teaching (London: Longman) 111-125.

Geoffrey Leech and Hilary Nesi

Moving towards perfection: The learners' (electronic) dictionary of the future

1 Introduction

The initial paper in this book, by Tony Cowie, has provided a historical account of the precursors of the present-day English learners' dictionary. It is appropriate, in this final contribution, to speculate on the learners' dictionaries of the future. Other preceding papers have made it clear that, in spite of the major advances in lexicographic practice that learners' dictionaries have made over the past two decades, such dictionaries fall well short of perfection. This is unavoidable, as far as the present generation of learners' dictionaries is concerned. Practical considerations determine that publishers have to produce a dictionary of a certain price, and of a certain size, which precludes the perfection of providing all the information which learners might ideally need. At the same time, economic opportunity has justified the considerable and continuing investment which publishers have put into these dictionaries, leading to the remarkable improvements we can already admire, particularly in tailoring the content and presentation of dictionaries closely to the needs of its users.

Among the sources of improvement, the development of electronic tools and resources, particularly corpora, has made the most groundbreaking contribution. In this respect, the learners' dictionary has set new standards: its example of responsiveness to the user's needs and accountability to linguistic evidence is increasingly being followed by older and more traditional branches of lexicography. Further, modern computational methods of information storage, text processing and book production mean that the existence of a learners' dictionary as a book of printed paper is almost secondary to its existence as (part of) an electronic databank. In fact, a number of different paper dictionaries - shaped to the purposes of this or that particular user-group - can be offshoots of the same lexicographical information bank. The developing market for electronic dictionaries now means that the paper dictionary is a secondary product. It is no longer essential even at the user's end: it can be replaced by a CD-ROM (such as those recently produced by Longman, COBUILD and Oxford University Press) or even by a tiny IC card, perhaps as an extension of an electronic notebook or personal organizer.

It is not surprising, then, if our vision of the future focuses on the fast-evolving opportunities of the new age of electronic communication and information technology. It would be unwise here to speculate about the demise of the printed book, an adaptable survivor from the Gutenberg technological breakthrough of the fifteenth century. The paper dictionary no doubt has a long and worthwhile future ahead of it - although it is unclear how far forces of inertia will serve to prolong its vitality in the next millennium. What does seem certain is that it will face growing competition from the electronic dictionary, which will provide increasing advantages as the price of hardware continues to drop and the power and convenience of the computer continues to increase. Hence in envisaging new horizons for learner lexicography in the next fifty years, we predict the electronic dictionary to be a better bet than the familiar 'hard-copy' dictionary, which we all know and love, but which appears to offer limited possibilities of further technological progress.[1]

As always, in dealing with the pioneering and experimental stages of new technologies, there are strong negative points balancing the positive ones in favour of innovation. Like the motor cars of the early 1900s, electronic dictionaries, with the backup technology they require, are on the expensive side, and have their teething problems. It will be a long time, for example, before electronic dictionaries are available in the majority of primary schools in the world. Likewise, although search and retrieval software is getting cleverer, it does not do all of the things we would like it to do. But to judge the future potential by present achievement is to make the cardinal error of traditionalists through the centuries. So let us, at this point, summarise the main advantages of the electronic dictionary, not limiting our attention to what has been done so far, or worrying too much about some short-term limitations of current products. In passing, we will return to a number of points mentioned in previous contributions to this book.

2 Advantages in information access

The types of advantage noted in this section are those which apply to many areas of the electronic information revolution, not only dictionaries.

2.1 Storage capacity

In considering the perfect learners' dictionary in relation to current learners' dictionaries, the image comes to mind of a giant octopus being confined inside a wooden box. The perfect learners' dictionary, one which answered all users' needs, would have to be a vast open-ended information source. It would need to extend its tentacles in many directions from the central core of a dictionary to other types of lexical information which might be required by this or that learner: e.g. lexico-grammatical, multilingual, visual, encyclopaedic, etymological. But the paper dictionary confines this open-ended requirement to a fairly strict limit. What Bolinger wrote in reviewing the OALD4 is just as apt today: "I suspect that hard-copy vademecum dictionaries of this type have about reached their capacity. Any really dramatic advance would burst their covers." (1990:144) Many of the comparative

---

1 On the range of electronic learners' dictionaries already available, and a review of their strengths and weaknesses, see Nesi 1996 and 1999.

arguments about whether this or that dictionary is preferable ultimately come down to issues of priority: how much room do we have for this kind of information rather than that? On the other hand, electronic storage media have massive capacity compared with storage on paper. A single CD-ROM can contain the most gigantic dictionary of English ever written: the twenty-volume *Oxford English Dictionary*. Currently, paper learners' dictionaries, although weighing over ten times as much as a CD-ROM, have less than a twentieth part of the capacity of the OED. In consequence, by transferring a learners' dictionary to CD-ROM, one could cram in at least 200 times as much material. This can allow the expansion of an existing learners' dictionary to a much larger size, or the addition of further reference information sources (such as are currently provided by the *Longman Interactive American Dictionary* and the *Collins COBUILD on CD-ROM*): for example, a visual library, a grammar, a usage dictionary, a dictionary of common errors, a large corpus of texts.

2.2 Multimedia

Apart from text and illustrations, the electronic dictionary is already beginning to use channels of information not available to the book dictionary: sound, flexible vision (including moving images), as well as text. *OALD on CD-ROM*, *The Longman Interactive English Dictionary* (LIED) and the *Longman Interactive American Dictionary* (LIAD), for example, all provide audio recordings, and LIED and LIAD also include a selection of video clips.

Contributors to this volume have at various points noted the limitations of making meanings clear on the printed page. Learners' dictionary lexicographers have done their best, using definitions with a limited defining vocabulary, usage boxes and illustrations showing special visualizable fields of vocabulary. But many expressions (the example of *make the bed* was used earlier) are difficult to explain in simple language, and the restrictions of the defining vocabulary may result in some verbose and clumsy definitions. However, the availability of animation can change all that: in principle, the depiction of action in real time will enable any physical action, process, or change of state to be directly portrayed to the learner. This potential has not yet been fully exploited, but some of the most recent electronic dictionaries such as LIAD are now beginning to use animation in a limited way to illustrate verb meanings. Similarly, the great advantage of the direct auditory representation of a word over its phonetic transcription scarcely needs to be laboured. Hearing any vocabulary item pronounced "at the click of a mouse" is a far better alternative to phonetic transcription, a bugbear to many learners. LIED, LIAD and *OALD on CD-ROM* provide audio recordings of every dictionary headword, and LIAD also offers a record and playback facility, enabling learners to compare their own pronunciation with the dictionary recording. With a "sound picture" of each word or phrase in a dictionary, phonetic transcriptions are hardly necessary. However, rather than banishing phonetic transcriptions from the electronic dictionary, one would like to keep them as an optional extra - as a kind of information which is made available only when it is needed and for the benefit of those who need it - see 3.3 below.

2.3 Easier and faster access

It is far easier to type a few characters on a keyboard - sufficient to find the headword you are interested in - than to ruffle through more than a thousand pages in order to home in on that same word. Access to an entry in an electronic dictionary is (normally) relatively instantaneous, whereas looking up in a printed dictionary is an inefficient, hit-or-miss, often frustrating process. The printed book is essentially a linear storage device, whereas conceptually, a lexical information resource is multi-dimensional. The alphabet, which has tyrannised over dictionary arrangement and access for centuries, ceases to be a tyrant when your dictionary is electronic.

Ironically, it has been argued (see Sharpe 1995: 50) that the very speed and convenience of access is a drawback of electronic learners' dictionaries, because information so easily extracted may be just as easily forgotten by the user! On the other hand, research by Guillot and Kenning (1994) has found that students using an electronic dictionary show "an increased capacity for sustained effort," with much exploratory browsing of the dictionary and more multiple searches than would otherwise take place.

We return to accessing issues - specifically to variable paths of access - in 3.3 below.

3 Advantages in terms of needs and resources

Turning now to advantages of the electronic learners' dictionary which are related more to educational value, first, let us consider a simple model of dictionary use in terms of **needs** and **resources**. A learner (here we are thinking of an EFL learner who is not a native speaker) uses a dictionary especially when trying to solve a communicative problem - one either of comprehension or of production. This is the **immediate** need for the use of the dictionary, but there is also a more **long-term** need or objective: the dictionary is a tool to improve the learner's competence in the target language. This is a goal that may be gradually attained over many years of learning.

A dictionary is a **resource** that may be consulted or accessed, in order to help satisfy the needs mentioned above. Those who compile the dictionary, however, may rely on more fundamental resources - such as a corpus of written texts and spoken transcriptions, or a citation bank. These are what may be called **primary resources** - direct evidence of the use of the language. Compared with them, the dictionary itself is a **secondary resource**: a compilation of lexical information about the language, systematically organised so as to be readily available to the user. The general relation between the dictionary and the dictionary user is represented in Figure 1, which shows **means of access** as the channel linking the user to the dictionary.

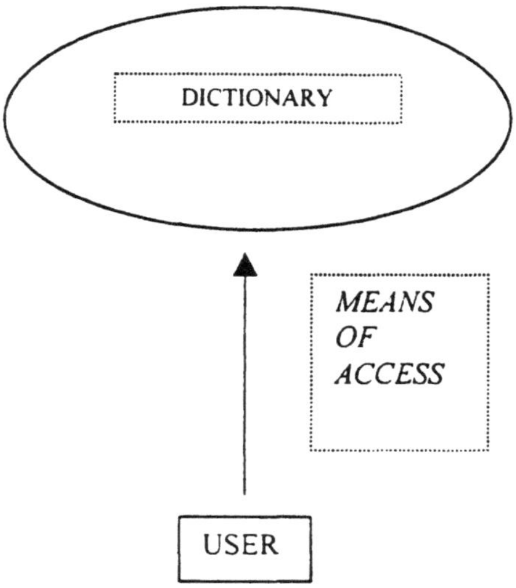

In the case of a printed dictionary, the three components of Figure 1 are relatively fixed, whereas in the case of an electronic dictionary, possibilities of variability are potentially very large. It is this **multi-access** potential, with its adaptability to need, that is a major advantage of the electronic dictionary.

3.1 Variability of access points

Let us consider first the learner, the dictionary user. The English learners' dictionaries chiefly considered in this volume (OALD5, LDOCE3, COBUILD2, and CIDE) are all roughly comparable in the level of learner that they cater for. Their lower bound of user competence is determined by the fact that these are monolingual learners' dictionaries: all the explanatory materials, as well as all the words and phraseologies to be explained, are in English, the target language. Their upper bound, although fuzzier, is imposed by the limited list of headwords they contain (entries for rare, archaic, or highly technical words being generally omitted), and perhaps also by the use of a limited defining vocabulary. In spite of the user-friendly aspects of these dictionaries, which make them rather enjoyable to use, a user with near-native competence would probably want to "upgrade" to more comprehensive or specialised native-speaker dictionaries. The user population, for these learners' dictionaries, is therefore confined to a broad band of intermediate-to-advanced learners, as shown in Figure 2.

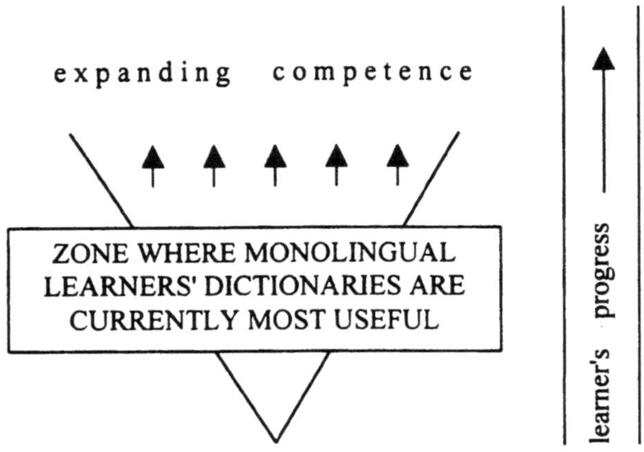

Learners excluded from this band include both those who are "too elementary" and those which are "too advanced". Extending the band of users downwards, to include elementary learners, would necessitate invading the territory of the bilingual dictionary, and giving access to the information in the dictionary via the learner's native language (or a second language the learner knows). This would not only be an *open sesame* for less advanced learners, but would also overcome the problem, for dictionaries employing a limited defining vocabulary, of unhelpful over-long definitions for something that could be more easily and economically explained in the learner's own language (see 2.2 above).

There is no obvious reason why future electronic learners' dictionaries should not provide such variable access points. For example, for speakers of French, a core list of headwords in French (with main sense and phraseological subdivisions within each headword) would provide a more accessible "front end" to the English dictionary vocabulary for productive use. For receptive use, the English defining vocabulary could be cross-referenced to equivalents for the major world languages. Of course, these NL-specific add-ons would take up space, but we have already noted that this would hardly be a problem for electronic dictionaries of the future.

Learners "too advanced" or specialized for current learners' dictionaries would have dictionary needs similar to those of native speakers. They would want to be able to extend their vocabulary into more peripheral areas of the lexicon: for example, into technical terminologies, archaic terms, slang expressions, dialectal forms and so on. Consider just one area where it has been noted that current learners' dictionaries leave much to be desired: the lexical characteristics of different national varieties of English. At present (see Heath this volume) learners' dictionaries make only limited efforts to cover national varieties apart from American and British English. Regrettably, there can be little room to spare for detail on Australian, New Zealand, Caribbean, Singaporean and other regional variants.[2] But again, if we "think electronic," there is little danger of dictionaries running out of space. Various national vocabularies can be add-on resources, supplementing the lexical databank with information optionally available to the user.

Another example of variable access points is the provision of a "sound like" facility, whereby the user can access a word via a word similar in pronunciation. LIED, *COBUILD on CD-ROM* and even some of the smallest hand-held electronic dictionaries provide this facility. Given the vagaries of English spelling, this is bound to be something of a hit-or-miss affair. However, developments in automatic speech recognition open up the possibility of the purely auditory look-up of a word. If this seems futuristic, there is already the device (for example, in LIED, LIAD and *OALD on CD-ROM*) of providing a word's pronunciation automatically on look-up, as an immediate auditory feedback to the user. Other approximate look-up procedures, such as the partial spelling of a word using wild-card characters, are also helpful. Such procedures can be an escape from the limitations of traditional orthographic look-up, where paradoxically a student needs to know how to spell a word in order to look it up (and find out how to spell it!).

3.2 Variability of destinations

The preceding paragraph has already introduced the idea of variability of destinations: different users, with different needs, will need to track down information from different lexical resources. Already, electronic dictionary producers are thinking pluralistically, combining a number of different resources in the same CD-ROM package: a dictionary accompanied by a grammar, a usage dictionary, an error dictionary, a corpus and so on. At present, however, there is a temptation to use the space on the CD-ROM rather like shelf space for books in a library: simply combining coexisting reference resources, without integrating them. The facility to access more than one resource from the same user interface is only a first step towards integration. There is much more to the integration of lexical resources than this. There is need for "multi-referencing": for simultaneous signalling to the user that the same query item is to be found in a number of different resources. At present, many of the teething troubles of electronic dictionaries, promising as they are, are to be found in the imperfect integration of a number of resources.[3] For example, there is clearly a pedagogical difficulty of integration between a dictionary and a corpus, where the corpus (consisting of authentic, unpreselected text or discourse data) inevitably contains many items which are not represented in the dictionary, and vice versa. No doubt it would be better to provide, not a "raw corpus," but an extensive citation bank, in the form of a concordance in which each item in the dictionary is illustrated by a set of examples in context. There is also an absurdity, for example, in providing a single route of

---

[2] But there are regionally specific dictionaries produced in some of these English-speaking countries. An example, for Singaporean usage, is the *Times-Chambers Essential English Dictionary*, Singapore and Edinburgh: Chambers Harrap & Federal Publications, 1997.

[3] See Nesi 1996 on the difficulties of cross-referencing.

access to both a learners' dictionary and a pronouncing dictionary, where the latter has many more headwords than the former, but supplies only pronunciation.[4] Such problems of integration can lead to much frustrated searching for information which turns out to be unavailable. But they can be overcome if the multiple-database provides signals to the user of the available sources of information for a given item at the point where the query is made. There should also be an easy way of "switching off" a given information source (say, a regional dictionary of British English, or a pronouncing dictionary) where these are not needed by a particular person or for a particular application.

Existing printed dictionaries suffer from problems of information overload: too many different types of information in the same dictionary can clutter the page and distract the reader from the information quest in hand. Especially grammar codes and phonetically transcribed pronunciations can be disproportionately distracting to users for whom these more technical features have no relevance and are difficult to handle. There is a big difference, here, between linguistically sophisticated users (typically teachers?) and linguistically naïve users (typically students?) who may nevertheless have a good practising knowledge of the target language. For the former, grammar codes and phonetic notation may be meat and drink; for the latter, meaning, spelling and phraseology tend to be the major concerns, and grammar and phonetics can be baffling and offputting. Of course, one can argue that students *ought* to be interested and enthused by grammar and phonetics, and so should be continually exposed to these types of information. But this argument loses its force if the result is to put the students off using their dictionary entirely.

One way to hide information of no importance to the reader's current concern is, as already said, to switch off or mask the information types not needed. Another is to use a hypertext structure for the databank, so that a user who wants to explore more detail can optionally explore links (say) to a concordance of corpus examples, or to a list of collocations associated with a given item. Hypertext referencing also helps to solve another problem of information overload. One of the difficulties of conventionally printed dictionaries is the great size and complexity of entries for some very common words, such as *in* or *get*. But for these, a hypertext information structure can provide not merely cross-referencing, but layering of information at different levels of detail, so that a top-level panoramic single-screen view of an entry (like the summary entries in the *Longman Language Activator*) can supply the reader with links to further details in terms of subsenses, multi-word expressions, and so on. It is true that current printed learners' dictionaries have become sophisticated in the simultaneous presentation of many kinds of information. But the various devices learners' dictionaries use to reduce information overload include not only features such as typography and layout, but also simplifications which verge on oversimplification. Simplifications which reduce the amount of information available (and most simplifications do) are unnecessary if an electronic dictionary makes use of hypertext methods of managing the presentation of information and other methods available with a modern windows-based user interface.

---

[4] See Nesi 1996 on the LIED problem in this respect.

3.3 Variability of search or access paths

Again, we have anticipated this type of variability in the above paragraphs. The multi-access feature of electronic dictionaries not only includes multi-referencing to different resources, but also extends to cross-referencing (e.g. via hypertext links) within and between resources. This means, for example, that on looking up the word *brave* in the dictionary, we can immediately click on one of a list of synonyms (*courageous*, *valiant*, *bold* etc.), and be able to compare the two synonym entries in separate windows on screen. Or it would be feasible to have a reception-oriented learners' dictionary cross-referring to a production-oriented dictionary like the *Longman Language Activator*, which provides detailed information on the choice between synonyms or quasi-synonymous words. The production-oriented dictionary, on the other hand, because it tends to cover a smaller vocabulary in greater detail, would benefit from cross-references to less common synonymous expressions in a reception-oriented dictionary, where meanings and examples for these expressions could be sought. In fact, in the longer term one could envisage a merging of the dictionary (essentially reception-oriented) and the thesaurus (a production-oriented lexical reference resource), providing access links via realisation (spelling or pronunciation) or by similarity of meaning as required. The difference between a dictionary and a thesaurus is basically a question of whether form or meaning is the access route to the lexical information which both types of publication ideally provide.

Possibilities of cross-referencing are numerous. At present, the dictionary shelf of the library contains many lexicographical tomes with overlapping information, but also with different areas of specialization. The need is to combine these so that cross-reference between the different special sources of information is easy. For example, a dictionary of *faux amis* between native language and target language is useful for learners, as is also a dictionary of common errors. Such dictionaries already exist as separate paper volumes. But to make the most of the information they contain requires cross-referencing, so that clicking on the flagged word in one dictionary will automatically bring up the relevant information in the other. Pushing this way of thinking a little further, we reach a stage where, for the user, different dictionaries do not exist as separate entities: rather, there is a single lexical database with links between the different categories of information associated with the same headword entries.

A final point about variable routes of access is that there should be links between primary and secondary resources. An obvious implementation, in a multi-access electronic dictionary, is a link from the dictionary item to corpus material - providing, for example, frequency data (including collocations) or KWIC concordance listings. The opposite link - going from corpus word to dictionary entry - could also be a possible and valuable type of connection, enabling the learner to use the bank of texts stored with the dictionary as a set of materials for reading comprehension, for example.

4 The interactive dictionary

Having elaborated on the advantages of variability in the electronic dictionary, we move on to a final advantage, closely associated with variability, viz the truly **interactive** potential of the electronic dictionary.

The printed book is not interactive: it is an inert resource, passively waiting to be consulted by the reader. On the other hand, an electronic dictionary offers a wide range of choices to its user - in terms of the points of departure, destinations, and search routes. Perhaps there is too much choice for some users: but for those who want to take a more active stance, there is a great opportunity for developing dictionary-using skills. The electronic dictionary can provide a stimulating environment for exploring the lexical resources of the language using their own initiative, and developing their own word power. Exercises and tasks comparable to those provided by CALL [computer-aided language learning] courseware can be integrated with the dictionary, and with the concordance materials which may accompany it. The *Electronic Wordpower Dictionary* and *OALD on CD-ROM* already include vocabulary games such as crosswords; more elaborate electronic dictionaries of the future might provide more focussed feedback on vocabulary learning activities, with suggestions for further exploration. In other words, the dictionary is adaptable for the needs of the learner, and to the learner's changing behaviour.

In another sense of "interactive", the electronic dictionary can interact with other computer tools and applications. These can vary from CALL materials and concordancing software (two already mentioned) to printers and word processors. From a word processor it is already possible, in existing packages, to access a dictionary or a thesaurus on-line. In this way, the dictionary becomes a writing aid comparable to a spelling or grammar checker, only more educationally useful. Similarly, it is already possible to link up a dictionary and a printer, allowing selective print-outs. Where students do not have individual access to computers, these provide, for example, multiple copies for classroom activities and study tasks.

5 Conclusion

As much of this paper has painted a rosy picture of future technological progress, it is time to end on a more sober note of re-appraisal. We are now in the period of **first generation** electronic learners' dictionaries, which are heavily influenced by the printed dictionaries from which they originate. It will not be surprising if many who use them have reservations about their superiority to printed dictionaries. In part, this is because the potential of the electronic dictionary is only beginning to be exploited. In part, it is also due to technological conservatism, especially among the older generations of dictionary users, which include many teachers. In part, too, it may be because we appreciate the familiar advantages of the printed dictionary and do not entirely appreciate how an electronic dictionary could ever match them.

Paper dictionaries are relatively cheap and accessible. We do not have to acquire special equipment or know-how in order to use them. We can casually dip into them, or scan them in a "browsing" mode, without using electronic implements such as a mouse. A paper dictionary is felt to be more ornamental, in one's living room, than a PC or a CD-ROM. It can be carried around the world (e.g. by air) without fear of serious damage or loss of functionality. Moreover, oddly enough, although a printed dictionary is an example of yesterday's technology, we can feel relatively confident that it will not become obsolete so quickly as the latest up-to-the-minute hardware and software. Finally, at least for some people, books can have some of the fetish value of a cuddly toy: we can treat them lovingly and take them to bed with us. It will be a long time before a computer with a CD-ROM drive will compete on all these fronts.

However, it is worth thinking here about hardware in the practical delivery of lexical information. Our assumption, up to now, has been that the computer plus CD-ROM will be the main mode of delivery. But we cannot look decades into the future, any more than a computer pioneer in the 1950s could have foreseen the age of terminals, keyboards, personal computers, diskettes, CD-ROMs, and all the other things that have become familiar to the average child today. Bolinger (1990: 145) was probably right, for example, to say that "the dictionary-consulter of the future will tap out inquiries on a hand-held computer." Already there is a growing market for electronic dictionaries as hand-held devices. Although these tend to be neglected by the educational and academic sectors as being lexicographically beneath serious notice, they are highly popular in certain student markets, and in the near future could well improve substantially in coverage, quality and price. If so, the problem of expense and portability associated with the first generation of learners' electronic dictionaries could well be on the way to solution. Another likely mode of delivery in the future is on-line, via the Internet, where the problem of information capacity can be ignored. It would not be too difficult, in view of current technology, to predict the advent of hand-held electronic dictionaries which can also interact by remote communication with large data resources on the World Wide Web. We can only speculate where technology will take the electronic dictionary in the future, but it seems unlikely that most of their current limitations, which may loom large in people's experience of electronic dictionaries today, will persist in the future.

There remains, therefore, a large gap between the promising (but limited) pioneering developments of the present, and the likely achievements of the future. Further, this gap cannot be bridged merely by technological advances. It is clear that first-generation electronic learners' dictionaries have some shortcomings which cannot be remedied without considerable expenditure of effort and money. Much of this progress - e.g. towards the optimal cross-referencing of resources - may turn out to be labour-intensive. The human and technical resources which have been expended on printed learners' dictionaries in the past twenty or thirty years will need to be applied, with equal dedication, to the development of the electronic dictionaries of the future. If that is done, it is likely that the overwhelming advantages *in principle* of electronic learners' dictionaries will become overwhelming advantages *in practice*. Although the perfect learners' dictionary will always remain imaginary, moving towards perfection will have become a reality.

Bibliography

Collins COBUILD on CD-ROM (1995). – Worthing: HarperCollins.
Longman Interactive American Dictionary (1997). – London: Addison Wesley Longman.
Longman Interactive English Dictionary (1993). – London: Longman.
Longman Language Activator (1993): Della Summers (ed.). – Harlow: Longman.
Oxford Advanced Learner's Dictionary (OALD4) (^{4}1989): Anthony P. Cowie (ed.). – Oxford: OUP.
Oxford Advanced Learner's Dictionary on CD-ROM (1997). – Oxford: OUP.
Oxford English Dictionary on CD-ROM (^{2}1992): – Oxford: OUP.
The Electronic Oxford Wordpower Dictionary (1994). – Oxford: OUP.
Times-Chambers Essential Dictionary (^{2}1997): Elaine Higgleton, Vincent B.Y. Ooi (eds.). – Singapore, Edinburgh: Chambers Harrap & Federal Publications.

Bolinger, Dwight L. (1990): "Review of Oxford Advanced Learner's Dictionary of Current English". – In: International Journal of Lexicography 3/2, 133-145.
Guillot, Marie-Noëlle, Marie-Madeleine Kenning (1994): "Electronic monolingual dictionaries as language learning aids: a case study". – In: Computers Education 23 (1/2), 63-73.
Nesi, Hilary (1996): "Review article: For future reference? Current English learners' dictionaries in electronic form". – In: System 24/4, 537-557.
Nesi, Hilary (1999): "A user's guide to electronic dictionaries for language learners". – In: International Journal of Lexicography 12.1.
Sharpe, Peter (1995): "Electronic dictionaries with particular reference to the design of an electronic bilingual dictionary for English-speaking learners of Japanese". – In: International Journal of Lexicography 8 /1, 39-54.

Appendix: German and French abstracts

Flor Aarts

Syntactic information in OALD5, LDOCE3, COBUILD2 and CIDE

Zusammenfassung

Im Zentrum dieses Beitrags stehen die syntaktischen Informationen in OALD, LDOCE, COBUILD und CIDE, insbesondere die zur Verbsyntax. Es wird ein Vergleich angestellt bezüglich des Artikelaufbaus, der verwendeten Symbole und der verschiedenen Kodierungsarten für syntaktische Angaben.

Résumé

Cet article met l'accent sur l'information syntaxique dans OALD, LDOCE, COBUILD et CIDE et plus particulièrement sur la syntaxe des verbes. Il compare la microstructure des articles-verbes, les symboles utilisés dans les codes constructionnels et la façon dont l'information constructionnelle est codée.

John Ayto

Lexical evolution and learners' dictionaries

Zusammenfassung

In diesem Beitrag werden Veränderungen der Wortschatzauswahl in OALD, LDOCE und COBUILD in den letzten 20 Jahren untersucht, wobei besondere Aufmerksamkeit auf den Wörtern liegt, die in representativen Ausschnitten der Wörterbücher in den Ausgaben neu aufgenommen oder weggelassen wurden. Die Wortschatzerfassung von CIDE wird ebenfalls in die Untersuchung mit einbezogen. Es wird gezeigt, daß neben einer Tendenz genereller Ausweitung (trotz der Konzentration auf Neologismen in der Publizistik) die Nützlichkeit für den Benutzer ein ebenso wichtiges Kriterium für die Aufnahme und die Nichtaufnahme eines Wortes bildet wie die Aktualität.

Résumé

Cet article examine les changements de macrostructure - intervenus durant 20 ans dans OALD, LDCOCE et COBUILD - en comparant les mots ajoutés et supprimés dans des échantillons représentatifs des éditions successives. La macrostructure de CIDE est également regardée de près. L'article montre qu'à côté de la tendance générale à l'expansion et malgré l'accent mis par la publicité sur les néologismes, l'utilité des informations pour l'utilisateur est un critère d'addition ou de retrait au moins aussi important que l'actualité.

Klaus-Dieter Barnickel

Political correctness in learners' dictionaries

Zusammenfassung

In diesem Beitrag werden die englischen Lernerwörterbücher unter dem Gesichtspunkt der *Political Correctness* untersucht. Dabei werden die einzelnen Wörterbücher und vorherige Auflagen im Hinblick auf Sexismus, Rassismus etc. verglichen.

Résumé

L'article examine les *learners' dictionaries* du point de vue du «politiquement correct» (sexisme, racisme, etc.). Il compare les dictionnaires entre eux, ainsi que l'évolution qu'on constate d'une édition à l'autre.

Henri Béjoint

Compound nouns in learners' dictionaries

Zusammenfassung

Wie werden die Komposita in den englischen Lernerwörterbüchern bearbeitet und welchen Aufschluß geben die Definitionen über das Verhältnis von Form und Bedeutung? Der Artikel zeigt, daß einige der Komposita schwer einzuordnen und zu erklären sind und ihre Bearbeitung dementsprechend großen Schwankungen unterworfen ist.

Résumé

L'article se propose d'examiner le traitement des noms composés dans les dictionnaires anglais pour apprenants, et plus particulièrement la façon dont les définitions rendent compte des spécificités des relations entre leur forme et leur sens. Il montre que certains de ces noms composés sont difficiles à catégoriser et à expliquer, et constate en conséquence de grandes variations dans la manière dont ils sont traités.

Gisela Böhner

Classroom experience with the new dictionaries: OALD5, LDOCE3, COBUILD2, CIDE

Zusammenfassung

Es wird untersucht, wie einsprachige Wörterbücher des Englischen (besonders OALD und LDOCE) von unseren Schülern verwendet werden, welche Anforderungen sie an diese Art von Wörterbüchern stellen und inwieweit diese Anforderungen von den einsprachigen Wörterbüchern erfüllt werden können.

Résumé
Cet article essaie de trouver une réponse à la question de savoir comment nos élèves utilisent les dictionnaires monolingues (surtout les dictionnaires OALD et LDOCE), ce qu'ils en exigent et dans quelle mesure ces dictionnaires sont capables de satisfaire leurs exigences.

Paul Bogaards
Access structures of learners' dictionaries

Zusammenfassung
Dieser Artikel befaßt sich mit den Schwierigkeiten, die sich Benutzern stellen, wenn sie eine bestimmte Art von Information in einem Lernerwörterbuch suchen. Dabei stellen sich je nach der Art der gesuchten Information ganz unterschiedliche Probleme. Beim Lesen ist der Ansatzpunkt eine Wortform, zu der semantische Information benötigt wird. Diesem Nachschlagebedürfnis entspricht die Konzeption von Lernerwörterbüchern. Für Produktionszwecke sind die Zugangsstrukturen jedoch weitaus schwieriger. In diesem Beitrag werden verschiedene Methoden diskutiert, dieses Nachschlagebedürfnis zu erfüllen.

Résumé
Cet article traite des problèmes que peuvent rencontrer les apprenants qui cherchent une information particulière dans un dictionnaire d'apprentissage. Ces problèmes sont assez différents selon le type d'information recherchée. Dans le cas de la compréhension écrite, les formes des mots donnent directement accès à l'information sémantique souhaitée. Quand l'apprenant doit produire un texte dans la langue étrangère, par contre, il est beaucoup plus difficile de trouver les mots nécessaires. Plusieurs techniques qui ont pour but de faciliter l'accès aux mots inconnus sont discutés.

Anthony P. Cowie
Learners' dictionaries in a historical and a theoretical perspective

Zusammenfassung
Dieser Beitrag beschreibt die Entstehung und frühe Entwicklung des einsprachigen Lernerwörterbuchs vor dem Hintergrund lexikologischer Forschung, die in den 20er und 30er Jahren, vor allem in Japan unter der Führung von Harold Palmer, durchgeführt wurde. Besondere Betonung liegt dabei auf der Verwendung eines begrenzten Wortschatzes, auf der Konzeption anschaulicher Beispiele, auf Michael Wests Entwicklung eines begrenzten Definitionswortschatzes und auf der Phraseologieforschung, zu der A.S. Hornby einen bemerkenswerten Beitrag geleistet hat und die von weitreichender Bedeutung sein sollte, sowohl innerhalb der Lernerlexikographie als auch darüber hinaus.

Résumé
Ce chapitre décrit la naissance et les premiers développements du dictionnaire pour apprenants monolingue, avec pour toile de fond les recherches menées surtout au Japon sous la direction de Harold Palmer au cours des années 20 et 30. Il aborde principalement les recherches consacrées au développement de vocabulaires restreints, la conception des exemples, l'élaboration par Michael West d'un vocabulaire définitoire restreint et les recherches dans le domaine de la phraséologie, auxquelles A.S. Hornby a contribué de façon remarquable et qui devaient avoir des effets considérables, tant sur la lexicographie pour apprenants qu'au-delà.

Jonathan Crowther

Encyclopedic learners' dictionaries

Zusammenfassung
Zu Beginn dieses Beitrags wird nach einer Begriffsbestimmung des enzyklopädischen Lernerwörterbuchs (ELD) erörtert, in welchem Ausmaß Wörterbücher für Muttersprachler in verschiedenen Ländern traditionell enzyklopädische Informationen beinhalten. Im Anschluß daran wird diskutiert, inwieweit es wünschenswert ist, daß enzyklopädische Lernerwörterbücher, assoziative und konnotative Bedeutungselemente im Hinblick auf Benutzer, die mit beispielsweise britischer oder amerikanischer Kultur wenig vertraut sind, aufnehmen und welche Schwierigkeiten es gibt, derartige Informationen zu bestimmen und zu vermitteln. Beispielsweise stellten sich die Fragen, in welchem Ausmaß enzyklopädische Lernerwörterbücher "populäre Kultur" und "hohe Kultur" berücksichtigen sollten und was die eigentlichen Bedürfnisse der Studierenden sind. Zum Abschluß werden Perspektiven der zukünftigen Entwicklung enzyklopädischer Lernerwörterbücher auch im Hinblick auf die elektronischen Medien aufgezeigt.

Résumé
L'article examine d'abord le terme de *encyclopedic learners' dictionary* (ELD) (Dictionnaire encyclopédique pour apprenants) et se demande dans quelle mesure les dictionnaires généraux monolingues de différents pays ont toujours inclu des informations encyclopédiques. Il se pose ensuite la question de savoir dans quelle mesure il est désirable d'inclure des informations connotatives ou associatives au profit d'un étudiant peu familier de la culture britannique et américaine et dans quelle mesure l'identification et le traitement de telles informations est possible. Faut-il, par exemple, tenir compte de la culture populaire autant que de la culture des élites? Où sont les vrais besoins des utilisateurs ? L'article termine en réfléchissant au devenir des ELDs et à l'évolution des versions électroniques.

Burkhard Dammann

Teachers' demands on learners' dictionaries

Zusammenfassung

Die Schule stellt spezifische Ansprüche an *Learners' dictionaries*. Obwohl im modernen Oberstufenunterricht Texte aller Art (von Shakespeare bis hin zur Boulevardpresse) besprochen werden, sind ganz praktische Erwägungen wie Klarheit der Darstellung, Didaktisierung des Angebots, ganz allgemein Benutzerfreundlichkeit, wichtiger als enzyklopädische Aspekte. Der folgende Text hebt auch hervor, warum aus examenstechnischen Gründen ein Lernerwörterbuch sogar "zu gut" sein kann.

Résumé

Le texte suivant insiste sur les aspects pratiques exigés par le lycée (niveau baccalauréat). D'un côté il faut un dictionnaire qui aide à comprendre des textes extrêmement divers, d'un autre côté la clarté didactique est préférable à la perfection encyclopédique. Le contexte scolaire demande des restrictions particulières.

Dieter Götz

On some differences between English and German (with respect to lexicography)

Zusammenfassung

Das Schreiben eines deutschen einsprachigen Lernerwörterbuchs bringt aufgrund bestimmter Eigenschaften der deutschen Sprache andere Fragestellungen und Probleme mit sich als das Schreiben eines entsprechenden englischen Wörterbuchs. So gehören z.B. Wörter lateinischen Ursprungs im Deutschen nur selten zum Kernwortschatz, Komposita und Affixe spielen eine größere Rolle, metasprachliche Erklärungen nehmen mehr Raum ein. Neben einsprachigen Lernerwörterbüchern können *bridge dictionaries* dazu beitragen, die Lernenden in einer für sie leichter verständlichen Weise mit den relevanten Informationen zu versorgen.

Résumé

A cause de certaines propriétés particulières à la langue allemande, la rédaction d'un dictionnaire d'apprentissage allemand entraîne d'autres problèmes que celle de son homologue anglais. Ainsi pour l'allemand, les mots d'origine latine font rarement partie du noyau lexical, les affixes et les mots composés jouent un rôle plus important et les explications métalinguistiques sont plus nombreuses. A côté des dictionnaires monolingues, des *dictionnaires-ponts* pourraient avoir leur utilité pour fournir à l'apprenant l'information pertinente d'une façon plus lisible.

Franz Josef Hausmann
Semiotaxis and learners' dictionaries

Zusammenfassung
Semiotaxis untersucht, inwieweit die Wörter ohne Kontext definierbar sind bzw. inwieweit sie zur Definition auf Kontext angewiesen sind. Daraus ergibt sich lexikographisch, ob die Kollokation links oder rechts von der Definition zu stehen hat und ob eine Definition im Artikel des Kollokators überhaupt einen Sinn hat. Ist es sinnvoll, *to make the bed* im Artikel *make* zu definieren? Im Beitrag werden verschiedene Beispiele aus den Lernerwörterbüchern diskutiert.

Résumé
La *Semiotaxis* examine dans quelle mesure les mots ont besoin de contexte pour pouvoir être définis. Elle décide de la place – à gauche ou à droite de la définition – d'une collocation dans le dictionnaire et du bien-fondé de la définition dans l'article du collocatif. Est-il raisonnable de définir *to make the bed* (faire le lit) à l'article *make* (faire) ? Plusieurs exemples tirés des *learners' dictionaries* sont présentés.

David Heath
The treatment of international varieties

Zusammenfassung
Dieser Beitrag zeigt, daß ein Lernerwörterbuch nur britisches und amerikanisches Englisch in bezug auf Orthographie, Aussprache und Morphologie systematisch behandeln kann. Behauptungen, daß auch andere Varietäten ausführlich dargestellt würden, können nur dazu führen, daß die damit verbundenen Erwartungen enttäuscht werden, da sie ausschließlich auf der unsystematischen Behandlung varietätenspezifischer Bedeutungen beruhen.

Résumé
Cet article montre qu'un *learners' dictionary* ne peut décrire de façon systématique l'orthographe, la prononciation et la morphologie que de l'anglais britannique et américain. Prétendre ajouter le traitement exhaustif d'autres variétés ne peut qu'entraîner la déception des utilisateurs, car de fait on ne trouve, pour ces autres variétés, que des informations peu systématiques sur certaines significations spécifiques.

Thomas Herbst

Designing an English Valency Dictionary: combining linguistic theory and userfriendliness

Zusammenfassung

In diesem Beitrag werden die Konzeption und die theoretischen Grundlagen eines Valenzwörterbuchs für das Englische, das in den letzten Jahren an den Universitäten Erlangen, Reading und Augsburg erstellt wurde, dargelegt. Insbesondere wird darauf eingegangen, welche Konflikte sich zwischen dem zugrundegelegten Modell der Valenztheorie und den lexikographischen Anforderungen der Benutzerfreundlichkeit ergeben. Mustereinträge des neuen Valenzwörterbuchs werden vorgestellt.

Résumé

Cet article expose les conceptions et les bases théoriques d'un dictionnaire valenciel (constructionnel) de l'anglais, élaboré ces dernières années à Erlangen, à Reading et à Augsbourg. Il insiste sur les conflits produits par certaines contradictions entre le modèle théorique appliqué et l'impérieuse convivialité de l'outil. Des entrées-témoins sont ajoutées.

Robert F. Ilson

The treatment of meaning in learners' dictionaries – and others

Zusammenfassung

Ein Vergleich der Erklärungen einiger fast gleichbedeutender Wörter aus einsprachigen Wörterbüchern des Englischen, Französischen und Deutschen, sowohl für Lernende als auch für Muttersprachler. Der Zweck der Übung ist zu untersuchen, ob die Qualität solcher Erklärungen in den Lernerwörterbüchern minderwertiger ist als in den Wörterbüchern für Muttersprachler und ob die englischen, französischen und deutschen Erklärungen bedeutend verschieden sind.

Résumé

L'article compare les explications de plusieurs mots semblables qui se trouvent dans des dictionnaires monolingues de l'anglais, du français et de l'allemand – conçus tant pour l'apprentissage de ces langues que pour l'étude de la langue maternelle – pour savoir si les dictionnaires conçus surtout pour les étrangers offrent des explications inférieures à celles des dictionnaires de la langue maternelle et si les explications des trois langues mentionnées se distinguent sensiblement.

Michael Klotz

Word complementation in English learners' dictionaries – a quantitive study of CIDE, COBUILD2, LDOCE3 and OALD5

Zusammenfassung

Quantitative Studien kommen in der Wörterbuchkritik trotz ihres hohen Aussagewertes nur selten zur Anwendung. Die vorliegende Studie will hier einen Beitrag leisten, indem sie die gegenwärtig aktuelle Generation von Lernerwörterbüchern auf das Enthaltensein von insgesamt 1260 Patterns zu 151 Verben, Adjektiven und Substantiven untersucht. Die Auswertung zeigt, daß alle vier untersuchten Wörterbücher etwa die gleiche Menge an Patternangaben enthalten, die enthaltenen Patterns dabei jedoch nicht identisch sind. Dies legt den Schluß nahe, daß keines der vier Wörterbücher alle relevanten Patterns auflistet. Darüber hinaus zeigt sich, daß alle vier Wörterbücher die Konstruktionsmöglichkeiten von Verben wesentlich umfassender behandeln als die von Adjektiven und Substantiven, wobei letztere oft auch nicht explizit kodiert und nur aus den Beispielsätzen entnehmbar sind. Obwohl alle vier Wörterbücher eine beeindruckende Anzahl von Patternangaben enthalten, sind also vor allem im Bereich der Adjektive und Substantive Verbesserungen durchaus noch möglich.

Résumé

La critique des dictionnaires a le tort de n'être que rarement quantitative. Voilà pourquoi la présente étude examine l'actuelle génération de *learners' dictionaries* quant à la présence ou l'absence de 1260 patrons syntaxiques de 151 verbes, adjectifs et substantifs. Il en résulte que les quatre dictionnaires dépouillés contiennent à peu près le même nombre de patrons sans que ce soient partout les mêmes. Il est donc probable qu'aucun ne fournit la totalité de l'utile. On constate aussi que les dictionnaires sont unanimes à privilégier la description des verbes au détriment des adjectifs et des substantifs dont les constructions manquent souvent de codage explicite et ne figurent que dans des phrases-exemples. On reconnaîtra donc le nombre impressionnant d'informations constructionnelles dans les quatre dictionnaires, mais on conclura aussi qu'il est possible d'améliorer considérablement le traitement des adjectifs et des substantifs.

Geoffrey Leech and Hilary Nesi

Moving towards perfection: The learners' (electronic) dictionary of the future

Zusammenfassung

Dieses Kapitel befaßt sich mit der Zukunft von Lernerwörterbüchern für das Englische. Es setzt voraus, daß die Hauptmethode zur Verbesserung zukünftiger Lernerwörterbücher die Entwicklung elektronischer Wörterbücher sein wird. Trotz des geringen Erfolges momentan erhältlicher Produkte werden die elektronischen Lernerwörterbücher der Zukunft extrem große Vorteile haben. Dennoch wird das gedruckte Wörterbuch noch nicht aussterben: das Zeitalter Gutenbergs ist noch nicht vergangen.

Résumé

Ce chapitre porte un regard sur l'avenir des dictionnaires pour étudiants débutant dans l'apprentissage de l'anglais ou dictionnaires pour apprenants. Il émet l'idée que, dans le futur, le principal moyen d'améliorer les dictionnaires pour apprenants sera le développement de dictionnaires électroniques. Malgré le succès limité des produits actuels, le dictionnaire électronique pour apprenants aura d'immenses avantages. Toutefois, la version imprimée du dictionnaire a encore une belle vie devant elle: l'âge de Gutenberg n'est pas encore révolu.

Brigitta Mittmann

The treatment of collocations in OALD5, LDOCE3, COBUILD2 and CIDE

Zusammenfassung

Die Berücksichtigung von Kollokationen hat bei der Herstellung aller vier 1995 erschienenen Lernerwörterbücher eine große Rolle gespielt. Dennoch ließen sich die darin enthaltenen Kolloktionsinformationen durchaus noch verbessern. Eine Untersuchung von 120 Kollokationen zeigte Probleme und Lösungsmöglichkeiten auf.

Résumé

Les quatre *learners' dictionaries* parus en 1995 prêtent indéniablement une attention particulière aux collocations. Malgré cet effort, l'information collocationnelle est loin d'être parfaite. L'examen de 120 collocations révèle les problèmes et suggère des solutions.

Rosamund Moon

Needles and haystacks, idioms and corpora: Gaining insight into idioms, using corpus analysis

Zusammenfassung

Im Mittelpunkt dieses Artikels stehen englische Idiome. Diese seltenen Erscheinungen werden manchmal als nur von marginalem Interesse betrachtet und von Lexikographen häufig vernachlässigt. Im ersten Teil des Artikels geht es um Idiome und Korpora. Es wird aufgezeigt, welche Aufschlüsse Korpora ermöglichen, im Hinblick auf die Frequenz von Idiomen, ihre Auftretensformen, grammatischen Konstruktionen, ihre Vorkommenskontexte und ihre Diskursfunktionen. Der zweite Teil beschäftigt sich mit der Behandlung von Idiomen in Wörterbüchern und geht der Frage nach, welche Typen von Informationen in einem perfekten Wörterbuch zu Idiomen gegeben werden sollten.

Résumé

Cette communication traite des expressions idiomatiques en anglais, expressions rares, parfois considérées comme présentant un intérêt limité et souvent negligées par les lexicographes. La première partie est consacrée à un examen de la place des expressions idiomatiques dans les corpus: leur fréquence, leur forme, les modèles auxquels elles se rattachent, les contextes dans lesquels elles sont utilisées et leurs usages discursifs et pragmatiques. La deuxième partie examine le traitement des expressions idiomatiques dans les dictionnaires et envisage les types d'information qu'il faudrait faire figurer à leur sujet dans le dictionnaire idéal.

André Moulin

The advanced learners' dictionary: syntax cum semantics

Zusammenfassung

In der heutigen Linguistik besteht u.a. die Tendenz, Syntax und Semantik in Beziehung zueinander zu setzen und z.B. das syntaktische Verhalten eines Verbs durch seine semantischen Argumente zu erklären (vgl. die Valenz). Wer aber Universitätsstudenten eine Fremdsprache lehrt und ein Lernerwörterbuch zusammen mit einem Grammatiklehrbuch gebrauchen will, hat es nicht immer leicht. Die zwei Typen von Nachschlagewerken unterscheiden sich nämlich nicht nur terminologisch, sondern auch in den vorgeschlagenen Erklärungen, die oft einen unterschiedlichen Komplexitätsgrad aufweisen und nicht notwendigerweise miteinander vereinbar sind.

Résumé

Une des tendances actuelles de la grammaire est d'associer syntaxe et sémantique et d'expliquer, par exemple, le comportement syntaxique d'un verbe (valence) en termes d'arguments sémantiques. Dans cette optique, il peut s'avérer difficile, lorsque l'on enseigne une langue étrangère à des étudiants universitaires, d'utiliser de concert manuel de grammaire et dictionnaire d'apprenant: ces deux types d'ouvrages divergent non seulement au niveau de la terminologie, mais surtout en ce qui concerne la complexité et la compatibilité des explications qu'ils proposent.

Kerstin Popp

Lexical units, suffixation, suffixes in OALD5, LDOCE3, COBUILD2 and CIDE

Zusammenfassung

Einige der auffälligsten Neuerungen in der neuen Generation von Lernerwörterbüchern zeigen sich in der Struktur, die einen besonders zentralen Aspekt für die Benutzerfreundlichkeit darstellt. In diesem Beitrag werden strukturelle Vor- und Nachteile der unterschiedlichen Vorgehensweisen der verschiedenen Lernerwörterbücher analysiert, wobei auch diskutiert wird, welche Struktureinheiten für eine quantitative Analyse relevant sind. Hierfür wird das Konzept der *lexical unit* nach Cruse auf seine Anwendbarkeit in der Lexikographie untersucht.

Résumé

Parmi les innovations apportées par la nouvelle génération de *learners' dictionaries*, une des plus remarquables concerne leur structure, c'est-à-dire un aspect primordial au niveau de la convivialité. Cet article analyse les avantages et les inconvénients des différentes structurations et pose également la question de savoir quelles sont les unités structurelles pertinentes pour une analyse quantitative. Pour ce faire, il examine la notion d'*unité lexicale* (lexical unit) de Cruse quant à son applicabilité lexicographique.

Gabriele Stein

Exemplification in EFL dictionaries

Zusammenfassung

Dieser Beitrag behandelt die mangelnde Systematik in der Exemplifizierung in englischen Lernerwörterbüchern. Es wird aufgezeigt, daß zahlreiche Bezüge zwischen deskriptiven und demonstrativen Bestandteilen der Wörterbucheinträge und zwischen Benutzer-Zielgruppe und Lexikographen bestehen, und erarbeitet, wie diese als Grundlage einer konsequenteren Beispielpraxis dienen könnten.

Résumé

L'article explore le manque de critères pour l'exemplification des mots dans les dictionnaires anglais pour apprenants étrangers. Il met en évidence les relations multiples qui existent entre la part descriptive et la part démonstrative d'une entrée, entre les usagers et les lexicographes, et montre comment celles-ci pourraient servir de base pour une pratique d'exemplification plus systématique.

Della Summers

Coverage of spoken English in relation to learners' dictionaries, especially the Longman Dictionary of Contemporary English

Zusammenfassung

Dieser Artikel befaßt sich mit den Korpora gesprochener Sprache, die alle Lernerwörterbücher, insbesondere aber LDOCE, bereichert haben. Demonstriert wird ihre Nützlichkeit bei der Auswahl der zu behandelnden Einheiten, bei Beispielen, Phraseologismen und *usage notes*.

Résumé

Cet article se penche sur les corpus oraux qui ont fécondé les *learners' dictionaries* et notamment LDOCE. Leur utilité pour la sélection des unités traitées, pour les exemples, pour les phrasèmes et pour les *usage notes* est démontrée.

Jan Svartvik
Corpora and dictionaries

Zusammenfassung

Die Qualität der Lernerwörterbücher hat sich im letzten Jahrzehnt enorm gesteigert. Ein Grund hierfür ist darin zu suchen, daß Lexikographen heutzutage intensiv mit Korpora arbeiten. Traditionelle Wörterbücher erfüllen jedoch nicht alle Bedürfnisse fremdsprachlicher Benutzer, etwa im Bereich der Kollokationen. In diesem Beitrag werden einige dieser Bereiche vorgestellt und es wird für einen direkten Korpuszugang durch die Studierenden plädiert, um diesen Informationsbedürfnissen gerecht zu werden.

Résumé

La qualité des *learners' dictionaries* a fait ces dernières années un bond en avant. Une des raisons en est que les lexicographes profitent maintenant pleinement de corpus électroniques. Toutefois les dictionnaires traditionnels sont incapables de satisfaire tous les besoins des utilisateurs étrangers, par exemple dans le domaine des cooccurrences. Pour pallier à ces insuffisances – dont certaines sont présentées – l'article plaide en faveur d'un accès direct de l'apprenant au corpus.

Bei Fragen zur Produktsicherheit wenden Sie sich bitte an:
If you have any questions regarding product safety,
please contact:

Walter de Gruyter GmbH
Genthiner Straße 13
10785 Berlin
productsafety@degruyterbrill.com